Latin American State Building in Comparative Perspective
Social Foundations of Institutional Order

Latin American State Building in Comparative Perspective provides an account of long-run institutional development in Latin America, which emphasizes the social and political foundations of state-building processes. The study argues that societal dynamics have path-dependent consequences at two critical points: at the initial consolidation of national institutions in the wake of independence and at the time when the "social question" of mass political incorporation forced its way into the national political agenda across the region during the Great Depression. Dynamics set into motion at these points in time have produced widely varying and stable distributions of state capacity in the region. Marcus J. Kurtz tests this argument using structured comparisons of the postindependence political development of Chile, Peru, Argentina, and Uruguay.

Marcus J. Kurtz is an Associate Professor in the Department of Political Science at Ohio State University. He is the author of *Free Market Democracy and the Chilean and Mexican Countryside* (Cambridge, 2004). He has had articles published in the *American Journal of Political Science, World Politics, Comparative Politics, Comparative Political Studies, International Organization, Journal of Politics, Politics & Society, Comparative Studies in Society and History*, and *Theory and Society*.

Latin American State Building in Comparative Perspective

Social Foundations of Institutional Order

MARCUS J. KURTZ
Ohio State University

CAMBRIDGE
UNIVERSITY PRESS

32 Avenue of the Americas, New York NY 10013-2473, USA

Cambridge University Press is part of the University of Cambridge.

It furthers the University's mission by disseminating knowledge in the pursuit of education, learning, and research at the highest international levels of excellence.

www.cambridge.org
Information on this title: www.cambridge.org/9780521747318

© Marcus J. Kurtz 2013

This publication is in copyright. Subject to statutory exception and to the provisions of relevant collective licensing agreements, no reproduction of any part may take place without the written permission of Cambridge University Press.

First published 2013
Reprinted 2013

A catalog record for this publication is available from the British Library.

Library of Congress Cataloging in Publication data
Kurtz, Marcus J.
Latin American state building in comparative perspective : social foundations of institutional order / Marcus J. Kurtz.
p. cm.
Includes bibliographical references and index.
ISBN 978-0-521-76644-9 (hardback) – ISBN 978-0-521-74731-8 (paperback)
1. Latin America – Politics and government. 2. Nation-building – Latin America – History. 3. Latin America – Social conditions. I. Title.
JL966.K87 2012
320.98–dc23   2012028450

ISBN 978-0-521-76644-9 Hardback
ISBN 978-0-521-74731-8 Paperback

Cambridge University Press has no responsibility for the persistence or accuracy of URLs for external or third-party Internet Web sites referred to in this publication, and does not guarantee that any content on such Web sites is, or will remain, accurate or appropriate.

For Sarah, Chloë, and Anneliese

Contents

Acknowledgments		*page* ix
1	The Difficulties of Studying State Building	1
2	The Social Foundations of State Building in the Contemporary Era	18
3	State Formation in Chile and Peru: Institution Building and Atrophy in Unlikely Settings	66
4	State Formation in Argentina and Uruguay: Agrarian Capitalism, Elite Conflict, and the Construction of Cooperation	95
5	Divergence Reinforced: The Timing of Political Inclusion and State Strength in Chile and Peru	131
6	The Social Question and the State: Mass Mobilization, Suffrage, and Institutional Development in Argentina and Uruguay	176
7	Conclusions, Implications, and Extensions: Social Foundations, Germany–Prussia, and the Limits of Contemporary State Building	227
References		251
Index		271

Acknowledgments

Some portions of Chapters 2 and 3 have been adapted from "The Social Foundations of Institutional Order: Reconsidering War and the 'Resource Curse' in Third World State Building." The final, definitive version of this paper has been published in *Politics & Society*, Vol. 37:4 (2009):479–520. Copyright © SAGE Publications Inc. All rights reserved.

I begin these acknowledgments where my entry into the social sciences began – working with David and Ruth Collier decades ago at Berkeley. From them I learned the importance of history, an openness to the possibility of long-term path dependencies, and the centrality of research design to any successful social-scientific scholarly endeavor. Whereas this book, unlike my last, was not conceived under their guidance, I hope that their influence shows across its breadth.

Of course, in the writing of any book there are always myriad debts – intellectual, personal, and professional – that are accrued. This book is no exception. Many of the ideas that ultimately worked their way into this manuscript emerged in conversations, often in unrelated contexts over unrelated matters, over the course of several years. Ken Dubin, Sebastián Etchemendy, Ken Greene, Victoria Hui, Pauline Jones Luong, Vicky Murillo, Michael Ross, and Aaron Schneider all provoked insights or changes in my thinking during the development of this book. They may not see their influence in the pages, but the book is stronger for the intellectual conversations that I have had with them. Kurt Weyland and the Comparative Politics Workshop at the University of Texas, Austin, gave me very important advice on the argument and framing of the first half of this book, as did the editorial collective at *Politics & Society*, which was generous enough to publish a preliminary version of the book's argument with respect to Chile and Peru. Scholarly works are always made stronger through the mechanism of debate and constructive disagreement. I am delighted to have been able to trade ideas back and forth with both Ryan x *Acknowledgments*

Saylor and Hillel Soifer over the past few years – and I very much look forward to continuing these conversations both in print and in person in the coming years. Deborah Boucoyannis was kind enough to help me with some of the vagaries of Prussian history, and hopefully kept me from venturing too far off the path as I explored this decidedly unfamiliar terrain.

Two individuals deserve special mention. Ken Shadlen has had the kindness to read drafts of every chapter of every book manuscript I have worked on, and his comments have always been both penetrating and productive. They are not always easy to address (nor necessarily successfully addressed, alas!), but they always shine a light on the goal of what the book should be rather than what it is. Andrew Schrank has probably heard more about this book than any human being should and has always been willing to read, respond, and engage in ways that have surely made me a far better scholar over the years than I have any right to be. The general and specific intellectual debt I owe to him is beyond measure.

I am lucky enough to have Sarah Brooks as a partner and spouse, for she at once has been my strongest supporter, most trenchant critic, and source for inspiration. At the same time, she has very successfully reminded me that there is more to life than simply the book that one is working on. And that one's book will often be made better for recognizing that fact. Finally, I believe it was James Scott who pointed out in an acknowledgment that his family was no help at all in completing a book, and that for this he was extremely thankful. My daughters, Chloë and Anneliese, have taken on this role with aplomb. They, with no infrequency, remind me that it is more important and a lot more fun to go to the park than to work at the office. And for that I am grateful.

Marcus J. Kurtz
Columbus, Ohio

I

The Difficulties of Studying State Building

On February 27, 2010, an earthquake of magnitude 8.8 struck just off the shore of Chile in the vicinity of the southern city of Concepción. This was a massive event, killing 521 people and injuring a further 12,000 (US Geological Survey 2011a). Unfortunately, this was not the first major earthquake to strike southern Chile; they are endemic to the region. Indeed, a previous earthquake of magnitude 9.6 struck in roughly the same region on May 22, 1960, killing 1,655 people and injuring a further 3,000. The latter was, in fact, the most powerful earthquake ever recorded anywhere in the world, and its energy release was "about two orders of magnitude larger than the mean annual seismic energy release in the world" (Lomnitz 2004, 374–75). Slightly more than a month before the 2010 earthquake in Chile, a much smaller magnitude 7.0 temblor struck Haiti. This vastly smaller seismic event resulted in the deaths of 316,000 people and the injury of a further 300,000 (US Geological Survey 2011b). Shockingly, the 2010 Chilean earthquake was approximately 500 times the strength of the Haitian temblor, even as its human and infrastructural toll was only about 0.17 percent as great (Kurczy et al. 2010). And the enormous 1960 earthquake was more powerful still: it released almost 8,000 times as much energy as the one that devastated Haiti but caused a small fraction of the latter's human and infrastructural toll.[1] Why was the least powerful of these seismic events by far the most lethal? The reason for this difference is quite clear: at least since the 1920s, the Chilean government had instituted and implemented building codes designed to guard against earthquake damage, notably through enforcing the use of shear walls (Lomnitz 2004, 368). No similar codes had been legislated in Haiti, nor could they in all likelihood have been effectively enforced.

---

[1] Importantly, this remains true even adjusting for the different populations of the two affected regions.

2 Latin American State Building in Comparative Perspective

This is not the only instance in which state capacity has been critical in matters of life and death. In 1991 and 1992, a cholera epidemic struck much of Latin America, but extensive infection was ultimately centered in Peru. By the time the bulk of the epidemic had run its course in that country, there were more than 301,000 reported cases, 114,000 hospitalizations, and 2,840 deaths. Peru's Andean neighbor Chile, by contrast, suffered a total of 41 cases and 2 deaths (Suárez and Bradford 1993, 4). Cholera, which had not seriously afflicted Peru for almost 100 years, reached that country and the rest of Latin America in the 1991–92 period – but did it not afflict both regions equally. Why was cholera able to run rampant in Peru while being quickly contained in Chile?

The answer to this question has two parts. The first is that basic water infrastructure in Peru was in a parlous state. One study of the city of Trujillo – Peru's third largest city and the epicenter of the outbreak – indicated that the public water distribution system was not chlorinated, was vulnerable to contamination from myriad illegal taps, suffered from leaks owing to inadequate maintenance, and relied on a storage system vulnerable to contamination (Tickner and Gouveia-Vigeant 2005, 497). The results were catastrophic, and efforts to combat the disease ranged from largely ineffective to almost tragic – as when then-President Fujimori went on national television to encourage the population to continue to eat ceviche (raw fish), a Peruvian national dish. This almost certainly cost lives. By contrast, when the Chilean government realized that cholera had entered the country and was being disseminated via seafood and vegetables commonly irrigated with untreated wastewater, it immediately took steps to stop the disease in its tracks. In and around Santiago, the capital, the use of wastewater for irrigation was banned, and enforcement was strict, involving inspections, barricades, and the destruction of contraband crops. The sale of raw seafood and vegetables in restaurants was banned, and a public information campaign was initiated (Venczel 1997, 33).

What do cholera and earthquakes have in common? They are both catastrophes derived from natural causes – the movement of seismic plates and infestation of the *Vibrio cholerae* bacterium. They are also the sorts of natural catastrophes that competent, but not necessarily wealthy, governments can prevent or effectively mitigate. The differences among Chile, Peru, and Haiti as their governments confronted disaster are not principally functions of the nations' levels of development – Haiti is obviously quite poor, but Chile began to become noticeably wealthier than Peru only in the 1990s. Instead, the shocking differences in the mortality attributed to these natural events come down to a simple set of capacities: the ability or inability of states to create appropriate basic infrastructure, impose regulation in construction and food production and distribution systems, or respond effectively and expeditiously to well-understood public health emergencies. In each case, the tools required to cope with catastrophe were both widely available and well within the means of even comparatively poor states. Indeed, the low mortality of the 1960 earthquake in Chile demonstrates that this capacity was long-standing – for the

The Difficulties of Studying State Building

stock of buildings in that year was certainly constructed over a long period of time that predated it, and the low levels of mortality for this gigantic temblor make plain that much of it was properly constructed.

It is contrasts such as these – and examples extend far beyond earthquakes and epidemic disease – that served as the initial motivation for this study. For they raise the obvious question of why some states are so much more able to achieve effective governance than others. What can account for the enormous variations we observe in the ability of states to impose the rule of law and implement basic public policy – variations that have often defied, rather than mirrored, variations in the level of development in the South American region? In short, this book asks what makes states strong and what makes them weak in terms of their ability to manage basic functions, impose core public policies, and regulate private behavior.

The most obvious answer to this question might suggest that state capacity is largely a question of wealth – in rich countries, states will have more resources and thus, in principle, ought to be able to perform more functions better. In Latin America, and much of the developing world, however, there is no clear relationship between national wealth and the strength of the state. What are widely seen as the most effective states in the region – such as Chile, Uruguay, and Costa Rica – are not necessarily the wealthiest. Others, such as Argentina, have been bedeviled by institutional ineffectiveness, despite consistently leading the continent in terms of per capita income and long-run development. How can this be? Differences in the capacities of states to, inter alia, provide public goods, regulate their economies,or respond to crises are fundamentally about the differential abilities of state institutions to reach deeply into society and shape or constrain individual behavior. This is not always fiscally costly, and the mere existence of a wealthy economy in and of itself does not make state institutions effective or even particularly likely to improve. Thus, institutional effectiveness must have other causes – and elaborating its sources is the goal of this book.

The question here is about *institutional* power – the ability of the state to induce residents, firms, and organizations to act in ways they would not in the absence of its regulatory and administrative presence. Examples of this governance power abound at the micro level – the citizens of institutionally strong states are more likely to refrain from creating illicit connections to water or electrical grids and they are more likely to pay the taxes they owe, serve in the military when called on, or use their property in a manner permitted by law. At the macro level, this is reflected, for example, in the uniform imposition of the rule of law, the provision of public goods, military effectiveness, and the ability to generate the tax resources to enable all of these. The infrastructural reach of state power – and much more will be said about this concept and how to measure it in the next chapter – thus matters.

In fact, the strength of state institutions matters for much more than the implementation of public policy. Indeed, implicitly or explicitly, scholars have long recognized that the effectiveness and the depth of penetration of public institutions are of paramount importance across a wide variety of other political domains. In the scholarship on ethnic conflict, for example, Horowitz (1971, 240) has pointed out that "the degree of governmental penetration of the hinterland and the degree to which the country is united by interregional communications" have a powerful effect on nationalization of formerly local intergroup ethnic conflict. Lijphart (1969) has pointed out that deeply penetrating and effective political institutions are essential to the construction of consociational approaches to the management of severe ethnic, class, and/or religious cleavages. Heller (1996) notes that in the Indian state of Kerala, the very high levels of social capital and cross-ethnic associational life are important consequences of state activity, and Varshney (2001) has shown that in India, such cross-ethnic formal (and informal) associational life is tied to the mitigation or avoidance of ethnic conflict and communal rioting.

The strength of state institutions has similarly had a powerful role to play in discussions of the foundations for long-run economic performance. Many in the economics community tend to emphasize the ability of the state to impose the rule of law or protect private property rights as a central determinant of comparative growth (e.g., Dollar and Kraay 2003; Acemoglu et al. 2005). Others, in the literature on the so-called developmental state, have taken a different tack, arguing that strong states are able to maximize growth because of the way they can deliberately get the prices "wrong" in an effort to spark rapid industrialization and the creation of new comparative advantages, while at the same time shaping and constraining the activities of powerful economic agents in ways that prevent inefficiency and rent seeking (e.g., Amsden 1991, 284; Haggard 1990). Chang (1999, 198–99) has gone so far as to suggest that even in the contemporary era of liberalization and international economic integration, it is the systematic strengthening of state institutions – not retrenchment and market deregulation – that will be critical to superior long-run economic performance.[2]

Beyond development and ethnic conflict, state-building outcomes have also been linked to popular support for democracy, the quality of democratic governance, the stability of political regimes, and myriad other political dynamics, including the ability to tax and, perhaps most critically, national survival and military effectiveness in an anarchic world. But what remains poorly understood, and is the topic of this book, is what accounts for the wide variations in state institutional strength that we see in the contemporary developing world in general and in South America in particular. For although there are existing explanations for differing patterns of political development – emphasizing

---

[2] It is important to note that no position is taken here as to the validity of these claims – only that otherwise very dissimilar perspectives on economic development have nevertheless emphasized the centrality of strong state institutions. They might differ on *which* institutions are of greatest import, but development and administrative capacity are theoretically tightly related.

The Difficulties of Studying State Building

international strategic conflict, natural resource endowments, culture, or institutional structure – we will see that their ability to explain these outcomes is at best very limited.

WHAT DOES MAKE A STATE STRONG?

How do nations go about constructing durable and effective institutions of government? This is an old question that has recently begun to draw substantial new attention – particularly in literatures that move beyond the canonical studies of the state-building process in Western Europe. As attention has turned from the dynamics of state formation in Early Modern Europe that gave birth to this literature to more recent experiences in Latin America, Africa, and Asia, new questions and new perspectives have emerged. Are the dynamics highlighted in the European cases more broadly applicable, or were they applicable only to that admittedly unusual region in the distant past? What role does world historical time play – from the ability of newer states to observe the institutional models implemented in earlier state builders to the near-complete end of the persistent, full-scale interstate warfare that has been a central causal factor in traditional accounts of institutional development?[3] And finally, are state-building outcomes the long-run products of underlying social or structural factors, or are they a consequence of more contemporaneous pressures, including the political effects of natural resource wealth, the necessities of interstate conflict and competition, institutional design, or party politics and political leadership?

As might be suspected, it has been impossible to approach a consensus as to the factors that produce or make possible a successful state-building effort. And as the opening vignette suggests, moreover, there is extraordinary, and extraordinarily consequential, variation in the quality, reach, and efficacy of public institutions around the globe. On the one hand, we have the wealthy, massive, deeply penetrating, and comparatively honest governments of northern Europe. On the other hand, we have the impoverished states whose governmental institutions have failed altogether (as in Somalia) or have been little more than a form of loosely organized kleptocracy (as in the Haiti of the Duvaliers or the Zaire of Mobutu). And of course, one can also observe virtually everything in between. Perhaps most interesting, however, are the states that have remarkably effective governmental institutions despite their comparative poverty (as in Chile and post-1953 Korea) or, alternatively, surprisingly weak governmental institutions despite their comparative wealth (as in Argentina or the dawn-of-the-twentieth-century United States). Although there is widespread consensus that the contemporary advanced industrial countries have comparatively strong

---

[3] Indeed, Tilly (1975, 81), a central figure in the European state-building literature, flatly states that the "European state-building experiences will not repeat themselves in new states" largely because the available models of state building and their promoters have changed dramatically.

6   *Latin American State Building in Comparative Perspective*

administrative institutions, they still differ substantially among themselves, and there is no agreement either on the direction of a possible causal connection between wealth and institution building or whether one exists at all. And despite quite a variety of prominent potential empirical exemplars of effective government, neither pressures from reform-minded institutions nor diffusion through emulation or learning have produced substantial convergence in the effectiveness of political institutions in the developing world.

The organizing question for this book – what makes a state strong?[4] – is a broad one that requires some delimitation to be theoretically and empirically tractable. The focus of this book, thus, is more narrow, examining the institutional development of a selection of states on the South American continent from the time of their independence into the contemporary era. In so doing, this book places the theoretical emphasis on the wide variations in institutional depth and efficacy to be found in countries that are in other important ways broadly similar: they share colonial legacies, initial levels and patterns of economic development, and strategic and economic positions within the international system. The explanation put forward in this book – and elaborated in Chapter 2 – takes a society-centric view of political development, linking long-run outcomes to underlying social and political dynamics at two critical moments: the initial consolidation of national political institutions after independence and the first large-scale electoral incorporation of nonelite civil society in the tumultuous decades in and around the Great Depression. This book contends that these two critical periods produced *trajectories* of political development that, once launched, became exceedingly difficult to alter in a fundamental way. These periods are also sequenced: the results of the first critical juncture powerfully condition the range of options available at the time of the second critical juncture.

ORDINARY STATE BUILDING

One of the central goals of this book, then, is to examine the state-building process in *ordinary* contexts. By contrast, much existing scholarship has focused on empirical cases that produced unusually penetrating and effective states that emerged in two very atypical contexts: in Early Modern Europe, under conditions of sustained, sovereignty-threatening interstate war and the collapse of feudalism, or in the developmental states of East Asia, in the context of some of the most serious, persistent security threats of the Cold War era and with an unprecedented level of direct and indirect support from the United States.[5] The

---

[4] As will be made more explicit in Chapter 2, state strength here has to do with the ability of political institutions to penetrate deeply into society and effectively regulate the social, economic, or political behavior of citizens.

[5] Particularly with respect to the European cases, the observed clustering of a group of very wealthy, administratively strong states is potentially deceptive. What is less commonly acknowledged in discussions of state building is that the emergence of these states occurred as institutionally weaker states were defeated in war or absorbed by their more powerful neighbors. After

The Difficulties of Studying State Building

emphasis has thus largely been on exceptional cases of institutional development – and a focus on variations among such cases may lead us to overestimate the import of some causal factors, while potentially missing others altogether.

Far fewer studies, by contrast, have examined the institutional development of the more typical states of postcolonial Latin America, Asia, Africa, and the Middle East.[6] Within these regions, even among states with a shared former colonial metropole, or similar levels of economic development, we can observe wide and enduring differences in the strength of governmental institutions. And it is in explaining these variations that the greatest theoretical and practical advances in our understanding of the processes of state building and administrative development can be achieved. It is this basic objective – understanding the variations in state building in comparatively commonplace contexts – that frames the research design employed here.

The specific empirical focus of this book is thus on the process of state building in four South American countries: Chile, Peru, Argentina, and Uruguay. Much can be held constant in these comparisons: these cases were selected in part because they are broadly similar in terms of economic development, position in the international division of labor, colonial heritage, and geographic location, but quite dissimilar in outcomes. Two of them, Chile and Uruguay, have been widely acknowledged to have had comparatively extensive and effective public bureaucracies dating at least to the late nineteenth and early twentieth centuries, respectively. Argentina, by contrast, for most of its history has been the wealthiest country on the continent, but since at least the 1940s, it has been saddled with a comparatively weak administrative infrastructure that is prone to populist and antipopulist cycling but not to effective taxation or governance. And Peru, since a national state was formed in the independence era, has found itself on a trajectory of political development that is nearly immune to effective administrative reform. Dedicated efforts to improve governance there – under democratic and authoritarian regimes alike, in contexts of wealth and crisis – have repeatedly foundered. The theoretical challenge posed by these cases is thus twofold: (1) any theory of political development covering them must account for the relative strength of state institutions as they emerged in each of these cases and (2) it must simultaneously explain the general stability of these relative positions once they emerge, for in the Latin American region, the comparative hierarchy of state institutional effectiveness has been very stable over a long period of time.

As should be clear, the theoretical ambition of this book is not necessarily to provide an account of state building that applies equally everywhere. Although

---

all, the roughly 500 state-like polities of the early modern era have produced roughly 25 states in the contemporary era. This was an intense, sustained, conflict-driven selection process that has been characteristic of few other times and places in world history.

[6] Herbst (2000), Centeno (2002), and Hui (2005) are laudable exceptions, and Soifer (2006) and Saylor (2008) have produced excellent PhD dissertations that focus on Latin American and African cases.

8   *Latin American State Building in Comparative Perspective*

the empirical evidence is drawn from the experience of four cases in the South American context, the theory is meant to be broadly informative for countries in the developing world whose institutional genesis is of comparatively recent vintage. In developing this examination, the theory is explicitly contrasted with the canonical approaches to state building drawn from the European and other experiences that emphasize the effects of war and resource wealth as they would apply to these Latin American cases. In the conclusion, the scope of this book's social–foundational approach to state building is probed by reversing this strategy and examining the extent to which it can help inform an understanding of the Prussian case, long taken as a paradigmatic example of the conflict-inspired pattern of state making.

WHAT IS TO COME?

Of course, a new theory of state building is unnecessary if the existing explanations are largely applicable. But the regnant approaches – emphasizing war or the deleterious effects of resource wealth – suffer from serious lacunae when they are focused on the experiences of the contemporary developing world. An emphasis on the causal effect of interstate war, for example, must contend with the wide variation in observed outcomes across cases in highly conflictual times and places, and the persistence of variation over the past century despite the fact that meaningful interstate war (e.g., in Latin America) has all but disappeared. Alternative bellicist accounts that emphasize war as a selection pressure but not a direct cause suffer from similar applicability problems in the contemporary period but are by contrast underspecified in conflict-ridden times – for they do not tell us *which* states will successfully adapt via institution building to the sovereignty-threatening realities of war and which will be eliminated by that war.

Alternatively, approaches that identify political underdevelopment as a typical consequence of high levels of natural resource wealth must contend with the reality that many states with just such endowments in fact used them to support the process of economic and political development (as in the United States, Australia, Canada, and Chile). While theories of the rentier state make prima facie plausible claims about the potential deleterious political effects of resource wealth for contexts like Peru, they do not effectively differentiate those who succumb to this risk from those who succeed in the effective use of such exogenous positive income shocks. And of course, they are yet further hampered in accounting for why, at the same time, administrative development is so uncommon in resource-scarce states despite the absence of so-called easy patronage and the alleged functional necessity of administrative improvement.

To foreshadow, this book takes a very different, society-centric approach to state building. It begins with the empirical observation that state building, in Latin America, at least, appears to be a long-term historical process that is subject to substantial, and substantially constraining, path-dependent branching

The Difficulties of Studying State Building

points. But what defines the paths of institutional development down which the region's states have moved? The argument here is that two critical watersheds effectively shape institutional trajectories and long-run political development.

The first has to do with the social relations and political dynamics that characterize the period in which national political institutions are first durably established. Specifically, what matters is whether labor is free or servile and whether elites cooperate in the delegation of political authority to the center. Where labor relations are free and elites cooperate to form an exclusionary oligarchy, a trajectory of institutional development can be initiated. Where prevailing social relations are unfree or elites are locked into a zero-sum struggle for control of national politics, the institutionalization of national administrative systems will be retarded and potentially subject to atrophy. The reasons are comparatively straightforward. Where servile labor relations remain important, economic elites rely on *local* control over the official coercive apparatus: they must be able to both prevent the flight of involuntary labor and confront the rebellions that are endemic in such systems. For, to centralize political and coercive authority, a necessary first step in the state-building process, would put elites in both economic and physical jeopardy. But free labor conditions are not sufficient, for elites in such contexts will only make costly investments in central institutions if they can be reasonably certain that the fruits of these investments – which can be substantial – will be shared, and shared widely, among the elites contributing to them materially and politically. And it is for this reason that mechanisms of power sharing and cooperation across elite factions are a second critical part of the initial trajectory of political development.

Once states initiate a dynamic of central state building or institutional atrophy, this trajectory interacts with a subsequent critical moment: the initial electoral incorporation of the broad mass of the middle and working classes. If popular-sector electoral incorporation comes late (during or after the Great Depression), an alliance between middle-sector and working-class parties becomes possible, organized through the expansion and strengthening of state institutions around a developmentalist, import-substituting, and economically interventionist development strategy.[7] In such cases, middle-sector employment is typically very state centric and oriented toward managing the protectionist developmental state. And in organizational terms, both white-collar and blue-collar unions make common cause around the strengthening of the state and the deepening of protection – for their employment and social status depend on it. By contrast, where especially middle-class political inclusion comes early, the formation of such an alliance becomes impossible, and the stabilization of

---

[7] This is similar to what Collier and Collier (2002 [1991]) call a *populist alliance*, a term that is avoided here because of the unfortunate connotations that *populism* holds for some with respect to institutionalization of the rule of law and the rational–legal organization of the public administration. As a descriptor of the class composition of the political alliance, however, it is quite accurate.

Latin American State Building in Comparative Perspective

powerful institutions is blocked (though in different ways, depending on the preexisting institutional trajectory). In particular, a middle class that entered politics before the Great Depression is typically centered in the private economy and is brought into politics by political parties strongly tied to the free trade policies hegemonic at that time. Of course, this complicates any potential subsequent alliance with working-class actors based in nascent industrial sectors, who have need of economic protection and state support if they are to grow rapidly. But for private-sector–linked middle-class actors, the state is as much a source of taxation as it is employment, and protectionism does little more than raise the cost of living, making a working class–middle class alliance around public-sector strengthening therein very difficult to achieve. And without such an alliance, any gains in institutional development and expanded state capacity are likely to be ephemeral at best. The specifics of this argument cannot, of course, be developed in a few short paragraphs, and it is to the task of theory development that we will turn in Chapter 2. But before moving to a detailed discussion of the theory here proposed to explain the quite varied state-building outcomes in the Latin American region, we must first have an overview of the breadth, depth, and stability of this variation.

THE LAY OF THE LAND AND THE LONG-RUN NATURE OF THE STATE-BUILDING PROCESS

One of the most surprising features of postindependence political development in South America has been the very long-term stability of the *hierarchy* of institutional capacity. That is, by various metrics, including tax capacity, education provision, or infrastructural development, the Latin American states with the strongest, most-penetrating public bureaucracies at the end of the nineteenth and the beginning of the twentieth centuries have remained in that position into the contemporary era. For example, Soifer (2009) has shown that Chile very early – in the second half of the nineteenth century – developed a national system of public education, in large measure because of the strength of its bureaucracy. And other metrics confirm this – and continue to place Chile at the top of a wide variety of governance and economic rankings in Latin America and among developing countries more broadly.[8] That is not to say there has been little change in the capacity and strength of political institutions in the region; naturally, there has been. But the *relative* position of states has been remarkably stable – far more so than, for example, institutional, partisan, or leadership-based accounts of political development would lead one to expect. Indeed, given the repeated political regime transformations in so many

---

[8] E.g., Standard and Poor's (2011) rates domestic Chilean debt as AA, only one notch below that of the United States. Worldwide Governance Indicators' (2011) Government Effectiveness rating places Chile first in the Latin American region, followed by Uruguay and Costa Rica; they are at least, thus, perceived to be effective by investors and elites.

The Difficulties of Studying State Building

TABLE 1.1. *Tax Capacity in South America, 1920–2000*
(Central Government Revenue as a Percentage of GDP)

	Top Tax Revenue Capacity, 1980–2000	Tax Revenue Capacity, 1920–40
Brazil	29.1	8.7
Uruguay	25.4	7.0[a]
Chile	25.0	9.3
Venezuela	22.2	10.8
Mexico	15.8	6.25
Ecuador	15.5	12.5
Peru	14.3	5.3
Argentina	12.6	7.6
Colombia	12.3	5.6
Bolivia	12.1	n.d.
Paraguay	11.7	n.d.

[a] GDP data for Uruguay are calculated from Nahum (2009, 272) for GDP in constant US dollars; from the Oxford–Montevideo Latin American Economic History database (http://oxlad.qeh.ox.ac.uk/search.php) for exchange rates; and from the US Bureau of Labor Statistics (http://www.bls.gov/data/inflation_calculator.htm) for US inflation rates.

Note: All cases save Uruguay's GDP are calculated based on tax receipts and GDP figures taken from the Oxford–Montevideo Latin American Economic History Database (http://oxlad.qeh.ox.ac.uk/search.php).

of the Latin American states, this stability is decidedly surprising and at first blush seems uncorrelated with the democratic or authoritarian character of the relevant political system.

To get a sense for the stability of political development in the region, consider, for example, Table 1.1, which compares 20-year averages of the states' tax receipts as a percentage of gross domestic product in 1920–40 and 1980–2000.[9] What we see is that – with a pair of exceptions – the states most capable of extracting revenue from their citizens in one period remain the ones most capable of doing so in the contemporary era. And indeed, the gaps between the two groups have expanded sharply over time. This is consistent with the presence of path dependencies in the underlying trajectories of political development hypothesized in this book – initially smaller differences will magnify over time through the positive and negative feedbacks operative on each path.

[9] Limitations on cross-national data availability account for the starting period selected. Twenty-year averages are used to smooth out the inevitable fluctuations that occur because of short-term revenue surges tied to commodity booms, for example, or the effects of cyclical economic upturns and downturns.

The exceptions to the general pattern are also worth discussing. Most notably, Venezuela and Ecuador stand out for their unusually high tax to gross domestic product ratios, particularly given the general consensus that their public bureaucracies are not continental standouts. The reason for this mismatch has to do with the overwhelming centrality of the extremely lucrative (and easy-to-tax) oil sector – over the long haul – for both countries. In Venezuela, for example, personal and corporate taxes (this principally includes royalties from the oil sector) accounted for 84.2 percent of all revenues in, for example, 1966–68. This was more than twice as large a proportion as the next closest country (Chile, at 35.3 percent) for which data are available, and it dwarfs the 0.31 percent coming from hard-to-collect property taxes, virtually no sales tax, and even the 6.8 percent of revenues coming from comparatively easy-to-tax international trade (see Chelliah 1971, 320). Thus, while aggregate tax capacity is a good first measure of the institutional reach of the state, it is imperfect and prone to potential error in specific settings – where massive easy monies are available to the fisc from resource booms or other external inflows. And it further highlights the importance of examining the composition of taxation as well, alongside nontax measures of capacity, before drawing definitive conclusions as to the relative infrastructural power of a given state.

The other exception is Argentina, which, in the early period, had a moderately high capacity to tax but, by the contemporary era, is squarely among the weak performers. This is a case that will be explored in great detail in subsequent chapters, for it embodies one of the few cases in which an initially favorable state-building trajectory was deflected into what ultimately proved to be a pattern of persistent institutional instability. It will be crucial for any theory of institutional development that implies a stable, long-run hierarchy of outcomes to explicitly accommodate apparently deviant cases like this, and it is why the Argentine comparison is crucial to the overall hypothesis-testing efforts of this book.

But these data are admittedly indirect, and to have real confidence in them – however stark the differences they show – confirmation on other grounds is required. Consequently, we next consider the expansion of primary and secondary education in the postindependence era. Education is a useful metric for the capacity of states in early- to mid-twentieth-century Latin America for several reasons. First, virtually every state in the region saw the provision of education as a vital state function; naturally the *means* employed (public, private, religious) varied substantially, but all involved very substantial promotion and expenditure on the part of the state. Second, mass education is a large-scale, administratively challenging task, involving the creation of extensive physical infrastructure, the training and allocation of teachers, and the ability to reach a population that was heavily (but to different degrees) concentrated in scattered rural settings. And of course, to this must be added the large continuing outlays required to maintain the teaching and support staff necessary to produce broad educational capacity.

The Difficulties of Studying State Building

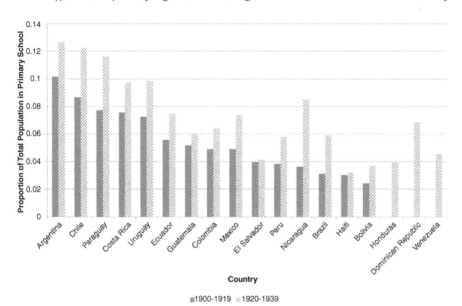

FIGURE 1.1. Students enrolled in primary education as a proportion of the population.

Consequently, the sooner states were able to accomplish this task (and by the late twentieth century, most had managed to do so to a large degree, especially in the arena of primary education), the more effective their institutions can be inferred to be. Empirically, I examine public-sector performance in this arena by measuring the proportion of the total population enrolled in primary and secondary education across several 20-year time periods.[10] A caveat is in order here. The absence of comparable and period-specific breakdowns of the age structure of the population makes it impossible to consider an enrollment ratio that measures the proportion of school-aged children who are actually enrolled. By using total population as the denominator, a similar age structure is assumed across countries. This will tend to *overestimate* the performance of countries that have a younger age structure (typically the poorer, more peasant-dominated countries) relative to those with a greater proportion of their population beyond school years.

In Figure 1.1, data on the proportion of the population enrolled in primary school are presented for the entire Latin American region over two 20-year periods (1900–19, 1920–39). These periods represent the era in which the mass expansion of primary education became possible – but was not necessarily

---

[10] Enrollment is a superior metric to literacy for this purpose, for it measures the capacity of the state to educate pupils at a particular point in time. Literacy is a strongly lagging indicator of this – for many (older) citizens, it reflects the consequences of state educational capacity in the distant past. Although it is a good measure of the stock of human capital in the economy, it is weak as a measure of the contemporaneous institutional capacity that is of interest here.

achieved.[11] Several features of these data immediately stand out. The regional leaders, Argentina, Chile, Paraguay, Costa Rica, and Uruguay, all manage impressive results from an early period, and four of these five – in this early period – are widely seen as having quite effective state bureaucracies, given the realities of the day.[12] Two of the cases identified in the taxation data – Chile and Uruguay – are also among the top performers in primary education. Venezuela is not, further confirming the likelihood that its score in the revenue metric was driven by oil royalties and not by a genuine ability to tax its population via a high-capacity state. Brazil, which performed well in terms of taxation, achieves only middling marks in primary education. The perplexing case is Paraguay, which appears to perform well in these data but which has limited ability to tax and is certainly not thought of in the contemporary era as having particularly effective public institutions. It is possible that the data on this case are misleading, however, as a knock-on consequence of the catastrophic demographic implications of the War of the Triple Alliance, in which it is estimated that between 60 and 69 percent of the total population was lost and an imbalanced population of between four and five women per man remained at war's end in 1870 (see Whigham and Potthast 1999, 185). This would leave Paraguay some 30 to 60 years later with a highly unusual demographic structure, leaving the data on its educational achievements presented here very hard to interpret.[13]

The data on secondary education largely confirm our expectations (see Figure 1.2). Once again, Uruguay and Chile are the regional star performers, with Colombia and Argentina forming a second tier. The remainder of the Latin American region made little progress in the expansion of access to secondary education before 1940. Naturally, quite a few made substantial progress thereafter, but we are interested here in those states that managed the task when it was comparatively most difficult. And this provides further confirmation that Chile and Uruguay have long had among the most deeply penetrating public administrations in the region. This is particularly surprising, since the educational metric is likely to some extent biased against them – they are likely not the countries with the largest available school-aged populations (being more urban and less peasant dominated); they would tend to have an older age structure. Yet they have more pupils in school (as a share of the population) than their regional compatriots.

At the dawn of the twentieth century in South America, no public good was more important from the perspective of state building (and economic

---

[11] Later periods are less relevant as primary education ultimately expanded everywhere, undermining its utility as a metric that discriminates among degrees of state capacity in the region.

[12] This characterization will come to change with respect to Argentina, the causes of which will be a central empirical matter considered in this book.

[13] There has been a very contentious debate on exactly how great the population losses were as a consequence of the conflict and the disease and famine it unleashed, but all agree it ranged from large to extremely large.

The Difficulties of Studying State Building

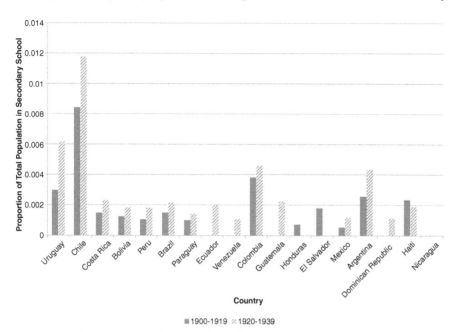

FIGURE 1.2. Students enrolled in secondary education as a proportion of the population.

development) than the construction of a national rail network, for rails at this point in time were the only efficient way to transport people and goods over substantial distances where riverine transport was not available, and they were effectively the arteries that cemented territorial unity and the formation of a single national market. Indeed, because railways permitted the central state to effectively project force throughout the national territory – which in the past was exceedingly difficult because the movement of troops over large distances was very costly and slow – the endemic regional rebellions on the continent began to come to an end. But the creation of this infrastructure did not occur at anything like an even pace across the region. In Figure 1.3, we see that four countries – Argentina, Uruguay, Chile, and Mexico – far outperformed the rest of the region in terms of the construction of railway infrastructure. This was, of course, accomplished in a variety of ways – owing to distinct policy choices on the part of states – either through the subvention of private actors, direct national ownership, or varied combinations of the two. But creating a national railway grid entailed creating a state strong and credible enough to obtain either massive direct foreign investments or credit on a similar scale, for the up-front costs of railway construction were enormous and would not be forthcoming without a plausible medium- to long-term time horizon during which to recoup them. The most extensive railway networks were built in Uruguay and Argentina, closely followed by Chile and Mexico. Here, again, we see principally the same states atop this metric of state building.

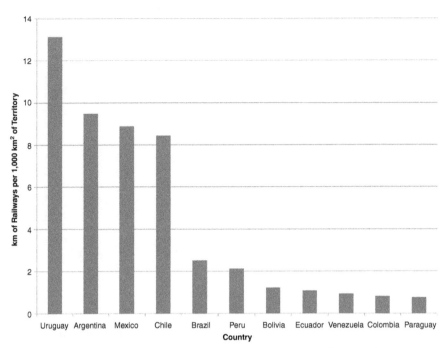

FIGURE 1.3. Railway network achievement as a proportion of national territory in South America, 1900–20.

Taking a step back, then, across a variety of metrics, a very similar group of countries is at the top of a series of quite different measures of state capacity from as early a date as 1900. And it is important to note that the hierarchies remain relatively constant over time as well. As we saw, in terms of tax revenues, the performance of the high-capacity states, if anything, becomes even more starkly distinct from the rest. In terms of educational reach, for example, Uruguay and Chile still top the region in terms of gross secondary enrollment ratios in the 1980–2000 period (World Bank 2011a).[14] In terms of social development outputs, Mahoney (2010, 5) identifies Uruguay, Argentina, Costa Rica, and Chile in the top category in the region from the late nineteenth century to the present.[15] And as we saw earlier, these can at least in part be seen as rough indicators of state building and capacity as well.

The central puzzle that this book addresses thus began with a simple observation – that the hierarchies of political development in South America have

---

[14] The gross secondary enrollment ratio is the number of pupils enrolled in secondary education as a percentage of the age-eligible population.
[15] In this context, social development is taken to mean performance measures of "health, education, and other social indicators" (Mahoney 2010, 6).

The Difficulties of Studying State Building

been strikingly stable over a very long period of time. The theoretical explanation for this pattern of development is presented in detail in the next chapter, and it must account for both the emergence of important initial differences among the newly independent former Spanish colonies of the continent and the stability of these relative differences over a long period of time.

2

The Social Foundations of State Building in the Contemporary Era

Chapter 1 posed a broad theoretical question: what accounts for the comparative success and failure of state-building efforts on the South American continent? Empirically, long-run South American state-building outcomes provide a series of paradoxical results that must be accommodated in any viable answer to this question. First, the strongest of state institutions emerged in some of the most unlikely of settings: the impoverished, colonial backwaters of Chile and Uruguay. At the same time, the wealthier colonial centers of Peru and Argentina (and Mexico in the north), despite higher levels of human capital (and thus larger pools of literate, skilled individuals available to staff their bureaucratic structures) and a legacy of much deeper institutional development from the era of Spanish colonialism, ultimately produced much less successful public administrations. While Argentina initially, if belatedly, began the development of strong national institutions at the end of the nineteenth century, by the 1940s, institutional development had devolved into a near-irreconcilable conflict over the proper scope and role of the state that left its institutions weak and subject to persistent cycles of populist expansion and antipopulist retrenchment. And despite a comparatively much higher level of economic development than the rest of the continent, and thus in principle more resources with which to build institutions and manage conflict, a durable institutional settlement was never achieved. Finally, Peru began its independent life as a weakly institutionalized state, characterized by administrative inefficacy and persistent civil conflict. And despite repeated efforts to alter the fundamental structure of its governmental institutions, it remained a continental laggard in this regard. This range of variation is quite typical of differences among the state administrative structures found in the late developing nations, and it begs critical questions as to what brings it about and why the relative differences tend to persist for long periods of time. It is to that task that this book now turns.

18

The Social Foundations of State Building in the Contemporary Era 19

This is far from the first book to wrestle with the causes of state building and state atrophy.[1] Indeed, there is an extensive and compelling literature that has considered, for example, the ways in which interstate warfare can serve as a critical impetus to the development of strong, penetrating, and effective state institutions. The role of conflict has varied in such accounts, ranging from a direct cause of institutional development to its emergence as a quasi-functionalist response to an existential external threat to an evolutionary selection mechanism that removes those states that do not successfully adapt to the demands of conflict – by rationalizing their bureaucratic structures, creating modern systems of taxation, or improving their property rights structure, inter alia – through defeat and dismemberment. Another literature, oddly disconnected from the first, has instead considered the causes of state institutional failure, highlighting the role of large stocks of easily taxed natural resources as a paradoxical foundation for weakness. In such ecological accounts, large natural resource endowments, most notably oil, make it possible through the windfall revenues they are said to provide for states to avoid the difficult tasks of administrative modernization and domestic taxation. Still others have focused on a variety of questions of institutional design, suggesting that the incentives that arise from alternative structures – whether political systems are unitary or federal, whether local government was directly ruled from the center or involved the mediation of local elites, or the rules of electoral competition, for example – induce or impede the strengthening of states over long periods of time (see, e.g., Soifer 2006; Saylor 2008). And finally, some have emphasized the role of culture and values in the construction of effective state institutions, either in the vein of the hoary modernity–tradition dichotomy of modernization theory or more Weberian-inspired accounts of the rise of rationality and bureaucracy in ways linked to particular strands of European Protestantism (e.g., Gorski 2003).

It is also crucial to differentiate the goals of this book from other work with which it bears some structural similarities, but also important differences. While the task here is to examine the dynamics of political development, this is meant in the specific sense of institution building and administrative reform. This is not a book that is directly concerned with the origins of distinct political regimes (even if they do, on occasion, have indirect implications for the claims made here with respect to state building). And while this book shares some structural similarity and an emphasis on path dependency in explanation with the magisterial work of Collier and Collier (2002), including in part a focus on a labor and popular sector incorporation in the Depression era, both the specific meaning of incorporation and the causal dynamics that follow from it differ quite substantially from the usage in that work. This is, of course, to

---

[1] That said, this is a literature that has overwhelmingly (but not entirely) focused on the earliest examples of effective national state formation and bureaucratic rationalization in central and northern Europe.

be expected given that the focus here is on administrative institutions that are very often conserved in strength and reach even as political regimes change with time, and which are cross-nationally not obviously correlated democratic or authoritarian regime outcomes.

THE STATE-BUILDING DEBATE: WHAT WE DO AND DO NOT KNOW

This book was spurred by the conviction that there are very serious lacunae in the conventional approaches to understanding national political development. It was also written in part out of a concern that the passing of world-historical time has in fundamental ways transformed the challenge facing new states as they endeavor to build and consolidate administrative institutions. Although – as will see later – there are important insights to be gained from the traditional examinations of the state-building process that highlight, for example, conflict, ecology, or institutions, it is not until these are married to an analysis of underlying social and political dynamics that a truly compelling account of contemporary Latin American political development can be constructed, or one that successfully confronts the new empirical puzzles laid out in the contrasting patterns of political development and underdevelopment in the "late developing" parts of the world. In the section that follows, the insights and inadequacies of the extant approaches to the understanding of state building will be examined with an eye to making the case for the centrality of *social* dynamics, rather than ecological, institutional, or international-systemic factors, in laying the long-run foundations of institutional order.

The most well-developed theoretical literatures on state building and decay – emphasizing conflict as the motor of institution building and resource wealth as the cause of institutional corrosion – have developed in near-complete isolation from each other, even as they seek to explain opposite sides of the same theoretical coin and suffer from similar methodological problems. To begin, some of the theoretical claims of prominent bellicist and resource curse accounts of political development suffer from incomplete specification of their central causal mechanisms. For example, often missing is a direct explanation of the factors that determine when and if war or resource wealth is a blessing or a curse. Instead, institutional development or atrophy is sometimes attributed to the demands of a strategic or ecological context in a quasi-functionalist sense. This theoretical strategy, however, must confront the reality that many resource-wealthy states have sharply improved their governmental institutions – including some of the wealthiest, most administratively strong states in the world, such as the United States, Norway, Canada, and Australia. Similarly, warfare has far more commonly been associated with institutional collapse than with long-run state building. The approach taken in this book will be to develop a society-centric account of institutional development that can also elucidate the conditions under which war and resource wealth do (and do not) have important consequences for institutional development.

The Social Foundations of State Building in the Contemporary Era

War and Political Development

It is commonplace to view war and/or the threat of war as a force driving the strengthening of states, or even, for that matter, the emergence of the nation-state as the dominant form of political organization (e.g., Tilly 1990; Centeno 2002; Hui 2005). This line of argument traces its roots at least to the early-twentieth-century writings of Otto Hintze (1975, 183, 199). Military competition in this conception drove increases in the tax capacity of the state and, over the longer term, forced institutional changes that facilitated economic modernization and industrialization (Hintze 1975, 201). It also, as a consequence of these efforts, ultimately created state institutions that were robust enough to place demands even on powerful societal actors.

Tilly (1990, 20) has among the best statements of this perspective, arguing that "preparation for war . . . involves rulers ineluctably in extraction. War builds up an infrastructure of taxation, supply, and administration that itself requires maintenance and often grows faster than the armies and navies that it serves." Whether and how this results in the construction of strong national states depends heavily, however, on the conflicts that emerge between the state and society over the terms of this extraction, thus implicating social structure critically in the charting of the course of national destiny.[2] International competition and the diffusion of organizational knowledge eventually made possible a convergence around what Tilly calls "capitalized coercion" in national–state administrative form – because of its comparative advantage in military conflict. Nevertheless, the different roads to this outcome left behind decidedly different public institutions. In this reading, strategic position is basically prior; political and social conflict merely shape the specific trajectory of underlying political development induced by it.

Conflict-centric approaches have formed the dominant perspective on the formation of strong and effective national states in Europe. For example, Porter (1994) echoes Tilly in highlighting state development as a competitive response to military–strategic innovations outside national borders. He shows greater sensitivity, however, to the possibility that states may simply *fail* to respond effectively to external challenges, a fate, for example, that befell Poland during the Great Northern War (1700–21) and resulted in its dismemberment as an autonomous political entity. Inevitability is thus removed, but without a clear specification of the causal processes that determine *which* states will effectively respond to external challenges from a conflictual environment. Spruyt (1994)

---

[2] Tilly discusses this in terms of three possibilities derived from differing patterns of state–society interaction. In *coercion-intensive* situations, rulers could subdue society (especially the nobility) and erected massive extractive structures. In *capital-intensive* systems, rulers were at the mercy of the voluntary contributions of capitalists for the funds through which to construct mercenary armies for defense or conquest. Where holders of power and capital were relatively well balanced, he argues, capitalized coercion emerged, in which domestic elites were incorporated into the leadership of newly constructed national states that in part reflected their interests.

goes one step further and argues that state formation is not simply a product of the Darwinian struggle for survival in a world of intense military competition; other often nonviolent mechanisms, such as international exchange or mimicry, could be at work as well. Others contend that the absence of substantial inter-state war makes African or Latin American state building unlikely at best (Herbst 2000; Centeno 1997, 2002). The converse has also been argued – that sustained peace will likely at least partially erode the scope and/or cohesiveness of state institutions (Desch 1996). As, however, the prevalence of interstate war of a scale sufficient to threaten national sovereignty declines into near-nonexistence (Mueller 2009), bellicist perspectives tend to produce distressing and distressingly invariant predictions about the prospects for state building in the contemporary era.

And even in the anarchic contexts for which they were developed, many bellicist accounts are missing a clear causal mechanism that would distinguish success from failure. Why do elites necessarily respond to external threat in an institution-building fashion? Or, if effective response is not taken as inevitable, what explains the path taken? Without clear answers to such questions, hypothesis testing is necessarily incomplete, and evidence can be at best only loosely consistent with any account. Indeed, where careful attention is paid to causal mechanisms within the bellicist camp, further complexities emerge. For example, Cohen et al. (1981) have suggested that strategic conflict may be *initiated* by states to build a more powerful foundation for political control over society. This raises two very interesting issues: (1) conflict's effects may be asymmetrical based on state vulnerability – is it external threat or opportunity for conquest that matters? – and (2) conflict may thus become endogenous; it may be purposefully pursued by modernizing, authority-centralizing elites to make state building politically viable rather than being a (exogenous) force inducing an institution-building response.

One excellent response to some of these problems is that of Hui (2004), who begins by thinking systematically about the *different* ways in which states may respond to external threats. She points out that their responses can include immediate self-defense expedients that are self-strengthening (that enhance administrative capacity over the longer term) *or* self-weakening (mobilizing "immediate resource holders" but at a long-term institutional cost). This approach implies that conflict is of continued theoretical importance, but without the implicit teleology of other works. A key issue still not fully answered is to specify the political conditions that shape the trajectories that states take in response to external threats. Implicitly, this is a question of where public resources come from, for military–strategic defense is very costly. The resulting patterns of revenue extraction have been tightly linked to state-building outcomes. It is here that a connection to the resource curse literature is manifest, for it is in its purported effects on the revenue system that natural resource wealth may induce pernicious institutional and political dynamics.

Natural Resource Rents and Politics

It is not hard to see the prima facie case that underlies the connection made between natural resource abundance, the creation of "rentier states," and consequent political and institutional calamity. After all, massive resource wealth in Zambia and Congo has been associated with moderate to extreme political chaos and decades of economic decline. Even greater rents accruing to oil exporters after the OPEC embargoes of the 1970s have become associated with institutional chaos in Venezuela and Indonesia; civil insurrection in Algeria; and instability, underdevelopment, and bloated but ineffective states across the Middle East. At the same time, Japan, Taiwan, and Korea, among the states most widely recognized for their exceptional ability to guide their societies and economies and the unusual efficacy of their bureaucracies, are contexts usually seen as largely devoid of valuable natural resources.

This conventional wisdom may not be as plausible as it at first appears. The logic of the rentier state thesis holds that the presence of large mineral rents induces a series of pernicious outcomes in the state. Public resources are redirected to inefficient and costly consumer subsidies, to the creation of "white elephant" industries, and to the construction of patronage and clientelistic networks to sustain elites in power. These practices are said to induce private agents to reallocate their activity away from efficient production and toward the conquest of rents, often resulting in the societal capture of state institutions. And finally, because of the availability of "easy money" in the natural resource sector, the very administrative capacity of the state – particularly that involving the collection of taxes – is undermined, since the generation of "internal" revenues is no longer necessary to fund ongoing activities. There is a close affinity of causal mechanisms with the bellicist approach here: both take as central to state building the creation of an effective and penetrating public revenue bureaucracy.

The question is, however, where large resource rents are to be had, must states fail, or do other possibilities exist? Here, again, the problem is one of causal mechanisms: we need to know *why* easy wealth necessarily causes political elites to make choices that spur institutional decay. If there are other realistic choices to be made, especially if some of them lead eventually to the *construction* of higher-quality bureaucracies and stronger states, the resource curse thesis in its usual formulation is open to serious doubt. Instead of insisting on the inevitably pernicious effects of natural resource rents, we must then inquire into the factors that condition the use of such rents: when do they underwrite stronger states, effective bureaucracies, and national integration, and when do they induce predation, rent seeking, clientelism, and corruption (e.g., Kurtz and Brooks 2011; Jones Luong and Weinthal 2010; Dunning 2008; Karl 1997)? But if this is the case, and resource effects are not inevitable, the critical causal factor is not natural resource abundance but rather the factors that condition its use.

But indeed it is the case that quite a few major natural resource–intensive political economies ended up producing very effective states characterized by high levels of bureaucratic probity and deep institutional penetration of society. Mineral wealth, for example, was and is central to the Australian political economy from the colonial era forward; it was certainly dominant during the critical period of state building. Natural resource exports – including ores, oil, and renewable resources – did and do characterize the Canadian economy. Massive and sudden oil revenues since the 1970s have not, by most accounts, produced a marked decline in the quality of the British or Norwegian civil services. And ultimately, even the United States at different points in its history was heavily dependent on its enormous natural resource wealth. Indeed, with respect to the last, Schrank (2004) has demonstrated that the effects of resource abundance in the United States were critically shaped not by the resources themselves but rather by the social property relationships in which they were situated in different states.

The linkage in the literature between natural resource wealth and weak states has been founded in part on conceptual and measurement confusions. For scholars working in this paradigm, a common strategy has been to identify resource-dependent countries by the ratio of natural resource exports to gross domestic product (GDP) in the contemporary era. While at first glance, this measure seems reasonable enough, it is not consonant with the concept implied in theory – that access to easily collectible mineral rents promotes bloated, patronage-producing state structures. It is access to easily extractable rents that matters and not access specifically to foreign exchange – for citizens typically can also be bribed, employed, or bought off in domestic currency (Stijns 2005, 2006). What matters, then, is production, not exports.

But the denominator is also problematic – it is not clear why the resource share of GDP is appropriate as the point of the argument is about the amount of natural resource wealth available for political distribution and not that there is quite a lot of it *relative to* the size of the overall economy. Why would large amounts of distributable wealth be less politically pernicious in a richer versus a poorer country – as long as one makes no assumptions as to the inherent quality of governance in relationship to national income? If both of these measurement considerations are not taken into account, countries that have potentially very large natural resource sectors, but that don't tend to export them (instead they consume them domestically), or countries that are quite well off would tend to be coded as resource scarce, despite having enormous natural resource sectors that produce large politically allocable rents. Indeed, if we consider the top 10 least corrupt governments as defined by Transparency International in 2012, we find that at least four have enormous natural resource sectors (Canada, Norway, New Zealand, and Australia), and Denmark is an energy exporter with notable proven reserves.

This is only the beginning of the problem, however, for a form of what Schrank (2004) has recently described as "temporal selection bias" is also

The Social Foundations of State Building in the Contemporary Era 25

a potential cause of serious error. Where resources contribute positively to economic growth, they are progressively depleted during the course of development, leaving such states apparently resource poor later in their developmental trajectory; but wealth did not inhibit growth.[3] Indeed, the same logic applies even if resource wealth is unrelated to economic growth – depletion over time would still induce a false correlation between resource scarcity and development. Moreover, if the measure of resource dependence used is a ratio of resources to GDP, these states would appear to be decreasingly resource dependent, even if the resource sectors were not depleted. And if economic and political development are positively correlated, this temporal process will have a tendency to produce strong false negatives with respect to the relationship between resource wealth and state efficacy in contemporary-era cross-sectional (or short–time series) analyses.[4] Thus, even a better measure of the size of the contemporary resource sector is not enough to permit a valid test of the natural resources–political underdevelopment linkage. It becomes clear that any such design must encompass a long historical sweep, and indications of resource intensity of economic life must be considered at the *start* rather than the culmination of the process of political development and state building.

The causal dynamics posited in resource curse arguments also warrant scrutiny.[5] If the claim is that natural resource rents induce the creation of "rent-seeking societies" and corrupt bureaucracies, then this can only have meaning if this outcome is more likely in their presence than in their absence. But it is precisely this comparison that is seldom properly addressed – are developing countries that *lack* natural resources any less likely to suffer endemic corruption and clientelism? Should one be surprised that Haiti, Paraguay, and Kyrgyzstan have ineffective states despite the fact that they are "blessed" with an absence of massive exported natural resource wealth? Are they institutionally better off than Ecuador, Bolivia, or Kazakhstan, which have such wealth? For that matter, should our hopes for improvements in governance and public institutions in Bolivia be raised given the collapse of its once-dominant tin industry two decades ago, or should they decline as its vast natural gas reserves are developed?[6]

---

[3] E.g., the recent closure of the last coal mine in France should not suggest to us that France developed economically because it is resource poor but rather that development is at least in part the cause of its contemporary relative resource scarcity.

[4] We could note, for example, that the United Kingdom was a very important coal and copper producer early in its development; Germany had large coal and copper reserves that helped make it the industrial powerhouse it is today. Neither are major coal producers today. Similarly, the United States has a deep history of resource-induced development. See Wright and Czelusta (2003, 2002).

[5] Perhaps the best and most-nuanced treatment of the resource curse argument is that of Ross (2012).

[6] To put this in causal inference terms, what is the effect of oil wealth? Perhaps the best way to approximate this is to examine dynamics over time within a single country, observing the response of institutions to changes in resource discovery and exploitation patterns. Alternatively,

26 *Latin American State Building in Comparative Perspective*

The literature linking natural resource wealth and political underdevelopment is extensive and nuanced. But at its core, it turns on a simple and compelling idea, summarized by Ross: in such contexts, politicians seize control over the ability to distribute the natural resource windfall and then "divert state assets into patronage, corruption, and pork barrel funding . . . [and] once they hold the ability to reshape resource institutions to their advantage, they may use the opportunity to create additional, allocable rents to meet their patronage and corruption needs" (Ross 2001, 35–37). The implication is that rents, once available, help consolidate political control, which then makes possible the further corruption of the state bureaucracy in a downward spiral of malgovernance, slow growth, cronyism, and patronage politics. Natural resource wealth is said to have associated effects on public institutions, undermining the resource extractive (tax) side of the state while permitting the construction of an oversized but often-captured distributive apparatus. The implication of both dynamics – though not always explicitly stated – is that where rents are not available, politicians *must* use other means to maintain support, including modernization of the state and economy or the provision of public goods. Similarly, the hard work of constructing effective institutions of taxation to provide necessary revenue both requires strong penetration of society and, as a consequence, induces citizens to demand accountability if it does not, for example, provide commensurate improvements in public services (Huntington 1991, 65; Anderson 1987; Ross 2004).[7] Both contentions are functionalist, and the implicit causal mechanisms are underspecified; it is unclear why politicians will steal or misuse rents simply because they exist, nor is it obvious why the absence of wealth induces improvements in performance (or if it doesn't always, what conditions whether it will). Nor are citizen demands for accountability inevitable simply because the efficacy of taxation improves. Moreover, sustained failure would seem all too real an option where resources are scarce. And effective use of resource wealth (or self-enrichment through mechanisms that also provide public goods) is a possibility as well.

The most powerful version of this argument, however, sidesteps the question of elite beliefs or state capture altogether. Instead, the claim is made that because the natural resource provides the state with a large and readily taxable stream of wealth, normal institutions of taxation become small and weak relative to the development of the national economy (Chaudhry 1989, 143; Shafer 1994, 13). Because revenue agencies are understood to be costly (in political and economic terms) to construct, states will not build such institutions unless

---

one could consider closely matched countries that differ over the presence of a major resource sector, though the problem is that appropriate matches are decidedly hard to come by. An excellent recent treatment utilizing the first strategy in a cross-national econometric frame has already cast serious doubt on a related conventional wisdom linking natural resource (and oil) wealth to authoritarian political regime outcomes (Haber and Menaldo 2011).

[7] Indeed, such bargains have a long history, as in the promulgation of the Magna Carta, which ultimately led to consultation of Parliament before the levying of new taxes in England.

The Social Foundations of State Building in the Contemporary Era   27

they have to. Chaudhry (1994, 5; see also Chaudhry 1989, 107) does add a qualification that this is likely the case only when "the construction of basic state institutions *coincides* with large inflows of external capital [emphasis added]." Sequencing is thus crucial, and here the claim is that natural resource wealth undermines the process of state building only at its inception. Already institutionally well-developed states thus are not likely to suffer from newly found wealth to anywhere near the same extent. This is consistent with Karl's contention that natural resource flows were institutionally corrosive in the cases she examined, except in Norway, where strong state institutions predated its oil boom (Karl 1997, 13). A critical implication of both scholars' work is that the effect of resource wealth on political development is profound *only* at a critical juncture early in the state-building process. Of course, this does not solve the conundrum of the emergence of very effective states in contexts that have always had a very important natural resource sector, as in the United States, Canada, or Australia. Nor does it really address the micrologic behind this distinction: why wouldn't politicians in states that come to resource wealth late have incentives to use it for patronage or populist purposes and to sharply curtail taxation?[8]

Where resource-curse scholars do try to fill in the causal mechanisms in their account, they come to strikingly opposed conclusions over whether an abundance of resource wealth produces an excessively strong society or state. Some argue that such wealth produces a set of social actors – especially entrepreneurs in the export sector – that captures public institutions, renders the state incapable of pursuing a coherent "national interest," and makes it wholly dependent on the success of the mineral sector (Shafer 1994; Karl 1997). Others suggest that it is typically the state and not society that is too strong, arguing that the availability of vast sums permits politicians to displace private-sector elites or make them dependent on public largesse, while the high sunk costs associated with natural resource (especially mineral) extraction can weaken business in relationship to the state over time (Moran 1974, chapter 6; Vernon 1977, 171; Chaudhry 1989, 1994). These twin causal mechanisms that underlie resource-curse arguments are thus diametrically opposed. Either the access to rents empowers the incorporating state, or it empowers the rent-seeking society. The antinomical character of the posited causal mechanisms suggests that resource-curse theory is closer to shorthand for an observed correlation than for a causal relationship, and as we have seen, there is also substantial room to doubt the validity even of the observed correlation.

---

[8] Indeed, such arguments face difficulty explaining why, for example, the discovery of oil in Norway did little to change the country's status as one of the highest-taxation economies in the world, while in Alaska, for example, contemporary oil discovery led to a radical decline in the tax burden, from the twelfth highest in the nation in 1977 to the lowest in the nation every year since 1981 (Tax Foundation 2011). Moreover, Alaska is one of two states in the United States that have neither an income nor a statewide sales tax (Howe and Reeb 1997, 117).

28   *Latin American State Building in Comparative Perspective*

Finally, both the simple and the path-dependent form of the resource curse argument relies on the assumption that elites will misuse resources in an institutionally detrimental manner simply because they can. Even where elites are fundamentally self-interested, this is not necessarily the case. They may well pursue private gain or the provision of rents for their cronies, but this in no way precludes them from doing so through the provision of the sorts of public goods that can modernize the state over time. Politicians may, for example, create and distribute rents by engaging in large-scale transportation and communication infrastructure provision, educational expansion, and military modernization. Even if the contracts for such work are awarded to cronies of the government, or access to employment in such projects is distributed as patronage, the long-term effects are the same: roads and rails are laid, schools are built, pupils are educated, telegraphs and telephones unite the national territory, and the coercive face of the state is strengthened.[9] These are likely to reduce domestic transaction costs, promote national integration, strengthen national defense and/or make possible colonial expansion, raise levels of human capital, increase the rate of economic development, and broaden the scope of the central government. This in turn may ultimately create new social groups with vested interests in the modernization of governance – from middle-sector groups and public employees to new entrepreneurial elements that operate in nonresource sectors to reform-minded military officers. Rent seeking thus does not have to be absent for an influx of resource wealth to have salutary effects on state building, if the way in which rents are distributed has the effect of inducing changes favorable to state building as they accumulate *over time*. The static and dynamic institutional effects of resource wealth can thus be opposed.

Institutionalist Accounts

As the preceding makes clear, this book takes issue with some of the contentions in the regnant literature on the long-run development or underdevelopment of state institutions. Much more recently, an institutionalist account of state building in the Latin American region has been developed by Hillel Soifer (2006, 2011). By contrast with the ecological and bellicist approaches, Soifer's institutionalist account is complementary to the society-centric theory developed here.

This institutionalist approach begins with the observation that in the nineteenth century, Latin American states took two basic approaches to the establishment of governing institutions in their more peripheral regions. The implementation of state policies required the development of local structures of

---

[9] It is crucial, however, that the rents be extracted via the actual provision of the public good rather than through a wholesale process of theft wherein private actors receive contracts and payments for infrastructural or public goods provision that is not in fact ever delivered.

The Social Foundations of State Building in the Contemporary Era

administration and raised the question of how they would be staffed. In some cases, Soifer (2011, 10ff.) points out that central states *delegated* authority to local elites. In others, they *deployed* agents directly as bureaucratic representatives of the central state. This in turn created a set of incentives that had profound implications for national political development: delegated authority relied on elites whose income sources were typically "from landholdings or other aspects of their status in the local community," which in turn made them less dependent on the central authorities and created important principal–agent problems for governance. Conversely, deployed agents not only relied on the center for their incomes but also had an incentive to induce "cooperation with the effort to expand the reach of the state" (Soifer 2011, 10). This in turn, over time, aggregates into a pattern of local institutional practices that either facilitate or impede state building over the long haul. Deployed agents, thus, were much more compatible with effective institutional development.

This is an important point, and these institutional choices likely played the role assigned them by Soifer. The difference between the society-centric approach taken here and Soifer's institutional one has to do with the starting point. Whereas Soifer treats these institutional developments as structured but exogenous choices, the approach here would suggest that they are effectively conditioned by underlying social realities as highlighted in this book. Elites may alternatively select deployed versus delegated rule, but this is not necessarily a meaningful choice. Delegated rule, from the perspective of the center, all but guarantees difficulty in governing, collecting revenues, and mobilizing soldiers, and as such, it is hard to imagine that any national executive would prefer it to a deployment strategy. But deployed rule must overcome efforts by local elites to resist it. Where the institutional account meets the societal account presented in this book is on precisely this issue: the social relations of local production will shape whether local elites will see the imposition of deployed rule as an existential threat or a burden that may also have potentially quite lucrative implications. That said, further exploration of the societal–institutional interaction at the local level is very much a productive avenue for future research.

What Should We Do Next?

Earlier, a series of theoretical and empirical lacunae in the existing scholarship on state building and atrophy were identified, and theoretical advance will require that some of these gaps be filled. But there are also additional challenges that must be considered, particularly when considering the development of national administrative institutions in the late developing countries, and it is with this task that the next section begins. Thereafter, a theory of long-term institutional development and decay will be presented that seeks at once to supersede or subsume important portions of the existing literature, while at

30 *Latin American State Building in Comparative Perspective*

the same time contending with the distinctive challenges involved in explaining state-building outcomes in the postcolonial era.[10]

ADDITIONAL CHALLENGES FOR A THEORY OF CONTEMPORARY STATE BUILDING

The problems in the extant literature on state building identified previously do not exhaust the challenges that face any attempt to construct an alternative theoretical account applicable to the experiences of state building in the period after that of the canonical examples in Early Modern Europe. First, any such account must clearly distinguish itself from explanations of long-run economic outcomes, for at least in the late developers, political and economic modernization do not necessarily occur in the same times and places. Second, it must adequately address the issue of *time* itself, in two senses: political development unfolds over a long period of time, and the relative hierarchies of institutional strength that emerge tend to persist. That is, state building is a long-term process that likely involves substantial path dependence. As important, attention must also be paid to the ways in which the emergence and development of governmental institutions in the "late institutionalizers"[11] are quite different from the conditions that prevailed in the earlier cases of state building. It is inappropriate to assume – and empirically unlikely to be the case, as we shall see – that the dynamics that long ago provoked institutional modernization remain the principal drivers of the substantial variation we observe in the contemporary era. Causal heterogeneity by historical era is a distinct possibility, as, for example, critical conditions in the global economy and the strategic environment in which states find themselves have changed sharply.[12]

Economic versus Political Development?

Because so many (though notably, not all) advanced industrial countries are thought to have comparatively effective bureaucracies and were by and large located in the European cradle of economic and political development, there

[10] This term is meant broadly and is understood to include both the cases of nineteenth-century national liberation in the South American context and the twentieth-century decolonization and institution-building experiences of Africa and parts of Asia. There are also obvious differences among these contexts as well, but they share the experience of attempting to build national institutions in a world in which powerful and wealthy states already exist.

[11] This term is deliberately intended to evoke a parallel with the way in which *late developers* has been used. The critical point here is that like economic development, the challenge of creating effective administrative institutions is different for the countries not in the first wave of political modernization.

[12] Most notably, states are much more economically integrated in the context of late, and especially late, late development, and the military struggle for national survival characteristic of the anarchic state system of Early Modern Europe has all but abated in the post–World War II era (and much earlier in places like Latin America).

The Social Foundations of State Building in the Contemporary Era 31

has been a tendency to assume that economic and political development are quite tightly related to each other. This is perhaps most clear in the economics literature that largely conflates the development of effective governmental institutions with the emergence of strong or efficient property rights, the latter themselves seen as inherently growth producing (e.g., Acemoğlu et al. 2001). But as long as we are careful to hew to an *institutional* as opposed to policy-based notion of what state strength actually is, there is a much weaker empirical foundation for this connection. This is not a claim that strong political institutions cannot contribute to growth by effectively implementing appropriate economic policy. They surely can. But the factors that determine the economic strategies that states select are not the same as those that condition the strength of their political and administrative institutions, and economic improvement can come well before institutional development, if the latter comes at all (Glaeser et al. 2004, 298). For example, in terms of wealth and social development, Argentina was for the most, if not all, of the twentieth century Latin America's wealthiest country and among its best educated, most egalitarian, and least poverty stricken. At the same time, its political regime was among the most unstable in the region, and its governing institutions stand out for their comparative inefficacy. Similar points could be made about the United States: very substantial economic development took place in the Gilded Age after the Civil War, in the context of a state that did not seek to govern the economy and a judiciary that was regularly "subverted" because "money and power influenced the path of justice" (Glaeser and Shleifer 2003, 404). For the first century of its existence, the American state was characterized by a "radical devolution of power accompanied by a serviceable but unassuming national government," and it was only between 1877 and 1920 that *national* institutions "first emerged free from the clutches of party domination, direct court supervision, and localistic orientations" (Skowronek 1982, 15, 23). Einhorn (2000, 157; 2008) concurs, pointing out that the signal characteristic of the American national state until the twentieth century was its weakness.[13]

Similarly, as we shall see subsequently, Chile and Uruguay comparatively early on developed effective, central systems of political administration. But we will also find that the development of these institutions was intimately connected to the construction of an economic policy regime predicated on very high levels of public employment, government ownership of industry, and the maintenance for over a half-century of a broad-based and high-level tariff protection. The last, in particular, is a decidedly questionable policy choice in the context of economies of such small scale. And even in Korea, one of the paradigmatic cases connecting a highly effective state to spectacular economic development in the postwar era, Cumings (2005, 223) points out that governmental institutions had been highly centralized and bureaucratized

---

[13] Indeed, Einhorn (2000, 160n25) notes that, outside of emergencies, the US national state "taxed nothing but imported goods before the Civil War" and that the "tariff dominated until WWI."

32 *Latin American State Building in Comparative Perspective*

for a very long time – but it was only after 1960 that persistent sharp increases in economic output were recorded.

The Question of Time

Meaningful state building, at least in most accounts, is something that takes place over the long term. How long is of course not a matter of consensus, nor need it be identical across cases. But the factors that condition the ability of states to centralize and bureaucratize their public administrations do not produce observable results overnight. Why is this the case? First, there is the question of the state of existing knowledge, which was a principal issue for the early modernizers. It is perhaps too easy to forget, but the structure of modern bureaucratic organization had to be developed and perfected over a long period of time – and then it had to become adopted into the administrative machinery of government and ultimately prove its superiority in political, military, and fiscal terms. Only after this had occurred could it serve as a credible model for administrative reform. For this reason, Rueschemeyer contends that the emergence of strong, modern bureaucratic states in northern Europe took nearly a millennium, beginning with the foundation of the University of Bologna and becoming completed only in the nineteenth century (Rueschemeyer 2005, 144). Indeed, the process of the development of organizational and managerial knowledge is central to Ertman's (1997, 28) discussion of the influence of strategic conflict on institutional development – for the earliest modernizers had to increase the extractive capacity of their states when only feudal or ecclesiastical models of large-scale organization were available, leading to a reliance on decidedly suboptimal institutional forms like venal office and tax farming. Those who faced this challenge later, conversely, had available other forms of administration as well as a much larger supply of appropriately skilled labor. And in a world of transaction costs and imperfect subjective models, the diffusion and adoption even of institutions that provide *obvious* advantages in governance is far from automatic or rapid (see, e.g., North 1990, 8).

The question of time becomes even more pressing in arguments about state building that rely on processes of selection (in the evolutionary sense) – and many do – to sort out "better" from "worse" institutions. This is of course most central in the bellicist approach to state building, wherein it is the reality of war and conquest that overwhelms states that do not improve their administrative structures, thus over time transforming the states system and inducing convergence around better practices. But any fundamental reorganization of state and society driven by such an evolutionary[14] mechanism requires a long time frame, for not all rivalries produce conflict, not all defeats imply

---

[14] The term *evolutionary* is here understood in the natural science sense of change in a population that is driven by a selection process that induces differential survival – in this case of institutional forms. It is not meant in the colloquial sense of "gradual" or "incremental."

The Social Foundations of State Building in the Contemporary Era   33

dismemberment of states, and not all suboptimal institutional responses result in defeat.[15] But alternative selection mechanisms such as North's (1981) emphasis on economic competition or Spruyt's (1994) focus on institutional superiority of the sovereign state in making credible commitments and managing interunit political interaction are logically even slower. For they do not very directly implicate the survival of the national political unit and thus the lives and fortunes of the elites who govern it.

But it is not enough to make the point that the development of strong institutions takes time – especially if their institutionalization requires either the development of new normative structures (as in Rueschemeyer 2005), quasi-voluntary compliance and cooperation (as in Levi 1989), the creation of powerful supporting constituencies capable of carrying the institutions into the future, or the creation of settler versus extractive colonial economies and institutional structures over the course of one or more centuries (as in Acemoğlu et al. 2001). It not only thus takes time to build durable institutional structures, but we saw empirically in the opening chapter that the relative levels of institutional development tend to be quite stable over long periods of time.

This is consistent with a variety of theoretical approaches that have highlighted long-term stability of the hierarchy of institutional strength linked to discrete moments of substantial change as a species of "punctuated equilibrium" (Spruyt 1994, 24). Indeed, Acemoğlu and Robinson (2006, 326) point out that institutional stability is often maintained, even when some formal political structures are transformed, through the emergence of countervailing forms of informal de facto power that preserve the core of ex ante practices and norms.[16] Others have pointed out that institutions create vested interests that tend to perpetuate their patterns of operation even when environmental factors or changing social or technological structures make them decidedly suboptimal (e.g., Ertman 2005, 168) or, alternatively, transaction costs and information unavailability might drive the persistence of poor institutions (North 1990, 52). While there is much debate as to the underlying causes for the observed pattern of long-run institutional stability, there is a substantial group of scholars who argue that the state-building process involves path dependencies – differences at critical initial moments generate institutional patterns that become

---

[15] This is an important point that is explicit in Hui's (2004, 184) contention that states can respond to international strategic rivalry with institution building and taxation or through long-term self-defeating expedients like excessive indebtedness. But it is not at all difficult to see how such expedients might help states to overcome an immediate crisis and delay still further the selection effects involved in international conflict. Indeed, according to her, states utilizing such expedients can even sometimes defeat competitors who adopt better approaches (though this is probabilistically less likely).

[16] E.g., they point out that the post–Civil War South remained in institutional terms not terribly different from its antebellum patterns, with the replacement of chattel slavery by a more informal, semiservile labor system enforced by the Ku Klux Klan and Jim Crow.

self-reinforcing over time. If this is the case – and it is the contention of this book that it is – the further implication follows that the causal dynamics involved in state building exhibit hysteresis. That is, the effects of particular independent variables depend importantly on what has come before, and thus factors that might have initiated a virtuous circle of state building at one point in the development of national–state institutions will *not* necessarily have that effect should they emerge later. Windows of opportunity, thus, can close.

The challenge thus is to produce a theory of institutional development and underdevelopment that can account for long periods of stability punctuated by periods of change in specific critical moments. It must also develop a theoretical account that can explain why the factors that were hypothesized to induce a particular trajectory are *not* determinative outside of these critical moments. And finally, empirical evidence must be brought to bear that can evaluate a path-dependent explanation in its own terms, compare it against explanations taking a more traditional contemporaneous cause–effect form, and show that timing is essential to the causes of state building such that subsequent efforts to change institutional trajectory are ultimately powerfully impeded.

State Building in the Late Developers

At least since Gershenkron (1962), it has been argued that economic development in "late developers" involved fundamentally different challenges from those faced by the first generation to make the transition to modern industrial capitalism.[17] This book contends that a similar dynamic – distinctive challenges of political development for late developers – characterizes the state-building process, making it dangerous to rely too heavily on the foundational literature that focused on the first states in Early Modern Europe. The differences that are essential have to do with information and the powerful selection pressures ascribed to interstate war.

The first difference – the global informational environment – represents a clear "advantage of backwardness." For the diffusion of administrative forms allowed late developers to gain the advantages of institutional innovation without paying the costs involved in experimentation, discovery, and repeated reform. Indeed, by the nineteenth and twentieth centuries, it had become clear that Weberian, meritocratic bureaucracy was a decided improvement on traditional feudal, ecclesiastical, or patrimonial alternative models of political administration. These advantages can be seen in the ability of states to raise revenues, solve principal–agent problems that impede governability, and raise the efficiency (cost relative to output) of producing public goods. And by the second half of the twentieth century, there was no shortage of international institutions endeavoring to transmit this information, promote administrative

---

[17] Indeed, Gershenkron's (1962) argument suggested a set of complementary differences in the development of state institutions that were linked to the challenge of late economic development.

The Social Foundations of State Building in the Contemporary Era

reform, and even subsidize or punitively incentivize the transformation of corrupt or patrimonial political systems through the provision or conditioning of aid and loans.

The second major difference hinges on the causal status of interstate war. The leading proponents of conflict-centric approaches to political development highlight the effect war is said to have in forging elite unity, driving the formation of powerful revenue bureaucracies, and selecting out of the system those states that do not adapt and focused their work almost exclusively on the period of national state development in Europe. But as Hui (2005) has pointed out, this was an almost unique environment of near-constant, severe conflict over the course of centuries. Most regional state systems, in fact, have not been characterized by anything like this degree of conflict. Some have argued, however, that more common and more limited "interstate rivalries" might be sufficient to drive state building (e.g., Thies 2005, 456; 2004).[18] But as such, these theories imply at most very limited actual conflict and minimally little more than posturing and the display of force. It is hard to see therefore how they are parallel in theoretical terms to the centuries of war-as-existential struggle that characterized the European continent.

In the Latin American context, specifically, two features of the strategic environment are notable. First, while there was some interstate conflict of a severe character in the nineteenth century, most conflict was civil rather than international. And by the twentieth century, interstate war had all but ceased to exist in Latin America. Indeed, only one meaningful war occurred in South America in the entirety of the twentieth century (the Chaco War between Bolivia and Paraguay). This is a global trend that Mueller has forcefully demonstrated, declaring boldly, "War has almost ceased to exist." In particular, he finds that interstate conflict that actually alters territorial borders (i.e., conquest and consequent state death for the losing party) has become almost extinct (Mueller 2009, 307). And of course, it is precisely this last sort of war that is hypothesized to drive state building in most bellicist interpretations.

This leaves us with two possibilities. Either the process of political development has been radically undermined by the absence of interstate conflict – and the pressure this takes off of states to modernize their bureaucracies, increase their tax revenues, or better organize their administrative systems – or other factors are principally driving the (large) variations in administrative capacity to be found in the contemporary developing world. The theory developed next is designed to do precisely the latter – explain the development of states in a world in which war to the death is not the state of nature.

---

[18] To qualify as an enduring rivalry for Thies, states need only engage in six *militarized interstate disputes* (MIDs) within a 20-year period. MIDs in turn are defined in such a way that the mere threat or display of military force is sufficient to constitute a militarized dispute. For the complete operational definition, see Ghosn et al. (2004).

36 *Latin American State Building in Comparative Perspective*

THE SOCIAL FOUNDATIONS OF INSTITUTIONAL ORDER

For late developers, the initial critical juncture has a comparatively noncontroversial starting point. Decolonization and independence required the creation of an initial set of national political institutions by Creole elites to replace the administration of the former colonial metropole. This institutional settlement – *or* a pattern of fragmentation and regionalism if elite agreement on the basic structure of national government could not be achieved – would powerfully condition the way subsequent institutional development unfolded. This initial branching point in the construction of postindependence governmental institutions would be followed by a second decisive moment as these preexisting structures faced a powerful new challenge: electoral and/or insurrectionary mobilization that aimed to initiate the incorporation into political competition of the representatives of nonelite citizens in the middle and working classes. This would introduce a further deflection of trajectories of state building that would decisively condition the relative scope, depth, and efficacy of South American governmental institutions into the contemporary era. In the sections that follow, the theoretical argument undergirding this two-stage, path-dependent explanation will be laid out.

Theory I: Launching a State-Building Trajectory

What we first focus on, then, are the conditions that shape the developmental trajectories that states face at their birth as independent national-state units. In the Latin American region, this first critical juncture took place early in the process of economic modernization of all the countries in the region. As a consequence, agriculture and mining were typically the dominant economic sectors, for industrialization was at best small scale and limited in extent. And it would be the social relations that govern the operation of agriculture – where the bulk of the population found employment – that were thus critical to the possibility of effective state building.

But what is the linkage between social relations and institutional development? This book argues that where a local elite organizes a labor-repressive agrarian economy, effective political development, even in the face of war or wealth, is very unlikely.[19] But free labor is not sufficient to produce a positive institutional trajectory. A second condition is required; that is, the incorporation of upper-class actors from all major factions into the national political

---

[19] Such an elite could be a settler population, a traditional feudal aristocracy, or simply a locally dominant upper class. The notion that rural social relations importantly condition long-term political outcomes is not new, being central to Moore's (1966) discussion of regime dynamics and Brenner's (1977, 1987) explanation of European economic development; see also Aston and Philpin (1987). The emphasis here on the role that free vs. unfree labor has in the development of state institutions is inspired directly from the recent pathbreaking work of Schrank (2004) that considers the role of social structure and resource wealth in US economic development.

The Social Foundations of State Building in the Contemporary Era 37

system – while maintaining the exclusion of the popular sectors – is crucial to enabling cooperation in state building and public goods provision activities, despite whatever cleavages might otherwise divide them. When both conditions obtain, and this sometimes came about only after a substantial period of conflict, elites will come together to centralize power in national institutions that are able to penetrate and control society to an ever-increasing extent, while simultaneously building national infrastructure, imposing substantial taxation, and providing substantial collective and individual benefits to the oligarchy that created them. An overview of this part of the argument can be found in Figure 2.1a. But why are these two conditions critical?

Social Relations. Hearkening back to Moore (1966), I contend that the absence of labor-repressive relations of production is critical to the long-run development of, not regimes, but effective political institutions. This distinction is emphatically not between capitalist and noncapitalist forms of production, for there are quite a few ways of organizing the economy that do not involve the exchange of land, labor, and capital on markets but that nevertheless do not require labor coercion (e.g., labor service tenancy, sharecropping, common property systems, or cooperative forms of production, inter alia). The emphasis here is specifically on the mechanism by which labor is recruited and employed in production – is it an inherently coercive process, or can workers leave the farms or mines free of any practical or de jure encumbrances? Where rural elites recruit their workforces through servile or semiservile means (through, for example, slavery, formal serfdom, indenture, labor corvées, or legally enforced debt peonage), administrative centralization and state building are decidedly unlikely.

Why is this the case? Labor-repressive systems leave local elites extremely vulnerable to the centralization of authority, as they imply the possibility that national governments may eventually be unable or unwilling to maintain the strict social control and labor repression on which the agrarian political economy (and potentially elites' own physical survival) depends. Even more critically, in such contexts, agrarian elites will also resist the taxation necessary to support even military modernization or collective defense against external aggression, to say nothing of paying the costs for other central state institutions. Labor-repressive economic systems are of notoriously low productivity (giving elites little margin for added fiscal contribution) and are inauspicious settings for most productivity-enhancing investments. Coerced labor forces rarely efficiently adapt and employ improved technologies, and elites are in any event very unlikely to permit (or pay for) the generalized educational improvement necessary to support such modernization. To do so would empower workers whose disempowerment is the cornerstone of economic production. And finally, there is the distributional question: ceding taxation authority and control over coercion to the center would be particularly risky in contexts where urban interests, competing regions, or other social classes might gain control or influence. They

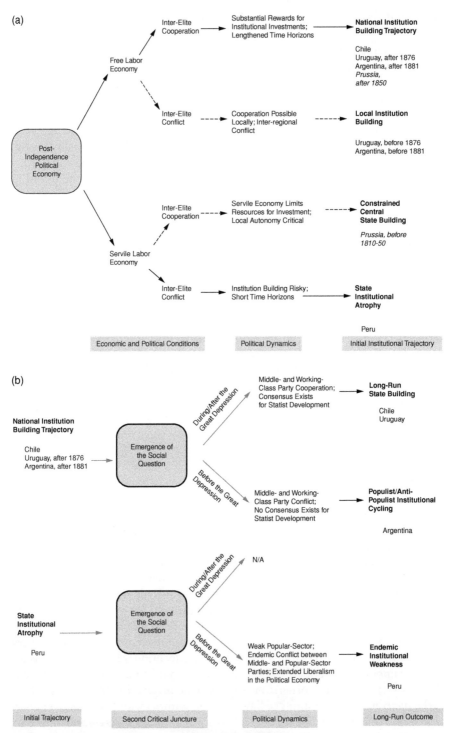

FIGURE 2.1. The argument in brief: (a) the first critical juncture; (b) the second critical juncture.

The Social Foundations of State Building in the Contemporary Era

might well, after all, form distributive or redistributive coalitions that exclude agrarian elites or some subset of them and would thus immediately threaten the rural social order.

This last threat is quite plausible, for urban-oriented governments have often moved to incorporate political actors beyond the elite strata as part of a strategy to build the political foundations for industrialization – which generally would require economic and social reforms anathema to rural elites, including, most notably, land reforms and direct resource transfers. Or more likely, because Latin American governments historically have overwhelmingly represented the interests of the powerful, agrarian elites might simply have to contend with efforts designed to promote industrialization at the rural sector's expense. Industrialization requires workers, and profitability in nascent industries requires low wages, an urban labor surplus, and cheap food. In servile systems with labor effectively bound to the countryside and to low-productivity agriculture, no such labor force can be recruited, and food prices remain comparatively high. Thus even capitalist industrialization threatens such agrarian systems with radical transformation. And if industrialization requires foreign exchange that can only be obtained from the export earnings of the agricultural sector, permitting centralization and institution building would also detonate a straightforward sectoral clash – as the state seeks to transfer foreign exchange earnings from agro-exporters to local industrialists.

Where labor is not servile – and this must be considered broadly to include any form of tenure in which a peasant has the practical legal right to leave the farm – the development of a modern army and the centralization of power are not life-or-death threats for local elites. Such situations would naturally include agrarian social structures characterized by independent family farms or capitalist agribusinesses employing wage labor but also noncapitalist, traditional large holdings staffed by peasants sharecropping, working for usufruct, or working as labor service tenants, as long as they had the legal ability to depart should they so choose. Some, but certainly not all, such settings have also been linked to better economic performance and at a minimum greater efficiency in the allocation of labor at least in comparison to servile systems. Elites in free-labor settings are frequently accustomed to paying something approaching market prices for labor, but that said, they also have the real potential to invest in labor-saving technology should such costs become onerous; these are investments that are irrational in servile systems. And, critically, military service by peasants would not risk the social instability it can bring to servile political economies when peasants, with newly acquired skills in warfare, return.

National Elite Politics. Although rural politics and rural elites are important, they do not alone define the amenability of a polity to successful state-building processes. Equally important are the linkages between the state executive and the upper classes as a whole. The critical factor here is that elites *beyond* the governing faction must have achieved meaningful political incorporation – and a share in political power. Where central authorities are at odds with powerful regional or local elites, or where the central state is dependent on the tax-collecting power of provincial strongmen or holders of venal office, political centralization will be blocked, and the expanded resource extraction that drives both state building and human capital formation cannot be imposed; it founders on the short-term self-interest of uncoordinated elites. But where elites are incorporated – either through cooperation in the form of an "oligarchic democracy" or through imposition in more absolutist bureaucratic settings – their collective interests can be organized within the state, and even difficult choices that have principally longer-term payoffs can be made. This is particularly true when they are made in the context of external challenges that, if unmet, would threaten the collective survival of the elite itself. My argument does not imply that state building is impossible (or even less likely) in federal systems, for the existence of subnational political units does not itself imply that local elites are not simultaneously effectively incorporated in the overarching national political system. The key question is whether regional interests are meaningfully included in national political institutions in ways that don't permanently benefit or marginalize one elite subgroup or region.[20]

What matters is whether the interests of the central state and those of powerful regional or local elites are harmonized or at least not directly threatening to each other. An absolutist road to political development would do so by making status as a member of a local elite dependent on administrative appointment, salaried employment, or military service, as defined by the central state (this could be Soifer's [2006] "deployed" strategy or militarized authoritarian dependence as in Vormärz Prussia). In such contexts, the center has discretion over who has access to such employment – positions are neither freely purchased, nor held as individual property, nor inherited – and the resources supporting the positions (and thus their status and power) come from the center. The alternative path, more typical of Latin America, to elite coordination involves a much less powerful central executive – one in which local elites effectively hold shared sway. This is the case in "oligarchic democracies" where the central state becomes the venue in which the collective interests of the upper classes are defined and articulated, and as such it can credibly be seen as a provider of collective goods for the elite without simultaneously threatening its independent authority – by sharing power across factions and/or credibly enabling the alternation of political control. This is most feasible when contending elite factions and parties are at least somewhat heterogeneous, and thus cross-cutting, in their sectoral and/or geographic composition. Should elites manage this, they would then form what McAdam (1982, 38–39), following

[20] While one could hypothesize that federal systems might be more prone to intractable conflicts among competing (regional) elite groups because they reify regional differences, this remains an interesting empirical question that should be addressed.

The Social Foundations of State Building in the Contemporary Era 41

Gamson (1968), called a "competitive establishment."[21] However, much as they may be at odds with each other over some of the issues of the day, they are united in their desire to avoid the expansion of the political arena to include subalterns and favor using the state to provide public goods broadly beneficial to elite interests. Importantly, the provision of public goods can also be used to generate private benefits – through the allocation, for example, of government contracts and the distribution of resulting employment through patronage and clientelistic channels. And in this way, selective incentives can also come to bear to mitigate the potential free riding of elite beneficiaries of these public goods. Of course, an often substantial part of the cost of the provision of these public goods can also be imposed on the middle and working classes (who have little say in selecting what is provided) through regressive forms of taxation.

Where elite inclusion and popular sector exclusion obtain, the time horizons of politicians can lengthen, and policy choices that at once enrich the upper classes but also produce long-run developmental benefits (e.g., expansion of rail infrastructure, education, economic promotion, or industrialization) become more likely. Critically, political bargains that create institutions that undergird elite cooperation are important in this context. They embody an effort to create an intertemporal agreement that prevents the extreme abuse of power by incumbents and thereby facilitates longer-run decisions that create policies that are "more effective, more sustainable, and more flexible" (Spiller et al. 2008, 6) than where such durable bargains cannot be struck.

Of course, this is generally possible only where the political system is effectively and exclusively dominated by upper-class interests, ensuring that newly empowered public institutions cannot be used in a redistributive way by middle-class or popular-sector actors. If democratization occurs early and nonelite social classes achieve real influence, this interelite cooperation around institutional development may quickly break down, and the political and material resources necessary to underwrite state-building efforts will not be forthcoming. None of this implies an absence of political competition – indeed, the struggles among contending elite factions are frequently vigorous. But once real mass suffrage becomes part of the equation, the possibility of launching an institution-building dynamic becomes more remote, for the now-real threat of redistributive politics undermines elites' willingness to support the construction of institutions strong enough to be able to impose serious costs on them aimed at promoting nonelite interests.

The vertiginous development of Latin American state institutions – where it occurred – empirically happened at two important moments. The first was,

---

[21] A similar distinction is made by Higley and Burton (2006, 14–15) between "disunited" and "consensually united" political elites. The former are locked in zero-sum struggle, whereas the latter are linked by interlocking social and communications networks that, while they contain factions that regularly oppose one another, embody the dominance of no particular faction and are founded on an "underlying consensus about most norms of political behavior."

as we have seen earlier, in the political settlements that gave birth to viable national governments (sometimes in the wake of more than a half-century of postindependence civil conflict). The second, however, occurred as part of the effort by these states to cope with the emergence of the middle and working classes as political forces that could no longer simply be excluded from political participation – at least not at an acceptable cost. This challenge induced a variety of responses by elites – or the contending actors themselves – to organize this political incorporation, with a powerful long-term effect on the character of institutional development. It is to this second critical juncture that we next turn.

Theory II: Economic Crisis, the Rise of Mass Political Participation, and the Postwar State

The first critical juncture – the social foundations and political dynamics that structured the initial formation of national political institutions – launched a trajectory for Latin American states, either in the direction of improved, more deeply penetrating governmental institutions or toward persistent weakness, regionalism, and a central state whose authority was geographically circumscribed and often questioned by important societal segments. This initial branching point does not, however, serve by itself to determine long-run outcomes. For the institutional structures created in the era of national-state formation all inevitably faced a second challenge, generally sometime between 1900 and the 1940s, of managing the political incorporation of the urban middle- and working-class masses into politics. This part of the argument is summarized in Figure 2.1b.

This challenge from below, commonly identified as the "social question," would permanently transform the terrain of Latin American politics in authoritarian and democratic contexts alike. And the manner in which it unfolded was central to the long-run development of state institutions – even those not directly related to managing cross-class political conflict. Why is mass political incorporation a moment in which fundamental institutional trajectories can be altered? The incorporation of the voices of (at least the urban) popular sectors fundamentally transforms political contestation by placing the question of *redistribution* squarely in the center of political debate. Middle- and working-class actors all across the Latin American region mobilized in the first half of the twentieth century to demand a greater share of the economic pie, a voice in public policy, and, in many cases, a transformed and expanded role for the state. But the way in which public institutions were actually restructured to accommodate and/or control this irruption from below varied widely. But once created, these institutional patterns, or indeed the inability to construct institutions with any longevity, persisted over the long haul. Consequently, the next step is to explore the causal dynamics that account for the trajectories of political development that were a result of these institutional outcomes.

The Social Foundations of State Building in the Contemporary Era   43

We cannot, however, abstract away from the first critical juncture, and this implies that the second critical juncture embodies a form of hysteresis: the same basic patterns of emergence of the social question produced decidedly different outcomes depending on the preexisting trajectory on which the state found itself as a result of the first critical juncture. The second critical juncture thus *deflects* the initial state-building trajectory into alternative long-run outcomes but does not uniquely determine what they might be. This second theoretical stage would not be necessary, however, if the character of the irruption of the masses were in fact constant across the cases or reducible to the factors produced by the resolution of the first critical juncture – but it is not.

The timing and manner in which the masses demanded and gained entry into national politics varied importantly across the region, and the four cases considered in detail here, in ways that are exogenous to the institutional and societal dynamics that gave birth to national institutions in the postindependence era. The emergence of the social question on the national political agenda was, after all, typically driven by mobilization from below. Contingent political struggles were an important part of the determinants of popular-sector mobilization and the ability to force inclusion. That said, the timing of the political engagement of middle- and working-class citizens also had a demographic and geographic foundation – they would first have to come to exist in sufficient numbers (to be able to effectively press their case). Moreover, patterns of mobilization and inclusion also reflected how concentrated the population was, or, for example, the urban population proportion and its immigrant versus citizen composition. None of these factors follows obviously or necessarily from the resolution of the first critical juncture. The point is that while the way in which mass incorporation was initially achieved matters importantly, it is not a product of the first wave of state building and varies independently across the positive and negative institutional trajectories that emerged from the first critical juncture.

The emergence of the social question as an unavoidable political problem – and the subsequent initial political incorporation of middle-class or working-class actors – occurred at different times in different contexts. Part of this difference in timing owes to the characteristics of the national economy in the early twentieth century, for some agricultural systems – as in grain and ranching in Argentina – had generated significant associated export processing industries, while others had few such industrial linkages or were, like mineral production, typically only able to generate at best modest employment. The critical dividing line is whether popular-sector emergence came well before the onset of the Great Depression (and the near-total collapse of the liberal international economy that it entailed) or during and after this period. For this moment marked a conceptual sea change that fundamentally shaped the underlying material interests that these actors brought to the political system. Where the middle classes, for example, emerged in large numbers *before* the Depression, this was a consequence of their linkage to a vibrant, private export economy. For this was the era of global laissez-faire and free trade, and if large numbers of such middle-class positions were created, it was because the private – principally export – economy was thriving and created associated sectors employing large numbers of relatively educated middle-sector workers. Where the middle class emerged later, during and after the Depression, this possibility was precluded. In that context, the bulk of middle-sector occupations was created within the public sector and linked to the expanding, protected, domestically oriented industrial sector or tied to administration, education, health care, or other public goods provision.

Why was this distinction of first-rank political importance? Where the middle sector was firmly centered in a booming, private export economy of the pre-Depression era, this would typically produce a political vehicle that favored the general outlines of that political economy: the gold standard, convertibility, free trade, and limited public-sector regulation. There were certainly critical reform demands often made by these new middle-class parties, including the democratization of the political system and the elimination of corruption, patronage politics, and vote rigging. But the scope and reach of state institutions were not a major axis of elite–middle-sector divisions, for their material interests were comparatively reconcilable with each other. By contrast, when a middle sector principally grew out of the state bureaucracy, which emerged politically after the economic tsunami of the Great Depression hit, its political representatives would be much more amenable to protectionism (itself in any event inevitable in the short term as trade collapsed), statism, and developmentalist economic strategies. For at this point in time, not only was the export economy devastated but free-trade economic policies were in near-universal disrepute. The attractiveness of an alternative rooted in the substantial expansion of the public sector and an increase in its power and prestige for a middle class already centered in the public bureaucracy were obvious. And the dominant, nonsocialist development model available – state-managed, import-substituting capitalism – would accomplish precisely this. Thus, middle-class parties came to have common ground with the emergent working-class parties and unions in the protected industries. Where differences occurred, they were over the level of redistribution. But this was a bridgeable gap, and strongly redistributive policies were not typically part of the bargain – nor were they essential features of statist industrialization. What mattered in this critical juncture for long-run political development, however, was whether the political representatives of the middle classes could or could not reach a durable state-building accommodation with parties tied to the working class and urban poor. And this was linked to the timing of their emergence and whether the economic center of gravity of the middle class was in the private or public sector; only where both middle and working classes had much to gain in the expansion and strengthening of the central state was political accommodation likely. For as the private sector at the time was largely export oriented and nonindustrial,

The Social Foundations of State Building in the Contemporary Era   45

if the middle classes were located principally there, they faced a zero-sum conflict of interest with a nascent and typically protected industrial sector focused on the domestic market.

The incorporation of working-class parties into national political competition often came somewhat later than that of the middle classes (though sometimes they were relatively coterminous). But the politics of the industrial working class were usually fairly clear: by the time of the Great Depression, the labor movement and its political representatives typically backed a vigorous policy of economic reorientation toward the domestic economy, protectionism, subsidized industrialization, and the creation of myriad social and economic benefits (i.e., a public role in the provision of pensions, health care, housing, and education).[22]

It would be an understatement to say that the pressure that this joint emergence of the popular sectors into national politics put on state institutions – which were themselves often of comparatively recent vintage – was intense. For the first time, powerful political voices were demanding major distributive policies, at the same time as they were advancing a political–economic agenda that also threatened to reorganize economic winners and losers along sectoral lines. Traditional elites – typically tied to the agro-export sectors – found themselves under threat both economically as the Depression devastated trade and politically as often-radical, working-class actors demanded public industrial investment and protectionism, sometimes in conjunction with emergent middle-class parties as well. And a large portion of this statist developmental effort would have to be financed through taxation directly or indirectly levied on traditional exporters. Such an effort could be rendered politically stable only where a broad, cross-class popular sector coalition could form to support it; it necessarily faced very powerful opposition.

The way in which this crisis of representation was resolved involved the interaction of the preexisting institutional trajectory with the politics of the emergent middle and working classes. In cases in which the initial path of political development was favorable to the development of strong institutions (Argentina, Uruguay, and Chile), the foundation existed for a major expansion of the reach and power of the central state. But it was far from inevitable, for the political dynamics that could *consolidate* a major expansion of state institutions were quite different from those that might simply bring it about.

---

[22] This was not necessarily a redistributive policy – though by increasing formal sector workers' cash and social wages, it was perhaps modestly so. The beneficiaries of these reforms in the formal sector working class, especially its unionized component, were, in Latin America, a relatively privileged stratum when compared to the majority of the population that languished in the urban informal sector or comprised the peasantry. Seen only in relation to the traditional oligarchy, this was a redistributive outcome but not one that favored the unorganized urban and rural poor.

For countries on an initially favorable path coming out of the first critical juncture – with cooperation among elites and nonservile social relations inducing the formation of viable national institutions – if the timing of middle-class political incorporation predated the Depression, in policy terms, middle-sector workers were typically tied to the oligarchy-dominated export sector economically and to free trade and laissez-faire politically. By contrast, working-class interests, not similarly centered in the agro-export economy, would promote economic redistribution and protectionist industrialization. So if major expansions of the scope and reach of the state were to take place, they were generally initially carried by the working classes and their political representatives, acting alone, and only when and where they could achieve power alone. Moreover, even in the comparatively rare cases in which presidents came to power with a principally working-class base, and implemented major reforms to the institutions of the state, a variety of problems would emerge that would militate against the long-run consolidation of these reforms. First, the staffing of the rapidly expanding state bureaucracy would of necessity be dominated by allies of this single political faction. Private sector–based middle-class parties would not initially cooperate with such an effort, and in turn their adherents would be excluded from the employment and other benefits of massive public-sector expansion. Without middle-class party cooperation at the outset, thus, the large employment gains would tend to exclude partisans of this sector, reducing the interest middle-class parties might have in subsequent cooperation, for the stabilization of these institutions would not particularly benefit their constituents. This made such institutional changes a matter of ongoing political conflict, not a parameter within which politics was carried out.

Should middle-class parties subsequently return to power, of course, the situation would be reversed, and they would seek to staff the bureaucracy at the expense of the incumbents who were largely partisans of their working-class opponents. And as a consequence, both the structure of public institutions and the civil servants that staffed them were subject to substantial volatility. Real, lasting institutionalization of such major institutional changes requires a broad, cross-class supporting coalition that in this context would be decidedly difficult to obtain or construct. With the middle classes largely outside the public sector, lacking a leading role in the design of developmentalist policy, and with material interests largely tied to the agro-export elite, the formation of an antioligarchical cross-class coalition behind the strengthening of the state and public interventionism was too difficult a political lift. Instead, politics would become a struggle in large measure over the legitimacy of an expanded state role and over who would control the institutions of the state (and the employment it represented). Policy would spiral between populist and antipopulist extremes, with no permanent, widely accepted institutional solution in the offing, for neither side was likely to win decisively or be permanently defeated. Nor would, for example, cooptation of a mobilized working class be an option, as the costs

The Social Foundations of State Building in the Contemporary Era 47

of such a strategy would be immense, and it would require powerful institutions that by definition did not yet exist to contain and channel their interests.

These dynamics did not take place where middle- and working-class political entry came late. In this context, an already-consolidated national state confronted the inclusion of middle- and working-class political parties, both of which were pushing for major expansions in public-sector activity. To be sure, the politics of these two groups were not identical, and middle-class parties were typically not terribly interested in redistributive policies. But on the core issues of economic management – economic protection, state ownership of industry, social welfare policies, and state direction of the economy – the material foundation for a lasting middle-class–working-class accommodation could be found. A statist development strategy would give middle-class sectors major expansions in employment opportunities and improvement in the material conditions of life as the state administration expanded its economic reach, enhanced its tax-generating capacity, and began to provide important social benefits, especially for the white-collar workers in the public sector itself. Members of the formal working class as well as domestically oriented industrialists benefited from the provision of state support as well as extensive economic protectionism, leading to rapid industrial expansion and increased employment tied to production for the sheltered domestic economy. This created a broad-based developmentalist coalition that provided crucial cross-class political support for effective and deep state institutions – support that was sufficient to make possible the consolidation of this major expansion of the institutional reach and capacity of the state and to be able to enforce its revenue demands in large measure on the traditional export oligarchy. This coalition in fact could often also count on some elite support, coming from the expanding industrial sectors that were reliant on protectionist policies and state-subsidized inputs.

The worst of all possible worlds – from the perspective of strong state institutions – came in a context where public institutions began on an already feeble foundation and were suddenly confronted by myriad redistributionist and statist demands by newly organized middle- and/or working-class actors. This trajectory began with political elites implacably opposed to the expansion of the state's infrastructural power, a position that became all the more determined as demands for heightened taxation, government regulation, and, most important, redistribution came to be voiced explicitly and powerfully in national politics. For acquiescence to such an institution-building policy during the era of the Depression would necessarily imply the imposition of substantial taxation on agro- and mineral-export elites. By contrast, with limited ex ante industrialization, an alternative elite coalition based on the industrial sector was unrealistic, for this group remained as yet underdeveloped and thus of limited political and economic importance. Similarly, without a history of statism, or strong central institutions, what middle-class actors that had emerged were not especially supportive of redistribution or statist developmentalism, tied as they were to the only important economic pole in the economy – the

48　　Latin American State Building in Comparative Perspective

agro-export sector. And even were the emergent working classes to come to power in such a context, there would only be a very limited institutional foundation on which to build, one too weak to constrain elite and middle-class resistance.

Thus an alliance with middle-sector political actors could not be a viable path to state building, for the material interests of middle-sector and working-class groups diverged sharply. Bringing the middle sectors into the coalition after launching such an institutional trajectory would also be difficult, for the expansion of the state would have been accomplished by, and *staffed* by, partisans of the incumbent government. To make room for a serious ex post accommodation with middle-class parties, the fruits of public employment and other patronage distribution would have to be redistributed among erstwhile political enemies, and questions of longer-term interparty trust would further bedevil such an arrangement. The only way room for this sharing of resources could be made would require a curtailment of existing jobs and other resources for partisans of the working-class–backed incumbent party that launched a statist trajectory of political development. Such a bargain would thus purchase an uncertain ally at the cost of weakened political control, the sharing of decision-making power, and internal division for the incumbent.

Instead, a powerful elite and middle-sector coalition would in these political contexts likely remain committed to the restriction of the reach of the central state's institutions and to the prevention of developmentalist or redistributionist economic policy (*even* during the Great Depression). And it would usually face a comparatively small mobilized working class incapable of instituting or institutionalizing state-building changes on its own.[23] Instead, a more limited state reach, policy gyrations, and weak institutions would remain the long-term outcome.

RESEARCH DESIGN AND PLAN OF THE BOOK

Eric Nordlinger (1968) noted more than 40 years ago that the study of political development was at least implicitly historically oriented, and most scholarship made claims that at a minimum required examination of outcomes that emerged over long periods of time and that the sequencing of key independent variables was often a critical element in determining them. This is as true today as it was then – though contemporary scholarship has been more self-conscious about the implications that the path-dependent character of arguments has for the testing of theory. For example, as Mahoney (2003, 53) has pointed out in the context of the path dependencies involved in understanding long-term economic development in Latin America, "explanations of differences

---

[23] After all, the premise of this path was a relatively limited process of industrialization in the pre-Depression era, which of needs restricts the size and thus potential economic and political power of the working classes.

The Social Foundations of State Building in the Contemporary Era 49

among units that draw on the current attributes of those units will often be inadequate." And of course, the matter becomes still more complicated when theories founded on substantial path dependencies must be evaluated against alternatives that are contemporaneous in their structure and are premised on the absence of hysteresis.

The implication is that an adequate theory of political development must of necessity consider a long historical sweep – if only to meaningfully accommodate the testing of alternative theories that are at issue. In fact, some theoretical claims require even more than the examination of the political development of contemporary states over the *longue durée* – most notably, the bellicist contention that conflict and the threat of conflict drive institution building. Here a long time frame is required even for the specification of the appropriate universe of cases, for a proper understanding of the effect of war making on state building cannot be founded on the observation (however accurate) that most effective contemporary nation-states were forged in the crucible of international conflict. What is missing here is the fact that state collapse was at the critical moment in European history a likely outcome of violent international conflict (Fazal 2004). The consequence is that war or the threat of conflict may be an enabling condition for initiating a process of state formation and strengthening, but much scholarship sees this as operating through an evolutionary selection process rather than a proper causal force. To wit, war may make states, but it seems to do so only occasionally. Scholars of state formation – by emphasizing the historical development of actually existing states – have fallen into the trap of selection bias by virtue of the fact that the states for which war sparked collapse (or which likely responded to external threats with what Hui calls "self-weakening expedients") were often dismembered and thus selected out of the contemporary sample (Hui 2004). While for those that survived, war appears to have been an important motivator for institutional improvement, to correctly assess its causal weight, one must focus on the universe of states present at the initiation, not denouement, of the state-building process.

An Intertemporal, Two-Stage Research Design

The approach to hypothesis testing taken here involves a series of structured comparisons. At the first level, the four country cases are divided into paired comparisons, each of which is designed to emphasize a different critical aspect of the social–foundational explanation proposed here. In addition, intertemporal comparisons within cases are made to highlight the specific effects of variables (e.g., social relations, elite politics) that change during the period under study. The design is two stage insofar as each paired comparison is evaluated at each critical juncture – the initial formation of viable national political institutions and the period of the initial political emergence of the middle sectors and working classes. And since the argument is path dependent, implying that at later stages, departures from the trajectory of political development on which a case finds itself are exceedingly difficult, the second stage analysis also highlights the specific moments in which determined efforts at path departure were undertaken by executives. These moments demonstrate the intense difficulty involved in successful path departure and that variables that at an earlier period were sufficient to drive state-building outcomes were unable to redirect trajectories later in the process, once the mechanisms that reproduce outcomes had been firmly established. Indeed, some of the most powerful authoritarian regimes on the continent tried, and failed, to institutionalize changes to the pattern of political development.

Why is hypothesis testing in this book centered on comparative historical evidence? The justifications for such an approach are both theoretical and practical. In the first case, arguments about the relationships of war, wealth, and/or politics to state building are cast here (and by most other scholars) in path-dependent terms. This precludes at least simple large-N cross-sectional research designs, insofar as putative causes and effects are hypothesized to be connected only given the outcomes of prior events, which are of necessity not recorded in contemporary data.[24] In principle, given data sets of long historical sweep, it might be possible to adequately model theories of this kind in large-N quantitative data. But even so, it would imply complicated functional forms and would pose a series of econometric and data challenges. In the absence of such long-term historical data, efforts to test such theory in cross-sectional (or short–time series) data would be nonsensical – they would either so oversimplify the theory in the effort to make it empirically tractable as to vitiate the hypothesis tests themselves or would be heavily biased with respect to key hypotheses.[25]

The Formation of National Institutions

The formation of recognizable, and fairly stable, national political institutions occurred in South America generally in the second half of the nineteenth century. The ultimate outcomes reflect quite substantial institutional divergences among the former Spanish colonies of the region. The theoretical account developed in this book to explain these initial differences focuses on two principal factors: the prevailing social relations of economic production (especially in the countryside) and the patterns of elite conflict or cooperation. At the same time, this approach is cast against alternatives emphasizing the causal effects of war and resource wealth, and it challenges the exogeneity of explanations that begin with institutional variations to explain long-run outcomes.

---

[24] In contexts where causal dynamics involve critical junctures, cause and ultimate effect are often widely separate in time, and indeed the "cause" may no longer be present at the time at which the effect is observable.

[25] I would argue that both are critical problems for approaches, such as those of Thies (2004, 2005), that test state-building arguments in cross-national data of quite limited time span.

The Social Foundations of State Building in the Contemporary Era 51

Figure 2.1 scores the state-building outcomes in this first period – the initial trajectories were everywhere established by the end of the nineteenth century. The variations highlighted in this figure were then used to structure the paired comparisons considered in this book: Peru and Chile, on the one hand, and Argentina and Uruguay, on the other. In the first period, the analytical focus of the Chile–Peru comparison emphasizes the polar overall outcomes (state atrophy versus substantial state building) that arise from differences on both the key independent variables. The contrast on the independent variables is very striking and characterizes essentially the entirety of the postindependence period for both countries. At the same time, this same comparison is used to shed light on several of the most plausible alternative explanations. For instance, Peru and Chile were, in the nineteenth century, in a regional environment characterized by substantial interstate conflict and rivalry. Indeed, they were among each other's principal political and military foes throughout this period, and they fought two major wars. The last, the War of the Pacific (1879–83), involved a definitive defeat of Peru by Chile and the temporary occupation of Lima. Both countries were also – and they remain so to this day – very important natural resource–exporting economies. In the nineteenth century, these exports were very heavily concentrated in nitrates; in fact, they were literally the very same nitrate deposits, for these very valuable mineral territories were annexed into Chile after the War of the Pacific. Not only does this contrast then permit us to examine the social–structural theory presented in this book against the regnant alternatives, it also allows us to consider the question, empirically, as to *when and if* war and resource wealth induce or impede national political development.

If Chile and Peru are very dissimilar cases in terms of the independent variables in this first period, Argentina and Uruguay are not. Not only were their basic political economies of the period almost identical (being principally ranching countries that would later also become major grain exporters), but both relied almost exclusively on free-wage labor for production in the postcolonial era. The cases are critical, however, insofar as the comparison (both within and across) sheds light on the critical role of elite politics. For only very late in the nineteenth century were their elites able to reach the sorts of compromises that made possible the construction of domestically and internationally recognized political institutions. To be sure, this was accomplished in different ways. In Argentina, one faction of the elite effectively militarily defeated its opponents and was able to impose a more or less hegemonic project – coupled with sufficient moves to incorporate the defeated side to stave off severe future disturbances. In Uruguay, two vituperatively opposed political parties – the Blancos and Colorados – ultimately came to a broad pattern of power sharing (called coparticipation) that was in a variety of forms able to survive from the late nineteenth through most of the twentieth centuries. And critically, the very rapid increases observable in the indicators used to measure the scope and extent of the institutional reach of each state take place in the immediate wake

Intra-Elite Political Dynamics

Zero-Sum/Non-Exclusionary   Competitive Establishment

		Institutional Atrophy	Constrained Central State Building
Social Relations	Servile	Peru	
	Free	Inter-Elite Conflict and Local Institution Building Argentina, to 1881 Uruguay, to 1876	National Institution Building Chile Argentina, after 1881 Uruguay, after 1876

FIGURE 2.2. Scoring the cases on the initial trajectory.

of these political settlements – highlighting the crucial role of elite politics even in a setting not saddled with a large segment of unfree labor.

The Rise of the Popular Classes

The analysis of the second critical juncture seeks to accomplish a somewhat different task. In theoretical terms, these two critical junctures are sequenced moments, and thus the outcomes of the second critical juncture depend in part on the path a state is on when it enters the period of mass electoral incorporation. As we see in Figure 2.2, three of our cases were on a favorable trajectory of institutional development (Argentina, Chile, and Uruguay), and one was not (Peru). From this starting point, the second set of empirical chapters examine the ways in which these trajectories were deflected or reinforced under the intense pressures of initial mass political incorporation – which generally took place in South America between the 1900s and the 1940s.

As Table 2.1 makes clear, a key axis of differentiation is the timing of this entry into real competition for national political control. In Argentina, the middle classes entered politics early, and this electoral incorporation produced a political party that was able to seize executive power well before the Great Depression. This would, ironically, have decidedly unfortunate implications for the pattern of national institutional development, as it laid the foundation for an inability to arrange a lasting accommodation between the middle sectors and a late-entering working-class party. The consequence was a cycling between populist and antipopulist institutional expansions and retrenchment that characterized the bulk of the post–World War II era. In Chile and Uruguay,

The Social Foundations of State Building in the Contemporary Era   53

TABLE 2.1. *Scoring the Cases in the Second Critical Juncture*

	Country Institutional	Timing of Middle-Class Electoral Entry	Driving Force behind Initial Effort at Major State-Building Program	Long-Run Outcome
Initially strong institutions	Chile	Late (during/after Great Depression)	Middle-class–working-class accommodation	Effective state building
	Uruguay	Late (during/after Great Depression)	Duopoly of multiclass political parties	Effective state building
	Argentina	Early (after First World War)	Working-class (Peronist) party alone	Populist/antipopulist institutional cycling
Initially weak institutions	Peru	Early (before Great Depression)	Not successfully imposed	Persistent institutional weakness

by contrast, widespread mass political participation came substantially later. Indeed, in the former, suffrage was decidedly restricted for much of the first half of the twentieth century, and well into the 1950s, even basic reforms like the secret ballot that would enable meaningful political participation had not yet been instituted. This set the stage for the emergence of middle- and working-class political forces that were able to collaborate – through quite different institutional vehicles – in the formation of vastly expanded state institutions in the context of the developmentalist protectionism of the post–World War II era.

But showing the different effects of the timing of initial popular-sector entry into real electoral contention is only part of the goal of the analysis of the second critical juncture. At the same time, in all these cases, elites initiated multiple efforts to change the institutional trajectory on which the states found themselves. I use these efforts to directly explore the constraining effects of institutional path dependence. Thus, in Chile, one can examine efforts in the 1950s under President Alessandri, and the exhaustive effort by the Pinochet dictatorship (1973–89), to radically shrink and weaken state institutions. If the path-dependent specification is correct, however, this task should prove to be all but impossible for executives *even in the context of almost-unchallenged authoritarian rule.* Similarly, this book examines the inability of the Uruguayan military to reverse the scope and penetration of its national state, even as it applied a tremendous amount of police and military coercion to effect its state-weakening goals, which were themselves consonant with advice and pressure emanating from the international system. And in Peru, we see the most decisive effects of the sequential character of the state-building process. For, in this case, we examine a military government that (in the 1967–80 period) actually managed to effectively reverse the structural impediments to institution building identified for the first critical juncture by using corporatist institutions to force effective national-level political coordination, while at the same time imposing serious structural reforms (radical land reform and the empowerment of workers) that effectively put an end to the servility so long characteristic of Peruvian labor relations. But this effort came very late and well after mass political incorporation had taken place. Ultimately, the military was unable to put the genie back in the bottle – weak institutions, ironically, proved remarkably resilient. These efforts at path departure help to test the sequential character of the argument, which is an essential component of any path-dependent theoretical formulations.

WHAT IS STATE BUILDING?

Before proceeding with the empirical analysis in subsequent chapters, however, it is crucial to be very clear about what is meant by state building. State building and state strength are not easy conceptual targets, and indeed, it has taken a variety of different meanings in the political science context. In some contexts, the emphasis is on *military strength*, regardless of the underlying economic and political institutions on which the military relies.[26] In other contexts, state building is conflated with nation building – the creation of a national identity, mass political participation, or, for example, cultural unification (see Tilly 1975, 70). While these sociocultural outcomes are potentially the consequences of a state-building experience, from the perspective of this book, they do not define it. Finally, some think of state strength in terms of formal institutional structures, classifying systems that fragment authority or employ a decentralized federalism with overlapping jurisdictions as inherently weaker than more unitary, centralized political systems. This also is a conceptualization not employed in this book.

The approach taken here – and it is widely shared in the contemporary comparative politics scholarship on state building – departs from a basically Weberian understanding of the state as the monopolist of the means of legitimate violence in a defined territorial area (Weber 1978, 54–56). Joining Giddens (1987, 20), however, I deemphasize the Weberian insistence on the legitimacy

---

[26] E.g., an emphasis on military capabilities would suggest that late Capetian France was quite strong, whereas an emphasis on the ability of the allegedly absolutist monarch to govern and tax would suggest quite the opposite (see, e.g., Ertman 1997).

The Social Foundations of State Building in the Contemporary Era 55

of this monopoly on violence as a definitional aspect of the state; this is a potential consequence of state building but is not necessarily constitutive of "state-ness" itself.[27] The aspect of the state that is crucial from the perspective of understanding the state-building process is the character of public institutions. For all states worthy of the name have a public administration of some sort – for good or ill – and the fundamental challenge of state building is the construction of institutions that are effective.

But what, then, is efficacy? In part, it implies an efficient solution to the principal–agent problem involved in governance. Scholars have long recognized that the incentives confronting front-line staff may be at odds with the policy goals of political executives or their administrative superiors. These differences could produce anything from active opposition and bureaucratic sabotage to an indifference that manifests itself in delay, avoidance, or error. While political leaders (the executive, sometimes the legislature) are charged with setting public policy, it is the public administration that is tasked with the actual implementation of political decisions – and depending on the way in which these institutions function, policy-as-implemented may or may not bear much resemblance to the choices made by politicians. There is, however, quite a lot more to it than this. For the coordination of the actions and behavior of the individuals working within the public administration[28] is only the beginning step for the implementation of policy. And indeed, the principal–agent problems within administrative agencies so frequently highlighted in the literature are sometimes far from the critical issue: policies must also be *imposed* on the societies governed by the state. And important policies almost always have powerful societal opponents. Moreover, the decisions of political leaders – to impose taxes, redistribute incomes, provide public goods, impose industrial or development strategies, inter alia – all imply the creation of very substantial winners and losers. The question from the perspective of state building is, however, how able (and at what cost) are public institutions to enforce these decisions, especially on societal actors who have vested interests in resisting them and substantial amounts of economic and/or political power? Thus, separate from the question of motivating administrative staff to seek policy implementation is the question of whether public institutions are sufficiently strong and penetrating to enforce compliance – this requires the ability both to efficiently detect societal evasion and to impose appropriate sanctions on malefactors.

Indeed, individuals in civil society frequently struggle to avoid the reach of the central state. One way this is accomplished is through the effort by elites to

---

[27] As Rueschemeyer (2005, 147) rightly points out, the norms and beliefs that would undergird legitimacy are in fact typically coercive impositions enforced by state officials.

[28] I specifically avoid the term *bureaucrats* here, for bureaucracy is only one – though generally the most effective – way in which a public administration can be structured. And as Evans (1992) has noted, it is generally in rather short supply.

shape public policy toward their private benefit – or to the detriment of their competitors (e.g., Krueger 1974). Or, alternatively, elites and the masses alike may engage in efforts to avoid compliance, for example, with the payment of their juridically defined tax burdens, especially where they are unconvinced of the benefits or the proportional contribution of others (Levi 1989). This is particularly the case when it is clear that revenue systems are transparent in their distributional consequences or where they violate deeply held, and materially defined but culturally experienced, norms about appropriate types and levels of extraction (e.g., Bates 1981; Scott 1990, 111; Ibid. 1987, 29, inter alia). The critical question from the perspective of state building, then, is the question of the institutional capacity of states to impose and effectively enforce the revenue and policy initiatives of their leaders. It is what Mann (1993, 59) in a more general sense calls "infrastructural power," which

> is the institutional capacity of a central state, despotic or not, to penetrate its territories and logistically implement decisions. This is collective power, "power through" society, coordinating social life through state infrastructures. It identifies a state as a set of central and radial institutions penetrating its territories.

State building, then, is the process by which the institutions of public administration are strengthened in their scope and penetration of society. By implication, such infrastructural power implies low levels of corruption and inefficiency, for these would render line civil servants poor agents of central authority. And administrative structures must also have a substantial degree of insulation from particularistic societal pressures not channeled through the formal political system, ensuring that a true decision-making hierarchy is maintained and that political choices are not reversed by ex post "lobbying" of administrative staff charged with implementing them.[29] Achieving these goals is not simply (or even largely) a question of institutional design per se, be it federalism versus unitary structures or overlapping versus discrete jurisdictions, though these can potentially have some effects on the infrastructural power of a central state. But it *is* critically about the *central* state: strong states must be able to impose policies throughout their national territories. And statelike entities without a meaningful center (as in, e.g., the United States under the Articles of Confederation or leagues of city-states in European history) cannot, in the sense of this book, be "strong."

Interestingly, much as the term *bureaucracy* is decried in contemporary discussions, state building inevitably involves the construction of bureaucratic institutions. Indeed, the very invention of modern bureaucratic administration was a breakthrough of world historical proportions, emerging in rudimentary form only around the seventeenth century in Europe (Ertman 2005, 166). Some have suggested that it provided organizational advantages that could even be decisive in international warfare, from a superior ability to raise revenues

---

[29] This is roughly what Fukuyama (2004, 8) considers the "strength of institutional capabilities" in his discussion of the state-building process.

The Social Foundations of State Building in the Contemporary Era 57

to the organizational and logistical improvements it brought to armies themselves. Further highlighting that building a bureaucracy is no mean feat, despite the contemporary availability of institutional models of efficient bureaucracy and substantial international promotion of best-practice institutional forms, it remains in remarkably scarce supply throughout much of the developing world (Evans 1992, 1995).

What State Building Is Not

Before embarking on a discussion of measurement strategies, it is important to be clear about what state building is *not*. Most critically, political development producing "strong" states in the sense employed here has no implication for the sort of policy choices (beyond the institutional configuration of the public administration) made by political elites or the type of regime within which they are undertaken. Thus, for example, it is widely held that the protection of private property rights requires a strong, effective state apparatus. But the former does not entail the latter – and thus measurement strategies that judge the quality of institutions based on the protection of property rights (or worse yet, the assumed consequences of particular levels property rights protection) will go astray.[30] Powerful institutions can support any number of property rights systems, not all of which will involve strong protections of individually alienable, fee-simple property.[31] Some – as in state socialist systems – may deny private property rights entirely.

---

[30] Acemoğlu and Robinson (1996, fn. 1) are explicit about their elision of policies and institutions, contending that many of the factors that affect property rights enforcement are policies but will nevertheless be treated as "economic institutions" by them.

[31] Indeed, it is important to note that many contemporary discussions treat private property rights as simply a continuum from "less protection" to "more protection." But this construction is essentially ignorant of the lesson that North (1981, 36) has taught us: that property rights are alternative bundles of rights and responsibilities attached to the notion of ownership, and that the key distinction from his perspective is their comparative "efficiency" versus "inefficiency" in an economic sense. Not all property is individual or individually alienable, and not all strong property protection is useful from a developmental or governance perspective. Consider that excessively strong individual property rights can impede the regulation of critical externalities, and the strongest form of property rights – allodial title – would render a market economy scarcely functional. Individual ownership should not be assumed, either. Earlier forms of property rights – especially those of the feudal era in Europe – entailed different rights attaching to distinct individuals for the same piece of property (e.g., lords were entitled to labor from resident serfs, certain fees and taxes, and a portion of the agricultural output, but peasants typically had enforceable unsufructory rights over a quantity of land and secondary rights even over demesne territory, e.g., gleaning and grazing rights [the right of shack, or agistment when applied to a royal forest], estovers [rights to collect wood], turbary [the right to cut turf for fuel], prohibitions on lords to fully cut their crops to facilitate grazing and gleaning, or prohibitions on enclosing the land to prevent the movement of peasant livestock or to restrict access to the commons). See, e.g., Markoff (1991, 172) on France and Manning (1977, 18 and fn. 2) on England.

In a similar vein, one cannot assume that effective bureaucratic institutions will produce good policy choices – be they in the realm of development strategy, fiscal management, public employment, or taxation levels. Effective public administrations should implement policies efficiently and with a minimum of graft or penetration by rent-seeking societal interests. But the choice of policy strategies is ultimately a question for the political system, not the public administration. And there are myriad examples of strong governments enforcing decidedly suboptimal economic policies (from the tariff escalations that helped deepen the Great Depression to the intense small-country protectionism of Uruguay in the 1950s and 1960s to the fiscal and monetary policy errors that characterize the contemporary deflationary period in Japan).

Ultimately, the conflation of policies with institutions makes analysis intractable. Acemoğlu et al. (2001, fn. 3) indeed provide the limiting and illustrative case. For them, the public "institutions" that are critical to long-run economic performance include "constraints on government expropriation, independent judiciary, property rights enforcement, and institutions providing equal access to education and ensuring civil liberties." Only some of these can reasonably be thought of as institutions – others are policy choices made and implemented through institutions (like mass education or political rights). But the factors that produce effective bureaucratic apparatuses by no means necessarily imply mass educational expansion, much less broadened civil and political rights.

We must similarly be careful to avoid the trap of concluding, like Rueschemeyer (2005, 146), that the emergence of cultural practices that facilitate efficient administration need be thought of as part of the state itself or as a characteristic of "state building" or "full institutionalization." It is for this reason that the Weberian notion of authority (legitimate power) was excluded from the definition of the state employed here. High-quality public institutions may sometimes propel the development of normative practices that support compliance with legal and policy enactments, but they are not constitutive of them. Thus, this book follows in part the perspective of Evans and Rauch (1999, 749), who emphasize the importance of what they call "Weberian state structures" – meritocratic recruitment into bureaucracies and long-term career trajectories that reward performance. While such structures might more effectively deliver public goods – and this over time could induce ideological or cultural patterns of compliance or cooperation like Levi's (1989) "quasi-voluntary compliance" or North's (1990, 47) "informal constraints" on interaction – they cannot tell us what mix of public goods will be selected for provision, nor do they ensure the emergence of complementary norms and practices.

Measurement

This focus on the institutional features of the state, while narrowing the conceptual terrain, does not set up an easy measurement task. As we will see,

The Social Foundations of State Building in the Contemporary Era   59

this is particularly true for this book given its focus on long-run patterns of political development in Latin America. For not only is a tractable set of cross-nationally valid measures of the institutional capacity of states required but these metrics must also exist in the historical record from roughly the early independence period onward. As we will see subsequently, all the available options are imperfect, so it is critical to utilize the best available data in a way that honestly examines the theoretical claims at issue, while being sensitive to the limits that the data imply. Conversely, to permit data availability to influence – consciously or otherwise – the elaboration of theoretical claims or conceptual structures undermines the hypothesis-testing process altogether. Either crucial variables will be omitted – specification error – or they will be defined in operations that are inappropriate, inducing random and/or systematic measurement error.

In thinking about developing metrics to capture the capacities or efficacy of state institutions, we are essentially confronted with two sets of choices. The first is whether to rely on "objective" indicators[32] of state capabilities or on *perceptions* of them. Both approaches are commonplace, and in the contemporary literature, indeed the most commonly used metrics are indeed subjective, perception-based ones. Notably, especially in the economics literature, scholars rely on indicators of state efficacy largely derived from perceptions of firms, international investors, investment consultancies, other "experts," and occasionally the views of the mass public; they are called on to assess the quality or probity of public administrations. So, for example, Transparency International's Corruption Perceptions Index is widely used to rank nations according to the perceived level of graft in the public administration. Alternatively, Political Risk Services, a business consultancy, produces the International Country Risk Guide, which includes an indicator of what they call "country risk" – ostensibly a measure of property rights security, which is frequently used as a proxy for the overall quality of state institutions (as in Acemoğlu et al. 2001). Perhaps the most comprehensive such metrics are included in the World Bank's (2011b) Worldwide Governance Indicators, which combine a broad swath of different perception-based metrics to construct aggregate measures of governance across six dimensions (see Kaufmann et al. 2009).

The perception-based approach will not do for both methodological and practical reasons. It has been widely demonstrated that perception-based approaches to measuring governance are subject to important selection biases, conflate policy measures with institutional measures, are limited in their scope, and are commonly subject to positive and negative halo effects related to recent economic performance (see, inter alia, for discussions of the problems of these indicators, Thomas 2010; Kurtz and Schrank 2007a, 2007b; Arndt and Oman

---

[32] The implication here is, of course, not that such indicators are without errors of measurement. Rather, the point is that they rely on concrete, measurable features or outputs of public administration.

60   *Latin American State Building in Comparative Perspective*

2006). In addition, perception-based indicators have only a narrow temporal sweep – the earliest dating back only to the 1980s, and there only with very limited coverage. As we will see, our theoretical contentions will require data over a much longer historical time frame, rendering these metrics inappropriate.

If we are to rely on objective metrics, this immediately raises the question of which metrics. One quite valid approach is that of Evans and Rauch (1999; also Rauch and Evans 2000). Their approach is to utilize a survey instrument applied to multiple country experts per case – cross-nationally – to assess not perceptions of governance but rather the objective, "structural" features of core bureaucratic agencies in 35 countries.[33] In principle, a direct measure of the institutional features of government is optimal. But for our purposes, this will be problematic, for it is not possible to engage in a similar consistent characterization of Latin American public bureaucracies from independence through the present – the historical sweep necessary for the argument developed earlier in this chapter. While there is some available direct evidence – documenting the actual on-the-ground operation of public administrations – its availability is haphazard. In the comparative empirical work that forms the core of this book, this information will naturally be used to validate the more consistent but indirect measures that form the core metric used here. It is also important to note that historical descriptions of the formal rules governing the operation of public bureaucracies are of at best limited utility given the many and extensive divergences (many of which continue into the present) from them that render them poor metrics of actual features of the operation of state institutions.

The main approach taken here – which is broadly shared in the historical literature on state building – relies on the measurable and documented inputs and outputs of public-sector activity. This is what Soifer (2008, 236) has identified as a "national capabilities approach" to measuring state infrastructural power. It takes as its starting point that an administrative organization that is weak (fragmented, inefficient, riddled with patronage and corruption, etc.) will do a comparatively poor job of accomplishing the tasks assigned to it. To be a useful measure of public-sector capacity, however, these outputs must be carefully selected so as to be sure that cross-national differences reflect principally variations in the capacity to produce them rather than policy choices over alternative priorities. As such, the best measures would be of the sorts of activities that all (or nearly all) states consider to be of primary importance – for these can be assumed to be pursued vigorously across contexts, and variations in success will depend principally on variation in the effectiveness of institutions, not on opportunity costs or political will.

---

[33] Evans and Rauch (1999, 755) are very clear about not asking their informants to characterize the quality or performance of the bureaucracy. They seek only descriptive information about objective features of bureaucratic institutions such as the mechanism for entry, the promotion process, or job tenure.

The Social Foundations of State Building in the Contemporary Era 61

One such metric – and it is indeed a powerful one – has to do with the ability of the state to tax the citizens and firms that engage in economic activity within its borders. At least since Schumpeter (1954, 17), taxation has been seen as central to the state's political reach. Indeed, he argued that "[t]axes not only helped to create the state. They helped to form it. The tax system was the organ of [state] development of [sic] which entailed the other organs." And it is widely used in contemporary scholarship as a measure of state strength (e.g., Cohen et al. 1981, 905; Gallo 1991, 8; Centeno 2002, 116–26; Thies 2005; see discussion in Soifer and vom Hau 2008, 220).[34] There are considerable advantages to considering the ability to tax as a plausible indicator of the overall level of state strength.[35] First and foremost, it is an activity in which virtually all states engage of necessity.[36] And of course, it is one that is intensely difficult: effective tax collection requires an effective bureaucratic apparatus that is capable of, for example, measuring economic activity, recording myriad transactions in the domestic market, estimating property and land values, ensuring the accurate reporting of incomes, and then extracting the relevant resources from economic agents of all types. In the Latin American context – characterized as it is by generally very high levels of inequality – this further implies that any state that manages to extract high levels of resources must of needs be deriving an important portion of them from the wealthier and more powerful members of society. For that is where the resources are. This is important, for the definition of state building used here emphasizes the ability to enforce policies not only on subaltern members of society but also on society's strongest. Of course, in wealthy, high-institutional–capacity contexts, taxation levels eventually come to reflect policy choices as well as the limits of institutional capacity. But for our cases, the level of extraction is principally defined by the capacity to tax (indeed, this capacity remains a critical limit on tax receipts even for some wealthy countries such as contemporary Italy or Greece).

The empirical approach of this book thus begins with an assessment of the tax capacity of countries in the Latin American region. But it goes well beyond this as well, for as Campbell (1993, 177) has pointed out, "both the *form* and the *level* of taxation influences [sic] state building." In the empirical discussions of our four cases, thus, analysis of over-time changes in the level of taxation will be complemented by discussions of the *types* of taxes that are employed. This variation is quite informative, for it is a much simpler administrative

---

[34] Indeed, Cohen et al. (1981, 905) flatly declare, "We shall use tax revenue to measure state power." Centeno uses taxation levels to underscore what he sees as the weakness of Latin American states, whereas Gallo focuses more on the type of taxation (foreign trade vs. broad-based internal taxation) to draw inferences about state capacity.

[35] It is worth noting that revenues derived from mineral production and/or export (excises, royalties, and income taxes) are included in the broad definition of tax revenues.

[36] The only important exceptions would be states that derive virtually all their resources from international transfers or the proceeds from investments, but this characterizes none of the states or time periods examined here in the Latin American context.

challenge to collect revenues from, for example, export and import taxes than it is to impose broad-based taxation on domestic transactions (as in a sales tax or a value-added tax), and of course, taxing income, profits, and wealth is administratively and politically difficult to impose. Indeed, it is precisely the fact that the means of revenue collection also matters, which underscores the use of tax capacity – ordinary revenue as a share of GDP – in an ordinal fashion as (one) of the set of metrics by which states are compared. To assume that such data were accurate at the interval level is simply not plausible: it is far administratively harder to lift tax receipts from 40 to 41 percent of the economy than from 4 to 5 percent – for the former necessarily entails imposing difficult-to-collect income, wealth, or broad-based consumption taxes, whereas the latter does not.[37] The reason is easy to see. Easy-to-collect taxes like tariffs and some excise taxes, were set at high enough levels to theoretically capture this proportion of GDP, would be high enough to impede imports or sales altogether, making them self-defeating. A revenue tariff would thus very quickly become a protectionist tariff and generate little in the way of tax receipts.

Several caveats are in order here, however. First, it should rightly be noted that the burden of domestic taxation that is imposed is only partially a question of administrative capacity; it is also a political and policy question concerning the appropriate level of extraction. Thus, it is possible that tax receipts as a share of the economy may be low as a result of a political choice to pursue a limited state rather than the incapacity of governmental institutions to collect such revenues were tax increases to be enacted. This is, however, a phenomenon much more likely confined to the advanced industrial countries. While it certainly accounts for the variation between the comparatively small state (in taxation terms) of the United States relative to, for example, social democratic Scandinavia, policy differences do not appear to account for much of the variation in the Latin American context, particularly in the nineteenth- and twentieth-century periods that most concern us here. The principal difficulty is actually collecting taxes that are owed, not imposing them in a de jure sense. As we will see in the next section, the comparative hierarchy (as measured by taxation) among Latin American states has been very constant for quite a long period of time, and within countries, extreme swings in the political ideology of executives, the regime type,[38] or severe economic crises do not generally appear to have major medium- or longer-term effects on comparative taxation levels. By way of illustration, the arch-liberal military government of Augusto Pinochet in Chile taxed at far higher levels than the developmentalist and redistributive "Revolutionary Government of the Armed Forces" in Peru

---

[37] This has not prevented some scholars from implicitly making the assumption that data are accurate at the interval level (as measures of state strength). See, e.g., Thies (2005).

[38] Slater (2008, 254–55) makes the case more generally that democracy and expanding state capacity can coincide, even as "authoritarian leviathans" are also a possibility.

The Social Foundations of State Building in the Contemporary Era   63

of the same time period![39] And of course, that state executives are essentially revenue maximizers (at least before the very contemporary era) is a foundational assumption of most of the literature on the development of taxation (as in, e.g., Levi 1989; Olson 1993).[40]

Taxation is, of course, not the only way to measure the capacity of states. And where available measures are necessarily indirect, it is appropriate to validate findings using alternative indicators. Usually, this requires analysis based on public goods production, which tends to be relatively well recorded in the historical record. The difficulty in using measurable public-sector outputs to judge the capacity of state institutions is that one must make the accessory assumption that the states in the sample are all pursuing the output that is being measured at a comparatively similar level of priority and that the task is potentially at least a large and complex one (i.e., one that puts substantial demands on the state and its institutions). But this implies that we must identify major activities in which all states engage. The two principal candidates employed here – since they apply well in the Latin American region – are education and infrastructure provision. While the precise form that both took varied across countries in Latin America, it was state support that undergirded the massification of education and the expansion of roads, rails, and telegraphs. And as an indicator of capacity, increasing rates of literacy or school enrollment match the increasing administrative challenge. It is easier to educate students in urban settings where scale economies, the supply of teachers, and transportation infrastructure are well developed. As literacy expands, however, it must necessarily penetrate the countryside, and in a very decentralized fashion – this is a much costlier task (financially and administratively) and involves the recruitment and placement of teaching staff in oftentimes undesirable, remote settings. Thus, improvement on this indicator does not simply represent the horizontal expansion of the state but also an improvement in its administrative and penetrative capacities.

For the Latin American states during the era in which state building began in earnest (from the mid-nineteenth to the early twentieth centuries), the provision of infrastructure, specifically rail infrastructure, was a critical task. It, in two very different senses, provides a measure of state capacity. On the one hand, like education, it was an economically valuable but administratively, financially, and technically challenging task to undertake, and it was one that was almost never managed without explicit or implicit state promotion (either through state ownership or varieties of public subsidy of private infrastructure

---

[39] Of course, the Pinochet period was characterized by far lower taxation than the immediately preceding socialist government of Salvador Allende. The point, however, is that even as late as the 1970s, the variation that is produced by shifts in policy is insufficient to reverse a long-standing hierarchy founded on differences in the *capacity* to tax.

[40] They are, of course, maximizers subject to constraints. But it is these constraints that help make the measure useful – for the stronger the state, the better "taxation bargain" it can strike with the societal actors from whom it takes revenue.

provision). It is certainly the case that some rail infrastructure was privately built and operated (as in Argentina) – but its existence nevertheless required extensive state participation in the form of loan guarantees, subsidies, land grants, tax exemptions, or favorable rate schedules, inter alia. Rail infrastructure measured the sinews of the state in a more literal sense as well, as it also physically connected the sometimes-remote portions of the national territory in a single political economy (and market) that could be governed from the center. For as much as rails unify national markets and improve communications capacity, they also make the essence of the central state – coercion – much easier to apply by removing geographic remoteness as a barrier to the imposition of central authority over often restive regions. They facilitated the movement of information, troops, and bureaucratic personnel.

What Is to Come?

Any new effort to explain the emergence and divergence of state institutions and their capacity in the South American region thus faces a daunting set of theoretical tasks. On the one hand, any treatment must be able to account for the emergence of strong institutions in unlikely places – after all, places like Chile and Uruguay inherited virtually no administrative infrastructure from the colonial period, and those areas that had been colonial centers (most notably Peru but also Argentina) did not produce the most effective states. But the account must also be able to explain the persistence in these relative differences over the subsequent century and a half. Moreover, it must directly engage the existing, vibrant literature on conflict-induced state building, especially the pathbreaking work on the formation of national states in Europe.

It is to this empirical and theoretical task that we next turn. In the paired comparisons that follow, the central hypotheses of this book will be explored and contrasted in their implications with the regnant alternative accounts. The empirical discussion proceeds in two steps: the first is concerned with the emergence (or failure to emerge) of an initial state-strengthening trajectory in the postindependence era, whereas the second examines the ways in which a second critical juncture sparked by the political incorporation of the middle and working classes reinforces or deflects the initial trajectory and reproduces the path of political development through, often severe, subsequent political and economic shocks. More specifically, in Chapter 3, a paired comparison of Peru and Chile – polar outcomes in terms of long-run state power – during the initial period of national institutional formation is used to elaborate the origins of their distinct long-run trajectories. In Chapter 4, the cross-time and cross-country comparisons of Argentina and Uruguay are used to establish the political side of the foundation of national institutions. In Chapter 5, the consolidating and deepening effects of the emergence of late and early middle- and working-class political participation are explored in Chile and Peru, respectively; in the former, it served to deepen and strengthen

The Social Foundations of State Building in the Contemporary Era   65

administrative institutions, whereas in the latter, it cemented their inadequacy. Finally, the politics of mass incorporation will be tied to the divergence in Argentine and Uruguayan political development from the mid-twentieth century onward in Chapter 6. Chapter 7 concludes the book and examines the potential reach of the theory to a paradigmatic and well-explored case of state building in the European context: Prussia–Germany.

3

State Formation in Chile and Peru

Institution Building and Atrophy in Unlikely Settings

The empirical portion of his book begins with an unlikely contrast. Postcolonial institutional development in Chile and Peru has proceeded along trajectories that were quite unexpected given the colonial-era foundations on which they were built. It was Chile that launched a trajectory of effective, long-run institutional development, while Peru suffered persistent, almost irremediable stagnation. But it was Peru that was the colonial center and began with substantial advantages – it was a viceroyalty in the Spanish colonial administrative system, and Lima was home to an important Audiencia (a superior court that also had some legislative functions). And it was Peru that experienced extensive colonial-era immigration, allowing Spain to establish "numerous and deep footholds" (Mahoney 2010, 67). This not only entailed a much stronger governing bureaucracy and its associated coercive apparatus but also a much higher level of basic human capital – the literate, educated individuals on which a postcolonial state would have to rely.[1] Not only were colonial institutions well developed in Peru, they had been undergoing a process of successful administrative reforms since the 1750s, abolishing venal office and imposing meritocratic norms on governmental bureaucracies, inter alia, that Mahoney (2010, 45) characterizes as "a resounding success in Mexico City and Lima." This legacy of human capital and powerful institutions did not, however, lead to successful subsequent state building.

---

[1] Mahoney (2010) also very powerfully makes the case that these institutions were not ultimately favorable to long-run economic and social development, for they were mercantilist in origin and created property rights structures and guild and trade systems that were impediments to the capitalist rationalization that would be necessary for long-run development. The question here is about *administrative* development and state building, which is not necessarily correlated with economic performance, and for which experience with extensive bureaucratic organization of even this variety is quite favorable.

State Formation in Chile and Peru 67

Chile, by contrast, was a colonial periphery. Not only was it nearly the most geographically remote part of the Spanish Empire but it was also thinly populated by Spanish immigrants, including the arrival of very few women. This led inevitably to miscegenation, which transformed the indigenous population of the Central Valley (estimated at between 800,000 and 1,200,000 before its decimation by disease) into a large mestizo populace dominated by a very small Creole and Peninsular class (Collier and Sater 2004, 3, 8). And while its colonial institutions were formally similar to the rest of Spanish America in their initial reliance on coercive production systems and enormous *encomienda* grants of control over indigenous labor, the Spanish did not invest enough military resources to conquer the Mapuche Indian population south of the Bío-Bío River or even to impose basic stability in the Central Valley until after the indigenous population had been largely decimated by disease or absorbed through intermarriage. As Mahoney (2010, 86) sums it up, "like Uruguay and the littoral of Argentina: the territory lacked arrangements that could sustain powerful merchants, entrenched landed elites who controlled huge pools of dependent labor, and an economically and politically significant church."[2]

The contrasts between the colonial-era institutions in Chile and Peru stand in sharp juxtaposition with some fundamental similarities in the postcolonial era. In terms of their basic political economies, both postindependence states were overwhelmingly dependent on mineral exports (of, especially, silver, nitrates, and copper) and, secondarily, on agro-exports (sugar and cotton in Peru and wheat in Chile). In geostrategic terms, both were, in the nineteenth century, surrounded by hostile military competitors, including not only their geographic neighbors (and each other) but also their former Spanish colonial rulers. Yet these similarities on several of the dimensions thought to be critical to state building do not at first blush lead us far in explaining the divergent postcolonial institutional trajectories that emerged. Why did Chile – with its inauspicious colonial-era institutional legacy – ultimately develop a state with comparatively high levels of infrastructural power, while Peru, with a more favorable legacy and similar resource base and strategic profile, was trapped in a cycle of persistent institutional calamity?

The argument of this book holds that the key to understanding the initial trajectories of political development that emerged in postcolonial Chile and Peru hinges on two critical features of the state-building era: the character of prevailing social relations in agriculture (and mining) and the ability of elites of different factions to cooperate, while at the same time maintaining the exclusion of nonelite groups from political power. We will see later that Chilean elites were remarkably able to do so, and factions regularly alternated in power – even

---

[2] While this would prove very beneficial for long-run social and economic development – relative to Peru, where the opposite was the case – it by no means laid the foundation for state building. There was no legacy of a strong colonial-era government, and the colony had low levels of human capital and quite limited wealth.

68 *Latin American State Building in Comparative Perspective*

though they were often quite bitterly divided over the issues of the day. This, in turn, facilitated the construction of a strong central administrative system. And despite relying on a noncapitalist (but nonservile) agrarian system that did not generate substantial economic returns, they managed to cooperate around extensive investments in governmental institutions, public education, and military modernization and conquest. In Peru, we will see that local elites – reliant on inherently restive servile labor in both the highlands and on the coast – jealously guarded their local control over coercive assets and were unwilling to invest in the formation of effective national institutions or even in collective national defense against invaders. And while the possession of tremendous – if short-lived – wealth in the form of a global nitrate monopoly in the late nineteenth century did not underwrite the formation of a strong state in comparison with Chile, the period of this guano boom was actually one of the better ones for Peruvian institutional development. Natural resource wealth could not create a strong state in this unfavorable terrain – but it clearly was not the reason for Peruvian political underdevelopment. Indeed, it probably helped on the margins.

THE OUTCOMES

It is important at the outset to establish the extent of the differences between Peru and Chile that emerged during the critical period in which national political institutions took coherent shape in the postindependence era. A telling first cut at this question can be seen in the data on tax revenue collection over time. The data in Figures 3.1 and 3.2 show the development of marked differences in the capacities of the Peruvian and Chilean states to collect revenues through the First World War. Particularly in less developed contexts, taxation capacity is a commonly accepted indicator of the efficacy and penetration of national institutions – indeed, domestic revenue extraction is *the* key indicator of state strength in bellicist and ecological accounts of political development (Tilly 1990; Chaudhry 1994). What is most clear from these data are the long-run trends in taxation. Direct comparison of levels is more difficult as the nineteenth-century Peruvian data cannot be rendered in constant *soles* (for no appropriate inflation time series could be found), nor could they be converted to a comparison currency (e.g., pounds sterling), as the necessary exchange rate data are similarly unavailable. That said, the key results for both cases are clearly visible in the available over-time trends (see Figures 3.1 and 3.2). With some plateaus early in the Republican history of Chile, per capita *real* tax receipts increased considerably. From roughly the 1850s until the global depression of the late 1870s, real tax income per head roughly doubled. Then, after a dip associated with the depression, they resume an upward trajectory – even more steeply – in part due to the acquisition of very valuable and easily taxed nitrate fields from Peru in the War of the Pacific (1879–83). Indeed, even a civil war in 1891 produced only a brief downturn in revenue collection,

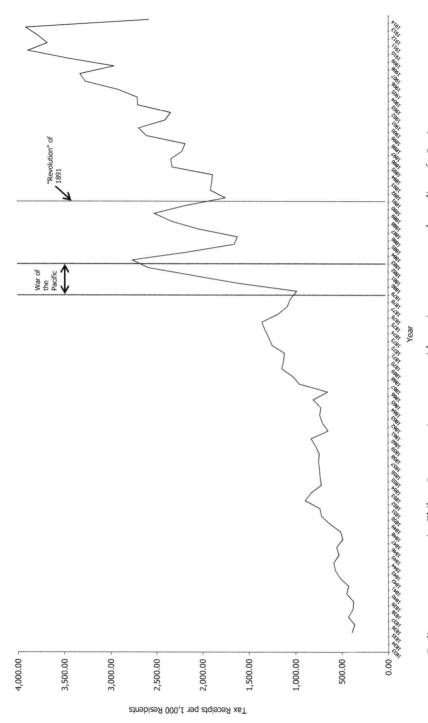

FIGURE 3.1. Ordinary tax revenues in Chile, 1833–1914 (per 1,000 residents, in constant pounds sterling of 1833).

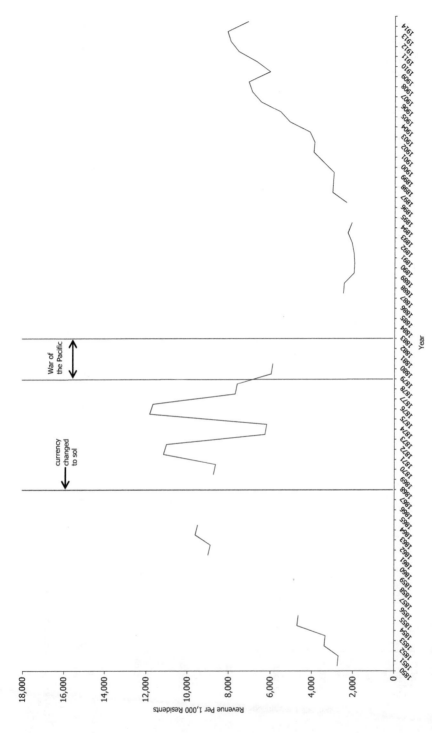

FIGURE 3.2. Government revenue in Peru, 1850–1914 (current pesos of 1868 and current soles of 1869–1914 per 1,000 residents).

State Formation in Chile and Peru   71

followed by a return to growth in fiscal resources, until the collapse of global trade attendant on the start of the First World War undermined Chilean tax receipts. It should be added that these data are necessarily underestimates: they exclude important direct taxes (on income *and* wealth) that were turned over to municipalities after the War of the Pacific and thus ceased to be included in national accounts, although they were still being collected. Indeed, the very existence early on of hard-to-collect direct taxes on income and wealth is itself an indication of the comparatively high quality of Chilean public administration that contrasts sharply with a Peruvian state still reliant on such primitive revenue tools as tax farms.[3]

By contrast, the Peruvian data tell a tale of collapse (see Figure 3.2). Indeed, the comparative absence even of data on public revenues itself suggests a much-less-developed Peruvian administrative capacity. Between 1833 and 1846, the Peruvian treasury did not even manage to record basic information on either revenues or expenditures (Tantaleán 1983, 48). While state revenues briefly improved during the era of the guano and nitrate booms,[4] once these territories were seized by the Chileans in the War of the Pacific, public revenues suffered a catastrophic decline. Indeed, throughout much of this era, the Peruvian state resorted to unrestrained monetary emission (printing paper money unsupported by gold or silver reserves or expanded economic activity), tax farming, and usurious loans in a largely unsuccessful effort to fund the basics of national government. The Peruvian state simply would not or could not impose even a modest level of domestic taxation. Thus, during the 1880s and 1890s, tax receipts averaged little more than a quarter of their prewar levels. It is very important, as well, to keep in mind that these data have *not* been adjusted for inflation, as no nineteenth-century price index is available for Peru – an important omission in a period of currency debasement. Thus, it is quite likely that the increase in tax revenues after roughly the turn of the century reflects price inflation as much or more than real increases in government receipts. By contrast, the Chilean data are in constant pounds sterling of 1833, and thus Chile's long-run increase in revenue – roughly a real quadrupling on a per capita basis between the 1850s and 1910s – reflects sharp actual increases in the ability of the state to tax its citizens.

It is thus clear that postindependence-era Peru and Chile were on decidedly different trajectories of political development – at least as measured by the

---

[3] The magnitude of the challenge of collecting such taxes should not be underestimated. Even the United States found it difficult to impose direct taxation. An income tax, for example, was not imposed in the United States until the time of the Civil War and was later ruled unconstitutional. Not until the passage of the Sixteenth Amendment in 1913 would it be possible to impose such a tax, and effective collection awaited the implementation of withholding during the New Deal.

[4] Until the invention of artificial nitrate fixation during the First World War, guano from the Chincha Islands off Peru and nitrates mined from the Atacama Desert were the only sizable and cost-effective sources of nitrates for use in artificial fertilizers and munitions to be found anywhere in the world.

72   *Latin American State Building in Comparative Perspective*

ability of the state to extract taxes from its citizens. It is also the case that they were ultimately taxed at vastly different levels. Using 1901 data, the first year for which comparable exchange rate data are available, Peruvian tax receipts per 1,000 residents amounted to roughly £392, while the equivalent number for Chile in that year was £2,327.[5] The difference in taxation was not a function of national wealth. While Chile was – in constant dollars, at purchasing power parity – slightly more than twice as wealthy as Peru on average in the 1900–10 period, it taxed at almost six times Peru's level (calculated from Oxford Economic History Database 2011).

WHY DIDN'T PERU BUILD A STRONG STATE?

Peru's colonial history suggests that it should have had a relatively well-developed administrative and coercive infrastructure (Tantaleán 1983). The Viceroyalty of Peru was a locus of Spanish control in lower South America, and its coercive infrastructure had to cope with the possibility of insurrection among the largest, and most organized, indigenous population south of the Mayan regions of Central America. Certainly by comparison with a backwater such as Santiago de Chile, Peru had decidedly more advanced colonial-era political and military institutions. While the Spanish colonists in Peru had effectively subjugated the once-mighty Inca Empire, in Chile, they invested so few resources that they had not even succeeded in suppressing the comparatively small indigenous populations in the south – instead they conceded to the Mapuche Indians effective independence in part of the area between Santiago and Concepción. Similarly, while the absence of major wars is an often-cited explanation of the generally low level of administrative capacity in Latin America as a whole, it is a poor explanation for the relative incapacity of the Peruvian state compared with its regional neighbors. Peru after independence was among the Latin American countries most consistently threatened by international military conflict, alternatively with Chile, Colombia, Spain, and Ecuador. This conflict could and did implicate the lives and fortunes of its elites, yet it did not impel their cooperation around the formation of either an effective state or even basic military preparedness or modernization.

What, then, accounts for the persistent backwardness of the Peruvian state? The political effects of a servile rural political economy were crucial from the formation of the republic onward. Indeed, the very question of independence from Spain had deeply divided the Creole elite of Peru, and ultimately liberation was not won by Peruvians but rather imposed from without by Bolívar, O'Higgins, and San Martín. Historians have pointed out that much of the reluctance of Peruvian Creole elites – although they stood to govern Peru after

---

[5] Peruvian government revenue data are from Mitchell (2003, 693) and are converted to pounds sterling with the exchange rate reported for 1901 by Global Financial Data Inc. (2005). Chilean data are from Dirección de Contabilidad (1914).

State Formation in Chile and Peru

independence – to join the continent-wide move to independence was founded on the fears that the revolutionary movement utilized indigenous images, symbols, and even soldiers. The participation of armed Indians – and the consequent possibility of postindependence rebellion against local repressive structures – was sufficient to drive many Peruvian elites to the royalist cause (Fisher 1984, 467–77).

It might be objected that the servile political economy of postindependence Peru was the inevitable consequence of a logically prior factor: the presence of a large indigenous population available for this form of exploitation. Beyond its functionalism, there are other problems with this claim. There was at the time of conquest also a sizable indigenous population in Chile (Collier and Sater 2004, 4). And servile labor relations were initially imposed there as well, but they soon disappeared as a principal mechanism of recruiting labor for agricultural production. Empirically, it is by no means a sufficient condition to impel the utilization of coercive forms of labor recruitment and management. Mahoney (2010) makes a much more sophisticated argument on this score, contending that it was not the availability of a large indigenous population but rather the level of organization it had in Inca-era Peru that made servile labor attractive to the Spanish colonists. It is quite true that the Inca Empire and its subject peoples were more concentrated and vastly more politically organized than their nomadic counterparts in Chile. And indigenous subject peoples had been accustomed under the Inca to a regime of forced labor (though at much less extensive levels) through the *mita* system. This historically contingent pattern of preexisting social organization probably did encourage reliance on coerced labor in the Sierra. But it does not account for the reliance on African slaves in the coastal sugar plantations: if the critical factor in the imposition of economy-wide forced labor relations is the availability of an organized, governable, and large indigenous population, then why were they not used to staff the coastal plantations? And if they were too geographically remote, then why didn't free labor relations emerge in this regional, labor-scarce economy? Finally, when the slave trade ended and the local slaves were emancipated, why did Peruvian elites turn to indentured Chinese labor rather than the local Indian population or wage laborers? It was only after these two resources – slave and indentures – were precluded that substantial recourse was taken to coercive recruitment of indigenous labor from the highlands.

The presence of the large, organized indigenous population thus by itself does not imply in a functional sense that recourse to servile labor will occur. Or at least its absence does not imply that nonservile relations will emerge; in most cases, the results are indeterminate. Nor was the use of coerced labor in the coastal sugar plantations inevitable – alternative forms of labor recruitment in both more or less labor-scarce environments were viable as the Argentine and Uruguayan (free wage labor) and Chilean (labor service tenancy) experiences demonstrate. And we will see later that – parallel to the Peruvian case – the absence of servile labor was similarly not inevitable in Chile, for both chattel

74   *Latin American State Building in Comparative Perspective*

slavery and the classic coerced labor of the Spanish *encomienda* system were practiced there in the colonial era. Instead, meaningful choices were made that initiated in Chile the transition to a different, nonservile form of agrarian productive relations.[6]

The consequences of this difference in social relations were profound, and they helped to keep postindependence Peru deeply fragmented by race and class – distinctions that were at the very heart of the system of taxation and social organization. It had political implications as well, for even the omnipresent threat of indigenous insurrection was insufficient to promote cooperation among members of different factions of the Creole elite, which was profoundly divided along regional and sectoral lines. The resultant conflict and instability was so severe that Peru was unable to form any kind of lasting national administrative infrastructure until the mid-nineteenth century, which in turn reinforced the importance of *local* control over coercive institutions for elites' physical and economic security. Indeed, between 1821 and 1845, 53 governments, 10 congresses, and as many as 7 constitutional documents claimed – but did not have – effective political authority (Bonilla 1984). Instead, in the first half of the nineteenth century, fragmentation, state weakness, and patrimonialism carried the day as deeply divided, rent-seeking elites confronted a state unable to resist their pressures or impose its will (Quiroz 1988). This conflict culminated in the 1841–45 civil war, which reduced what little remained of Peruvian public administration to an "inherently predatory" state (Gootenberg 1989, 112).

The end of the civil conflict, and the rise to power of a more lasting caudillo, Ramón Castilla, in 1845 (president from 1845 to 1851 and from 1855 to 1862), brought with it the first real effort at state (re-)building. Castilla had the singular fortune of coming to power during a period of historically unprecedented wealth – during the guano boom.[7] Indeed, guano made Peru the world's only major source of nonanimal fertilizer for much of the last half of the nineteenth century, and the Peruvian state managed to retain an unprecedented 60 to 70 percent of the proceeds as its profit (Hunt 1985, 270–72). This sudden influx of wealth made it possible for Castilla to coopt southern elites, stamp out regionalist rebellions, and establish a more effective national military. Even a measure of elite cooperation was purchased as Castilla used guano proceeds to redeem otherwise near-worthless government bonds – that had

---

[6] In this sense, the patterns of prevailing social relations of agricultural production were, in both Chile and Peru, at least in important measure exogenous to the presence or absence of a large indigenous population, which itself was in part endogenous to preferences for servile labor, the consequences of disease and repression, and varying social practices with respect to miscegenation in the colonial era.

[7] Guano, the centuries-old accumulation of nitrates in bird excrement on the Chincha Islands, was rapidly controlled by the Peruvian state. As it was concentrated on a few offshore islands and extremely easy to extract and commercialize, even a state as administratively deficient as Peru retained effective control over the rents that resulted. See Berg and Weaver (1978, 72–73).

State Formation in Chile and Peru   75

been acquired at a small fraction of their face value by many members of
the upper classes (Gootenberg 1989, 81, 124). Some was also paid to agrarian elites as (often fraudulently overstated) compensation for manumission in
1854 (Basadre 1947, 236; Hunt 1985, 275). Guano wealth thus underwrote
the expansion of the Peruvian state, whose budget ballooned eightfold in the
span of 25 years. According to Peloso (1996, 194), nearly half of the guano
revenues went into the expansion of the military and civilian personnel of
the central state, and much of the rest was effectively transferred to domestic
and foreign bondholders. Resource wealth thus contributed to ending internal
conflict but was in very large measure dissipated as rents rather than being
invested in institutional expansion or improvement – or social development
that might ultimately impel or stabilize such state-building efforts. That said, it
still marked an administrative *improvement* relative to the era of greater natural resource scarcity, in direct contrast to the expectations of resource curse
scholarship.

Peruvian political stability and limited administrative development, however, had been mortared with the proceeds from guano exports, and when
these declined in the early 1870s, so did the reach of the central state (Berg
and Weaver 1978, 76). The timing was unfortunate, as it was at just this
moment that the external military conflict with Chile was heating up. A bellicist perspective on this conflict would suggest that faced with the threat of war
with Chile, the Peruvian elite might accept some centralization of authority
or increase in taxation to pay the substantial costs associated with building a
military effective enough to repel or deter the Chileans. Even the threat of war,
however, was not enough to make possible the creation of an effective revenue
system for the Peruvian state; the loss of guano revenues was not compensated
for by the imposition of effective domestic direct or indirect taxation.[8] Importantly, the issue was not just the ability to collect taxes but rather the explicit
unwillingness of elites in the Peruvian legislature to levy new taxes, even for
the national defense. Whether they would have been able to collect them, had
they been levied, remains an open question. Instead, Peru resorted to massive
monetary emission, more than quadrupling the paper money supply in a matter
of months at the onset of the war (Yepes del Castillo 1981, 100).

Far from provoking political modernization, the War of the Pacific (1879–
83) fought between a Bolivian and Peruvian alliance against the Chilean
invaders produced an institutional collapse. Instead of unifying Peruvians
around the defense of the nation, the war "generated not only ... confrontation

---

[8] Indeed, what direct taxes had existed were largely abolished during the guano boom, and those
taxes that were ultimately reinstated were typically extremely regressive capitation taxes on
the indigenous population. So onerous was this burden for the impoverished peasantry that it
sparked open rebellion (Berg and Weaver 1978, 71). At the same time, the very mechanisms used
to collect taxes were primitive in the extreme – tax farming was not abolished until the 1890s,
and even the abolition of the Indian head tax in this era was replaced by a no less burdensome
salt tax. See Klarén (2000, 205).

76   *Latin American State Building in Comparative Perspective*

between the ruling class and the subordinate classes as a whole, but also ethnic confrontation" (Bonilla 1978a, 106). The Peruvian elite in fact continued its refusal to approve tax levies to defend itself even as the Chileans actually invaded (Werlich 1978, 115). The war laid bare the fundamental social problem rooted in the countryside that made Peruvian political modernization all but impossible: the continued reliance on an enormous, and rebellious, semiservile labor force – the indigenous population of the Sierra and indentured Chinese laborers on the coastal plantations. Indeed, class and racial politics very quickly overwhelmed "national" loyalty as the Chilean invasion arrived. That is, elites were generally far more concerned that peasants remain under control than they were with contributing to the national defense against the Chilean invaders. The mayor of Lima himself openly hoped for a prompt Chilean occupation of the city out of fear that subalterns might rise in rebellion (Bonilla 1978b, 101). Moreover, as a few Peruvian patriots like Cáceres attempted to engage the Chileans in a guerrilla conflict in 1882–83, the agrarian upper class not only largely refused to support the effort but actively collaborated with the Chilean occupiers because of Cáceres's reliance on armed peasant *montoneras* (guerrillas) (Mallon 1987; Bonilla 1978a).

Elites were reluctant to resist the Chilean invaders, as doing so would require joining with and arming the (long-restive) local peasantry. It was thus the semiservile social structure of highland Peru that prevented the Chilean invasion from propelling a nationalist response among elites that might otherwise have made them willing to pay taxes toward their collective defense and permit the centralization of power that would have helped to create an even moderately competent military. But given a choice between nationalist fears of Chileans and class fears of an armed, mobilized peasantry, much of the Peruvian elite gave in to the latter, even at the cost of collaboration in their own nation's occupation (Smith 1989, 71). The point is not, however, that Peru was handicapped because it had a precapitalist agrarian system. The Chilean rural economy was by all accounts also extremely inefficient and clearly run along precapitalist lines. But Chilean peasants were free to abandon their estates should they so choose, and agrarian elites could thus support the construction of mass armies without risking social unrest, personal security, or economic catastrophe. The difference is that a labor-repressive agrarian structure like Peru's is an unsuitable social basis on which to recruit a mass army. But even one as traditional and economically unproductive as the Chilean can, by contrast, serve as such a foundation because the military apparatus is not simultaneously extensively used in a repressive capacity to maintain agrarian social control; indeed, military service can even be a first step in a process of social mobility through which peasants move to higher-status urban occupations. In Peru, landlords were neither willing to entrust local social control to soon-to-be-mobilized peasant troops, nor could they part with the labor that mass conscription would have entailed or the political and military empowerment of peasants it would have required. Fears of rebellion in Peru were well founded – at least four major

State Formation in Chile and Peru 77

popular insurrections occurred in the nineteenth century, in 1834, 1854, 1865, and 1895, as well as with great intensity again in 1915–16 and 1920–23 (on the former, Basadre 1947, 215; on the latter, Burga and Flores Galindo 1979, 8).

An explanation for Peruvian elites' insistence on maintaining local control over the coercive apparatus, even at the expense of national sovereignty itself, requires an examination of exactly how force was essential to the operation of the agrarian economy. While unfree labor was essential in both major agrarian political economies of Peru (the highland "Sierra" grain producers and sheep ranchers, and the lowland coastal plantations), it was very differently organized. It is also important to note that unfree relations were not confined only to the agrarian economy (which was, of course, at the time the most important) but also characterized much of the mining sector well into the twentieth century.

Coastal plantation agriculture is the clearest example of reliance on classic servile labor. These (often sugar) plantations initially relied on African slave labor until manumission in 1854, which was followed by the importation of Chinese indentured servants under similarly exploitative conditions until 1874 (Yepes del Castillo 1981, 186; Berry 1990, 41). When the supply of indentured labor ended shortly before the War of the Pacific, planters shifted not to wage labor but rather to an interregional system of debt peonage (*enganche*) (Klarén 1977, 241–42). In this way, they were able to draw on the labor surplus in the indigenous highland region rather than pay the comparatively high wages that would have been required either to attract it voluntarily or to recruit foreign workers.

The enganche system, variations of which were widely used in Latin America, involves the advance of cash by planters or their middlemen, who bind the recipient to a term of labor (in Peru, formally from three months to two years), during which, in theory, the debt and interest will be repaid. Of course, these terms serve as minima, as a wide variety of tools were used to increase their length or raise the debt level. Owners, for example, would pay in scrip redeemable only at (exorbitantly priced) company stores and would extend further credit in these facilities, they could falsify the debt records of the often illiterate labor force, and they would take advantage of individual misfortunes or cash shortages (for funerals, weddings, or the like) to encourage ill-advised further advances of cash and thus lengthen terms of indenture.

The linkage between the enganche system and the local control of coercion becomes more transparent when one recognizes that the labor recruiters (*enganchadores*) were themselves typically local political authorities in the highland communities from which workers were recruited. For these highland officials, landlords, and even clergymen, personal profit was intimately tied to their local control over the proximate Indian communities – for without this control, not only could Indians not be induced to accept the advances but they would also flee their servitude with great frequency, for the fundamentally exploitative character of this system of labor relations was quite apparent. As Klarén

(1977, 243) puts it, this system, especially early on, "was based far more on a mix of physical force and moral persuasion than on money incentives."

Coercion was also essential to highland agriculture, even though there existed in this region a local labor surplus (in contrast to the coasts, to which workers were literally forcibly transported). Here semiservile labor relations were less about labor recruitment alone or just the potential monetary expense of free wage labor. Instead, the violence inherent in Sierra agriculture was about controlling a restive population and, more importantly, protecting the very property rights of the landlords themselves. Highland landlords were effectively in perpetual conflict with surrounding Indian communities over the boundaries between their properties and Indian communal lands, for not only were their estates established as a consequence of the colonial seizure of Inca lands, but in subsequent years, encroachment on formally inalienable community lands became commonplace – and was subject to frequent counterattacks.

Unlike Chile's Central Valley, however, Spain's conquest of Peru did not eradicate or absorb via intermarriage the indigenous population or its independent communities – though decimate and impoverish them it did. And it was the survival of these communities, down to the present day, that made the ongoing violent conflicts over the control over land both possible and eventually inevitable. Whenever landlord coercive resources were at a nadir, they were immediately faced with the likelihood of violent efforts by Indians to reclaim their lands and reassert their rights – indeed, exactly such zero-sum conflicts over the control over productive land have long been identified as structurally conducive to endemic rebellion (see Paige 1975, 1997). And these conflicts were not simply a threat to the livelihoods of Sierra *gamonales* (traditional highland landlords) but also to landlords' lives. The threat of an Indian uprising alone, however, does not necessarily impede state building. In both Argentina and Chile, the postcolonial state fought long and brutal conflicts – especially so in Argentina's scorched-earth "Conquest of the Desert" – with indigenous tribes over control of land. But in these cases – unlike Peru – the conflict contributed to, rather than impeded, military modernization and political centralization. The key is the role that social relations played in the formation and use of national armies.

Economic development ironically only made matters worse in Peru, for the opening of the Southern Railway vastly increased the potential profitability of highland farms and ranches. But for it to pave the way for the definitive introduction of wage labor, it would have first required the even further dispossession of Indian lands and, more important, a clear end to any collective indigenous capacity to resist. As is, of course, made clear by the civil war in highland Peru as late as the 1990s, in the almost two centuries after independence, neither the foundation for indigenous grievances nor the capacity to rebel in pursuit of their redress has been removed. This, of course, sapped the willingness of these landlords to permit the centralization of force in the hands of a remote national army, and it made them even more reticent to tolerate the

State Formation in Chile and Peru

79

participation of indigenous Peruvians in the military defense of the fatherland, for they saw themselves as the likely next targets of the military skills and equipment indigenous peasants would acquire by doing so.

This reticence contributed to defeat in the War of the Pacific, which brought with it a critical territorial loss for Peru – the nitrate fields of the Atacama Desert – as Chile seized the southern Peruvian provinces of Arica and Tacna as well as Iquique from Bolivia. These nitrates had replaced guano as the world's principal source of fertilizer and nitrate inputs for munitions and were thus exceedingly valuable. Some have contended that the response of Peruvian elites to defeat by the Chileans should be an effort to reconstitute the state and professionalize the public administration (Quiroz 1988, 76). But national unity and political modernization were the last things on the mind of the Peruvian elite after the departure of Chilean troops in 1884. Instead, these collaborationist elites insisted that in exchange for their support, General Cáceres, who had led the guerrilla resistance to occupation, would have to use his forces to repress the very Indian peasants who had been his allies throughout the struggle against the Chilean invaders. With this he complied, in effect reestablishing both basic social control and the labor-repressive agrarian social structure that had prevailed since colonization.[9] It is possible that an opportunity to redirect Peru onto a path of more effective state building was lost in this choice.

The institutionally stunted path that Peruvian political development took then continued into the period after the end of the War of the Pacific in 1884 through roughly the end of the First World War (an era known in Peru as the "Aristocratic Republic"). While temporally largely coterminous with the Chilean oligarchy-dominated Parliamentary Republic, the internal politics of this period in Peru were quite different. While Klarén (2000, 213–15) has shown that this was a period in which a coherent oligarchical stratum finally emerged, forged out of an alliance among Lima businessmen, the export economy, and the landlords of the Sierra, unlike in Chile, the political system was unable to mediate intraelite divisions through the emergent party system. And the powerful political alliance between the *gamonales* (traditional landlords) of the Sierra and the sugar and cotton agro-exporters of the coastal region ensured that nothing would be done to undermine the reliance on semiservile labor (Yepes del Castillo 1981, 186; Berry 1990, 41). Partly as a consequence, economic underdevelopment persisted, and even a basic transition to capitalist production proceeded slowly. Burga and Flores report that even as late as 1946, agricultural employment relations had not yet been monetized in most of Peru – a national-scale market economy was thus still to be constructed even at this late a date (Burga and Flores 1979, 27). The ultimate effect was that neither economic development nor state building was likely to ensue, for both would

---

[9] Indeed, those guerrilla leaders under Cáceres's control paid with their lives for their patriotism; they were publicly executed on his orders in June 1884. See Bonilla (1978b, 114).

80   *Latin American State Building in Comparative Perspective*

have required a more powerful and centralized form of political authority than either agrarian elite group could tolerate.[10]

The imposition of a more economically viable, liberal pattern of economic and social organization would have required extensive investment by elites in national institutions. For its imposition in the Peruvian context would have necessitated, inter alia, the extinguishing of a host of extant property rights (of both the indigenous population and the Roman Catholic Church), a change in their fundamental form (including the abolition of collective property and restrictions on alienability), emancipation, new institutions to mobilize and regulate labor, and the removal of existing barriers to market competition and exchange.[11] However much some Peruvian urban elites, especially nascent industrialists, might have preferred this, in contrast to Chilean industrial interests, they were not as connected to their rural counterparts by economic or kinship linkages, and a power-centralizing compromise was never effectively on the political agenda.

The inability to incorporate competing elites in a stable and authority-centralizing oligarchic democracy during the Aristocratic Republic, which we will see that the Chileans managed during the same period, prevented the creation of political institutions in Peru capable of effectively pursuing even the collective interests of the upper classes, much less anything approximating a national interest. The effects are hard to overstate and administrative backwardness was profound – indeed, until 1895, the state did not even have a meaningful revenue bureaucracy, relying instead on various forms of tax farming (Yepes del Castillo 1981, 177). Seemingly the only alternative to overcome elite division so as to modernize governmental institutions would have required a more absolutist form of political centralization. And in practice, the first substantial moves toward the creation of forward-looking, truly national policy occurred under the dictatorship of President Augusto Leguía (1908–12, 1919–30), who seized power in a coup immediately on having achieved his second electoral victory. Leguía undertook to transform Peruvian institutions, beginning by closing the congress, imposing a new authority-centralizing constitution, and creating a militarized national police, the Guardia Civil.[12]

The 11 years of Leguía's second period of rule marked a serious effort at political development, albeit under increasingly authoritarian auspices. They also demonstrate its limits – even employing autocratic power – in such sociopolitically inhospitable terrain. On the one hand, after Leguía's entry into power for the second time in 1919, opponents were driven from the political field,

---

[10] Thorp and Bertram (1978, 321) have documented Peru's exceedingly slow long-run growth rate, estimating it at roughly 1% a year between 1890 and 1975. Berry (1990, 53) has pointed out the uncharacteristically small size of the Peruvian state into the 1940s, even after the substantial expansion during the second Leguía government (1919–30).

[11] Mahoney (2001, 35–39) has an excellent discussion of just how powerfully interventionist the state had to be to bring liberal economic and social policies in the Central American context – which mirrors the challenges faced in the rest of Spanish America.

[12] On the last, see Loveman (1999, 89).

State Formation in Chile and Peru 81

and the legislature was rendered subservient. Moreover, in terms of political and economic development, contemporary observers were struck by his efforts at the modernization and expansion of the military; the creation of a national reserve bank; and extensive investments in agricultural, transportation, and mineral infrastructure (Stuart 1928, 416–20). The stop that Leguía's authoritarianism put to open divisions among political elites (or at least the ability to voice them publicly) made some institutional development possible; between 1919 and 1927, state revenues quadrupled (from a low base), while the number of public employees expanded sixfold over the decade of the 1920s (Collier and Collier 2002 [1991], 139). Notably, this was accomplished without the spur of a major external security threat. This in turn highlights the importance of elite cooperation or acquiescence – achieved by bargain or coercion – to the initial state-building project.

Conversely, a transformation of Peruvian social structure that might have sustained political and institutional modernization was not undertaken; no effective effort was made to bring free labor relations to the countryside (not to mention agrarian reform), nor was the temporary sublimation of elite divisions under an authoritarian regime stable, for Leguía's rule was personalistic rather than institutionalizing and thus central authority could not survive his loss of power when the Great Depression swamped the Peruvian economy. Ultimately, Leguía neither definitively undermined the economic position of the agrarian oligarchy, nor was he able to render it politically subordinate along the lines of the successful continental European absolutist states. In the political liberalization after his fall, moreover, compulsory and secret balloting for all literate males aged 21 and above was introduced (Basadre 1976, 138). This laudable but precocious democratization brought about some incorporation of nonelite actors into Peruvian national politics (as will be shown in Chapter 5), further reducing the likelihood that rural elites would in the future cede power to a political center that now would include important nonelite political actors.

In the end, socioeconomic and political factors lined up in Peru to launch a trajectory of political underdevelopment. Neither threats of external conflict nor potential collective benefits from the modernization of state institutions were sufficient to permit an elite reliant on local coercive control over a hostile labor force to permit political centralization. And a divided elite was all the more incapable of bridging differences between factions or managing a viable strategy for long-run alternation in power or the development of a shared set of political and economic goals. Instead, localism, civil conflict, and regional divides left a legacy that made Peru decidedly unfavorable terrain for the modernization of the central state and the deepening of its penetration and control over society.

HOW DID THE CHILEAN STATE BECOME SO STRONG?

Chile, over the course of the nineteenth and twentieth centuries, moved squarely down the path of comparatively early and effective state building. But viewed from the perspective of its birth in the independence struggle from Spain, this hardly seems a likely outcome. Indeed, on a variety of dimensions, one might have expected Chile to take a different – and more common – path toward persistent internal conflict, administrative ineffectiveness, and territorial disunity. Instead, the Chilean state, even in the nineteenth century, was able to levy serious domestic taxes, field effective armies at great distances from its capital and sources of supply, provide critical public goods and infrastructure, and achieve both territorial unification and administrative control down to the local level. By contrast, Peru squandered the immense resources it acquired as the monopoly supplier of artificial fertilizers; was unable to gain the cooperation of its own upper classes either in support of national self-defense or for the construction of an effective bureaucracy that could provide essential public goods; achieved administrative penetration into local areas only very late; and to this day has developed a very limited capacity for economic governance, taxation, or the promotion of development.

Not only does Chile stand out in comparison to its Andean neighbor, it is also generally considered to have long been a continental outlier with respect to the effectiveness of its public administration, the efficiency and professionalism of its military, and its ability to govern its economy.[13] For all the consensus that exists as to the comparatively high quality of the Chilean public administration, conventional theoretical treatments of the origins of such capacity are decidedly unpropitious starting points for explaining it. On the one hand, Chile has been since independence highly dependent on natural resource exports for the overwhelming majority of its foreign exchange, a substantial portion of economic activity, and large percentages of its public revenue. On the other hand, at least in the nineteenth century, Chile was involved in strategic conflicts with Spain, Bolivia, Peru, and Argentina – that might have spurred its elite to cooperate in a modernizing effort driven by the need for collective survival (see Chapter 5). If this conflict is the key – and we saw earlier that the parallel threat had, if anything, negative effects in Peru – there is no explanation for why the development and modernization of the Chilean public administration continued apace (if not becoming more rapid) in the twentieth century when such military threats were almost completely superseded. Finally, in most of these conflicts, the Chileans were the aggressors, not those threatened.

An alternative account emphasizing cumulative advantages, favorable international position, or neocolonial parasitism on its immediate neighbors is also

---

[13] Centeno (2002, chapter 1). It should be pointed out that this capacity is quite independent of developmental strategy. The Chilean state was quite capable of undertaking state-led developmental efforts at least since the presidency of Balmaceda (1886–91) and most extensively in the era of import-substituting industrialization initiated under the Popular Front governments (1938–52) and continued until the fall of Salvador Allende in 1973. At the same time, effective arms-length market-regulating institutions were created during the neoliberal turn initiated by the military government of General Pinochet (1973–89), which were markedly strengthened in the posttransition's Christian- and social-democratic governments of the Concertación (1989–2007).

State Formation in Chile and Peru

not of much help. Chile entered the era of independence on decidedly shaky pilings. A backwater during the colonial era, it had developed neither a highly structured and effective bureaucracy nor the accompanying coercive institutions that characterized the Viceroyalty of Peru, centered in Lima. With brief exceptions – before the opening of the transcontinental railroad in the United States or the completion of the Panama Canal – Chile has also been far removed from the centers of global commerce and thus from any diffusion of innovation that extensive trade might have implied. It was geographically more remote from key markets in North American and Europe than any other part of the South American continent.

Why could, and did, Chilean elites, who were as politically divided as many others in Latin America over, for example, the role of the church, the powers of the presidency, the gold standard, or the centralization of authority, initiate the creation of an effective central state in the postindependence era that began a virtuous cycle of administrative development? Making this all the more surprising, the Chilean state was not even born as a territorially unified entity – for 50 years after independence, its southern provinces were cut off from the core of the state by an unconquered and well-defended Mapuche and other Indian territories that spanned the breadth of the country south of the Bío-Bío River.

The factor that opened the door to political development – though itself not sufficient – was the absence of a labor-repressive agrarian social structure. The ultimate reliance on free labor was not simply a legacy of population density or colonial-era practices. Chile had a substantial indigenous population at the time of conquest – and while it was decimated by disease and war, so was the highland Indian population of Peru. And as in Peru, coercive colonial labor recruitment institutions, including chattel slavery and the *estancia* system, were initially employed. While the local indigenous population of the Chilean Central Valley ultimately disappeared – through mortality and assimilation via intermarriage – it could have been, but was not, replaced by African slaves or indentured labor as on the Peruvian coast. Or, for that matter, it might have been supplanted by free wage labor as in Argentina or Uruguay. But instead, a very peculiar form of heritable labor service tenancy developed, relying neither on juridical coercion nor the payment of market-based cash wages to acquire labor. This development of a system of uncoerced labor, complex and contingent as its emergence was, would ultimately prove exceedingly consequential for long-run political development.

It is crucial to realize that the presence of nonservile social relations does not imply that Chilean agriculture was characterized by an agrarian capitalism of either large farms employing wage laborers or independent small and medium family farmers. It was a world of enormous estates worked on precapitalist terms by labor service tenants – called *inquilinos* – linked through traditional relations of asymmetrical reciprocity to their landlords (Bauer 1975, 80–81). In the first half of the nineteenth century, these peasants were typically of Creole or mestizo (mixed Creole and indigenous) origin. Imported indentured labor and slavery were not important contributors to production. By the second half of the century, their numbers were augmented by new peasant immigrants from Spain, the Basque lands, and, secondarily, Prussia–Germany. The critical point, however, was that these were *voluntary* tenancies – peasants could legally and practically leave at will. And indeed, even this traditional hacienda system in Chile was complemented by a substantial migratory and seasonal workforce (*afuerinos*) that provided supplemental labor during harvest periods (Blakemore 1993, 45). To be sure, such productive relations did not facilitate agricultural modernization in the way either capitalist or small-farmer systems would, but they were consonant with substantial improvements in the efficacy of the central government.

The postindependence Chilean agrarian political economy was as unusual as it was consequential. The system that developed – and ultimately persisted until the agrarian reforms of the 1960s and 1970s – involved the construction of a nonservile but simultaneously largely noncapitalist set of productive relations. That Chilean agriculture was based on immense landholding inequality and free labor is surprising; that it did so without transformation into a capitalist wage labor system is remarkable. There are certainly other examples of nonservile labor systems in Latin America, notably the far-more-common agrarian capitalism of Argentina and Uruguay. Critically, the political relations in the Chilean countryside also, despite this immense inequality and surplus population, lacked the endemic conflict that characterized Peruvian and countless other Latin American societies.[14] Although it was comparatively peaceful, this production system did not allow for economic growth founded on agricultural modernization, as in Argentina. Instead, it generally managed to produce little more than enough output to cover domestic food needs, and that not always.[15]

To understand how such a fundamental inequality in landownership was paradoxically combined with free labor and comparative social peace, one must examine the evolution of the system of labor service tenancy (*inquilinaje*) on which it was founded. After independence, Chilean rural elites were exceedingly land rich, but given the weak international competitiveness of their products and poor transportation infrastructure, they were generally quite cash poor (Bauer and Johnson 1977, 88). And unlike in Argentina and Uruguay, labor was generally not particularly scarce. These two facts worked against the establishment of wage labor relations, as landlords were neither easily able to pay substantial cash sums nor were they required to do so to attract workers. Importantly, and again in contrast to Peru, although there was a labor surplus in Chile, it was not in large measure resident in independent long-standing peasant

---

[14] On land inequality, see Comité Interamericano de Desarrollo Agrícola (1966); on rural protest levels, see Loveman (1976).

[15] This limited agricultural productivity was not a consequence of geographic or climatic constraints, as the massive export-oriented growth of the sector after land tenure and productive relations reformation between the 1960s and 1980s definitively demonstrate.

State Formation in Chile and Peru

communities; indeed, much of Chilean village life was actually internal to the large farms (haciendas). The exception, of course, was the indigenously controlled South, but this ceased to be exceptional after the conquest of the 1880s and the subsequent expropriation and forced resettlement of the remaining Mapuche Indians onto reservations (*reducciones*). The consequence, however, of this general settlement pattern is that it did not set up a long-standing, persistent land conflict: communities and haciendas were not perennially at odds over control over land. That battle, alas, had long since been decided: the haciendas already controlled much of the valuable, arable land. The haciendas were often surrounded by large numbers of small- and microholdings (*minifundistas*) on more marginal terrain, many of whose families provided them seasonal labor inputs (as their own farms were insufficient to produce year-round subsistence). *Inquilinaje* itself emerged gradually in the colonial era through the settlement on the haciendas proper of peasant families – initially to safeguard boundaries and later to provide more extensive labor (Bengoa 1990). As time went on, and peasant labor became more plentiful relative to demand, these arrangements gradually took on the character of heritable (but not transferable) labor-service tenancies rather than alienable property rights. That said, the tenancies were a hybrid form. They could not be sold, but they could be passed on to one's children (assuming an appropriately positive relationship with the landlord was maintained) and implied some basic social-service and old-age security obligations on the part of the landlord. As such, they represented better life conditions than typically confronted the migratory labor force.

The system that emerged out of this somewhat unusual confluence of initial conditions combined with a political economy that principally produced grain. The important point here is that this sort of production requires relatively low year-round labor inputs but substantial increases in the harvest season. The *inquilinaje* system accommodated these conditions quite well. First, it settled a year-round permanent labor force on the haciendas by means of a payment principally through usufruct. Each tenant family head was granted the right to farm – for himself, on his own time – two pieces of land. One was larger and oriented toward basic grain production (for peasants, often more labor-intensive crops such as beans, rice, potatoes, and lentils), whereas the other was smaller (*cerco*) and provided a space on which to build a dwelling as well as to grow fruits and vegetables. In return, the tenant (*inquilino*) was required to provide 270 days of labor on the hacienda, during which meals were provided. Seasonal spikes in labor demand were met through two different mechanisms. First, the *inquilinos* would make available the labor of *inquilino* family members (called *voluntarios*) in exchange for food on days worked and a modest cash stipend. In addition to this, a second source of labor relied on an outside floating labor pool – the *afuerinos* (literally, "outsiders"). These were a combination of impoverished migratory laborers (*peones*) and residents of nearby microfarms (*minifundistas*) that were not extensive enough to occupy all the owners' time or to provide for subsistence needs.

86 *Latin American State Building in Comparative Perspective*

The result was a system that was, at its core, a closed hacienda community. As Kay (1977, 104) points out, the system was as much cultural as it was economic – the haciendas frequently had their own schools, churches, and stores (*pulperías*). And the ties of asymmetrical reciprocity (with landlords undertaking, e.g., minimal social insurance functions in cases of illness or death) underwrote a system where "loyalty to estate and landlord were repaid by security of tenure" (Bauer and Johnson 1977, 96). Critical to this was the social (and life-chances) distinction between *inquilino* and *afuerino*. However difficult the lot of the former was, it paled in comparison to the hardships and societal disapprobation that were the lot of the latter. And of course, it introduced a social cleavage among hacienda employees that made cooperation to better their collective lot nearly impossible; this cleavage remained a persistent problem, even into the period of mid- to late-twentieth-century agrarian reform.

The critical consequence was that Chilean landlords did not require direct local control over the coercive apparatus of the state either to maintain their physical security or even to underwrite their economic security. The Chilean countryside simply never experienced anything like the endemic unrest that characterized the Peruvian Sierra and coast.[16] Nor did the economic well-being of the agricultural sector impose insuperable limits on policies to promote economic advancement in urban or mining areas. This was a diverse agrarian elite, which, by 1891, often had its foundational wealth from precisely these two nonagrarian sectors (Collier 1977). Indeed, its diversity was also its strength from the perspective of state building. There were no marked social or economic barriers to entry into agriculture for newly wealthy elites operating in other sectors of the economy. Instead, agrarian property ownership quickly became the gateway to entry into upper-class social circles (Collier 1993, 21–22). It also paved the way for participation in national parliamentary politics, for it brought with it clientelistic influence over the votes of hacienda peasants in a system of typically quite restricted suffrage – and by the late nineteenth century, electoral registries also came under the control of the wealthiest local taxpayers, often a local landlord (Remmer 1977, 214). Partly as a result, all major national political factions had economically heterogeneous, but elite, political bases that included agrarians. Nonelite parties, by contrast, could gain little meaningful entrée until well after the start of the twentieth century (see Chapter 5).

The absence of labor-repressive agriculture is, however, at its core only a necessary condition for effective state building. Merely stating that agrarian elites need not fear insurrection if they cede control over local coercive assets does not imply that they will do so. To take this next step requires that two conditions be met. First, there must be a compelling collective elite interest in strengthening the central state, and second, doing so must be reasonably understood as

---

[16] Even Loveman (1976), who is at pains to document that the Chilean countryside was not entirely quiescent, makes it clear that little protest occurred until the agrarian reform era of the 1950s and 1960s, and almost none of it was violent.

State Formation in Chile and Peru

nonthreatening to the fundamental material interests of nearly all politically relevant fragments of the upper class. If, by contrast, the central state is seen as the tool of one particular faction (be it geographic, social, or sectoral), then efforts at political centralization will likely detonate intense factional and civil conflict, as we saw in the Peruvian case, that can impede even collectively rational administrative modernization.

The foundations of elite support for the state-building effort can be found in the construction of what the Chileans call the "Portalian State" period, running from the 1830s through 1891. This was a political compromise among elites that created what might be called an "oligarchic republic" – a political system in which all major components of the upper classes had effective political representation and in which none could seriously contend for perpetual dominance.[17] The Portalian political system was founded on a strongly presidential basis but included one critical restraint: no president could be elected to more than two five-year terms (Blakemore 1974). And in any event, even a strong presidency was always confronted with quite public political opposition from the legislature, where representatives of other political factions could and did express their views and prepare for the next presidential contest. Still, the mere establishment of such a regime out of the postindependence political chaos was an accomplishment, one typically accounted for by the consolidation of the political dominance of the Creole landowning oligarchy (Cariola and Sunkel 1985), elite fears of persistent military anarchy and popular mobilization (Edwards 1976 [1927]), and the emergent "national" traditions and upper-class unity that were born in the struggle for independence (Krebs 1984).

The critical point is not that the oligarchy spoke with a single voice in the Portalian era (it did not) but rather that it created a system in which its internal conflicts could be managed in a way that did not lead to the destruction of the administrative structure of the state. Part of this was founded on the near-complete exclusion of nonoligarchical political forces from a substantial role in politics – with suffrage expansion waiting at least until the 1920s and in a large-scale way occurring only much later, by which time the institutions of a powerful central state had already been firmly established. Of course, the initial elite compromise that came out of the independence effort was not enough by itself to ensure the long-term cooperation necessary to build an effective state. Over time, clashes among the particular interests of different factions of the upper classes, at times crystallizing around ideological concerns over the role of the church in society or the direction of development, would lead to brief insurrections (in the 1850s and again in 1891), but in each case, the vanquished

---

[17] This last point is crucial, for it changes the game of politics from a one-off to an iterated game. While one or the other faction at different times was politically ascendant, the rules of political competition made it clear that this dominance was always subject to compromise, renewal, or replacement, and in no case could a single political figure govern indefinitely.

88 *Latin American State Building in Comparative Perspective*

elites were quickly reintegrated into normal politics. This precedent was itself quite important.

Institutionally, the foundations of interelite compromise were further facilitated by the establishment of a single-term presidency in 1871 (Collier 1993) and by the subjugation of the executive to the parliament after the "revolution" of 1891. The former heightened the iterative character of elite politics by ensuring that the defeat of any particular faction's presidential candidate was only a brief, temporary defeat and that new leadership would be selected within a five-year period. In practice, alternation among factions and parties controlling the presidency did occur with some regularity, and of course, as the transition from one leader to another in accordance with the constitutional schedule continued over time, it helped to make the commitments embedded in the constitution credible and binding. Similarly, even when political conflicts became severe enough to provoke brief armed rebellions, it was typically the case that the defeated side would be quickly reabsorbed into the political system (Blakemore 1974). Most notably, even after the most severe civil conflict – the deposition of President Balmaceda and the installation of the Parliamentary Republic in 1891 – political divisions were quickly overcome. The supporters of Balmaceda, while initially sentenced to 15 years' exile and the forfeiture of their properties, were quickly amnestied, reentering politics through the Liberal Democratic Party in 1892 and becoming the second largest political force in the substantially more powerful legislature by 1894.[18]

There was a social foundation to this interelite compromise as well. As noted earlier, while the Chilean upper class may have had its foundational wealth in distinct sectors (e.g., mining, industry–commerce, or landholding), there were few if any economic or social barriers to entry into other sectors. Indeed, it became the norm rather than the exception for holders of great urban or mineral wealth to then acquire substantial agricultural holdings. Indeed, these dynamics were so strong that Zeitlin and Ratcliff (1988, 176) contend that in Chile, ultimately, "the ownership of land and capital is indissoluble." And threats to the fundamental interests of major elite segments could thus not be generated from within the broader elite itself. Nor was Chile characterized by the comparatively strong regional differentiation of Peru (much less that of Argentina or Brazil). While the south had for a time a somewhat distinct sociopolitical identity from the politically hegemonic Central Valley, the comparatively similar economic profiles of regional elites, coupled with cooperation-inducing institutions, prevented the emergence of the sorts of overlapping regional-cum-sectoral-cum-policy cleavages that undermined Peruvian compromise. And of course, repetition of cooperation in the institutionalized transfer of power

---

[18] See Remmer (1977) and Blakemore (1974). Indeed, Remmer points out that this indicates a strong underlying unity among different parts of the Chilean upper class as well as the fact that there was no meaningful social reform implicit in what the Chileans call the "Revolution of 1891."

State Formation in Chile and Peru 89

among elite factions or parties only strengthened the coordinating power of the oligarchic–democratic equilibrium.

Thus, the structure of agrarian social relations and the *collective* hegemony (despite internal differences) of the oligarchic elite were the critical conditions that made the construction of a powerful state possible in Chile. But possibility is not necessity, and it is only when these foundational conditions interacted with the strategic arena that a process of real state building was initiated. In Chile, this was facilitated by the multisectoral wealth of the major upper-class families – and their tendency to have material interests in both city and countryside. At the same time, an unusually effective set of clientelistic practices (in the countryside) and suffrage restrictions (in the cities) would keep large-scale middle- and working-class electoral participation off the agenda until the late 1930s, and not meaningfully for the peasantry until the 1960s, when welfare expansions and unionization in the countryside broke the back of hacienda clientelism (Scully 1992). When political institutions were first founded and stabilized in the nineteenth century, elites were quite confident that their investments in these structures would be collectively and individually profitable, for a redistributive use of state institutions was not on the table. Similar exclusionary elite cooperation was also – as will be shown in Chapter 4 – critical in the eventually successful initial formation of strong institutions in Argentina and Uruguay, but only *after* extensive civil conflict was resolved via the definitive victory of one side in the former and through a complex political bargain – eventually institutionalized in a collegial executive – in the latter.

The Peruvian–Chilean comparison also highlights some of the difficulties involved in the application of more traditional bellicist or ecological explanations of administrative development. These alternatives are next examined.

WARS OF EXPANSION AND THE CHILEAN STATE

In the usual telling, it is the threat of international conflict that drives state building as it forces states to construct centralized mass armies to deter, or defend themselves against, potential external aggressors. This in turn necessitates an expansion in the capacity to tax that substantially deepens the penetration of the state into society and its capacity for domestic political control and economic monitoring. While strategic conflict played a role in the construction of an effective Chilean state, it is a role quite different from that attributed to it in this stylized account. And it could have this effect only because of the underlying political–economic environment described earlier.

It was the construction of an elite consensus in Chile around the desirability of *initiating wars of conquest* – from which the dominant classes expected to benefit – that turned military conflict into a component of the process by which an effective administration was constructed. Successive conflicts – with the Araucanian Indians to the south, with Spain, and repeatedly with Peru and Bolivia – were both initiated by the Chilean state and used to justify the

90 *Latin American State Building in Comparative Perspective*

expansion of public powers, the creation of an effective standing army, the imposition of substantial new tax burdens, and the creation of major public infrastructure. The first two conflicts brought new expanses of land into the hands of agrarian elites and regional strategic dominance, respectively, while the last war led to the annexation of the enormously valuable nitrate fields of the Atacama Desert. But these wars represented not external threats but strategic opportunities – investments in war – through which Chilean elites could and did enrich themselves and their country. These were wars that were sometimes costly in the short term to agrarian landlords if they absorbed too much peasant labor or required large tax increases – but these were costs that were handsomely repaid to the families of these same elites when new lands and nitrate profits became available for distribution to them by the state. And of course, even in the most severe conflicts, military recruitment focused on the de facto impressment of *peones* and *afuerinos*, only very late seriously affecting the core hacienda *inquilino* labor forces (Sater 2004, 137).

State expansion was thus not a response to an anarchic environment, contra bellicist expectations. Indeed, given the technological constraints on its neighbors in the middle to late nineteenth century, Chile was, as Blakemore (1974, 1) has called it, effectively an "island nation." Hemmed in by the Andes to the east, the massive and scarcely populated Atacama Desert to the north, and the Pacific Ocean to the west, none of Chile's neighbors had the logistical capacity to launch a serious attack on Chilean interests. Indeed, Argentina, Chile's only wealthier neighbor, had by the very late nineteenth century only barely managed to settle its internal question of national territorial unification – it was not a security threat at the time. Finally, although the Araucanian Indians in the south had long proved adept at avoiding conquest, they were in no position to do more than defend their remote southern territories.

Rather than being defensive, Chile's wars in the nineteenth century were instead wars of aggression. They were more or less explicitly aimed at pursuing regional strategic hegemony and seizing the valuable territories of neighbors. The former was the case in the war against the Peruvian–Bolivian Confederation (1836–39), which, although victorious, cost the founder of the Chilean state, Diego Portales, his life in an assassination (Donoso 1942, 17–19). Similarly, the naval war with Spain (1864–66) gave Chile effective regional dominance over the only meaningful North and South American cross-continental transportation and trade route until the opening of the transcontinental railway and the Panama Canal: naval shipment through the Straits of Magellan.

These wars demonstrated two critical capacities. First, the Chilean elite was capable of taxing itself – *in advance* – to the extent necessary to prosecute successfully these military endeavors, even at great logistical reach. Indeed, in the conflict with the Peruvian–Bolivian Confederation, the Chileans defeated the numerically superior armies of more populous foes in distant and hostile terrain. Second, the Chilean state was capable of raising a mass army able to travel great distances and willing to suffer substantial losses in the service

State Formation in Chile and Peru 91

of a nascent state – that is, it could conscript, train, and transport its soldiers using revenues taxed from its elites without engendering their opposition, even as it drew labor away from the hacienda economy or provided peasants with military skills. This point should not be understated. The initial independence struggle and these successive conflicts are widely seen as defining moments in Chilean history, through which a sense of national identity, bellicist pride, and allegiance to an independent state were born and deepened (e.g., see Góngora 2003, 66; Krebs 1984, 110–17; Nunn 1970, 301; Donoso 1942, 21). These mechanisms reinforced the path-dependent trajectory on which political development had been launched.

Indeed, in marked contrast to what bellicist theories of state formation would expect, having by the late 1860s removed any serious threats to its national security, the Chilean state did not recede into the background. Instead, the oligarchic elites who dominated politics had come to understand that a strong state could be used to serve their material interests, and they were capable of cooperation – despite substantial divisions over some of the questions of the day – to maintain the capacity for the effective projection of force and to impose the necessary tax burdens on themselves to finance this effort. It was in the two great conquests of the late nineteenth century that this dynamic – state building as an investment – most notably came to the fore: the (second) defeat of the Peruvian–Bolivian alliance in the War of the Pacific and the decisive subjugation of the Araucanian Indians.

The War of the Pacific came at a time of economic crisis for Chile. Beset by the global depression of the late 1870s, the agricultural and mineral exports that had hitherto underwritten the economy teetered on the verge of collapse. This was coupled with a sharp increase in interest rates, capital outflow, and a severe debt burden that threatened fiscal stability (see Monteón 1982, 19). It was in this context that the War of the Pacific exploded – and was fought, not coincidentally, for control of the vast and valuable nitrate reserves then part of Bolivia and southern Peru (Ortega 1984, 347).

Initially, Peru, Bolivia, and Chile were all militarily unprepared for the brutal conflict that was to ensue after the Chilean–Bolivian treaty dispute over nitrate taxation exploded into open warfare.[19] Indeed, in numerical terms, the two sides were comparatively evenly matched, and in many ways, the Peruvians ought to have had the advantage given that they were defending their home territory, while the Chileans were thousands of kilometers from their bases of supply and reliant on potentially quite tenuous nineteenth-century logistical support. Nevertheless, as we saw, the Peruvian elites were unwilling to provide the resources to defend their nation and, in some instances, found collusion with the invading Chileans preferable to the military mobilization of the subject Indian populations of their landholdings. The contrast with the behavior of the

---

[19] Peru was immediately dragged into this conflict as a consequence of the mutual-assistance treaty it had concluded with the Bolivians.

92   *Latin American State Building in Comparative Perspective*

Chileans was dramatic. Figure 3.1 shows the increases in domestic taxation that were imposed to pay the enormous costs of rearming and prosecuting a war at long distance – in the span of a year or two, the Chilean state's tax take increased by nearly 150 percent. Nor were these revenues simply extracted from the toiling masses (who, in any event, lacked the resources to prosecute the war). Indeed, by 1879, serious income, capital gains, and inheritance taxes were imposed, imposts that would only be paid by well-off individuals (Ortega 1984, 343–44). Notably, these taxes were applied not in times of plenty but rather during an economic crisis when elites' ability to pay them was at a nadir.

But material resources are not enough to prevail, and to prevail so decisively, in a well-matched military conflict. At the same time, ordinary Chileans could be effectively recruited to fight a war abroad – prima facie evidence of both the sort of national identification and patriotic sentiment that war making requires and of superior administrative capacity. Indeed, many observers – both at the time and in more recent scholarship – have directly attributed the Chilean success in the War of the Pacific to its vastly more solid and penetrating public administration and the organizational advantages that this produced in the arena of war.[20]

Victory in the war brought massive wealth to the Chilean republic in the form of control over nitrate-rich territories from Peru's south. From the perspective of most resource-curse scholarship, however, this bonanza should have proven to be a disaster in terms of subsequent state building and political development. Certainly the resources involved were of a magnitude similar to, for example, the twentieth-century oil booms, and they came relatively early in the state-building process. Taxes on nitrate and iodine (a by-product of nitrate processing) exports alone represented 5.52 percent of Chilean ordinary tax revenue in 1880 but exploded to 52.06 percent by 1890 (Blakemore 1993, 41). Not only did overall customs receipts surge massively but they became overwhelmingly important in the national budget until the trade collapse attendant on the First World War.

But this allegedly easy money had different effects than it had in Peru, and they confound the expectations of resource-curse theories. In the first place, the revenues themselves are evidence of a process of administrative modernization as such revenues had to be collected from powerful foreign-owned mineral multinationals and upper-class Chileans. These are hardly the easiest of targets for taxation as they are both politically and economically difficult to levy imposts on; yet the Chilean state did so at high and expanding levels (Mamalakis 1976). Nor did large tax inflows from trade spell the end of the Chilean state's ability to levy serious internal direct and indirect taxes or

---

[20] See Cariola and Sunkel (1985). Alberto Edwards (1976 [1927], 165), writing in 1927, referred to "the splendid administrative organization, the fundamental solidity of which Chile gave such an eloquent display in the War of the Pacific. . . . Peru and Bolivia were necessarily defeated by a country better organized."

State Formation in Chile and Peru

undermine the administrative capacity that this requires. Instead, these receipts (especially inheritance, agricultural, and income taxes) were turned over to municipal control and thus are not recorded in the national accounts data – though they were levied nonetheless (Bowman and Wallerstein 1982, 448).

Most interestingly, the marked increase in revenues available to the Chilean state was in large measure invested in the provision of public goods, the modernization of the military, and the expansion of public services. It is likely that such public goods' provision not only improved the profitability of Chilean enterprise in general as productivity rose and transaction costs declined but also was privately profitable for elites through rents available in the contracting, purchase arrangements, and employment it implied. What exactly were nitrate proceeds spent on? In large measure, they were expended on the construction of new or expanded state institutions. Cariola and Sunkel (1985) point out that in 1880, the Chilean state directly employed some 3,000 workers, a number that had expanded to 13,000 by 1900 and more than 27,000 by 1919. During this period, a national uniformed police service was built; mail and telegraph service was extended; and water, sewer, paving, and lighting services were brought to Chile's cities. The two most critical accomplishments of this period, however, were the massive expansion of public education – from some 20,000 students in public schools in 1869 to better than 500,000 in 1925 (Cariola and Sunkel 1985, 147–59). The consequence was an expansion in literacy rates from 28.9 percent in 1885 to over 50 percent by 1910 (Blakemore 1993, 61). This expanded state capacity only in the long term came back to haunt the elite that laid its foundations, first during the state-led industrial modernization initiated by the Popular Front and subsequent governments (1938–52) and later by Salvador Allende's (1970–73) brief socialist transformation that ultimately broke the back of the landowning oligarchy, even if it was itself overthrown in a bloody coup. But it also provided the administrative capacity that was crucial to the subsequent market-oriented turn in economic policy under both authoritarian (1973–89) and democratic (1989–) governments of widely varying political colorations.

CONCLUSION

This chapter began a set of paired comparisons that are carried through the rest of this volume. The cases were selected to examine specific components of the general argument about the centrality of the domestic *social* and *political* foundations of long-run institutional development in the South American region. They were also chosen for the way in which the contrasts speak to the dominant alternative explanations in the literature. The examination of the initial watershed in Chile and Peru, the formation of national political institutions out of the chaos of the postindependence period, highlighted the central contribution that contrasting patterns of agrarian economic organization – free versus servile labor – had for long-run institutional development. The Chilean case was also chosen as a contrast with Peru because its nonservile productive relations were also principally noncapitalist productive relations, which helps to differentiate the argument of this book from a more general claim that capitalist productive relations are necessary to serious administrative strengthening, either through the interests they create or as a functionalist complement to the property rights structure they imply. Capitalist agrarian relations certainly *can* be a foundation for long-run political development (as the Uruguayan and Argentine cases will show), but they are not required, nor are they the theoretically central variable.

This chapter told the beginning of the story of political development in Chile and Peru – the institutional start on which each political system was to be built. It also laid the foundation for a long-run argument about the way in which these initial differences became self-reinforcing, creating path dependencies that are the critical substrate on which a second watershed event – the emergence and resolution of the social question of worker and middle-sector political participation – would ultimately determine the fate of national political development. This second part of the story of Chilean and Peruvian state building will be taken up in Chapter 5.

The next chapter considers the initial critical juncture in two cases quite different from Chile and Peru. In Argentina and Uruguay, through different political mechanisms, a state-building trajectory was successfully launched. In these cases, the emphasis is on the *political* side of the coin, for Argentina and Uruguay shared the characteristic of being principally reliant on free (in this case, capitalist wage) labor. Institutional development, however, came only late in each case, tied directly to the resolution of persistent interelite conflict. It is this contrast, and an in-depth examination of the political side of the argument proposed in this book, that forms the central goal of the chapter that is to come.

4

State Formation in Argentina and Uruguay

Agrarian Capitalism, Elite Conflict, and the Construction of Cooperation

This chapter marks a move away from an exploration of the polar differences highlighted in the comparison between the dynamics of state building in Peru and Chile. In that context, a continental laggard stood in sharp contrast to likely the best performer in the region. Here a more subtle distinction is made in the contrasts within and between the Argentine and Uruguayan cases. Both countries quite belatedly initiated successful state strengthening trajectories in the postindependence period after almost a half-century of severe internal conflict. To do so, they each had to overcome long-standing elite divisions that prevented political cooperation, and they accomplished this in very different ways; through a definitive victory of one side in Argentina and quite differently through the construction of institutions of power sharing in Uruguay. The state strengthening trajectories that ultimately emerged would, however, diverge as each country faced the second critical juncture coming as a consequence of the initial entry of the middle and working classes into politics; this is an outcome that will be explored in Chapter 6. For the present, however, the contrasts within and between these cases highlight the centrality of elite politics as one of the two principal initial determinants of long-term national political development.

As a matter of research design, there are two broad sets of theoretically important comparisons to be made here. First, in each case, a long period of severe interelite conflict was associated with very little success in the construction of national political institutions. And then, over the course of decades, ultimately successful elite coordination and compromise made possible the initiation of a trajectory of political development in each. But in the Argentine case, it was a form of elite cooperation that had its birth in the force of arms, making lingering reluctance and regional resistance facts of life even as national political institutions took hold. In Uruguay, elite compromise was a pacted outcome negotiated between contending political parties that ultimately produced a quasi-consociational outcome that would undergird the collective dominance of these very same parties over the subsequent century. It also produced a remarkable level of institutional development and societal penetration by the state in a polity that began the era of independence in a nearly ungovernable form. The comparisons over time help to hold constant the distinctive features of each country that might have affected the outcomes, while the cross-national variation allows a further investigation of the implications of the means by which elite cooperation is achieved for institutional development.

On other potentially important dimensions in the initial postindependence state formation era, the cases are well matched; they had nearly identical political economies and shared an international strategic environment in which each was among the other's military or strategic rivals. Although both were export-oriented commodity producers, most notably in cattle ranching, neither was either blessed or cursed with substantial easy-to-tax natural resource wealth. And both were characterized since independence with a predominance of nonservile labor relations, effectively holding constant in comparison the other theoretically central factor highlighted in this book.

The testing of the sociopolitical theory of state building proposed in the opening chapters of this book thus continues here, with a focus on the politics of elite cooperation. Like the Chilean case examined in Chapter 3, both Argentina and Uruguay ultimately initiated a trajectory of effective institutional development and an expansion of the infrastructural power of the central state. But there are important contrasts with the Chilean case as well. Economic activity in postindependence Argentina and Uruguay occurred in a context in which servile labor had never been an important component of the agrarian (or urban) political economy. But rural labor relations also embodied important contrasts with the Chilean experience, for the Argentine and Uruguayan political economies were fundamentally organized around capitalist free wage labor, in contrast to the noncapitalist but juridically free Chilean system of heritable labor service tenancy. This contrast underscores the point that effective state building is neither sufficiently determined by the existence of agrarian capitalism nor is it necessary for it to occur. And of course, agrarian relations do not predict long-run outcomes on their own either, as we will see in Chapter 6's discussion of the ultimate outcome in Argentina. Thus, juridically free labor, but not agrarian capitalism per se, is a key variable in this initial critical juncture, but it produces an outcome only as it interacts with the character of elite political conflict and cooperation.

State building initially, however, seemed an unlikely outcome as elite politics in the postindependence era in Argentina and Uruguay took on a decidedly conflictual cast, inhibiting the cooperation and compromise necessary to establish powerful institutions. For nearly 70 years, in fact, the Argentine republic was unable to solve its persistent center-periphery cleavage embodied in the struggle between the province and city of Buenos Aires against the other provinces of the coast and interior. Throughout most of this period, both sides sought to establish their own hegemony and thus to try to build a national state

State Formation in Argentina and Uruguay 97

under the domination of one or the other main coalition. Elite cooperation was ultimately achieved, but it was not until the 1880s when something of a lasting settlement had finally been accomplished in part by force of arms, and this finally opened the door to the effective construction of durable state institutions. In Uruguay, the internecine conflict between the Blanco and Colorado parties ravaged the country with civil war, until it was ultimately (and only gradually) mitigated through the construction of a series of increasingly credible power-sharing institutions in the late nineteenth and early twentieth centuries.

State building thus came slowly to both countries. We will see in Chapter 6, however, that this long delay had the potential to cost more than time. For in Argentina, state building was too incipient to produce institutions strong enough to weather the next great political challenge: the expansion of suffrage and the entry of the working classes into national political competition. This marks yet another divergence from both the Peruvian experience of institutional underdevelopment and the Chilean and Uruguayan construction of extensive and effective institutions. Because of the tardy emergence of viable national institutions in Argentina, and the precocious and ferocious entry of the middle and working classes into politics, institutions there were much less well consolidated and ultimately unable to constrain societal interests or defend their own integrity as this political wave crashed into the polity, only to be followed by the economic turmoil sparked by the Great Depression. This ultimately induced a divergence into populist–antipopulist institutional cycling during the second critical juncture, contrasting sharply with the Uruguayan experience of delayed mass participation and the consolidation of state institutions supported by a cross-party and cross-class alliance committed to statist development. These outcomes are explored directly in Chapter 6. But here we begin with the long-delayed emergence of the Argentine national state and its golden age of effective institutional development and a similar process of political settlement and institution building in Uruguay.

ARGENTINA: PRECOCIOUS CAPITALISM, BELATED STATE BUILDING, AND PERSISTENT POLITICAL CONFLICT

Argentina has always been a perplexing case of institutional development. Indeed, from the perspective of traditional explanations, the comparative underdevelopment of its public administration is something of a puzzle. On one hand, Buenos Aires was an institutional center in the late colonial era, ultimately becoming the seat of the Viceroyalty of Rio de la Plata, which was created late in the colonial period. While lacking the history and institutional depth of the Viceroyalty of Peru, Buenos Aires still began the era of independence with greater experience in, and infrastructure of, governance than would characterize either Montevideo, in what would become Uruguay, or Santiago, Chile. Perhaps more surprising, Argentina has for a long time stood out as the wealthiest country on the South American continent – often by far.

Yet comparatively successful economic development has not been sufficient to drive enduring improvements in the strength of its institutions, nor has institutional weakness doomed it to poverty and underdevelopment. Instead, this juxtaposition underscores the contention of this book that the factors inducing long-run economic development and long-run institutional improvement are not necessarily the same. What makes this conjunction of comparative wealth and weak governance even more perplexing is that the Argentine economy produced wealth that *could have*, but did not, ultimately underwrite the more vibrant state structures like those found in, for example, Chile and Uruguay.

Nor was Argentine wealth simply a function of natural resource extraction, as would be expected in resource-curse accounts of political underdevelopment. While they are certainly reliant on vast stretches of suitable land – ranching and cereal production were and remain critical components of Argentine exports – these are hardly the "easy to exploit" and concentrated (in ownership terms) point-source resources (such as oil, hard-rock diamonds, and other minerals) highlighted by resource-curse scholars. And indeed, much of Argentine political history is consumed with the (often fruitless) effort to tax agrarian wealth and income, a task that appears no easier today than it was in the past century; it is at a minimum clearly not the easy money that produces and pays for clientelism and institutional weakness in resource-curse accounts of political underdevelopment.

Why, then, did the Argentine state suffer such a long and traumatic labor before being born in a form that ultimately was less able to confront subsequent institutional challenges? Stronger institutions emerged only after the 1880s, and they were too ill consolidated to handle the early entry of middle-class actors into contention for national power. Argentina's comparatively weak state is interesting because it represents a partial failure in what was an essentially favorable environment: Argentina was wealthy, was not beset by racial division as a result of the destruction of most of the indigenous population, had an economy organized along effective capitalist lines from an early date, and was certainly engaged in enough military competition and conflict to give elites a powerful reason to establish a viable central administration. But for nearly 70 years, workable and durably independent central state institutions did not emerge, foundering on the inability of elites to solve the question of how the interests of Buenos Aires and the other provinces could be accommodated within a single political framework.

Unlike Chile and Peru, Argentina thus changes values on a key independent variable in the nineteenth-century state-building era. Although it was never characterized by substantial unfree labor, it was plagued by a near-complete inability of competing elites to form any sort of stable political compromise for much of the postindependence era. But the fact remains that eventually, a viable political accommodation was reached. From the perspective of the expectations of this book, the state-building process should *at that late point* begin to move in a substantially more positive direction, for after the 1880s, Argentina would

State Formation in Argentina and Uruguay

finally have the social and political foundations for political development. So in contrast to Peru, where persistent administrative failure was the expectation, in Argentina, we should see the long-delayed onset of institutional development (and the capacities, inter alia, to wage war, collect taxes, and provide infrastructure that go with these things).

In the pages that follow, three central aspects of the sociopolitical argument of this book will be examined. First, is there evidence that Argentina's agrarian capitalist political economy provided potentially auspicious terrain for the centralization of authority and the construction of viable and penetrating political institutions? Since, of course, such development did not fully manifest in the pre-1880s period, this is a potentially difficult point to establish. That said, we will see that there is strong evidence that the Argentine countryside was dominated by an upper class at once willing to contribute to collective institution building (if at the regional or provincial level) and able to tolerate military service on the part of its labor force. On both scores, the contrast with Peruvian localism (and the causal mechanisms that provoked institutional underdevelopment) is stark. And ultimately, once the interelite political barriers to national unification were removed, the expected rapid expansion of public institutions and infrastructure ensued. A further crucial contrast is with Chile, which had a similarly free but noncapitalist agrarian economy. If anything, Argentina's agrarian capitalism was even more fertile ground for the development of an effective state – a point that will be made more fully in the discussion of Uruguay.

This, then, begs the second question: *why* was Argentina's elite for so long unable to form any sort of lasting political compromise, despite the potentially enormous collective and individual gains from cooperation, and what factors ultimately made an effective end to intraelite (armed) conflict possible? Finally, in the context of both explications, I engage the ecological and bellicist alternatives to show how they cannot account for state-building outcomes we observe. The starting point, however, is with the sociopolitical dynamics that at first blocked then ultimately launched the process of political development in Argentina.

Agrarian Political Economy

It is critical to recognize from the outset that unfree labor had little role in the postindependence Argentine agrarian order. This might at first glance seem less than obvious, given the comparative lateness of the formal abolition of slavery (in 1853, only a year before Peru). But in practice, slavery was never the backbone of actual production, and the Argentine republic was on a path to emancipation literally from its founding. Indeed, the postindependence Constituent Assembly in 1813 had already decreed the "free womb" (the automatic emancipation of the children of slaves) as well as the forced sale of slaves to the state (as a form of compensated manumission). The last were to serve a term in the military, to be followed by receipt of their freedom (Hinks 2006, 417). Similarly, participation in the international slave trade was also prohibited.

The practical effect is clear, insofar as any reliance on servile labor for production was from a very early date effectively precluded as a sustainable economic form. This is particularly important when we recall that Argentina was – rather uncharacteristically for most of the Latin American region – an area of long-run labor scarcity rather than surplus. In such a context, there are really only two ways to recruit an adequate labor force, particularly for arduous agricultural labor: servile techniques that tie labor to the land coercively and wage labor relations generous enough to compete with urban alternatives and ultimately to attract international migrants. It is this latter option that was undertaken in Argentina, which came to rely on massive waves of voluntary European immigration to provide the bulk of its agrarian and urban working classes. In this, it was much like the northern and midwestern United States. Moreover, that the nascent Argentine state was willing to recruit slaves into the military – from its earliest days – suggests strongly that after service, there was no intention (either via de jure or de facto means) to return them to bonded labor but rather to provide a pathway to actual freedom. It also makes very clear that the function of armies and militias – contra Peru – was *not* to enforce coercive productive relations, for armed former slaves would be most ill suited for that task.

Indeed, what emerged in Argentina was something akin to full-scale capitalist agriculture. To be sure (at least initially outside the environs of Buenos Aires) it was a bit of an odd form of capitalism, as logistical and transportation difficulties placed immense restrictions on access to markets and thus the productive employment of land. In fact, some traditional scholarship has suggested a certain precapitalist quality to early postindependence land tenure arrangements; most notably, scholars have pointed out the enormous swathes of land concentrated in comparatively few hands. And while it is true that early *estancias* were of enormous size, more recent scholarship has shown that it does not follow from this that ownership concentration was either inimical to capitalist agriculture or even necessarily conducive to severe income inequality. To begin, it is crucial to remember that under prevailing conditions in the early independence era, much of Argentina's land – because of the inaccessibility of markets – was essentially valueless in market terms. Instead, it was the cattle that grazed on it (and ranching is *always* a land-extensive activity) that had value; cattle could transport themselves to market in a way that cereals, for example, could not. And cattle ownership was distributed in a substantially different fashion than land, as many ranchers operated illicitly on others,' typically unfenced, property. Relative labor scarcity is, of course, the second key feature as it acts as a check on income inequality even where ownership is highly concentrated.

Moreover, while the postcolonial estancia system, especially in the interior provinces, was characterized by the production of most of its own internal

State Formation in Argentina and Uruguay

consumption requirements, it was at the same time also organized around generating a market-oriented surplus and was reliant on wage labor. Nor were the socioeconomic distinctions between labor and ownership rigid. On the one hand, even from the earliest days, middle-sector producers were important contributors to the agrarian political economy. On the other hand, landownership (or, more accurately, control) was often precarious enough, owing to underexploitation, that squatters on peripheral portions of colonial-era estancias could have a reasonable probability of ultimately gaining effective title, especially if military service to provincial militias were to have been thrown into the bargain (Barsky and Djenderedjian 2003, 118). Moreover, postcolonial agrarian expansion utilizing immigrant labor in the 1860s and 1870s often began in rental or sharecropping forms of tenure, but these were remunerative enough over time that they ended with direct landownership through purchase.

Two features of this early postindependence period thus stand out. First, not only was wage labor widely employed from the outset, but it was also sufficiently well remunerated relative to the cost of land that upward mobility through the class structure (from tenant to small farmer) was a realistic and commonplace outcome, even for immigrants. Second, at different points, military service (usually in provincial militias) was a road (or part of a set of conditions) to such mobility as well. This of course draws a line under the comparative readiness of the Argentine political economy to underwrite an effort at national state building. None of the dynamics – agrarian exploitation, coerced labor, and the overwhelming importance of local (instead of national or provincial) force – that stood in the way of centralizing authority in Peru were present in Argentina. Instead, quite the opposite obtained, requiring only an end to perpetual provincial–Buenos Aires political conflict for state-building potential to be realized.

As it happened, the unrealized comparative advantages of the Argentine agrarian economy in the early postindependence era in fact provided quite strong positive incentives for elites to cooperate around the formation of a powerful central state. For only such a state could extract or borrow the resources necessary to undertake the infrastructural investments required to link the fertile Pampa region to burgeoning international markets for cattle, hides, sheep, and later grains. In fact, the degree to which Argentine economic development took place before 1880 despite the inability of the governments of the day to launch coherent and penetrating "national" institutions to supplant the intensive regionalism of the provinces is testament to the extraordinary scale of these advantages. It is also the case that once such a national state was launched in 1861, after Mitre's victory in the battle of Pavón, and consolidated by 1881, a truly remarkable period of economic and political expansion was made possible.

In many ways, the regionalism–provincialism that dominated Argentine politics until national unification (c. 1861–80) was the mirror image of the localism that dominated the Peruvian agrarian political economy. In Peru, localism was fiercely defended by elites as control over force was the sine qua non for their economic and social survival in the face of a huge and restive servile labor force. By contrast, regionalism seriously inhibited prosperity for Argentine elites – even as they were politically compelled to defend it. In essence, regionalism prevented producers from effectively utilizing the immense comparative advantages in agriculture and ranching that characterized Pampean Argentina. Until national unification, rural producers would inevitably face a patchwork of interprovincial tariffs, a massively deficient infrastructure, an underdeveloped banking sector, and what could only be described as monetary anarchy – since many provinces (and banks!) were simultaneously in the business of currency emission and debasement. At the same time, the absence of a strong national army increased the threat that the indigenous population posed to elites' property rights in frontier areas, precluded the incorporation of Indian lands into national production, and engendered the almost ceaseless center–periphery conflict that was economically destructive for all involved.

The point that the agrarian economy would benefit mightily from the initiation of national unification and state building is made all the clearer through an examination of the period after 1880, when national institutions were in fact finally consolidated. Indeed, in a comparative sense, while both Argentina's and Chile's agrarian political economies were suitable environments for the germination of a sustained state-building effort, they were not equally so. The fact that the former relied on fully capitalist land tenure and labor relations opened the further possibility of mutually reinforcing dynamics of state building and economic development, whereas in Chile, the rural sector would remain an increasingly severe drag on economic (but not political) development into the late twentieth century. One way to understand this is to look at what happened when internecine political conflicts were finally resolved, and both the agrarian political economy and interelite political dynamics finally pointed to a successful institution-building outcome. Figure 4.1 tracks the expenditures of the Argentine national state almost from its meaningful inception in the 1860s through its initial consolidation and beyond.

What is striking from this figure is the degree to which the construction of national political institutions on a firm foundation in the 1880s facilitated a massive increase in public investment (which was intimately linked to an explosion of agricultural productivity and production). Indeed, in looking at the composition of public spending, Interior Ministry spending moves from accounting for a small portion of the total (and much less than that spent on the military) to an order of magnitude greater, occupying a much larger share of (much expanded) governmental outlays. Such investments – in port, rail, and other infrastructure – would have been difficult either to amortize or justify for a noncapitalist agricultural sector and had the further benefit of stabilizing national institutions by literally tying the provinces to Buenos Aires with roads and rails. It is also striking that this massive wave of state building was *not* related to the military, in sharp contrast to bellicist expectations that war and

State Formation in Argentina and Uruguay

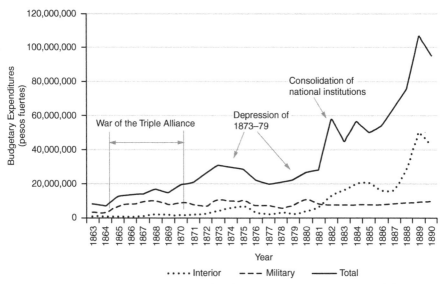

FIGURE 4.1. Argentine government spending by area, 1863–90. *Source:* Oszlak (1982b, 27).

preparation for it would drive state formation. Indeed, even the wrenching and protracted Paraguayan War[1] from 1864 to 1870 caused only minor changes in military and total expenditure. In fact, in real terms, military spending was essentially constant over the entire period – even accounting for prosecuting the war with Paraguay and the revenues required for the brutal and definitive subjugation of Argentina's indigenous population, the seizure of its lands, and the incorporation of these territories into agrarian production.

But if the rural upper classes had so much to gain – and little to lose in economic terms – from the construction of a viable national state, why was it so hard to organize? The theory presented here would suggest that the almost irremediable *political* conflicts between provincial and *porteño* elites were in fact the crucial barrier, though left thusly, it would beg the question of why such a strong common interest – in state building and the economic expansion that might result from it – was insufficient to render successful any of the myriad efforts at national consolidation attempted in the period between 1813 and 1880. The unfortunate fact was that provincial–center political conflict had, paradoxically, a strong material foundation in the very political economy that stood to gain from its superation. But as all elites had a long-run interest in some sort of solution to the problem of national unification, the potential for vigorous state building remained. But until province–center cooperation actually came about, it would remain in the arena of potential.

---

[1] This is also called the War of the Triple Alliance.

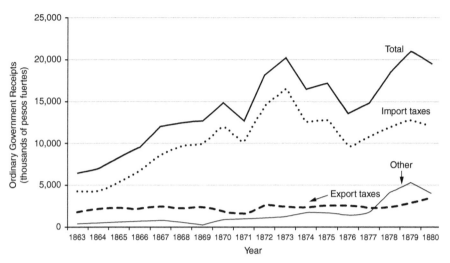

FIGURE 4.2. Argentine government taxation by source, 1863–80. *Source:* Oszlak (1982b, 27).

Unfortunately, several aspects of Argentine political and economic development firmly tied the interests of provincial elites to those of the provinces in which they resided – and therefore against those of Buenos Aires. First and foremost, almost all international trade – the very lifeblood of the Argentine economy – flowed through a single choke point: the port of Buenos Aires. This was coupled to an infrastructure of taxation that was almost entirely tied to taxes on that trade. Consider, for example, the composition of national revenues depicted in Figure 4.2. Until real national unification was actually achieved in the 1880s, virtually all the revenues accruing the Argentine state were received as a result of taxes on imports (principally) and exports (secondarily). But there was virtually no mechanism by which revenues received in the customshouse of Buenos Aires (and perforce controlled by that province or city) could reliably be shared in an equitable fashion with the remaining provinces, from whose activities much of the surplus was generated. This was as true of exports as it was of imports – all of which were likely to be taxed on arrival in the city. How could, for example, Entre Ríos or Córdoba maintain anything like coequal status in a federal system, or even minimal fiscal viability, if they were dependent on the good graces of the province of Buenos Aires for revenue transfers to fund essential activities? But any serious effort at national unification would require the abandonment of interprovincial tariffs, the emission of competing currencies, and thus virtually all of the meaningful independent revenue sources in provincial hands. By contrast, there was no possibility that the province of Buenos Aires would voluntarily cede control over the customs revenue to a national state that it did not itself dominate.

State Formation in Argentina and Uruguay 105

Landholders supported provincial governments for reasons that went beyond the political and fiscal viability of the latter, for of course, that was not their primordial concern. Perhaps more important, especially in an agrarian setting where titles to land were often legally and practically insecure, the fact that it was provincial governments that adjudicated and defended property claims was crucial. Elites were compelled to support provincial governments owing to their reliance on legal decisions as to proper title; this was particularly important as much squatting or irregular land occupation could and would regularly be converted into legally titled holdings. And of course, for those living in the vicinity of indigenous populations, provincial militias were the only reliable form of property rights protection and personal defense. And of course, to the extent to which landlords were also provincial political elites, the benefits they derived from this political role (and the largesse it produced) depended entirely on the maintenance of control over local revenue streams rather than their transfer to the very different elites of Buenos Aires or to a putative and distant "national" government.

That said, it is important to remember that regionalism in Argentina, as it was not founded on military control of restive labor forces, was far from the localism that characterized Peru. Indeed, Argentine provinces could, all too easily, cooperate with each other in opposition to Buenos Aires and raise funds to prosecute war with the indigenous population or external enemies (in Paraguay, Brazil, and Uruguay), and most commonly with Buenos Aires itself. Nothing about the agrarian political economy prevented interprovincial elite cooperation, militarization, the arming of peasants, or investments in conquest. This was not the barrier to state building. The failure was, rather, entirely political: because a cooperative outcome between the peripheral provinces and the province of Buenos Aires proved so difficult, only a definitive victory by one side or the other could create the elite cooperation that was the principal barrier both to national political development and economic progress. The achievement – through force of arms – of this elite cooperation is the story to which we next turn.

Political Conflict in Postindependence Argentina

The barrier to state building in what would eventually become Argentina was mainly a problem of almost irresolvable provincial–*porteño* elite political conflict. This exceptionally severe center–periphery struggle, however, was far from inevitable in a structural sense; to be sure, it had a material foundation, but one that was a consequence of idiosyncratic features of the postindependence political economy and geography. As the contrast with Uruguay will show, given somewhat different political conditions, a very similar economy was capable of very effective administrative development (not to mention survival as a sovereign entity surrounded by far more powerful states). Indeed, what makes the Argentine experience tragic is that the regional *and* Buenos

Aires upper classes both had long-run interests in successful state building. The problem was that the cooperation and coordination required to initiate the process could not easily be accommodated. Unlike the Chilean experience, neither the confidence-building experience of iterated cross-factional replacement of political executives nor a set of political cleavages founded on socioeconomically heterogeneous bases existed that might have undergirded the initial cooperation necessary to launch a sustained period of state building. And even the final recourse to creating elite cooperation and coordination – through the coercive establishment of the hegemony of one faction – proved impossible until the economic development of the latter part of the nineteenth century finally tipped the political and military balance in favor of the province of Buenos Aires.

The creation of the material foundation for protracted center–periphery conflict in Argentina was a product of the unintended consequences of the territorial excisions that occurred as the Spanish lost control over the former Viceroyalty of Rio de la Plata. Initially, this viceroyalty had spanned the continent and had united Andean highlands with the Atlantic territories south of Brazil, focused on the twin ports of Buenos Aires and Montevideo. Soon after independence, however, Paraguay, Alto Perú (Bolivia), and the Banda Oriental (Uruguay) declared themselves independent of the nascent Argentine territory. In particular, the secession of Alto Perú to form Bolivia was critical and an entirely reasonable consequence of the way in which its mineral wealth had been used to support faraway Buenos Aires and the costly Atlantic route for marketing its silver. Once independence came, Bolivia's exports were redirected through the far more geographically proximate Pacific ports, and the indirect drain that trade via Buenos Aires implied ceased (Klein and dos Santos 1973, 396).

Why did this territorial subdivision matter for state building *within* Argentina? Critically, it fundamentally transformed the economic structures that had grown up during the colonial era in ways that helped to create the material basis for severe center–periphery conflict. In the colonial era, the northwestern provinces of Argentina had been important conduits for the silver trade out of the Bolivian mines at Potosí. Indeed, silver was one of the few products valuable enough to be profitable despite the immense overland and riverine transport costs involved in bringing products to market down from the highlands to the Rio de la Plata River and out via the ports of Buenos Aires and Montevideo (the only Southern Atlantic ports in the Spanish colonial empire) (Alvarez 2001 [1936], 43–45).

The loss of the silver trade posed a dramatic problem for the northern provinces of Argentina, for until that time, they had largely survived on the expenditures it entailed during transshipment across their territories. First, the basic manufactures that this region produced could no longer find a home in Bolivia (which could now trade via much more accessible Pacific ports and could finally acquire cost-effective imports), and they were similarly unable to

State Formation in Argentina and Uruguay 107

compete against imported foreign goods in the expanding market in Buenos Aires itself.[2] This left interior provinces reliant on protectionism and inter-provincial internal tariffs for the survival of what little economic activity remained to them and for fiscal resources. Unfortunately, the province of Buenos Aires, having in part launched the independence struggle to break the shackles of Spanish mercantilism, stood to gain greatly from a liberal stance on international trade: its jerked meat exports found an easy market feeding the slave populations of Brazil and the Antilles (Alvarez 1938, 70). And conse-quently, duties on imports purchased out of these earnings provided a steady stream of resources to fill the Buenos Aires provincial fisc's coffers. For the inte-rior provinces, this was not simply a problem of economic viability – the very survival of their urban centers was at risk, central as they had been to the silver trade in the colonial era (Cortes-Conde 2001, 15). Not only were the interior provinces now denied the trade revenues consequent on colonial-era mercantilist regulations, but they also faced competition from foreign goods now freely imported via Buenos Aires.

The dissolution of the Viceroyalty of Rio de la Plata had one further – critical – effect hindering the prospects for postindependence elite cooperation in Argentina. It left the port of Buenos Aires as the sole remaining source of substantial tax revenue. For with the loss of revenue from the silver trade out of Bolivia, and the loss of Uruguay (and with it, the port of Montevideo), the Buenos Aires customshouse became the most valuable property in the nascent republic. This was an advantage that was a consequence of colonial policy and political accident, as the former had rendered Buenos Aires a (compulsory) mercantilist hub for colonial exports (thus impeding the development of alter-native ports), and the latter was transformed into a monopoly when Uruguay left the viceroyalty. This monopoly position – in international trade for Buenos Aires – was essentially a political construction, and it relied on politics to survive. For example, the province of Buenos Aires at various points tried to block international navigation up the Rio de la Plata River – to force provinces with connectivity to this waterway to operate indirectly through its port. For while Buenos Aires favored free trade with other countries, it behaved in a mercantilist fashion vis-à-vis potential domestic extraprovincial competitors.

Indeed, the effort to monopolize international trade – and increase costs for provincial economic actors by forcing transshipment via Buenos Aires – had no natural basis. And of course, this effort underscored the fact that the *porteño* commitment to liberal trade policies was hardly consistent or reflected anything other than self-interest. There was also no particular geographic foundation to Buenos Aires's dominance, for the port did not provide natural shelter from

---

[2] Indeed, Alvarez (2001, 46) points out that higher-quality products imported from the United Kingdom – despite ocean transport over immense distances – could still be sold at roughly half the cost of equivalents produced in the Argentine interior because of its exceedingly costly prerail land-based transportation system.

storms for ships anchored there, nor did it even provide (until the 1870s) deep-water access. The last implied that the costs of its use were high, as international freight would have to be off-loaded onto smaller ships for it to be transferred to the city's docks. But there was also a paradox here: to open an alternative port would be very costly, and the only source of funds sufficient to do so were to be found in the Buenos Aires customshouse itself![3] And of course, doing so would undermine the economic viability of the province of Buenos Aires were competition for control over international trade to take place. Instead, the status quo was very desirable for it, as imports to all of Argentina tended to enter via Buenos Aires, so its provincial tariffs acted as an indirect tax on the entire country, but its revenues were distributed only to the province of Buenos Aires's fisc.

Peripheral provincial governments responded to the political and fiscal chaos of the postindependence reorganization of economic activity by endeavoring to generate viable sources of government revenues and set up independent, less vulnerable regional economies. They thus quickly implemented provincial-level tariffs that served both to provide revenue and afford protection to local pro-ducers (Oszlak 2004, 205). Provincial banks were also established to undergird economic activity, and provincial-level currencies were created to give gover-nors greater measures of economic control. The latter was, unfortunately, also a revenue source of sorts, as resort to currency emission and consequent debase-ment of monetary values was a common occurrence, given the chronically inadequate fiscal resources available and the high costs of persistent conflict.

It is easy to see why provincial governments would have strong political con-flicts with the province of Buenos Aires, especially given its quest for unilateral political hegemony. It takes more explication to understand why peripheral landholders, ranchers, and producers were supportive of the provinces in their struggles with the center. After all, they stood to gain in the long run from territorial unification and the improvement of infrastructure. But in the nearer term, there was a series of tools – inter alia, violence and fiscal coercion – that would make opposition to provincial governors potentially exceedingly costly for landlords (Oszlak 2004, 47–49). Before at least 1850, there were further critical reasons for landlords to back provincial political elites. First, the local caudillo had substantial control over access to labor (which remained very scarce until the late-nineteenth-century wave of immigration) and other resources. Second, postcolonial property rights were often very poorly speci-fied (Alvarez 1938, 66). They required ongoing defense and public action either to be defined in the first place or to avoid post facto usurpation. And given the precarious stability of judicial institutions and the adjudication of land claims at the provincial level, even the direct control over physical property was reliant on the consent of the provincial government and the support of

---

[3] Equivalently, the Buenos Aires customs revenue was also the only tax source big enough to serve as surety for international loans on a scale necessary to build an alternative deepwater port.

State Formation in Argentina and Uruguay

its coercive capacity (Barsky and Djenderedjian 2003, 194, 205). This threat to landlord physical security was all the more important in regions where the indigenous presence – and thus constant conflict over land – implied reliance on provincial militias for physical and economic security. Indeed, indigenous tribes had quite successfully seized on the immediate postindependence period of chaos to reclaim lands that had been expropriated from them. And it was not until the 1880s that the conflict with indigenous Argentines was brought to a bloody close.

The next task is to understand what ultimately made possible the construction of viable national political institutions. Empirically, the strategy here is to explore three episodes of potential state building in the postindependence era – two of them unsuccessful and one ultimately viable – to demonstrate the centrality of elite political compromise and cooperation in the construction of viable national political institutions. The first of these, based on the power of Buenos Aires province under Juan Manuel de Rosas (governor from 1829 to 1852), was effective in building stronger *provincial* institutions but was unable to forge a viable set of national institutions that incorporated the other provincial power centers. The second effort, under General Urquiza, was based on the military might of the allied peripheral provinces after they scored a military victory over the forces of Buenos Aires. This produced the Confederación Argentina as a loosely knit effort to unite the national territory on what proved to be a weak institutional foundation, and that for most of its existence did not even include Buenos Aires. Finally, after the victory of Mitre and the forces of Buenos Aires at the battle of Pavón in 1861, the foundations were finally beginning to be laid for national institutions that could solve the problem of interelite compromise, and as a consequence, this opened up an unprecedented period of both state building and economic growth.

As was briefly mentioned earlier, the independence struggle in the former Viceroyalty of Rio de la Plata was a cause of political fragmentation, not the spur toward Creole political unification (in opposition to Spanish dominance) that it had been elsewhere. Indeed, this fact alone begins to cast doubt on conventional bellicist accounts of state building, as it has implications for the principal causal mechanism in this literature: is a life-or-death struggle with an external power likely to spur elite cooperation around the defense (or, in this case, creation) of national sovereignty? It did not, at least in this instance. Instead, out of the postindependence political chaos, what emerged was a strong sense of *provincial* sovereignty, leading first to de facto autonomy and then to further trappings of statehood. By the 1820s, the provinces were signing interprovincial treaties, setting up customshouses, and engaging in other similar national-state political activities (Criscenti 1961, 380, 389).

The first potential break in the postindependence wave of political fragmentation came upon the heels of the rise of a power-centralizing caudillo, Juan Manuel de Rosas, in the province of Buenos Aires. While Rosas, in part by dint of severe repression, did establish strong control over the province of Buenos

Aires – indeed, even a measure of institutional development and control over the hinterland in that province – this was *not* extended to the other provinces that would later compose the Argentine Republic. Indeed, according to Rock (2000, 183), Rosas "continually resisted convening a national congress, writing a national constitution and establishing a national government." Instead, inter-provincial relations were governed by the 1831 "Federal Pact," which gave the province of Buenos Aires authority over foreign relations (eminently sensible given the location of foreign delegations in that city) but otherwise involved a relationship among provinces more akin to independent nations than federal subunits (Criscenti 1961, 401–2). This only heightened provincial-level identification, and by the 1830s, according to Crescenti (1961, 407), "the province was now undeniably the *patria* [fatherland]" to its residents. This was, of course, reinforced by the efforts of Buenos Aires to effectively impose itself or its interests on the rest of the potential national territory, in essence provoking the active resistance and cooperation of provincial caudillos in opposition to its goals and, as a consequence, creating durable barriers to the creation of national institutions and identities (Trinidade 1985, 145).

Even within the province of Buenos Aires, however, Rosas's rule was not terribly institutionalizing. Instead, he governed more as a caudillo than as a president. Indeed, a careful examination of the institutional development of the province during his rule shows the problem. First and foremost, the organs of government were almost completely dominated by the coercive apparatus. For example, an analysis of Rosas's 1841 budget demonstrates that – net of interest payments on the existing stock of debt – some 81 percent of public expenditure was accounted for by the Department of War (Garavaglia 2003, 148). To clarify the stunning implications of this emphasis on coercion, even 86 percent of the staff of the Department of Government – which included, inter alia, provincial governance, schools, libraries, the judiciary, archives, public works, tribunals of commerce and medicine, university, and the police and guards – were accounted for by the last two categories (the repressive face of the state). A further 7 percent were members of the clergy paid for out of public funds, while a mere 55 employees, in total, staffed all the remaining functions (Garavaglia 2003, 151). If any serious effort to build institutions were to have been made, it would have been in this department, which was itself scarcely funded in comparison to the military. Rosas was indeed a caudillo par excellence – he made virtually no investments in institutions outside of the coercive apparatus of the state.

The second effort to overcome interelite, center–periphery differences took place after the defeat of Rosas at the battle of Caseros in 1852. In this case, a coalition of provincial forces led by General Justo José de Urquiza from Entre Ríos, with some Brazilian and Uruguayan participation, defeated the caudillo of Buenos Aires. And indeed, shortly thereafter, provincial elites gained their opportunity to construct national institutions of their own (naturally quite decentralized) design. This was embodied in the Constitution of 1853, which

State Formation in Argentina and Uruguay 111

gave birth to the Confederación Argentina (Argentine Confederation). While this marked an institutional improvement over the efforts of Rosas, it fell far short of either building a meaningful state or overcoming entrenched conflicts between center and periphery, and those among provincial governors. Indeed, while Urquiza certainly sought to create comparatively powerful institutions, "the provincial governors and the surviving [provincial] *caudillos* ... who were unwilling to sacrifice the autonomies of their provinces, blunted these ambitions" (Rock 2000, 185). So instead, only a loose confederation that delegated few powers (and even fewer resources) to the center was created.

Indeed, a notable feature of the Confederación Argentina was that despite its defeat at Caseros, the province of Buenos Aires was still able to resist formal incorporation. Indeed, Buenos Aires declared its independence and, for some years, functioned as a separate national state, largely out of fear that the Confederación would make an effort to take control of – or demand a large subsidy from – its customs revenues. Ultimately, Urquiza was able to force Buenos Aires into the Confederación, in 1859, but only on condition that its elites be able to continue their dominance of the provincial government, that a reduced authority of the national state over the provinces be embedded in the constitution, and that there be only a gradual financial integration of Buenos Aires into the national state (Halperín 1995, 54).

In the end, Urquiza was unable to establish the political cooperation (by force or negotiation) that would have made possible the establishment of strong, national-level political institutions. On the one hand, he sought to create a national state without disrupting incumbent provincial authorities or imposing political hegemony of a single province. And with Buenos Aires outside the Confederación for most of its existence, the fiscal resources that might have made possible an incentive-based integration of provincial elites simply did not exist. Indeed, most provinces were scarcely making the minimal required contributions to the national institutions they ostensibly supported.[4] And militarily, Urquiza could only reliably command the forces of his home province of Entre Ríos; the Confederación itself had not built an effective and independent "national" army, despite sustained efforts in this direction (Buchbinder 2002, 645–46; Rock 2000, 167). And in the end, this was not enough. When, in 1861, Bartolomé Mitre launched a rebellion backed by the forces of the province of Buenos Aires, Urquiza, "despairing of the future of the bankrupt, divided and therefore non-viable confederation," was defeated, leaving Mitre in effective control of the national territory.

It was soon thereafter that the Republic of Argentina was created, based on the resources and institutions of the province of Buenos Aires, and it would,

---

[4] See Oszlak (2004, 61–62). Indeed, the deck was decidedly stacked against a province-led effort at national unity, for as Oszlak (2004, 58) points out, their articulation was blocked by dispersion and isolation and limited population, limited communication and transportation infrastructure, monetary and fiscal anarchy, and persistent problems of security.

over the succeeding 20 years, finally put an end to the internecine center–periphery struggles that had impeded the construction of a national state from the dawn of independence. But for real cross-factional elite cooperation to occur, several things had to happen. First, the peripheral side of the conflict had to be weakened, at least enough so that it would no longer be able to viably challenge Buenos Aires in military terms. Second, peripheral elites would have to begin to develop interests in common – or at least compatible – with those of their *porteño* counterparts. Third, political institutions would have to be constructed that could plausibly intermediate future conflicts. And finally, coercive forces – a real national army – sufficient to back up national institutions and dominate or deter potential insurrections would finally have to be organized and be outside of provincial (including Buenos Aires's) control. Remarkably, all four of these conditions were achieved in the 1861–81 period, by the end cementing the long-elusive elite unity that had impeded extensive state building. What ensued was a belated but unprecedented period of both institutional development and economic growth that would not founder until the second critical juncture – the emergence of the social question of middle- and working-class political participation – bent the Argentine institutional trajectory in a populist rather than institutionalizing direction. But that is the topic of Chapter 6.

It was not just military victory or clever politics that made possible the substantial consolidation of the Argentine political elite across the center periphery divide. Indeed, were force alone enough, it might well have been accomplished far earlier. What made the 1861–81 period different, however, begins with a transformation of the political economy that brought with it a reorientation of provincial elites' material interests. While earlier, the peripheral economy was heavily invested in protectionism, and fought mightily against the free trade orientation of Buenos Aires, after mid-century, this began to change, and it did so with accelerating scale as the century ended. As the mechanization of textile and other production brought a massive surge in international demand for Argentine wool and hide exports, the littoral provinces that were major producers of these products experienced surging economic output and development (Barsky 2003, 247). This began to align their economic interests more in the direction of those of Buenos Aires, and they became less consonant with those of other peripheral areas in the west and south. This economic linkage, however, could not have occurred earlier as it relied on the expansion of the rail network. This linkage of littoral elites to the new regime was reinforced during the Paraguayan War, a consequence of which involved a large influx of Brazilian funds to support the Argentine war effort, in turn producing an enlarged market for food and ranching producers in the littoral provinces (Rock 2000, 188).

What this change in the underlying political economy did was open up divisions among the peripheral provinces. This by itself was not enough to impel a durable political compromise capable of supporting the development of strong political institutions. But at the same time, nascent national political

State Formation in Argentina and Uruguay 113

institutions were implementing policies that at once served to deepen the political–economic foundations of interelite compromise and to more tightly knit the country together. Most important in this regard was a massive expansion of the rail network. This expansion was debt financed through the national government and backed by the only source of revenue substantial enough to attract the massive foreign loans required: Buenos Aires's customs revenues. But by expanding the rail network – and thus massively reducing overland transportation costs – provincial agricultural and ranching producers were for the first time able to bring their goods to the international market at a cost-effective price.

This had four critical state-building effects. First, it immediately raised the incomes of rural landholding elites by providing them with a highly profitable outlet for their production – and the massive expansion of trade that this engendered can be seen in the national accounts. At the same time, it amounted to an enormous increase in landowner *wealth* by fundamentally revaluing agrarian property. Notably, such land was of nearly zero value in the immediate postindependence era, and in the wake of infrastructural development, it suddenly became exceedingly valuable, providing a massive windfall to provincial elites, one that was a by-product of national unity, even one created under the auspices of the province of Buenos Aires. Third, of course, trains move in both directions, and the creation of a transportation grid not only linked the vast territories of the Argentine Republic in a more socially and culturally coherent way but also facilitated the transport of federal troops in the event that the political compromise failed to hold sway in a particular locality. And finally, just as it had in Chile, the expansion of public infrastructure itself was a mechanism of resource transfer – in this case, from center to periphery – that served to link elite interests across this divide. This has been described as a system of elite compromise based on redistribution to provincial elites that helped purchase their cooperation. It functioned through mechanisms like lending, patronage employment, the profits from the assignment of public contracts distributed by provincial elites, and perhaps most important, the huge expansion of the educational system – as a subsidy to human capital formation and as a source of patronage and rents (Rock 2000, 22, 29, 192).

These moves created a situation in which elite interests from center and periphery could quite plausibly be harmonized, but this itself still is insufficient to produce a commitment to state-building investments on the part of these elites. Before this would be possible, viable political institutions that would guarantee the *long-term* interests of all important political actors would have to be developed; that is, a system to prevent the permanent hegemony of any particular faction, or the entry of nonelite actors into politics, would have to develop. Central to creating this was the utilization of an electoral system that had two critical features. First, it selected a (single-consecutive-term) president through an electoral college that gave very substantial (and disproportionate) weight to provincial interests. Second, it determined electoral outcomes in a highly elite dominant fashion by mandating public voting "under the [watchful] eyes of magistrates and military commanders," thus ensuring that outcomes favoring working-class or nonelite politicians would not transpire (McLynn 1979, 304).

The credibility of this system was demonstrated in its second application, when the anointed successor of Mitre, the effective founder of the Argentine Republic, was defeated in the election by Sarmiento, the candidate of a different faction. This demonstrated that the one-term rule was meaningful and that losses in one period for a faction did not imply permanent political exclusion. And perhaps most critically, as Rock has pointed out, it (and the subsequent 1874 election) demonstrated that the key to electoral victory "now lay in the ability of the candidate for president to forge a coalition in the provinces" that could be linked to a Buenos Aires base (Rock 2000, 191). Finally a political and institutional compromise among elites had arrived.

But institutions and institutional equilibria can be disrupted. Here is where coercion matters. Early on in the formation of the Argentine Republic, the prosecution of the Paraguayan War led to the creation of an increasingly professionalized national army (especially after 1876) (Oszlak 1982a, 1982b, 11, 23). This provided a tool through which local rebellions could be quickly quashed before gaining serious traction (Halperín 1995, 57). And soon thereafter, there was an enormous influx of new territory acquired via the near-extermination of the indigenous population, which provided the economic resources – access to land – that cemented provincial elites' loyalties to the nation. For newly acquired Indian territories were not distributed in small plots as homesteads for family farmers (as in the United States) but rather as large estancias to politically connected interests.

URUGUAY: CIVIL CHAOS, ELITE COMPROMISE, AND EXPLOSIVE INSTITUTION BUILDING

In many ways, Uruguay should never have existed. The late-colonial-era Banda Oriental (Eastern Strip) was originally conceived of as a buffer region between the Spanish Viceroyalty of Rio de la Plata and the Portuguese colony of Brazil. After independence, Uruguayan internal politics continued to be heavily affected by the political and military interventions of its new Argentine and Brazilian neighbors. But miraculously enough, this tiny republic not only ultimately managed to retain its independence perched precariously between these regional behemoths, but as López Alves (1996, 130) has noted, "in terms of governability... [it] became a model for the rest of the region."

This transformation from improbable republic to continental leader in institutional development is all the more perplexing when one considers its isolation, poverty, and institutionally deficient starting point. Certainly relative to neighboring Argentina (or Peru, for that matter), very little administrative infrastructure had been created in the colonial Banda Oriental. Indeed, outside

State Formation in Argentina and Uruguay 115

the capital of Montevideo, national political institutions had decidedly little sway. And of course, this characteristic became even more severe during the first 60 years of political independence, as protracted and recurrent civil and international conflict devastated the ability of Montevideo to govern the hinterland, reducing the provincial departments to a caudillo-dominated, semianarchic state. Nor, in contrast to Argentina, were comparatively plentiful external resources available for state building, for even when, late in the state-building era, the wool and refrigerated beef trades became viable, they brought to Uruguay nowhere near the sorts of economic returns that they did to Argentina.

Yet it was Uruguay, rather than Argentina, that would ultimately develop the stronger institutions. These differences were, however, only nascent in the state formation era after independence, for on many dimensions relative to political development, the two states were quite similar. Both countries developed export-oriented forms of extensive agrarian capitalism (in ranching, wool, hides, and jerked and frozen beef). Indeed, in some ways, the Uruguayan agrarian political economy was less favorable than the Argentine – it had less of an immigrant, small–medium farming and ranching sector, and what existed of the last was devastated by the form that land enclosure took in the 1870s, leaving behind a juridically free but economically very inegalitarian rural sector. The emergent rural oligarchs then became the backbone for the caudillo politics and persistent internecine conflict that characterized the Republic for the first two-thirds of the century after independence.

Yet at the critical time – and at roughly the same time as in Argentina – contending Uruguayan elites managed to come to a political settlement. It would turn out over the long haul that this belated settlement would prove more comprehensive and durable than that of Argentina and would ultimately serve as the foundation of a political compromise that would last in one form or another for over a century. Two critical factors gave Uruguay an edge on the political side of the initial state-building process. First, interelite conflict was organized around two very heterogeneous political parties: the Blancos (National Party) and the Colorados. Like the parties in Chile, they were regionally and socially heterogeneous, both having import components in Montevideo and the countryside.[5] There was thus no persistent regional dispute that turned politics into a clear zero-sum distributional game between them. And like the Chilean upper classes, Uruguayan elites shared similar foundations to their wealth – typically some aspect of export-oriented ranching. Thus neither a regional nor a sectoral division characterized the parties. The second major difference is that elite coordination was not (despite persistent violent conflict) achieved through force of arms but rather through negotiations that implemented political

---

[5] While the Colorados had somewhat more weight in Montevideo, and the reverse was true with respect to the Blancos in the countryside, both had politically important support in both the center and periphery of the country.

Latin American State Building in Comparative Perspective

compromises that would later come to be called *coparticipation* – the principle that the losing faction in electoral politics would nevertheless be granted access to meaningful executive political power and to public resources. While it certainly took Uruguayan elites a very long time to build up cross-party trust in this system, in iterated practice – most clearly undertaken during the Batlle presidencies of the late nineteenth and early twentieth centuries – the foundation was laid for long-run elite cooperation, the massive expansion of public institutions, and collective dominance of the two traditional parties that lasted throughout Uruguay's democratic history, until the election of a leftist candidate, Tabaré Vázquez, in 2004.

The Uruguayan State

The increasingly institutionally sound and society-penetrating Uruguayan state that emerged in the last quarter of the nineteenth century and the first quarter of the twentieth century could scarcely have been expected given the realities of the postindependence era. At independence, Montevideo was a secondary port city, it lacked a well-established colonial-era administrative infrastructure, and it was poorly connected in infrastructural, governance, or communication terms with the interior of the then Banda Oriental. Not only was the proto-state financially debilitated, controlling effectively only the customs revenue in Montevideo, but also the national territory was both ill-defined and underpopulated, leaving Uruguay "lacking all the attributes and a good portion of the resources of a modern state" (Yaffé 2000, 2; translation by the author).

From this inauspicious starting point, things grew rapidly worse. The postindependence era quickly came to be dominated by internecine war, often partly an extension of the political conflicts in neighboring Argentina. By the time of the 1851–52 Guerra Grande (Great War), the Uruguayan republic was in an economically and politically prostrate state. The economy was devastated, with the civil war reducing the stock of cattle – the principal form of wealth – from 7 million head in 1842 to as little as 1.8–2.5 million in 1852 (Nahum and Barrán 1972, 14). Exports collapsed from over 8 million gold pesos in 1847 to 937,00 in 1852 (Olivera 2002, 26), and as much as 34 percent of the population of the country had fled, while others moved to remote interior areas to avoid being pressed into military service (Olivera 2002, 15, 18). Conflict left the government with virtually no reach beyond urban Montevideo, private property rights were defined as little more than what various rural caudillos could defend with private forces, and the system of economic production had reverted to its most primitive form.

The conflict, however, had several unusual features that would ultimately lay the foundation for a much more stable political future. First, it was fought between two political parties – the Blancos and the Colorados – which, while frequently at odds, were not founded on social, regional, or class cleavages. During the Guerra Grande, they functioned in part as extensions of Argentine

State Formation in Argentina and Uruguay   117

political conflicts, with the Blancos lining up alongside the Argentine caudillo
Rosas and the Colorados aligned with the Argentine *unitarios* and the French
(López Alves 1996, 121). The war ended with a power-sharing agreement
(under the slogan "neither victors, nor vanquished") that, after a brief inter-
ruption in 1870–72, led to a more formalized power-sharing agreement that
guaranteed the minority Blancos control of 4 of 12 departments (provinces). It
was a foundation of interparty cooperation that would later become absolutely
essential.

The actual construction of strong state institutions proceeded in two critical
stages. The first occurred during the military government of Latorre, 1876–80,
and under subsequent presidents (called the *militarismo* period in Uruguay).
What the nonpartisan Latorre dictatorship was able to do was lay the foundation for a modern state, including the creation of a national-level judicial system
and civil registry, the establishment of a property rights regime and the means
to enforce it, a unified criminal code, a rural code, and a functioning system of
law and order (via the *jueces letrados de departamentos*) (Pivel Devoto 1942,
197). He also established a functioning system of public education, inducing a
sharp drop in illiteracy (López Alves 1996, 129).

The evidence that a national system of property rights was created and
effective juridical enforcement of them had become possible can be seen in the
evolution of the price of the land – for insecure property is of necessity far less
valuable than that which can reliably be held in fee simple. Figure 4.3 shows
the evolution of land prices in Uruguay (disaggregated by region). One can see
clearly that soon after Latorre's reforms were implemented, the value of land
surged as much as 20-fold. It is also notable that in the far north, the least
developed and most remote region, the penetration of the institutions of stable
property rights was most delayed, and the price gains were, commensurately,
smaller.

Of course, more than stable property rights affect the value of land. The
first substantial increase in land prices – roughly a sixfold increase from the
time of the end of the Guerra Grande to the emergence of basic property security – was due principally to this establishment of basic law and order. The
second phase of land-price increase was a product of the increasing accessibil-
ity of international markets, which in the nineteenth century was a question
of railway development. This rail expansion, however, is also an indicator of
the strengthening of public institutions, for railway development required not
only political stability, strong property rights, and the rule of law but also a
state capable of acquiring large sums of foreign investment. Such investment,
of course, would hinge critically on the credibility of public institutions – either
with regard to the ability and willingness to repay debt or to make good on
the terms of long-term concessions for the operation of rail lines. Reliance on
domestic resources as an alternative would be inadequate to the task. Uruguay
also plainly had no capacity to manufacture the inputs to railway infrastructure domestically, did not generate sufficient foreign exchange surpluses to

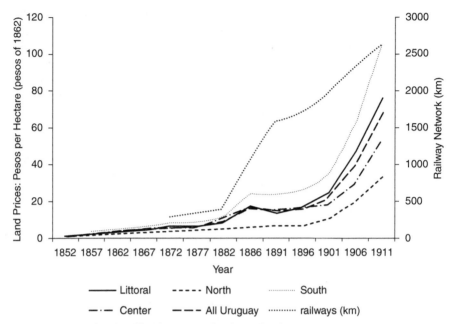

FIGURE 4.3. Evolution of land prices and railway development in Uruguay, 1852–1911. *Source:* Historia Rural del Uruguay Moderno, 1851–1885, Volume I, Part 2, apendice documental. Montevideo, Uruguay: Ediciones de la Banda Oriental, 1967, p. 318. For 1852–82, ibid., Volume II, 1886–94. For 1886–91, Juan Rial, *Estadisticas historicas de uruguay 1850–1930*, Cuaderno 40, Montevideo, Uruguay: Centro de Informaciones y Estudios del Uruguay, 1980. Data are adjusted for tabular misalignment.

directly purchase it, and lacked the domestic technical capacity to successfully construct a rail network. But foreign investment did in fact increase sharply as the *militarista*-era reforms took hold. In 1865, Uruguay had received British investment amounting to £1.1 million. By 1875, this had risen to £6.2 million, and by 1885, to £16.0 million (Olivera 2002, 60). These ongoing and large volumes (for Uruguay) of international borrowing imply a state that has managed to a substantial degree to tax its own citizenry. Naturally, were Uruguayan loans regularly in arrears, one would not see new lending on an increasing scale. And of course, the fact that Uruguay was able to maintain a gold (or bimetallic gold-silver) standard over most of a half-century, and to quickly reestablish convertibility after crisis-induced deviations (Olivera 2002, 29), is an indicator of a comparatively high level of state capacity in itself – fiscal discipline and prudent budgeting were possible there, in sharp contrast to Peru.

The two broad periods of state building can be seen in data on public revenues as well. In Figure 4.4, we see the progression of tax receipts in Uruguay. The first major increase in taxation occurs after the reforms of Latorre, with public revenues rising from about $U 7 million in 1875 to $U 17 million

State Formation in Argentina and Uruguay 119

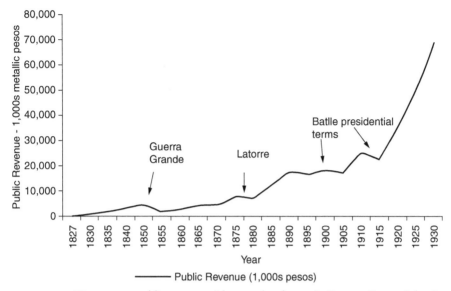

FIGURE 4.4. Uruguayan public revenue (thousands of pesos). *Source:* Buzzetti (1969, 233).

by 1890.[6] The second period of major state building corresponds to the two Batlle administrations (1903–7; 1911–15) – well known for the massive surge in institution building and nationalization they produced. Indeed, by the end of Batlle's second term, when further movement to increase the scope of the Uruguayan state stopped, a period of rapid and sustained increases in the ability of the government to extract revenue ensued. That is, the institutions of the state became ever more effective and penetrating.

How and why Uruguay managed such a decisive break from the chaos of the postindependence era is the focus of the remainder of this chapter. The explanation not only involves the *creation* – rather than the mere inheritance – of a nonlabor repressive agrarian capitalist economy out of the ill-defined and economically contradictory "property is what you can defend" environment of the postindependence era, riven as it was by civil conflict. In this, Uruguayan

---

[6] While these data are not adjusted for inflation, it is important to note that Uruguay, unlike most Latin American countries of the era, was consistently on a metallic standard for its currency. In the period from 1877, the currency was either silver coin or paper convertible at a fixed rate to silver. This was later converted to a bimetallic standard, followed by the adoption of the gold standard in 1896. The gold standard was briefly suspended as a consequence of the First World War, but even during this brief period of inconvertibility, the Uruguayan peso was frequently appreciated as depreciated against the US dollar. As a consequence, the data presented here are a rough estimate of the progression of real public tax revenues, not the results of the currency debasement so common elsewhere on the continent.

120 *Latin American State Building in Comparative Perspective*

rural social structure came to resemble that of Argentina, albeit with a substantially more inegalitarian distribution of landownership owing to the way in which property rights were initially defined under Latorre. But the explanation also acknowledges the central role of political compromise, especially iterated political compromise, among elites unencumbered by clear democratic links to popular pressures. While the institutions of Uruguayan political coparticipation were first introduced at the end of the Guerra Grande in 1852, it was not until the Batlle presidencies that they were sufficiently robust in practice to support a massive expansion in public power. But the precedent of power sharing despite the numerical superiority of one side or another was established. Ultimately, it helped produce an expansion of the state that would work to the benefit of both principal political factions – Blancos and Colorados – throughout most of the twentieth century.

Importantly, it was neither the pressures of strategic conflict nor the absence of natural resource wealth that was crucial to Uruguayan state building. With respect to the former, serious investments in the institutions of government principally occurred well after the major threats to the sovereignty of the Uruguayan republic had receded. Indeed, early on in its history, there were multiple – and extremely menacing – threats to the survival of the state, at one point leaving "independent" Uruguay reduced to control of little more than the core of Montevideo's old city. But these threats occurred in a period of persistent institutional failure, and it was only well after they receded, and territorial consolidation of the boundaries with Brazil and Argentina became institutionalized, that administrative and political development began in earnest. By contrast, the fact that Uruguay has virtually none of the mineral wealth that many contend impedes state building might at first seem to lend credence to ecological explanations. But the causal status of resource wealth is at best here uncertain. The absence of such wealth characterized the political economy both during periods of administrative catastrophe and periods of remarkable administrative development; this suggests that ecological forces are orthogonal to, rather than determinative of, political modernization. What is the real causal story? It is to this I next turn, considering first the transformations of agrarian social structure in the late nineteenth century that launched a trajectory of state-building reforms and then the political compromises that expanded it into the following century.

Agrarian Political Economy

For all their ultimate similarities, the postindependence agrarian political economies of Argentina and Uruguay had quite important differences. Indeed, of the two, the Uruguayan countryside provided a less auspicious setting for the establishment of rural social relations capable of underwriting an extended period of state building. Argentina, as we saw earlier, was virtually born a capitalist nation. For all its political woes, basic private property rights and wage

State Formation in Argentina and Uruguay 121

labor relations prevailed throughout most of the economy from the time of independence. While it is true that production in early Uruguay was also often characterized by free labor relations, they were not universal,[7] and it was *not yet* characterized by agrarian capitalism, at least in the normal sense of the term. The economic problem in Uruguay was property rights, not principally labor. For on independence, and worsening as a consequence of the ensuing endemic civil conflict, there was little public means to accurately identify ownership of, or defend individuals' control over, the two most critical forms of property for production: land and cattle. As a consequence, de facto possession (coupled with the ability to defend one's possession) became the most meaningful form of ownership, and it was a precarious form at best. This property-rights instability itself exacerbated economic problems as it made cattle rustling a viable way of life, both in terms of access to cattle through theft and grazing them through surreptitious encroachment.[8]

This is an admittedly unusual form of economic production without clear property rights, and it was probably at its most chaotic at the end of the Guerra Grande in 1852. By this point in time, the countryside – always short of labor – had become seriously depopulated, losing by one estimate 34 percent of its occupants between 1840 and 1852, as residents fled to avoid being press-ganged into military service (Nahum and Barrán 1972, 15). This intense labor scarcity was coupled with a countryside that was effectively unenclosed, having few if any man-made demarcations that would indicate actual ownership of land, nor having a geography that could prevent easy encroachment of outsiders' cattle herds on one's fields. The consequence (partly visible in Figure 4.3) is that land was exceedingly inexpensive, a consequence both of the insecurity of exclusive use and the difficulties in bringing agricultural products to international markets. By contrast, the principal form of wealth was embodied by cattle, as they could more readily be policed than land, were identifiable by brands, and were at least capable of transporting themselves to market. Agricultural products like wheat or other grains had none of these virtues.

In social-structural terms, this produced a variety of unusual features. On the one hand, there was a substantial middle sector of ranchers, many of whom earned their living by grazing their herds partially, or completely, on the properties of others without payment of rent or seeking consent. There were also very large-scale, landholding ranchers who were hard put to police the borders of their territories or protect their herds from rustling. In many ways, it approximated what Stinchcombe (1961, 175) defined as a ranching enterprise

---

[7] This is largely but not completely the case, as in the north (near the Brazilian border), servile and semiservile labor regimes persisted until the reforms of President Berro in the 1860s.

[8] Cattle raiding was by no means limited to Uruguay. But by contrast, cattle rustling in Argentina was most commonly a consequence of Indian raids on settler territories. This, however, marks a very distinct challenge that, instead of turning Argentines against each other, as in Uruguay, where theft and encroachment became a means to social mobility or subsistence, it united the Creole elites and masses against an external Indian "threat."

122   *Latin American State Building in Comparative Perspective*

economy, with its characteristic "free floating, mobile labor force . . . [that made up a] socially undisciplined element." Indeed, Uruguayan accounts have highlighted the massively insecure character of property rights, a product of "the superimposition of titles of distinct origin, and the generalized illegal appropriation of public lands" (Yaffé 2000, 2). Reinforcing this, local caudillo dominance and disorderly and violence-prone social conditions reigned supreme.

This agrarian order was not a foundation on which to build a state. For insecure property rights could never induce the necessary investment to promote the sustained expansion of the economy needed to pay for more effective institutions, and multitudinous, fragmented, and violence-prone caudillos would scarcely opt to cooperate in the centralization of what little authority they had – since regional control over coercion was essential to the "ownership" of land and livestock. State building could happen, but only after some form of reliable property-rights regime was firmly implanted.

There is something of a paradox here, of course. To effectively demarcate (and thus in practice redistribute) property rights and reliably enforce them is in itself an aspect of the state-building process. But of course, insecure property rights, and the consequent reliance of elites on regional power to defend their ownership, indirectly militate against substantial national state building. But this was not an insuperable barrier – as a reliance on servile labor, by contrast, would be – for were the state able to define and defend property rights, this would redound to the benefit of these same elites. The difficulty is analogous to a transaction cost and collective action problem rather than a conflict of material interest: if political forces could induce a shift to a new equilibrium of enforceable, nationally defined property rights, it would quickly become self-reinforcing. And it was the military government of Latorre – coupled with a crucial technological innovation – that finally enabled the creation of a basic national property system in Uruguay.

Why could Latorre manage what had eluded Uruguay for so long? After all, he was not the first to make the effort – President Berro made precisely such a push to clearly define ownership in 1860–63. But Latorre had several advantages. First, he came as the head of a military government that, at least in the short term, was able to impose outcomes on the country – or at least substantial portions of it – and had some credibility.[9] The creation of secure property rights would also be directly economically beneficial to current de facto large landholders: among other things, it would reduce the costs of maintaining

---

[9] This is, of course, crucial. For the effort is effectively to move from one equilibrium (the costly self-enforcement of property rights) to another (centrally enforced and defined property rights, with all the efficiencies that this entails). As the outcome state is collectively, and generally individually, beneficial for landholding elites, the principal question is demonstrating the credibility of the transition – and the participation of competing elites in it – which would render the maintenance of powerful independent local coercive force less important. And of course, this is precisely what a military government is capable of doing: signaling the ability to use force to enforce its key policies.

State Formation in Argentina and Uruguay 123

control over land and cattle, make possible profit-increasing investments like cross-breeding with imported specialty stock, and make viable investments in transportation infrastructure that would subsequently vastly increase the value of holdings. For these reasons, the creation of a secure, nationally defined property rights system was collectively extremely beneficial to agrarian elites. But the incentives embodied in the specific property regime proposed by Latorre were also immediately and individually beneficial to most large-scale agrarian landholders.

While establishing property rights was clearly a desirable goal, the mechanism by which to undertake it could produce a wide range of distributional outcomes – particularly since ex ante legitimate "ownership" was anything but clear. The key issue of the day was that of physical enclosure (in Uruguayan parlance, *el alambramiento del campo*). To the time of Latorre's reforms, rural land in Uruguay was largely valueless because it was mostly unfenced, and this made it virtually impossible to defend its borders from encroaching herds (or to prevent one's own herds from engaging in indiscriminate cross-breeding with inferior stock). But with the invention and large-scale importation of cost-effective barbed wire fencing (first patented in 1867 and then improved in 1874),[10] the enclosure of the Uruguayan countryside became a realistic possibility (prewire technologies would have been far too costly given the massive ranch sizes involved). The question then became, how should one impose property demarcation? Latorre's Codigo Rural, enforced as of January 18, 1876, was the state's answer to this question. The approach embodied in the Codigo Rural not only facilitated the enclosure of the countryside but simultaneously engendered a massive transfer of property in land to the largest and wealthiest of potential landholders – helping to ensure that they were among the state's most ardent supporters with regard to this policy.

How was this asset transfer accomplished? First, it is a geometric fact that the enclosure of a single large property (on a per hectare basis) is less costly than enclosing an equivalent area composed of smaller farms. And of course, although barbed wire was far cheaper than alternative means of fencing property, it was far from inexpensive given the resources available to Uruguayan ranchers and their limited access to (only high-cost) credit. Indeed, smaller property owners were very hard put to afford the up-front costs of enclosure, and it was also relatively less profitable for them to do so. They thus faced a serious transaction cost that impeded enclosure. The second issue was how the delineation of shared boundaries was to be accomplished. Had the law been silent on the issue, there would have been a tremendous incentive for landowners to free ride on the fencing activities of their neighbors – after all, why would one pay to fence one's own property when one can benefit from the equivalent activity performed by a neighbor? To prevent free riding like

---

[10] Joseph Glidden patented the improved form of the barbed wire fence on November 24, 1874. US Patent Office, Patent No. 157, 124.

this, the law created a shared mandate. Whenever the owner of one side of a boundary decided to fence it, the law required that the property owner on the facing side pay 50 percent of the cost. Concurrence of this second owner was not, however, required, nor were exceptions made if the costs of enclosure were unaffordable to him or her.

This seemingly technical mechanism was crucial. For not only would large landowners be more able to amortize the (lower per hectare) costs of enclosures for their properties, but in so doing, they could impose substantially higher immediate costs on their small- and medium-holding neighbors. Quite commonly, these costs exceeded what the neighbors could afford, leading to a forced sale of their lands and/or herds at fire-sale prices. The immediate beneficiaries were, of course, the adjacent large landowners, who had deliberately put the smaller property owners in this position in the first place. And as enclosure and the accompanying security of title led inevitably to substantial subsequent increases in the price of land (see Figure 4.3), a further windfall befell the large, enclosing landlords. Enclosure itself had a second key directly profitable component for large landowners: it allowed them to acquire the cattle of the relatively large number of small and medium ranchers who had, since independence, at least, been raising their cattle in whole or in part via encroachment on others' lands. As fences ended their ability to graze on others' property, they had little choice but to liquidate their herds – again, allowing the large landowners to acquire very valuable cattle at sharply reduced prices. And of course, it drove competing producers out of business.

The elimination of a large number of small and medium ranchers served a function in the establishment of modern agrarian capitalism beyond that which it played in the establishment of basic property rights. Certainly clear, well-defined property rights were critical, but beyond that, an adequate and reliable supply of wage labor would also be required. This was problematic in Uruguay, though while some workers had long been available in the countryside, they were comparatively scarce. Moreover, the expensive, nomadic, unreliable, and frequently restive gauchos (literally, "cowboys") who populated the lower classes of the postindependence era were inadequate to the task. But enclosure, by driving small and middling producers as well as encroachers out of the market, had the simultaneous effect of sharply increasing the available wage labor force. It also reduced the viability of alternative forms of employment dramatically, serving a vital disciplinary function with respect to the anarchic cowboy culture that had to that time prevailed in rural Uruguay. And since urban, industrial development in Uruguay was quite limited in comparison even to other contemporary Latin American countries, exit to the city for employment was also largely foreclosed. In the end, the pro-landlord Latorre government further aided the establishment of capitalist labor relations through the application of vagrancy laws to encourage wage labor employment among unemployed gauchos and former small and medium ranchers.

The enclosures and the establishment of full-fledged agrarian capitalism in Uruguay occurred at the same time that the structure of agrarian production

State Formation in Argentina and Uruguay

was profoundly changed by the arrival of the international sheep and wool trade. Indeed, this change was not particularly disruptive for producers, for sheep and cattle are complementary forms of agricultural production.[11] And as wool production required substantially more labor, this created an incentive to settle more population into stable communities in the countryside and further diminished reliance on the traditional gauchos that had dominated preenclosure cattle production. And with the decline of the gauchos came a decline in the power of local caciques, who had relied on them for their local quasi-military power (Nahum and Barrán 1972, 79).

The progress of state building and the penetration of public institutions and infrastructure followed the geographic progression of agrarian capitalism. It came to most of Uruguay (the center and littoral regions) first, and without substantial resistance. For however much agrarian elites were divided into the contending Blanco and Colorado parties, both parties had strong classically liberal currents that were supportive of the Latorre (and subsequent military government) property reforms. What the *militarista* era did, instead, was to seal the internal hegemony of the liberal, capitalist factions of both parties. Indeed, the ultimate suppression of the vestiges of unfree labor in the north of Uruguay came at the behest of these liberal agrarian elites, who objected to having to compete with the Brazilian-influenced northerners who had reduced their labor forces to semiservile conditions. And thus was the part of Uruguay that might have held back state building removed from political relevance – these northern, servile-labor estancias were either forced out of business or transformed into capitalist agribusinesses, like their southern and littoral brethren.

The key is that the economic chaos of the preindependence era was not a fundamental problem from the perspective of state building in the way that unfree labor was in Peru. Centralization of authority in Peru would have weakened landlord control over restive populations and threatened property rights. In Uruguay, it made possible the consolidation and efficient protection of property rights, while at the same time helping to eliminate threats to production from encroachers and cattle rustlers. While building a national private property regime had some public good characteristics and suffered from a coordination problem and free-rider dilemmas in the effort to shift to this new equilibrium, that transformation and the centralization of authority that it required was collectively and – as implemented by Latorre – individually profitable for Uruguayan landlords and as such was completed with alacrity once it was credibly initiated.[12]

---

[11] Indeed, exclusive sheep grazing destroys the natural prairies on which they feed. Cattle, however, are far less destructive, and if grazing land is rotated between them, then the grasses have time to recover sufficiently to support the next period of sheep ranching. See Nahum and Barrán (1972, 75).

[12] By contrast, the centralization of authority in a setting of unfree labor would have produced a persistent threat to property rights – rather than undergirded them – and was thus anathema to such traditional elites in Peru, or for that matter, the Uruguayan far north. In Peru, they

126 *Latin American State Building in Comparative Perspective*

Forging Elite Political Cooperation

Uruguay and Argentina ultimately achieved – after a long delay in each case – substantial elite unity around a program of further national institutional development. There was, however, one ultimately important difference in how this was accomplished. In Uruguay, elite cooperation would come to be organized around an increasingly institutionalized process of quasi-consociational political incorporation of the two principal political parties (called "coparticipation" locally). By contrast, in Argentina, political hegemony represented the victory of the Buenos Aires faction of the national dominant class, and subsequent political development occurred largely on its terms.

Although the initial postindependence wave of internecine political conflict in both countries might suggest that eventual political compromise was an unlikely outcome, there were good reasons even from an early period arguing for the ability of the agrarian elites to eventually be able to bridge their differences and cooperate in the construction of what ultimately would become very powerful and penetrating national institutions. To begin, the agrarian upper class in Uruguay was essentially economically homogeneous. While there were some differences in labor relations in the comparatively remote and economically unimportant north, all its main factions, across the partisan divide, were engaged principally in ranching activity – initially, cattle, and later, in a complementary fashion, sheep and wool. Indeed, socially and institutionally, different components of the upper class were similarly homogeneous. For example, when a newer, more capitalist set of producers entered agricultural activity after the Guerra Grande, they did not displace but rather integrated with the traditional upper class through the mechanism of marriage (Nahum and Barrán 1972, 129). And organizationally, as property rights developed under Latorre, the agrarian producers even of different factions and parties were united in a single organization – the Asociación Rural – that strongly supported the liberal reforms that consolidated and materially benefited the large property owners who were coming to dominate the Uruguayan countryside.[13]

Nor was the civil conflict of the postindependence era ultimately a barrier to elite compromise and state building, despite contentions as to its corrosive effects elsewhere on the continent (Centeno 2002). Civil conflict in Uruguay was, unlike that of most other cases, not necessarily a product of profound disagreement over the course of domestic politics or a distributional struggle across a major social cleavage. Instead, particularly in the most notable episode, the Guerra Grande, it was a reflection of differences in *external* orientation – either in support of Rosas and his expansionism in Argentina (Blancos), or alternatively, of Argentine Unitarios or Brazil (Colorados) (Gros Espiell 1966, 64).

dominated through the era of state building, whereas in Uruguay, they were a comparatively small group along the Brazilian border that was ultimately politically defeated.

[13] Zum Felde (1941, 175–76) points out that Latorre received support from both the Blanco and Colorado parties and was strongly allied to the Asociación Rural.

State Formation in Argentina and Uruguay

With the resolution of the underlying conflicts in Argentina, of course, any Uruguayan reflection would also cease to be problematic.

Indeed, the end of the Guerra Grande foreshadowed the exact sort of institutionalized interelite compromise that would eventually lay the foundation for the construction of a powerful Uruguayan state. That devastating conflict ended not with a victory but with a settlement that involved a power-sharing agreement among the warring factions under the slogan "neither victors nor vanquished" (*ni vencedores ni vencidos*). While this compromise did not end internal political conflict in Uruguay, it did set a template for resolving future conflicts. Thus, in the wake of the 1870–72 rebellion by Blanco party leader Timoteo Aparicio (*la revolución de las lanzas*), a settlement was reached that was even more explicit: the Colorados (the majority party) would concede political control of 4 of 12 departments to the Blancos.[14]

It is also the case that as Uruguayan institutions became more stable, they became more reinforcing of interelite political compromise. That is, they contained features that would facilitate long-term compromise and confidence building among elites, but they would not be relevant until the institutional rules came to have some sway over political outcomes. The constitution itself, technically in force from 1830 to 1918, was for much of this period largely a dead letter. But that said, a feature for which it was frequently criticized may well have proved later to be a crucial spur to compromise: it envisioned a comparatively weak executive. The constitution, for example, permitted a single (consecutive) four-year term (Gros Espiell 1966, 50, 58–59). The absence of reelection was, as in Chile, an important way to reassure political competitors that electoral defeats did not imply permanent exclusion from office and its benefits. And a comparatively weak executive increases the probability that a defeated opponent would accept loss and focus efforts on subsequent contests.

At the same time as institutions helped to reinforce the credibility of elite compromises, and pacts themselves demonstrated the viability of the "institutional" path of political contestation, the capacity for violent alternatives declined. As López Alves has pointed out, the reforms of the Latorre government decisively weakened the caudillos that had been the backbone of civil insurrection (and indeed, the scale of the remaining conflicts declined almost secularly after the end of the Guerra Grande) (López Alves 1996, 126). Equally crucial, the armed forces of the national government gradually came to be dominant and, later, after the Paraguayan War,

---

[14] This particular solution was also a precedent for resolving subsequent political struggles between Blancos and Colorados. In the wake of a failed electoral reform and a brief uprising, in 1897, El Pacto de la Cruz (the Pact of the Cross) was established, which included political amnesty, proportional representation, and an agreement that six departments be headed by Blancos. This, according to Juan Pivel Devoto, meant that the "principle of co-participation [first consecrated 25 years earlier] was ratified" (Pivel Devoto 1942, 388–89).

128   *Latin American State Building in Comparative Perspective*

hegemonic.[15] Not only did the war bring a surge of material resources from Brazil (enriching the national state and the dominant classes through Montevideo's important logistical role in the conflict), it also spurred the professionalization of the national army as a consequence of its participation in this long and bloody conflict. The national military, and by extension the central government, also gained a crucial monopoly over the importation and use of the newly invented (repeating) Remington rifle, making it technologically dominant over the arms available to rural caudillos (Nahum and Barrán 1972, 156). Given Montevideo's role as the only important port for international commerce, widespread illicit importation of military equipment was not viable. When this decisive technological advantage was coupled with a rail and telegraph infrastructure allowing the central government to project its force across the national territory, the possibility of successful insurrection was increasingly foreclosed. Even when occasional armed rebellion broke out, how it was treated is instructive – usually the defeated side was quickly reincorporated into national elite politics.[16]

But at the same time, the benefits of political participation and compromise became ever clearer from the perspective of elites. National political dynamics in the late nineteenth and early twentieth centuries included two main political parties that were – in ideological terms – barely distinguishable. Electoral rules came to embody proportional representation principles and, after the 1910 reform, were made even more so by the adoption of the "double simultaneous vote." The latter was a form of proportional representation that apportioned seats to sub- and cross-party lists called *lemas*, institutionalizing political conflict that distributed power not only across parties but also across factions within parties (Gros Espiell 1966, 76). This increased the factionalization of the two elite-dominated parties, and the ideological breadth within each, often leading to political competition between sides consisting even of cross-party alliances of subparty factions. Even more surprising is that the shift to this form of proportional representation was promoted by none other than the Colorado Party (in an explicit effort at conciliation), despite that it had a clear dominant position and could only stand to lose from such a reform (Pivel Devoto 1942, 344). It was, thus, in itself a powerful confidence-building tool.

One ingredient, however, remained for the absence of a social, economic, or political foundation for persistent division among elites to lead to a serious

---

[15] Also called the War of the Triple Alliance, this five-year conflict resulted in the conquest of Paraguay by a Brazil–Argentina–Uruguay alliance.

[16] The 1904 rebellion (one of the last important ones) of Saravia against the election of reformist José Batlle to the presidency, for example, ended in decisive defeat, a general amnesty, the electoral participation of the losing side, and even incorporation of the rebels into the national army. See Méndez Vives (1975, 127).

State Formation in Argentina and Uruguay 129

investment in state building. They had to be able to believe that a strengthened state would not subsequently be used in ways that were damaging to elite interests. Here is where Uruguayan political institutions completed the circle. For, as accommodating as they were to alternative elite interests, they were radically exclusionary when it came to nonelite political tendencies. Most notable in this regard was the suffrage law, which denied the vote to, inter alia, debtors, illiterates, criminals, soldiers, servants, and those without property. And of course, if this were not enough, voting was initially public and oral (López Alves 1996, 126).

In the end, a trajectory of effective state building was launched on the basis of a free-wage, capitalist economy in both Argentina and Uruguay. In each case, a very difficult and lengthy process of overcoming severe political divisions among elites was necessary before cooperation around the construction of a strong national state could ensue. And although the ultimate mechanism by which some measure of elite unity was obtained (victory or compromise and collective benefits) varied, in this initial period, the emergent trajectory of political development was quite auspicious. It would only be later, when long-excluded middle-sector and working-class political actors entered into contention for national power, that the trajectories of political development of these two countries would diverge, leading to a deepening of state building in Uruguay and a shift to cycles of institution building and destruction in Argentina. But that outcome is the empirical heart of Chapter 6.

With respect to the sociopolitical explanation for trajectories of state building developed in this book, the Argentina–Uruguay comparison makes a further important point: it is not impossible for a country to shift its position on a key independent variable. That is, both Argentina and Uruguay, after extensive struggle, were able to overcome the unfavorable political relationships within their elite classes and create a coalition capable of driving a state-building process forward.[17] What we see in the chapters that follow, however, is that the sequencing of critical junctures is important, for eventually, path dependencies do become extremely constraining. If, for example, political cooperation is achieved *after* the entry of the masses into politics in the second critical juncture, it will not have the same felicitous effect in terms of the promotion of institutional development. Similarly, as we will see in the Peruvian case, the ultimate destruction of the hegemony of semiservile and inegalitarian labor relations in agriculture would come too late to be a spur for state building, for the window of opportunity had closed. Because of the already-deep participation of the masses in politics, Peruvian elites would nevertheless resist

---

[17] We will also see in Chapter 7 that in Prussia, it was just barely possible to transform a servile agrarian system into one reliant on free labor. This was by no means an easy task, but as it was accomplished before mass political participation was achieved, it engendered the possibility of the effective state building for which the Prussian, and later German, state is so well known.

institutional reform. While the maintenance of rural control was no longer their concern, they now had – as a consequence of the second critical juncture – serious concerns that strengthened state institutions could be used against their interests by reformist, populist, or leftist political forces representing the disadvantaged sectors. And in this way, again, timing would be crucial.

5

Divergence Reinforced

The Timing of Political Inclusion and State Strength in Chile and Peru

We saw in Chapter 3 that Chile and Peru represented polar outcomes with regard to their initial state-building trajectories. But this represented only the first of two critical steps in the theory of long-run state building developed in this book. In this chapter, we consider the second major branching point in institutional development – the fashion in which the inclusion of middle-class and working-class actors as important players in national politics is structured. This is a sequenced claim, and outcomes depend on the interaction with the preexisting paths of political development on which each country had already been launched. It is only after this second critical juncture, coming around the time of the Great Depression in most of Latin America, that trajectories are most firmly established. The outcomes in Chile and Peru explored in this chapter are here again polar with respect to institutional development. Indeed, the second critical juncture in these cases reinforced and deepened the preexisting trajectories of political development: while the ultimate accommodation of the social question in Chile led to a further and dramatic expansion and strengthening of state institutions, precocious political incorporation in Peru only heightened the underdeveloped character of the public administration and locked in an infelicitous trajectory for decades to come.

In Chile, already possessing some of the most well-founded institutions on the continent, the entry of the masses into electoral politics came quite late – in large part after the start of the Great Depression and, for some, long thereafter. In a process that we see as well in the Uruguayan case (Chapter 6), what instead occurred was a development of institutions designed to accommodate mass economic and political mobilization well in advance of the reality of such autonomous large-scale participation. This had the effect of ultimately channeling political participation – when suffrage was finally extended to new groups – in ways that served to strengthen and expand these institutions rather than pose insurmountable challenges to them. By contrast,

131

in Peru, mass participation came quite early, before solid institutions existed and in a political–economic context far less favorable to the use of the state to accommodate emergent middle-sector and working-class political demands. The consequence was a highly polarized politics, a weakened state, and the inability to construct any sort of viable, penetrating, or lasting administrative structure under democratic or authoritarian auspices alike.

As we will see in this chapter and the next, in one sense, the rise of the social question is a constant: all the political systems examined in this book at some point faced – and responded to – demands for political participation on the part of middle-sector and working-class political actors. These class strata did not necessarily enter politics at the same time in any particular country – and this in itself had effects on the possibilities for cross-class compromise and cooperation. What is most crucial, however, is the issue of timing and economic context. The critical outcome – the one that determines the long-run impact on administrative development of popular-sector incorporation – hinges on the viability of a political accommodation being struck between middle- and working-class political forces at the moment that the social question comes to a final head. This in turn is structured by features of the political economy and by timing of incorporation in relationship to the onset of the Great Depression. Timing of incorporation, of course, here stands in for a series of social and political dynamics that are tied to the initial entry of popular-sector voters into electoral competition for the first time.

The question of "when" the middle and working classes enter into political relevance is at least in part a question of when they develop in substantial numbers and in relation to which specific economic sectors – keeping in mind that most of Latin America's political economies organized around quite inegalitarian agricultural and mineral sectors that generated comparatively little such employment. From this flow two principal issues that are extremely consequential from a state-building perspective. The first has to do with the basic material interests of the bulk of the middle sectors. In some cases, as in Argentina, the middle sectors developed first in large numbers in the private sector and in direct or indirect association with a vibrant agro-export economy in the pre-Depression era. In others, such as Chile and Uruguay, the middle class emerged later and principally in various forms of public employment. This differentiation is ultimately mirrored by the political representatives of the middle classes at the time of incorporation – middle-class parties very importantly differed on issues of economic protectionism and the merits of expanding the state's role in direct service provision and economic production. Where the middle sectors emerged early and were linked to the private economy, they came into politics in the era of the gold standard and free trade, tied to export sectors, and as such, they were typically initially hostile to protectionism, state institutional expansion, and developmentalist economic regulation. This put them in a poor position to reach an accommodation with rising working-class interests, which typically came into active political contention later, and by the time of the

Divergence Reinforced

Great Depression, they were committed to protectionism and state-supported industrialization – which would inevitably be paid for by precisely the export-oriented economic sectors to which the early-incorporated middle classes were linked. This was a recipe for severe contestation over the appropriate size of the state and created incentives for middle-class actors to form political alliances with traditional elites rather than mobilized working-class parties in an effort to keep the popular sector from achieving control over the course of national policy.

This early challenge of political incorporation can occur in cases in which the state is on an initially favorable state-building path – as in Argentina – or in a context that is inauspicious for institutional development, such as is the case in Peru. It is the latter situation whose consequences will be explored in this chapter. In this context, beginning the task of building effective and comprehensive state institutions became exceedingly difficult for both political and economic reasons. The rise of the social question reshaped the interests of the main contending political forces in ways that are even more inimical to national institutional development. To begin, it is important to remember that initiating a dynamic state-building process is a major task of political construction under the best of circumstances, for it is both fiscally costly and has the potential to create substantial uncertainty over the future course of policy. And it necessarily shifts the balance of winners and losers in domestic political–economic competition in sharp ways. Materially, where the middle and working classes' political emergence comes early, a large political coalition in favor of the strengthening of the state simply does not exist and is nearly impossible to assemble. Major elements of the middle sectors, as we saw earlier, do not rely on the state and are predisposed against economically intervention-ist and institutionally expansive policy. While state building and institutional creation would ultimately produce many new middle-sector positions, those actors who are not yet present in large numbers or politically relevant at the time of the *initiation* of the process, they exist only as a potential post facto support for public-sector expansion. Thus, while there may be a latent (future) constituency for state expansion and investments in institutional development, there isn't a concurrent one.

Where a history of poor institutions combines with early initial mass suffrage, the political elites who had heretofore resisted state building because of internecine political conflict and the personal and economic risks it entailed in a semiservile economy would remain implacably opposed, indeed more resistant, to the strengthening of the state. Not only do the factors that inhibited institutional development in the postindependence era still obtain – the need for local repressive control, a reticence to pay and inability to afford substantial taxation, and persistent interelite divisions that raise the specter of distributional coalitions – but a host of new barriers are added to the mix. Most notably, with the entry of the masses into politics, the question of *re*-distributive policy ceases to be a theoretical one and becomes a real potentiality. And not only would such policy – initiated in the Depression context – involve income transfers from the wealthy to at least the organized masses but it would also focus on transferring resources to industrial development, layering a sectoral clash atop an existing class-based conflict that only further raised the costs of institutional development for the traditional agro-export or mineral elite. For, any program of domestic industrialization would have to be financed in large measure out of foreign exchange and other tax revenues taken from these traditional export sectors. And with no preexisting, large indigenous industrial sector, forming a populist coalition around protected development is quite difficult. Indeed, the only actor with an interest in serious institutional reform would be the organized working class, but this would of needs be a comparatively small group in such a largely preindustrial setting, and politically, it would be difficult for its representatives to achieve power, much less successfully enact and institutionalize state-building reforms.

Notwithstanding all these pitfalls facing any putative state builder, there remains the further problem that extant public institutions were quite weak, making the generation of revenues to support successful developmentalism and state expansion much more difficult to come by, especially in the face of an implacably resistant upper class, even were stable national political control to be achieved by proponents of institutional development. We see this clearly in the case of Peru, where even when a powerful military government – capable of marginalizing domestic elites and redistributing their assets – seized control and embarked on an effort to sharply expand and strengthen public institutions in pursuit of a developmentalist economic strategy, it met with little lasting success.

By contrast, if the middle sectors developed later, they typically were centered in public-sector occupations (e.g., public administration, education, the judicial system, and health care) or as employees of state-owned enterprises. This distinct sectoral location tended to induce the emergence of substantially different political representatives, especially in terms of their orientation to the expansion and strengthening of public institutions. Moreover, as their entry into politics occurred during and after the onset of the Great Depression – which thoroughly discredited export-oriented models of development – and their material interests were tied to the public administration, they were in a strong position to form alliances with newly mobilized working-class actors around a joint program of statism, protected industrialization, and state-guided economic development. The Great Depression thus represented a political window for a wholly new political alliance to emerge, one that had real potential to attain and keep power in an open electoral process. If such a bargain could be struck, long-term collectively beneficial patterns of industrial and state expansion could be launched by a broad middle- and working-class coalition that would as a consequence be self-reinforcing. And in many cases, elements of the industry-linked upper classes could be brought on board as well, further broadening the cross-class cooperation needed to sustain state building. As such

Divergence Reinforced

bargains underwrote the expansion of the state and rapid import-substituting industrialization, and the size and power of the core constituencies behind this political bargain increased vertiginously once implemented – helping to lock in the trajectory for the indefinite future.

The combination of delayed mass incorporation and preexisting vibrant state institutions was thus especially favorable terrain for the further development of government institutions and their spread into substantial new competencies. Not only was there a material foundation for an underlying and broad-based bargain among middle- and working-class political constituencies to support this, there was also far less resistance from the more economically advantaged sectors of society. With the expansion of institutions coming in the wake of the Great Depression, and coupled with an already quite vigorous and demonstrably effective state, the alternatives for elites to some sort of protectionist development were substantially foreclosed. The export economy had, after all, all but collapsed. At the same time, threats of redistributive politics had not yet become substantial – for mobilized working-class actors were not yet anywhere near potentially politically dominant by themselves. And of course, the expansion of institutions in the previous era had ultimately proved both publicly and privately beneficial for such elites – and without redistributive politics clearly dominating political competition, many could credibly believe that they would be major beneficiaries of developmentalist and statist policies as well. They were not, as an empirical matter, wrong in this. This does not mean, of course, that they had no doubts about the wisdom of strengthening public institutions. The point is to compare the implacable opposition and divided support that is characteristic of the weak-state, early incorporation path to political development with one that begins with a stronger state and far less precocious democratization.

THE OUTCOMES

Very polar trajectories can be seen in the long-term political development of Peru and Chile. As we saw in Chapter 3, Chile had for much of the time between independence and the Great Depression been on an institution-building trajectory. Yet it was with the emergence of the social question during and after the Depression that the construction of political institutions took a further qualitative leap forward. In some ways, the Chilean political economy was particularly suited to the dramatic strengthening of public institutions. To begin with, state economic intervention had a comparatively early history, with relatively high and sometimes deliberately protective tariffs, emerging as early as the First World War. This was substantially earlier than was typical in most of the rest of the Latin American region. The socioeconomically heterogeneous elite quickly took advantage of this protection, and thus agrarian elites tended to have important ties to the nascent industrial sectors. By contrast, exports were dominated by British and American mineral interests in the nitrate and copper mining sectors, respectively, leaving only a small *domestic* constituency strongly wedded to economic openness. Indeed, even the agricultural sector – owing in part to its undercapitalized and inefficient production structure – was a supporter of economic protection, for except during momentary contingencies, it was generally incapable of exporting its output or effectively competing with foreign producers (especially in the grain and cattle sectors, in which nearby Argentina was a very efficient producer).

By contrast, mass-based political participation was very slow to develop in Chile. While there certainly was incipient labor mobilization, especially in the mineral sector, in the 1910s and 1920s, sustained labor-based collective action and organization would only arrive much later. Indeed, even the initial labor law (passed in 1924 and effectively implemented in the 1930s) created only a limited form of firm-level representation and effectively precluded organization in the countryside. Mass suffrage was similarly quite restricted, with the end of rampant vote buying occurring only after the 1958 secret ballot reforms and the advent of female suffrage coming in that decade as well. So gradual was mass political inclusion that illiterates (who long remained a substantial portion of the population) were unable to vote until 1970. And of course, members of the Communist Party could neither run for office nor vote during the 1948–58 period of juridical proscription. Institution building, however, began early, during the dictatorial interlude of Carlos Ibáñez (1927–32), and was dramatically expanded during the middle-class–centered Radical Party coalition governments of the Popular Front era and beyond (1938–52).

The trajectory on which Peru found itself differed sharply from that of Chile. Its elites had not managed to come to a lasting political accommodation among themselves, and the persistence of coercive labor relations in many sectors militated against efforts to centralize authority in national political institutions. And as the Great Depression struck, the divergences with Chile were only heightened. If Chile had already begun to develop a domestically oriented industrial elite that was a potential partner in a state-building effort, Peru had quite the opposite problem. Its industrial sector at this time was exceedingly limited, and the domestic elite was deeply committed to agro-export production and thus decidedly hostile to the sorts of statist and protectionist bargains that were possible elsewhere. This was a critical difference, for where we saw effective state building in the Latin American region, it was deeply connected to the creation of the political institutions undergirding protectionist development, national economic planning, and the mobilization and control of financial resources. As much as Peruvian elites resisted authority centralization in an earlier era to preserve their control over coercive assets, they further resisted it in the wake of the Depression as such centralization would also have implied a major transfer of their wealth (and strict control over their foreign exchange earnings) in support of a nascent industrial sector of which they were not a part.

Also in contrast to Chile, the initial development of mass-based political competition came comparatively early – middle-class and working-class

Divergence Reinforced 137

interests were decisive in the electorate as early as the 1930s – and made the institution-building calculus all the harder. For as a consequence, in addition to the long-standing reasons for elites to resist the construction of national institutions that might seriously constrain their power (and tax their wealth) came the possibility of *redistributive* politics as well. While it is true that the main vehicle for mass political incorporation at the time – Alianza Popular Revolucionaria Americana (APRA) – was frequently prohibited from electoral participation, it was also equally true that the loyalties of large middle-class and working-class constituencies to this party were visibly quite durable. In fact, it is the only really institutionalized, long-lasting political party to have developed in the Peruvian context to this day. And that made redistribution a real possibility whenever the authoritarian–democratic pendulum swung back to the latter. This meant elites always had to contemplate a future in which APRA might come to power – singly or in coalition. The result was an inability to create a broad, cross-class political constituency for the consolidation of public institutions, and we will see that even efforts by the military to impose such a solution were similarly unable to deflect Peru from its long-term trajectory of institutional underdevelopment and a weak state.

THE LONG ROAD TO STATE STRENGTH: POLITICAL PARTICIPATION
AND INSTITUTIONAL DYNAMICS IN CHILE FROM THE POPULAR
FRONT TO PINOCHET

How did the dynamics of delayed mass inclusion in Chile ultimately produce an exceedingly interventionist and unusually effective public administration that was ultimately put to use by first centrist and later leftist political forces in the 1960s and 1970s behind a campaign of moderate and then radical redistribution, only to be followed by the archetypal free-market authoritarianism of General Pinochet? Although Chile was certainly on the path to institutional development in its postindependence era, as we saw in Chapter 3, the conditions it faced as it entered the twentieth century were not at first blush especially auspicious. Its agricultural economy, while not servile, was trapped in a web of archaic productive relations and undercapitalization, leading first to stagnation and then later to outright decline. The principal sources of critical foreign exchange – nitrate and copper exports – were also rocked by twin crises in the early twentieth century. Cost-effective artificial nitrate fixation, invented by Germany during the First World War, put nitrate exports on a permanent downward spiral. And the economic calamity of the Great Depression all but destroyed the copper export economy; indeed, Chile was much more seriously affected by this global calamity than her Latin American peers. Moreover, through the late nineteenth and mid-twentieth centuries, overall economic growth was decidedly unspectacular; instead, by the 1950s, the Chilean economy had become plagued by persistently low growth and high inflation (Hirschman 1963). The expansion of the Chilean state in the twentieth century, then, was not funded by access to relatively large quantities of foreign exchange from the mineral sector – as it had been in the nineteenth century. Instead, it took place in the context of near-permanent fiscal resource constraints, a boom–bust economy, and fragmented politics.

Yet the state expanded and improved, and did so decisively. Even more surprisingly, the major institutional innovations that structured the expanded Chilean state took place well before extensive and autonomous, mobilized working-class electoral participation became a reality. Indeed, some of the initial social reforms – in the 1920s – were designed precisely to weaken, constrain, and institutionalize such potential working-class political participation. The institutional transformations that built the expanded and strengthened state – as we will see later – came in two major phases. The first – driven by pressure from reformist military officers – involved the breaking of a logjam in 1924–25 over the imposition of basic social welfare and labor laws and ultimately a new constitution that returned Chile to a strongly presidential form of government. The second, carried out especially in the early years of the middle-class Radical Party-led governments of the Popular Front and thereafter (1938–52) to build the infrastructure of a protectionist, entrepreneurial state and strict economic management in the service of developmentalist goals. The first phase thus laid the foundation for a large, quasi-Bismarckian system of social provision that included pension, health care, and housing provision in a series of occupationally and class-segregated systems. The second built an apparatus of economic intervention through the active management of credit allocation, extensive protection, subsidy, and foreign exchange controls. To this was added a large state-owned enterprise sector, especially in strategic industries like steel, petroleum, transport, and energy production.

The consequence was a dramatic expansion of the scope of the public sector – and the associated revenue-raising capacity that accompanied it. Figure 5.2 traces the comparative evolution of central government revenues in Chile in contrast to Peru. We can see from this figure, continuing the pattern set in the nineteenth century, that Chilean taxation was dramatically higher than that of Peru. Typically, the gap was at least 10 percentage points of gross domestic product (GDP), sometimes much more than that. And indeed, even after almost two decades of military rule after 1973, ostensibly dedicated to neoliberal minimalism, the Chilean state's revenue advantage over Peru remained stark. As we will see, the post-Depression Chilean state was an activist one, and one that accomplished even one of the most difficult tasks any government faces – imposing serious domestic taxation – very effectively from an early time. While the *policies* to which this capacity was applied would change dramatically over time, institution building and governance improvement continued in a more or less uninterrupted fashion across political regimes and executives of different partisan affiliations.

The remainder of this section will set out the ways in which the rise of the social question in Chile paradoxically produced a dramatic strengthening of an already improving state institutional infrastructure. Once the path was

Divergence Reinforced 139

firmly set in the 1930s and 1940s, even the most dramatic of political and economic swings were unable to fundamentally change trajectory. This will be the final empirical contribution of this chapter – an examination of the difficulties of changing institutional trajectories, even under governments quite committed to doing so. In particular, as a test of the mechanisms that reinforced the development of strong institutions in Chile, two specific periods of potential path departure are considered: first, the administration of conservative, oligarchy-backed Jorge Alessandri (1958–64), who pursued a sharp fiscal and institutional retrenchment in the context of persistent and rising inflation, and second, even more dramatically, with the collapse of democracy in 1973, a military government came to power that was ultimately committed to a dramatically reduced and weakened Chilean state, and it governed essentially unchecked until a return to democracy in 1989. But even the authoritarian Pinochet experience, although it shrank the economic and social role of the state somewhat, did *not* notably undermine the efficacy of state institutions. And indeed, the "neoliberal" Chilean state proved more capable of economic governance and imposed much higher taxation than most of its more "statist" peers in South America.

THE CHILEAN ECONOMY AT THE DAWN OF THE SOCIAL QUESTION

After the War of the Pacific and the conclusion of the civil conflict that ended with the deposition of President Balmaceda and the initiation of the Parliamentary Republic of 1891–1925, Chile found itself in a period of comparative external and internal peace and the new owner of exceedingly profitable nitrate-producing territories acquired from Peru and Bolivia. But this was also a period of comparative economic and social stasis – the Chilean political economy did not undergo the rapid transformations of, for example, Argentina. Experiencing neither Argentine-style rapid economic growth nor mass immigration, it instead experienced economic growth that barely kept up with population expansion, ranging in per capita terms from 1.1 percent in the 1890–1910 interval to 1.4 percent in the 1920s and 1930s (Monteón 1998, 17).

The revenues from the newly acquired nitrate territories seized from Peru initially underwrote a major expansion of infrastructure and public-sector investments in education. These export receipts, reaching almost $90 million in the period immediately before the First World War, for example, produced an increase in the national rail network from 1,000 to 5,000 kilometers between 1890 and 1920 (Faúndez 2007, 57). The major cities also underwent infrastructural improvements, and huge investments were made in the expansion of education – with literacy rising from 18.9 percent of the population in 1885 to over 50 percent by 1910 (Blakemore 1993, 61).

But this fiscal expansion was not accompanied by broad-based, rapid economic growth and began to falter in the face of severe challenges as early as the First World War. Although urbanization proceeded apace, it was still not until 1940 that a majority of the national population resided in cities. Similarly, population grew, but not at the vertiginous rates experienced by Argentina or Peru (see Chapter 6), rising from 2.5 million in 1885 to 5.0 million in 1940 (Arellano 1985, 400). The dependence on the mineral sector for foreign exchange and government revenues in this period was quite intense, and this made the broader economy and the fisc subject to the severe volatility characteristic of this economic sector (Faúndez 2007, 57).[1] And this volatility, in both of the two main mineral sectors, ultimately hit Chile very hard. Nitrate production underwent two major collapses in the twentieth century, the first after the end of the First World War, when artificial nitrate fixation created an economically viable competitor to mined Chilean nitrate (formerly a near-global monopoly). The consequence was a 62 percent decline in production between 1918 and 1922, followed by stagnation, a brief recovery, and a further 78.5 percent production decline between 1929 and 1932, as the Great Depression set in. The collapse of global trade in the early 1930s was similarly devastating to copper production, which declined vertiginously by 67.8 percent over the same period, while the price it fetched simultaneously collapsed alongside international demand (Ballesteros and Davis 1963, 165–66).

The consequence of this mineral–agricultural economic structure, and a political leadership that was dominated by the traditional oligarchy until at least 1920, was a decidedly slow pace of industrialization. Investments tended to go to the mineral enclaves of the far north rather than to nascent manufacturing sectors in Santiago. Nor were agrarian social relations altered, leaving the agricultural sector undercapitalized and of low productivity (Lower 1968, 292). This left a residual industrial sector that predominantly comprised small, often artisanal enterprises – as of 1927, 75 percent of "industrial" workers labored in firms of fewer than five employees (Davis 1970, 73). Unlike, for example, Argentina, which had a large industrial meat-processing industry tied to its cattle exports, mineral exports in Chile produced less in the way of associated industrial activity. Given the few domestic linkages of the export economy and the severe social inequality inherent in hacienda agriculture, it was public employment – supported by taxation on mineral exports – that was the principal location of a growing class of middle-sector workers comprised of professionals, technicians, bureaucrats, educators, and the like (Grant 1983, 152).

LABOR MOBILIZATION AND DELAYED POLITICAL INCORPORATION

As was pointed out earlier, Chilean social structure did not encompass a traditional large industrial working class in the period leading up to the Great Depression. It would be a mistake, however, to infer from this that labor mobilization was limited or unimportant. While it is true that there was virtually

---

[1] As Chile was at the time a largely preindustrial economy, the foreign exchange generated by mineral sales was critical to the broader economy's capacity to import necessary inputs and manufactured goods.

Divergence Reinforced

no labor mobilization in the countryside – which would remain true until the reforms enacted in the 1960s – there were other important instances of labor mobilization and waves of protest. But these mobilizations were met with two responses that ultimately dramatically undermined their efficacy and impeded an early political empowerment of working-class citizens as voters. On the one hand, they were met with often savage repression, and on the other, they were eventually legalized after 1925 (and effectively so only in 1932), but only in a fragmented and fragmenting fashion.

Part of the reason that labor mobilization was not effective in forcing the wholesale and autonomous political incorporation of working-class voters had to do with the unusual character of the Chilean economy. Labor mobilization and organization was concentrated in the peripheral parts of the country – the nitrate- and copper-mining areas of the north and the coal and port areas of the south. By contrast, lacking substantial large-scale industrialization, the Central Valley and Santiago proper were not the core of workers' organizational, electoral, or mobilizational strength (Faúndez 2007, 61). But peripheral areas were also more vulnerable to repressive responses, which, for example, characterized the 1906 nitrate and rail strike in Antofagasta and even more so the massive mobilization at the nitrate port of Iquique in 1907 – which was put down with machine guns at the cost of hundreds of lives (Blakemore 1993, 63).

After about 1910, the labor movement became more radicalized, and its principal representative, the Federación Obrera Chilena (Chilean Workers' Federation; FOCh) became associated with the Communist Party. But it is also the case that the FOCh, while sometimes capable of convening large protests, had a limited dues-paying organizational base, estimated at its peak in 1925 at between 25,000 and 30,000 members (Collier and Collier 2002 [1991], 75).

In political and electoral terms, the pre-Depression era was a period of near-complete exclusion for working-class and many middle-class voters. Indeed, Chile was an unusual country insofar as it systematically reduced suffrage in the years leading up to the Great Depression (see Figure 5.1). The proportion of the total population that was registered to vote and that actually voted peaked in 1912 at 17.6 and 8.7 percent, respectively. Shortly thereafter, voting became far more restricted, with a mere 5.3 percent of the citizenry registered in 1915, and with only gradual increases thereafter. Even by 1949, suffrage had not even reached meager 1912 levels, as only 10.4 percent of the population was registered to vote and only 8.3 percent actually did (Remmer 1977, 226). Not only was suffrage effectively quite restricted, but at least since 1891, elections had been subject to "government intervention at the polls, bribery on a massive scale, and the use of legislative certification to remove unwanted victors" (Monteón 1998, 19). This situation only became worse after 1925, when a new electoral law placed control over the electoral registries in the hands of local committees in each municipality, whose membership comprised the largest income-tax payers (Haring 1931, 10). This effectively put the oligarchy in charge of who was in practice permitted to vote, adding a further restriction to the long-extant bar on voting by illiterates or women.

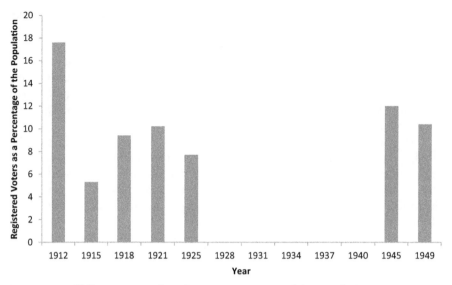

FIGURE 5.1. Chilean voter registration as a percentage of the population.

The near-complete exclusion of reformists and leftists in the pre-Depression era can be seen in the electoral results. In the 1912 elections, the middle-class Radical Party and the more leftist Democratic and Socialist parties combined to elect a total of 6 of 25 senators and 29 of 118 deputies. In 1915, they combined to elect 3 of 12 senators and 31 of 118 deputies. The remainder of the seats were dominated by the oligarchical Conservative and Liberal parties and the less ideological, more opportunistic Liberal Democrats (Remmer 1977, 220). This pattern of oligarchical dominance would continue until 1920, when the first major cracks in the political system began to appear.

The political watershed began with the election of 1920, which featured a reformist senator from the north of Chile, Arturo Alessandri, at the head of the Liberal Alliance. Alessandri ultimately won a very narrow victory in the election over the Conservative Luis Barros Borgoño, in a contested electoral college result of 177 to 176 that was ultimately decided in Alessandri's favor by a "Tribunal of Honor" (Olivarría 1962, 72). Alessandri's agenda included very substantial reforms, including increased income or land taxation to fund expanded infrastructure spending, expansion of free public education, national control over the banking system, and the creation of the first labor relations system in Chile, which envisioned a legal role for unions (Monteón 1998, 20; Haring 1931, 3). Conservative forces continued to dominate in the senate, however, effectively blocking the implementation of this agenda. This produced an effective stalemate that continued for most of Alessandri's presidency – until 1924 – when a definitive break finally emerged.

Divergence Reinforced 143

INSTITUTIONAL REFORM, THE MILITARY, AND THE GRADUAL RISE OF THE MIDDLE SECTORS

In Chile, as we will see was the case in Uruguay as well, the principal institutions that would govern the economy and institutionalize class relations were developed and implemented substantially *before* the entry into political competition of the representatives of the middle and working classes had been achieved. Indeed, the reforms of the first Alessandri presidency were finally enacted not because of pressure from organized workers or middle-class citizens but rather under the threat of military intervention. And it would be almost 15 years, and a new constitution, later before the first government led by the middle-class Radical Party would come to power, ultimately further deepening the penetration of state institutions into society and creating the new institutions that would govern the economy for decades to come.

The institutional crisis came to a head in 1924, when a group of mid-ranking officers, including Majors Carlos Ibáñez and Marmaduke Grove, packed the senate galleries and insisted that a comprehensive package of reforms be implemented – implicitly under the threat of a military seizure of power. The demands included income taxation, a labor code and social welfare legislation, and action on the national budget (Blakemore 1993, 75). Notably, their demands did not include broad and free mass suffrage. The legislation was forthcoming, but Alessandri continued to be shadowed by a military junta, prompting the president to tender his resignation and flee the country.

Soon after the departure of Alessandri, a new constitution was drafted that implied a major reorganization of power, a strengthening of the state and of the executive, and an increasing ability of public institutions to operate in ways autonomous of the dominant economic classes (Cavarozzi 1978, 257). Specifically, the constitution returned Chile to a strong presidential system, through direct elections to a six-year term, without immediate reelection. Church and state were formally separated, and most surprisingly, the state was empowered to alter property rights in the societal interest (Blakemore 1993, 79). The constitution did not, for all its reformist character, impose an increase in suffrage (Monteón 1998, 20). Indeed, the social and political reforms of the era were more about containing and channeling the political aspirations of subaltern groups than they were about responding to their grievances or permitting their free articulation.

The labor law finally approved in 1924 did legalize unions – though in effect only outside of agriculture – but it did so in a way that was designed simultaneously to keep them weak and fragmented. Unions and collective bargaining were permitted only at the enterprise level (and enterprises were overwhelmingly small in Chile at the time). At the same time, more politically efficacious federations and confederations of unions remained outside the bounds of legality. Similarly, other social laws were designed to fragment workers. Among other features, the law enshrined differences between *empleados* (white-collar employees) and *obreros* (working-class employees) and granted substantially greater benefits to the former relative to the latter. For example, the Caja de Seguro Obligatorio (the social welfare and pension fund for private-sector blue-collar workers) paid pensions so low that they were in the early days paid out as a simple lump sum. By contrast, white-collar employees in the Caja de Empleados Particulares (for the private sector) received far better health benefits, housing allowances, unemployment insurance, and a joint life pension annuity (covering the worker and his or her spouse) (Alexander 1949, 53–57). And of course, virtually no benefits were provided to the large numbers of agricultural workers who remained the captive clients of the landowning oligarchy. It was, in essence, a Bismarckian approach to social provision. Its provisions created clear divisions among social groups – indeed, in addition to the two main social welfare funds, there were by 1945 at least 42 other funds covering specific occupations, further fragmenting the interests of different occupational groups.[2]

The beginnings of a push to create new and more powerful administrative institutions, however, came at a time when the national political system was entering a period of crisis. After Alessandri's resignation and flight, effective power was in the hands of a short-lived interim government headed by General Luis Altamirano. Then, in January 1925, a junta led by Carlos Ibáñez and Marmaduke Grove seized power and acted to bring President Alessandri back to Chile (Nunn 1970, 45–46). After a bout of persistent conflict between Alessandri and the military, the former again resigned and was replaced by Emiliano Figueroa, a weak, oligarchy-linked figure. But increasingly, Ibáñez was the power behind the throne, and in 1927, he seized direct political control and ruled as president, essentially unchecked by any legislative or other authority.

The development of new and powerful state institutions was high on the agenda of President Ibáñez. In the brief interlude during which he ruled as dictator (1927–31), he managed to create a lasting institutional infrastructure, including the Central Bank, the Carabineros (the militarized national police force), and the Comptroller General (Contraloría General) (Cavarozzi 1978, 257).[3] The labor code was organized and implemented more effectively – though in this case as part of an ultimately unsuccessful effort to impose authoritarian corporatist institutional arrangements on labor (Collier and Collier 2002 [1991]). Perhaps as important, however, was a move to reorganize the staffing and operation of the public bureaucracy along much more technocratic lines. This change – in part brought about by a literal shift to the employment of engineers in public administration, from the ministerial level down, would

---

[2] There was a bewildering combination of funds in this group, including a large one for public employees and journalists, another for railway workers, and some as tiny as the one covering the mortgage bank of Valparaíso (Alexander 1949).

[3] This last office was more powerful than its North American analogues as it was constitutionally enshrined and charged with, among other things, assessing the constitutionality of decrees, laws, and appropriations.

Divergence Reinforced

continue among subsequent democratic governments and was in the eyes of one observer as important a change as the new Constitution of 1925 itself (Ibáñez Santa María 1981, 7, 11). So effective were these reforms, especially in the revenue apparatus, that according to one contemporary observer in a single year (1927–28), because of layoffs of redundant personnel combined with the improved collections of taxes, and the payment of market-rate wages to civil servants, a serious fiscal deficit was eliminated without recourse to increased taxation (Haring 1931, 23–24). The sum result of these reforms was that the "public technocracy began to exercise a decisive influence in the decision-making process in ministries, state enterprises, and the public administration at large" (Silva 1994, 284).

While many of the institutional innovations of the period of authoritarian rule under President Ibáñez continued over subsequent administrations and decades, politically, his government could not survive the calamity of the Great Depression, and by 1931, he was forced from office. After a brief period of instability, and of successive governments, including a 12-day "Socialist Republic" headed by Ibáñez's former collaborator, Marmaduke Grove, in 1932, Arturo Alessandri was once again returned to the presidency. President Alessandri, of 1932–38, was not, however, the reformer of the 1920–25 period. Instead, he governed much more in the mode of a traditional conservative. It was not until the next election, in 1938, that the first definitive cracks in the oligarchical dominance of Chilean politics appeared.

The mid-to-late 1930s marked the gradual economic and political emergence of a large middle class. At its core, as we have seen, this middle class was largely a creation of public-sector employment – which increased vertiginously as a share of the active labor force with the reforms of the 1920s, rising 81 percent between 1920 and 1930 (calculated from Ballesteros and Davis 1963, 176). As we will see, this change was crucial and late in coming. Grant (1983, 125) points out that "genuinely middle class elements probably did not appear in Chile until the beginning of the twentieth century," and after the Depression, "it [the state] created a middle class, the function of which was to serve as the bureaucratic managers or agents of capitalist development strategies and to provide the backbone of the consumer market." This was not simply the demarcation of a social group comprising public servants, however. Rather, at least by the time of the first available survey work in 1965, it was a group of workers who overwhelmingly (more than 70 percent) identified as middle class and were strong supporters of a mixed-economy approach to economic management (Petras and Grenier 1969, 75, 86). They would become the political and human capital backbone of the Chilean state.

THE RADICAL PARTY, THE MIDDLE CLASSES, AND THE POPULAR FRONT IN POWER

As we have seen, major steps in the strengthening of Chilean public institutions began before the complete inclusion of middle-sector and working-class citizens in the democratic polity. But the consolidation of this strengthened – and vastly expanded – dynamic of institutional development would come as these actors gradually entered the political arena during and after the Great Depression. The principal political feature of this period was the construction of a powerful consensus around the wisdom of an expansive and highly interventionist set of state institutions leading a protectionist industrial development strategy. This was a consensus that formed during the Popular Front government led by the middle-class Radical Party and that, in its basic form, eventually encompassed the vast majority of the Chilean political spectrum – including much of the political right – at least until the military coup of 1973.

This statist consensus was part of the critical accommodation between middle-class and working-class political actors that made long-run institutional development possible. In contrast to the Uruguayan experience, it involved compromise among clearly class-based political parties as opposed to cooperation between two multiclass traditional parties. But the key fact remained that major innovations in the structure and strength of state institutions were undertaken with an explicit cross-party and cross-class political compromise, and elite reactions to this turn to the mixed economy and substantial protectionism ranged from muted opposition to open support. The contrast with Argentina or Peru could not be more stark. While Argentina came out of the independence era on a trajectory of institutional improvement, when the social question came to the fore, political parties were unable to agree on either the appropriateness of protectionist development or a compromise on the actual building of public institutions. And the various, ultimately unsuccessful attempts to move Peru in an institutionalizing direction were all met with intense upper-class opposition.

The large-scale entry of nonelite political parties into Congress and later the executive branch occurred in Chile in a comparatively gradual fashion. But the defining moment was when the Radical Party came to win the presidency in 1938 at the head of a broad Popular Front coalition that also included the Socialist and Communist parties as well as other smaller political forces. The very formation of the Popular Front was a complex political undertaking, as its social bases were quite diverse. On the one hand, the Radical Party was quite factionalized, representing both progressive middle-class reformers and traditional landlords from the Chilean south. At the same time, they were in alliance with a fragmented and populist Socialist Party and the orthodox Marxists of the Communist Party.

The 1938 election was a watershed, fought between the representative of the oligarchy, Gustavo Ross, and Pedro Aguirre Cerda, a Radical Party member who had risen from rural poverty to become a teacher and a lawyer (Palma 1967, 211). In a sign of just how nascent the entry of the masses into politics was at this point, the electoral results were quite close: 222,700 for Aguirre and 218,609 for Ross, who contested the result but ultimately lost (Stevenson 1942, 88). At the same time, conservative forces (principally the Liberal and Conservative parties) retained a strong majority in the Chilean Senate and a

Divergence Reinforced

plurality in the Chamber of Deputies. This put President Aguirre in the position of creating compromises that could win widespread support – both on the left within the Popular Front and on the right within the legislature. It was a task that, with respect to the creation of strong institutions of economic governance and the implementation of a developmentalist approach to industrialization, he accomplished.

It is critical to note at the outset that Chile was unusually fertile terrain for the construction of such a statist, and state-building, consensus.[4] Unlike Argentina or Uruguay, nearly the entirety of its foreign exchange earnings came as a result of mining activity rather than agriculture. And the mining sector – especially the all-important copper sector – was largely foreign owned. What this meant, however, was that the economic elite was not very dependent on a liberal trade policy for its own wealth. Instead, the elite relied on the domestic market for the sale of agricultural output and on protectionist tariffs for the profitability of the nascent industrial sector. Indeed, Pike notes that in the early twentieth century, Chile had already begun to import wheat (its dietary staple) from Argentina, and as early as 1912, exports of animal and agricultural products were outstripped by mineral exports by an order of magnitude (Pike 1963, 19). And the agricultural trade deficit only worsened over time – by the late 1950s, food imports were consuming one-sixth of foreign exchange earnings (Feder 1960, 92). Muñoz Goma and Arriagada (1977, 18) pointed out that even the Sociedad Nacional de Agricultura (National Agricultural Society; SNA) – the archetypal representative of the rural oligarchy – contained important voices that defended *both* agricultural and industrial tariffs. More so, then, than in Argentina or Uruguay, the Chilean upper class had much to gain from protection and state intervention – for even the oligarchy-dominated agricultural sector relied on it for survival. Nor was it an unprecedented development under the Popular Front, for substantial protectionism had begun to characterize Chilean trade policy from the mid-1920s onward (Finer 1947, 7).

What the Aguirre government did was take a history of increasing protectionism, expand the policy, and organize it into a comprehensive program of import-substituting industrialization, centered around a new economic organization – CORFO, or the Corporación de Fomento de la Producción (Production Development Corporation) (Faúndez 2007, 79). The creation of this very powerful institution – which survives to the present day – has been seen as entailing a "transcendental reorganization of the Chilean state" (Muñoz

---

[4] It is also important to note that this was a consensus about state-guided industrialization and protectionism. At no point was there consensus about substantial redistribution of wealth – and Chile remained throughout the pre-1970 period a country of very severe inequality. It was also the case that the peasantry was, until 1967, entirely excluded from the institutions that composed the post-Depression consensus. Until the Frei government of 1964–70, peasant labor unionization was forbidden, social welfare benefits were not extended to the countryside, and consequent clientelistic dependence produced substantial electoral support for conservative political parties.

Goma and Arriagada 1977, 7) and has been characterized as the "most important institution created in Chile in this century" (Olavarría Bravo 1962, 388). But it also embodied a political compromise, as we will see later, that helped it to survive over the very long term.

But while the passage of the legislation in part took advantage of the unusual political conditions that obtained after the devastating 1939 earthquake near the southern city of Concepción, CORFO itself was designed – through careful compromise – to be an institution that lasted and was effective. To begin, governance was crucial, for CORFO was to play a major role in the allocation of investment, especially subsidized investment, in the Chilean economy, and it is worth noting that between 1940 and 1955, public investment represented the majority of all capital formation in the economy (Felix 1960, 17). Partly to gain the support of conservative forces in Congress, the governing board of the corporation included representatives of the most important peak business organizations tied to the economic elite, specifically the SNA, the Sociedad Nacional Minera (National Mining Society), and the Sociedad de Fomento Fabril (Society for Industrial Development) (Monteón 1998, 257). It also included a representative from the labor movement, with the remainder drawn from the ranks of government. Further cementing the need for broad consensus, its development plans were subject to a requirement of a two-thirds vote of the board for approval (Finer 1947, 14).

The creation of CORFO was important from the perspective of state building for two reasons. On the one hand, it was part and parcel of the process of state building itself, representing a new and powerful penetration of the state into the governance of the economy. It was also accomplished in a unique way: the voices of a wide spectrum of stakeholders were built into its governance, just as on the administrative side, it was considerably autonomous from day-to-day politics. Its funding was guaranteed, being provided principally by earmarked taxes, particularly a 10 percent tax on profits from copper exports (thus providing it with a dedicated source of foreign exchange as well). It did not rely on the political process for annual appropriations or require ongoing legislative authorization for its activities. Its staffing was highly technocratic – in many cases drawing on the same engineers originally brought into the government in the late 1920s by Carlos Ibáñez (Silva 2006, 182). The political bargain that created CORFO as an autonomous entity, however, came at a considerable price: an informal agreement was reached that in exchange for the right's support for the CORFO law, rural unionization would be effectively precluded, and thus the political bulwarks of conservative power would remain untouched until the land reform and peasant unionization laws of 1967 (Silva 1994, 288; Kaufman 1972).

The formal center-left coalition that made up the Popular Front was of short duration – it collapsed in 1941 amid acrimony between the Socialists and Communists (Stevenson 1942, 110). But the basic pattern of governance – an executive headed by a Radical Party president in varying coalition with parties

Divergence Reinforced 149

of the political right and left – would continue until 1952. Indeed, none of the three Radical Party presidents of the period – Pedro Aguirre Cerda, Juan Antonio Ríos, and Gabriel González Videla – would have been elected but for coalition support, and the Radical Party at no point between 1938 and 1952 had a congressional majority (Snow 1972, 92). Despite this, and as a sign of the breadth of support for expanded statism, the CORFO-led project of state-sponsored import substitution proceeded apace. At the same time, the enfranchisement of the popular sectors continued, but only very gradually and in fits and starts, with notable reversals along the way.

In terms of industrialization, this period saw a dramatic transformation of the Chilean economy. Relative to its position in 1929, just before the crisis of the Great Depression, industrial production had expanded 340 percent by 1957, while agriculture and mining were scarcely higher than the starting point – 137 percent and 111 percent of their 1929 levels, respectively (Ballesteros and Davis 1963, 160–61). It was a period in which CORFO undertook enormous investments aimed at launching a heavy industrial sector in Chile. In 1943, it created the Empresa Nacional de Electricidad (National Electricity Enterprise) as a public provider of electric power in an effort to sharply expand access to electricity for the population and to make possible major industrial development (Palma Zuñiga 1967, 236). One of the most important such creations was an iron and steel industry launched via the creation of the state-owned Compañía de Aceros del Pacífico (Pacific Steel Company), which was authorized by CORFO in 1946 and entered into production in 1950. This was, however, much more than a typical import-substitution white elephant industry. Foreign observers noted that the firm had been entirely handed over to Chilean management (after an initial learning period employing US advisors) and operated at a level of price and quality equivalent to international producers. Indeed, after satisfying all of Chile's internal demand, it was by the late 1950s exporting as much as 30 percent of its output (White and Chilcote 1961, 263–64).

In terms of mass political incorporation, however, the story was somewhat different and far less rapid. During the period of the Popular Front and subsequent Radical Party governments, labor union membership expanded alongside progress in industrialization, reaching 250,000 unionized workers in 1952, compared to 55,000 in 1932 (Correa et al. 2001, 78). At the same time as literacy expanded, so did suffrage rights that were conditioned on them, reaching 18 percent of the population registered to vote in 1952. This was, however, still limited suffrage for working-class and peasant Chileans, for illiterates (until 1970) and women (until 1949) were still barred from electoral participation, and ballots were not secret until 1958.

The barriers to full political incorporation of the popular sectors went beyond the limitations on suffrage. From 1948 to 1958, the Law for the Permanent Defense of Democracy enacted by Radical Party president Gabriel González Videla legally proscribed the Communist Party, removing it and its leaders from political contestation. This was particularly important as the

Communist Party represented a major player in legislative politics and commanded very substantial electoral support among working-class voters as well as being very well represented in the labor movement. And even for those mass-based parties for which electoral competition was still allowed, vote buying and clientelistic control by elites remained a serious problem. It was not until 1958, at the end of the (this time elected) second presidency of Carlos Ibáñez, that the secret ballot was implemented and the ban on Communist Party participation was lifted. In addition, voting was made compulsory, leading effectively to unencumbered, broad suffrage for the first time (Grugel 1992, 183).

Why was the gradual and tardy expansion of effective democratic participation important? It made it possible for successive presidents over a sustained period of time to increase substantially the scope and effectiveness of public institutions. The late entry of the middle classes into politics – behind a statist vision of governance from the outset – coupled with an upper class whose material interests were not particularly tied to a liberal trade arena created a supportive coalition behind postwar import substitution. And the multiple restrictions on the entry of popular-sector actors into politics prevented these institutions – at least until the 1960s – from having a substantially redistributive character. As Drake (1999, 68) has summarized, the

mild social reforms that were implemented [between 1938 and 1952] were restricted to the cities, thus placating landowning elites. . . . [And they] channeled the populist mobilization of the lower classes into a Marxist framework but also into the established network of political participation and bargaining. The economic, social, and political crisis of the early thirties now found resolution through integration of the left and labor, plus the urban and lower classes, into national governing institutions.

As this book has argued, one of the key elements in the building of strong states in Latin America was the ability to form enduring cross-class compromises over the creation and entrenchment of institutions to govern the economy and provide educational and physical infrastructure. This was a sometimes tacit, sometimes explicit outcome in the Chilean case, where political parties of all sides for most of the period from the Great Depression through 1973 were strongly supportive of this basic policy thrust. There were strong disagreements about the question of redistribution – and these would become acute in the late 1960s and early 1970s – but basic developmentalist institutions and premises went essentially unchallenged. This enabled these institutions to weather the crises that would inevitably beset them. Later, we examine two such periods in which the development of the Chilean state was seriously at issue. First, I consider the inflationary crisis and stabilization efforts undertaken by Jorge Alessandri (1958–64), Chile's last elected right-wing president until 2010. Second, I consider the effects of the 16-year period of military rule under General Pinochet (1973–89) – an authoritarian government explicitly committed to the dismantlement of the developmentalist state and a massive retrenchment of the public administration. We will see that in both cases – and shockingly

Divergence Reinforced

in the latter – the quality and efficacy of the Chilean state's institutions were largely unaffected, and its position at the top of the hierarchy of institutional quality in Latin America was preserved.

THREATS TO THE STATE-BUILDING PATH: STABILIZATION AND COUNTERREVOLUTION

The path of sustained institution building that Chile had long been on was challenged at two critical points in the postwar era. The first came as a consequence of economic crisis and stagflation that took hold as the "easy" phases of import-substituting industrialization were exhausted. Once markets for low-technology wage goods were saturated, further industrial development required ever greater investment, especially of scarce foreign exchange. As this investment was necessarily in more increasingly capital-intensive sectors, the sectors employed fewer workers and were hobbled by the small size of the domestic markets for their output. Elected in 1958, conservative president Jorge Alessandri responded to these problems by seeking to pursue a serious liberalization of the Chilean economy and to reduce sharply the scope and reach of the state. This effort was unsuccessful and was followed instead by a radical further deepening of the scope and penetration of state institutions under the subsequent Christian Democratic administration of Eduardo Frei Montalva and the three-year democratic Socialist experiment of Salvador Allende Gossens. The second – far more substantial – episode of retrenchment came during the period of military rule by General Augusto Pinochet, who not only sought to eradicate the popular-sector mobilization and Marxist politics of the 1970–73 period but also eventually launched what many have seen as a radical dismantlement of the state and many of its institutions. In the end, as we shall see later, neither of these experiences represented a departure from the overall institution-building path that Chile had walked since the postindependence era. Instead, although policies changed during these administrations, the effectiveness of governmental institutions was not fundamentally transformed or undermined, even if state activity in some arenas was deliberately restricted. And in some cases, the shrinkage of the state actually implied a further strengthening of governmental institutions, when, for example, privatization of public services or pensions required the construction of an effective arm's-length regulatory apparatus to replace direct ownership or control.

Alessandri and Democratic Retrenchment

The 1950s were difficult times for the Chilean economy, and they produced some unorthodox political outcomes. In 1952, after 14 years of Radical Party government, antiparty outsider (and former dictator) Carlos Ibáñez was elected on a populist platform but immediately confronted harsh economic realities. On the one hand, the end of the heightened international demand sparked by the Korean War brought about a sharp decline in the prices of Chile's export products, while at the same time, two decades of statist industrialization had taken fiscal demands to new heights – to pay for a government that now employed more than 200,000 and expended nearly 42 percent of GDP (Kofas 1999, 356). This economic downturn was not, however, purely cyclical. The limits of closed-economy industrialization and foreign exchange shortage had also produced persistently high inflation, necessitating a turn to automatic wage indexing in 1952 (Bailey 1961, 542). Continually rising prices – inflation surged to 88 percent in 1955 – led Ibáñez to impose an orthodox stabilization recommended by the US Klein–Saks commission, which, while it reduced price increases, also caused a severe economic downturn (Drake 1993, 125). It did not, however, reestablish either long-run price stability or economic growth.

The problem was in important ways structural. On the one hand, the easy phase of Chilean import-substituting industrialization had come to an end, and further industrial growth would be much more difficult and require substantially higher investment levels and increased access to very scarce foreign exchange (Grant 1983, 157–58). These were not easily forthcoming, as investment rates hovered at a low level of approximately 10 percent of GDP, with over half of this already-small amount reflecting public, not private, investment (Felix 1960, 117). And most of what remained was private bank credit made possible by the injection of funds from the Central Bank, both into the private banks and to directly finance the fiscal deficit, at a high cost in terms of inflation (Grove 1951).

Jorge Alessandri came to power in 1958 committed to reversing the trend of ever-increasing government control over the economy, restraining wages, and deregulating international trade (Angell 1993, 143). Coupled with this emphasis was an effort that paradoxically strengthened state institutions – a sharp increase in the employment of technocrats in place of traditional political appointees (Silva 2006, 181). The effort to hew the liberal, technocratic line did not, however, last for long, and by the middle of his term, he was exchanging cabinet positions for political support with the protectionist Radical Party (Faúndez 2007, 89). The attempted departure from the statist development model quickly ran into further serious problems, as exports did not respond to trade liberalization as anticipated, and debt levels had risen alarmingly (Angell 1993, 144). At the same time, so, too, did the number of legal and illegal strikes in response to the austerity measures Alessandri had imposed, increasing monotonically from 120 in 1958 to 564 at the end of his term in 1964 (Barrera 1980, 1286). This mobilization forced Alessandri to make concessions, and inflation once again rose to alarming levels. Thus, instead of initiating a departure from the state-centric, developmentalist path Chile had been on since the 1930s, if anything, this experience deepened that trajectory. Chile's persistent economic difficulties – given the political and institutional structure in which they were embedded – gave rise not to opposition to statism but to a political ideology of "underdevelopment" that prescribed *increased* and more

Divergence Reinforced

redistributive statism (Ayres 1972). Indeed, the two subsequent presidential administrations embarked on a path of dramatic expansion of the state's role in the economy, including, for the first time, a major redistributive element. This reached its peak after the 1970 election of a Socialist, Salvador Allende, to the presidency and ultimately induced political conflict so intractable that the democratic regime that had been in place since 1932 was unable to survive.

Military Rule and State Institutions

The second great challenge to state building in Chile, then, came as a consequence of the bloody 1973 military seizure of power. While the coup came at a time of economic crisis, it was fundamentally a political reaction to the socialist policies of the incumbent Allende government and the political conflict it stirred. The former included the nationalization of the commanding heights of the economy, dramatic land reform, expropriation of foreign mineral firms, and a sharply increased state role in the setting of prices throughout the economy. The latter involved mass mobilization of urban labor and peasant unions (which also experienced vertiginous membership growth), countermobilization by conservative and Christian Democratic forces, and at times near economic paralysis as a consequence of this conflict.

In one sense, this military intervention radically transformed the institutions of government – those that involved the political regime. But what is of importance here is whether the radical economic and political *policy* changes initiated by General Pinochet's government beginning in 1975 in any important way affected the long-term trajectory of institutional development in Chile. Indeed, it might be expected that they would for several reasons. Not only did the military government come to support a radical reduction of the state's role in society, impose severe austerity (including the dismissal of a substantial number of public employees and serious pay erosion for those who remained), and emphasize the reliance on market forces instead of administrative institutions wherever possible, but it also sought directly to undermine the organizational foundations of working-class and middle-sector organizations that were the political underpinnings of the era of expansive statism. We shall see, however, that while the size of the Chilean state did indeed shrink (relative to the immediate pre-coup period), and its patterns of interaction with society and the economy were transformed, it nevertheless remained a very strong, administratively capable state. And in comparative terms, even the neoliberal minimalism of the Pinochet era implied a far more penetrating, powerful, and interventionist state than had ever been found, for example, in neighboring Peru under statist and liberal administrations alike.

The critical issue here is that, notwithstanding the degree of commitment to neoliberal minimalism at times characteristic of the military government, and its destruction of institutions in the political arena, the basic trajectory of institutionalization and professionalization of the public administration in

Chile continued through the dictatorship and into the succeeding years (1990–) of democratic governance under both the center-left Concertación coalition and the political right. Some institutional structures, much economic policy, and most state–society linkages were certainly disrupted. But many institutions remained even as their functions were transformed, and indeed, very important new ones were created. To understand the relationship between the military period and long-run state-building dynamics, it is critical to make a sharp separation of policy choices from the institutional structures that are charged with implementing them.

In policy terms, the military government sought in large measure to rely on market forces instead of administrative planning and industrial policy for the guidance of productive investment and the provision of important social services. This, it contended, would both make for better economic policy and provide a mechanism by which citizens would cease to look to the state, instead of themselves as individuals, as a means to provide benefits. In the process, it was argued that an eventual return to democratic politics would be possible, having eradicated the underlying social bases for leftist policies and fragmented working-class and peasant constituencies most supportive of statism (Garretón 1982, 362; Kurtz 2004).

But the military regime – contrary to much conventional wisdom – was not simply about privatization, marketization, and individualization. It also made substantial institutional investments alongside the privatization and liberalization of large swathes of the formerly protected and state-guided (or owned) economy. Indeed, the military's vision of the future institutional order was first laid out publicly in a speech by General Pinochet at Chacarillas in July 1977. In it, he proposed "seven modernizations" to important facets of the state (including, e.g., social provision, labor law, education, public administration, and justice inter alia) (Loveman 1988, 266). These changes certainly amounted to a policy of individualization and an end to redistribution (or, more properly, a shift to more regressive redistribution) as matters of policy, but they also implied the creation and/or strengthening of myriad public institutions.

The 1970s were a period of tremendous change in the Chilean political economy, and the point here is that despite the transformation in the goals being pursued by state institutions, there was substantial continuity in the *capacity* of public institutions to engage in policy implementation and, in fact, substantial further administrative development. Contrary to conventional perspectives, this was a regime committed to regressive policies implemented by an efficient but smaller state. It was *not* a regime that undermined the state or its capacity to act. We can see this change in two clear, and very important, areas: taxation and social provision.

There are several important things to note on the taxation front. The first is that while the military regime substantially reduced taxation, it did not produce *low* taxation. Instead, as we can see from Figure 5.2, it returned the aggregate level of taxation to normal (but comparatively quite high) historical levels and

Divergence Reinforced

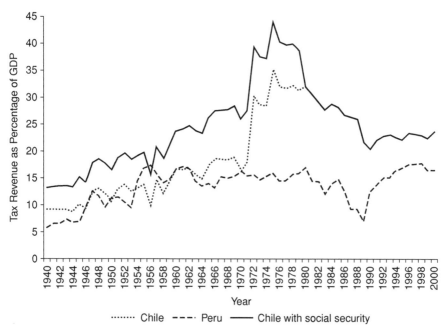

FIGURE 5.2. Tax revenue as a proportion of GDP, 1940–2000.

funded the state at a level compatible with very effective institutions. And the comparison with Peru remains stark: the allegedly minimalist Chilean military government, even at its lowest point, imposed revenue demands on society far higher than ever managed in Peru, even in the populist heyday of Alan García's first government (1985–90). And in overall terms, these generally were on the order of 25 percent of GDP, a comparatively high number for a country at this level of development and among the higher numbers in the Latin American region.

What the military did, instead, was consistent with a general pattern of policy change but continued institutional improvement. The taxation system was made stronger and more efficient, as well as more regressive, under military rule. For example, the military replaced an older sales tax with a very broad value-added tax in 1974. It also invested heavily in the Sistema de Impuestos Internos (the domestic tax collection agency), "which increased its registration and inspection capacities, significantly improved informational systems, [and] established a solid and cohesive professional team of administrators" (Bergman 2003, 606). And voluntary tax compliance levels are as a result very high (Bergman 2003). Tax collection continued to increase with the return to democracy, by an approximately 5 percent of GDP according to OECD (2011) estimates between 1990 and 2008, indicating that policy choice, not institutional capacities, was becoming the relevant constraint.

Similarly, the military regime was well known for its first-in-the-world full privatization of Chile's national pension system. This may at first seem to be an effort to rid the state of important functions and simply reduce public-sector capacity by ending the governmental provision of social insurance in favor of an individual compulsory savings system. But it is less widely recognized that the process of pension privatization actually implied very substantial *investments* in institutional capacity on the part of the military government. In fact, before the 1981 privatization of pensions, the military government undertook a massive modernization and rationalization of the fragmented (and class-divided) system of separate Cajas that had existed since the 1920s. Decree 3448 of 1979 created a uniform system of benefits and method of indexation (Borzutzky 2003, 87). This was a reform that had long been in the offing but had been blocked for political reasons in the democratic era. Even more important, however, after the privatization of 1981 was the creation of an independent and "highly efficient specialized supervisory body" for the pension fund and insurance industries that were created in the reform process (Queisser 1998, 40). This was both a costly and complex undertaking. And the neoliberal Chilean reformers did not opt for a minimalist regulatory scheme but rather undertook "Draconian" regulation in which the "pension supervisor issues investment regulations which list the instruments that are authorized for pension fund investment. They also establish quantitative limits with respect to the share of assets that a fund may invest per instrument as well as limits per individual issuer" (Queisser 1998, 44). Clearly the military was perfectly willing and able to invest in *new* state capacity, as long as it was consonant with the political–economic goals implicit in its policy choices.

In the end, the Chilean experience shows the importance of foundational moments for long-run outcomes. Indeed, it is all the more compelling insofar as efforts at institution weakening were in the end not particularly successful, despite the fact that this is typically a far less severe challenge than the inverse, the construction of strong institutions. Policies, governments, booms and busts, and even political regimes come and go, but the capacity of public institutions to undertake policy hews to distinct long-term patterns.

THE POWER OF PATH DEPENDENCE: EARLY MASS INCORPORATION, LATE INDUSTRIALIZATION, AND THE FAILURES OF STATE BUILDING IN PERU

The argument that is developed here about the limits of state building in Peru necessarily takes a very different form from the discussions of the intersection of mass political incorporation and political development in the other three cases – Argentina, Chile, and Uruguay. In each of these, an *initial* state-building trajectory was launched that was favorable to the development of effective political and governmental institutions. In one case, Argentina, this outcome was deflected onto a path of populist institutional cycling by the precocious entry

Divergence Reinforced 157

of the masses into political competition and the inability of middle-sector and working-class interests to come to a lasting accommodation around a shared policy of state strengthening. In Chile and Uruguay, through somewhat different political vehicles, such an accommodation was reached, and some of the most capable and extensive political institutions on the continent were constructed.

But Peru was different. As we saw in Chapter 3, it was decidedly not on a path to effective institution building, and the repeated failures to change this outcome in the twentieth century are as a consequence not entirely surprising. Thus, evaluating the role of the timing of the emergence of meaningful mass political participation requires a different strategy. We begin by examining two moments when there were serious efforts under democratic auspices to put together the sort of middle class–working class alliance that undergirded the successful development of state institutions in Chile and Uruguay but that ultimately made little headway. The final critical moment examines the effort by the 1968–79 military government to impose radical structural and institutional reform by suppressing political opposition rather than constructing political coalitions.

The first democratic attempt to change Peru's path came at the time of the 1931 elections, when APRA endeavored to create a winning electoral combination of organized workers and the new middle classes behind a program of statist development and institutional reform. This effort was frustrated before it got off the ground, when APRA was unable to overcome the conservative populism of Sánchez Cerro. The second moment came at the end of the Second World War, when José Luis Bustamante y Rivero was elected to the Peruvian presidency (1945–48) with APRA's support. This electoral coalition had strong majorities in the legislature yet was not able, despite trying, to initiate the institutional reforms and statist industrialization trajectories that were part and parcel of successful state-building efforts in other Latin American countries. Again, lasting political accommodation proved impossible, and neither economic development nor institution building resulted. The final critical moment from the perspective of the argument of this book is decidedly different and underlines the path dependencies involved in the state-building process. In 1968, a military government came to power in Peru that was quite different from the typical such regime: it was committed to wide-ranging structural reform of the political economy, including the imposition of the sort of land reforms that would fundamentally alter the underlying social dynamics in the Peruvian countryside in ways that more closely approximated the positive cases of state building discussed in Chapters 3 and 4. But they also serve to highlight the hysteresis that was here in play: because the timing of this social transformation long postdated the entry of the masses into political competition, the end of the servile agricultural economy did not – and could not – spark the effective institution building of the Chilean and Uruguayan cases.

The remainder of this chapter will lay out how the unlikely, and precocious, entry of the Peruvian masses into political competition further inhibited efforts at national political institution building and ultimately impeded it even when, belatedly, the underlying social foundations that had prevented the initiation of institutional development after independence had been transformed. It begins with an examination of the changes in the structure of Peruvian society at the time of the Great Depression and then moves to consider the way in which the political representation of middle-class and working-class voters came to be constructed. This is accompanied by a further discussion of the failures of elite groups to find meaningful mass-based political support – a dilemma shared by Argentina – and the consequent importance of coercion and military intervention to upper-class actors. We then move to a consideration of the political dynamics of the moments when very credible efforts at cross-class cooperation that was structured around the expansion and modernization of the state and economy were attempted – and why they failed. And finally, we consider the Revolutionary Government of the Armed Forces (1968–79) and why the very real structural transformations that it implemented – reforming land tenure and ending the large-scale presence of servile labor – were insufficient to launch a new state-building trajectory in Peru.

LATE INDUSTRIALIZATION AND EARLY MASS MOBILIZATION: A PERUVIAN PARADOX

The history of Peruvian labor mobilization presents something of a paradox. While by the time of the Great Depression in Peru, a recognizable manufacturing sector had emerged, a large-scale industrial working class had not. At the same time, however, given the comparatively weakly industrialized political economy, labor's political organization and mobilizational capacity were surprisingly strong. It was this early mobilization – which accompanied early political incorporation – that would help cement the conditions that impeded the formation of stronger political institutions throughout much of the twentieth century.

The Peruvian political economy at the dawn of the twentieth century had a substantial export focus, just as the economies of many of its peers did. Differences, however, are quite notable. In the Argentine case, export orientation had also led to the creation of a local industrial sector as well as the formation of a fairly extensive but outwardly oriented middle class. Unlike in Chile and Uruguay, the beginnings of a tariff-protected industrial sector in Peru had not emerged in any very substantial way in this era. Alternative, domestically oriented industrial elites were thus at best a weak group in Peru, and instead, an agro-export oligarchy opposing both institution building and centralization of authority was hegemonic among the upper classes.

The Peruvian economy could be broadly divided into three main components: on the one hand, comparatively efficient export agriculture, especially in cotton and sugar, characterized the coastal regions; traditional hacienda

Divergence Reinforced

dominance continued – and expanded – in the highlands of the Sierra; and finally, there was extensive participation by foreign interests in the mineral and oil sectors (Hunt 1971, 34). Indeed, much more so than was the case in other agro-export sectors, cotton production in Peru employed a comparatively large wage labor force and tended to be produced on small- and medium-sized farms in the 1920 and 1930s (Thorp and Bertram 1978, 154). At the same time, partly as a result of the road building and other infrastructural investment undertaken by the Leguía dictatorship (1919–30), highland haciendas grew in value as their access to markets improved, leading to their expansion – typically at the expense of nearby Indian communities (Stein 1980, 63).

On the industrial side, the pre-Depression era was one of substantial stagnation. There were two sides to this coin. On the one hand, overall economic growth was concentrated in the export sectors, with increasing participation of foreign direct investment on the part of US interests (North and Dos Santos 1970, 170). At the same time, Peru remained committed to a strong currency, and the sol was pegged to gold between 1898 and 1931, ensuring that devaluation that might improve the competitiveness of local manufacturers was impossible. The tariff system also failed to provide incentives for much local industrialization – in sharp contrast to the experiences of Chile and Uruguay. The Peruvians employed a tariff that was based on a fixed tax on the quantity imported, not one that was assessed on an ad valorem basis. And as a consequence, as international prices rose, the effective level of protection dropped sharply, from roughly 27 percent of the value of imports to 10 percent between 1902 and 1920 (Thorp and Bertram 1978, 125). Indeed, the only substantial revisions of the tariff scheme in this era raised protection on capital goods and intermediates – effectively *further* impeding local industrialization (Thorp and Bertram 1978, 126).

The end result was the creation of a formal sector that was centered neither in the state nor in domestically oriented industries. With respect to the former, even during the infrastructure-development push of the Leguía years before the Depression, the state was still comparatively quite small. For example, by 1929, fully 37.3 percent of government expenditure went to the coercive side of the state (the military, police, and courts), while only 11.7 percent was expended on education and 8.3 percent on development (calculated from Hunt 1971, 398). What infrastructural spending did occur was also not financed by domestic direct or indirect taxation. Instead, Leguía relied on the revenue tariff (further precluding the use of protective tariffs as a spur to industrialization) and, even more important, foreign indebtedness, which increased 10-fold from 1918 to 1929 (Pike 1967, 228).

The weakness of the industrial working class proper can be seen in the composition of employment in Lima – the principal manufacturing center – during this period. Stein notes that of the roughly 110,000 working-class jobs in greater Lima in 1931, employment in construction, informal service occupations (vendors, waiters, domestic servants, etc.), and artisans such as bakers, tailors, and cobblers were the most numerous (Stein 1980, 69–70). A key feature here was

160   *Latin American State Building in Comparative Perspective*

that very little working-class employment was in import-competing industrial occupations. The remainder of the working class could be found in explicitly export-oriented employment in the cotton and sugarcane fields as well as in mining. What there was not, however, was a substantial industrial working class or set of locally oriented industrialists who might have formed the foundation for the sort of statist and state-building coalition found in other contexts (Cotler 1978, 242). A similar story can be told of the middle classes. Unlike Uruguay or Chile, where middle-class occupations were very heavily concentrated in public employment, the limited scope of the Peruvian state precluded this outcome. Instead, the middle classes were concentrated in the ownership of artisanal production firms, which faced increasing pressure from foreign competition given the openness of the Peruvian economy (North and Dos Santos 1970, 170). Stein (1980, 74) reports that the most populous middle-class occupational category in Lima in 1931 was commerce, with 25,000 persons in that sector. By contrast, the public administration accounted for only 5,313 persons, and "engineers and technicians" only comprised 915. Clearly the middle class was linked strongly neither to the state and public employment nor, for that matter, to the dominant export industries (at least in Lima). The comparative statistics are stark. In data for 1925, Collier and Collier (2002 [1991], 67) report that factory employment as a share of the economically active population was 8.3 percent in Argentina, 7.0 percent in Uruguay, and 6.1 percent in Chile. By contrast, it was a comparatively paltry 1.2 percent in Peru.

What is striking, however, is how comparatively organized and mobilized the lower and middle sectors were in Peru, despite that industrialization was at best incipient in the years before the Great Depression. Rapid expansion of mining, especially through the United States–owned Cerro de Pasco corporation, fomented substantial labor unrest as early as the first decade of the twentieth century (Laite 1980, 321). Mobilization had also spread to metropolitan Lima, most notably when the longshoremen of Callao managed even to induce President Billinghurst in 1913 to intervene on their behalf and secure for them an eight-hour workday as well as to establish an office to impose compromise settlements where strikes grew too violent (Payne 1965, 38; Leite 1980, 322). This mobilization was taken to the next level when workers launched a successful general strike in Lima in 1919 that caused "the complete paralysation of activities in the capital" (Sulmont 1980, 22). In the end, the strike wave of the 1916–19 period, despite intense conflict and long odds, resulted in the implementation of the eight-hour day in Lima and Callao, and by presidential decree, for all public servants (Werlich 1978, 149; Anderle 1985, 86).

LABOR AND THE WORKING CLASSES ENTER POLITICS: APRA AND THE PERUVIAN POLITICAL SYSTEM

We saw earlier and in previous chapters that as the working classes and middle sectors emerged as important societal actors, they also – at different time

Divergence Reinforced 161

points and in different ways – entered institutionalized political competition and obtained representation in the political party system. This was sometimes in the form of catchall parties that represented cross-class combinations of workers, middle-class voters, and some elites, as in the Blanco and Colorado parties in Uruguay. In other cases, distinct political parties came to be based in these different social strata, for example, as in the Radical parties in Argentina and Chile, which were associated with middle-class interests, and the Peronists, who found a base in the Argentine working class, while the Socialists and Communists competed for this position in Chile. In different ways, the manner in which this political representation was organized helped to shape the possibilities for political cooperation around emerging state-building projects.

The parallel story in the Peruvian case, however, is quite different. In the era in which democratic political competition (however intermittent) came to Peru during and after the Great Depression, the formation of stable political party representation of important social actors posed a great challenge. Indeed, viewed from a distance, only one major political party in Peru has had anything like the durability of its counterparts in the other countries we have examined. In particular, large segments of the population have frequently been without effective, institutionalized political representation – including the burgeoning informal sector and, in many cases, the competing factions of the economic elite.

Peru was not, however, without any well-established political party representatives, for APRA, under the command of its charismatic founder, Víctor Raúl Haya de la Torre, for much of the twentieth century, developed a durable following and made a lasting imprint on Peruvian politics. Haya de la Torre's entry into politics – and later founding of APRA – was intimately connected to the rise of the Peruvian labor movement. Solidly middle class by background – his mother came from a landowning family in Trujillo, and his father was a teacher and journalist (Anderle 1985, 101) – Haya's political activity began in earnest at the time of the 1919 general strike. While he was a student at the University of San Marcos, it was Haya de la Torre who organized important student support for the workers in the strike. Thereafter, he was heavily involved in the launch of the "Popular University," which brought middle-class students to working-class areas to provide an education to which these poorer citizens would otherwise not have had access (Stein 1999, 102). This marked the start of the political activity for which Haya de la Torre was ultimately exiled in 1923 by the Leguía dictatorship (Werlich 1978, 176–77, 181). Indeed, it was during his exile in Mexico in 1924 that Haya officially first formed APRA.

Whom did APRA represent? While the party was cross-class in composition, it was not as comprehensive as, for example, the Colorados in Uruguay. With its strongest base in the north of Peru, the party initially counted as supporters parts of the organized working class, some middle-sector interests, and small and medium farmers in the north (Graham 1992, 25). Unlike the catchall parties of Uruguay, however, APRA never had an important base of support among the (themselves internally divided) Peruvian economic elites. Quite the contrary, they found themselves vehemently opposed to the possibility of APRA coming to power and frequently supported military intervention to prevent precisely that outcome.

There is some division over how best to characterize the ideological orientation of APRA, with something of a consensus that it became a substantially more conservative party as it evolved after the 1930s. The important feature of APRA's political program, from the perspective of this book, is the fact that it *could* in theory have served as the foundation for the consolidation of a stronger and more deeply penetrating state, much as we observed in Chile beginning under the Popular Front or Uruguay under Batlle. Its 1931 Plan Mínimo (Minimum Plan) outlined the parameters of what a putative APRA government might pursue. Elements of this plan emphasized expansions of education and social welfare, some (compensated) nationalization and tariff-protected industrialization, and the "technification" public administration and meritocratic civil service reforms, alongside comprehensive national economic planning (Cotler 1978, 236–38). By the standards of Latin America of the era, these were not radical proposals – they are in essence comparable to, if not more modest than, the reforms initiated in Chile and Uruguay under multiclass political coalitions.

A critical problem of the Peruvian political system of the time of the incorporation of the masses into electoral politics was that many elements of society did *not* have an effective, institutionalized electoral vehicle. While some elements of the middle class were comfortable with APRA (especially in the north among interests threatened by international economic integration), this was *not* more universally true. Indeed, a viable interlocutor for the middle sectors of the southern region, centered in Arequipa, did not emerge until the consolidation of Acción Popular by Fernando Belaúnde Terry in the 1950s and 1960s (Bertram 1991, 399). Meanwhile, as they did in Argentina, the Peruvian upper classes had tremendous difficulty in developing an electorally viable political representative. To begin, by the 1930s, they remained deeply divided between former supporters of the Civilista Party and the adherents of the former dictator Augusto Leguía as well as being cleaved along regional and sectoral lines over exchange rate policy (Cotler 1978, 232; Bertram 1991, 401).

Not only was there thus no viable political interlocutor with which APRA might cooperate in the interests of state building but the path of statist economic development and political modernization was further impeded by the decidedly small domestic industrial sector – leaving few members of the upper classes as potential beneficiaries and thus possible partners. By contrast, the political mobilization of Peru's masses came comparatively early, both in historical terms and in relation to the level of economic development. As a poor country, characterized by comparatively low levels of economic protection, Peru simply was far less industrialized than its peers at the time of workers'

Divergence Reinforced

163

political incorporation. The social foundations for a middle class–working class developmentalist alliance were also missing among the middle sectors. Not only were middle-class groups not particularly well organized, they were, as we have seen earlier, very heavily centered outside the public sector and thus had no material stake in either state-led industrialization or the expansion and strengthening of governmental institutions.

The early entry of the masses into electoral politics was thus doubly problematic for state building in Peru. Not only had the dilemmas that inhibited the modernization of the public administration in the postindependence period largely not been overcome – elites remained severely divided and free labor relations were not fully established – but the precocious transition to open electoral competition in 1931 further highlighted the risks to elites of constructing strong institutions: what would happen were they ever to fall into APRA's hands?[5]

THE POLITICAL IRRUPTION OF THE MASSES: THE 1931 ELECTION

Peru, like the rest of Latin America, was shaken after 1929 by the economic cataclysm that was the Great Depression. Its biggest effect in Peru, however, was perhaps not economic – for the country was less severely affected, and recovered more rapidly, than most of its Latin American peers.[6] With the onset of the crisis, which had a major financial component, the formerly plentiful foreign loans that had been employed by President Leguía to fund infrastructural development came to a sudden halt just as tariff revenues – the other principal source of revenue – were declining rapidly alongside the collapse of international trade (Villanueva 1975, 21). This brought the large program of public works, on which Leguía had staked his political credibility, to a sudden halt and sharply undermined the legitimacy of the dictatorship.

The political crisis came to a head, however, when a little-known lieutenant colonel, Luis Miguel Sánchez Cerro, took his Arequipa-based garrison into rebellion against the dictator in 1930. The rebellion rapidly gained steam and produced the ouster of President Leguía and his replacement by a junta that governed for six months, with Sánchez Cerro at its head. At that point, Sánchez Cerro was removed from the junta, which subsequently opened the way for the first comparatively free and fair national elections to select the next president.

This electoral contest – and APRA's Haya de la Torre and Sánchez Cerro were its principal contenders – was held under unusually free conditions. Not only were political parties, ranging from the formerly suppressed APRA and

---

[5] The answer would not become clear until 1985–90, but the economic consequences of this first APRA government were profoundly negative.

[6] Notably, Peru's export profile was less concentrated and thus less subject to the volatility inherent in the mineral-based dependence, for example, of Chile. See Thorp and Bertram (1978, 151).

Sánchez Cerro's political vehicle the Unión Revolucionaria, allowed to compete freely but the voting was conducted under conditions of ballot secrecy – in force since 1919 in Peru – with suffrage open to all literate men. This stands in sharp contrast to, for example, Chile, where the secret ballot came only in 1958. In Peru, free suffrage was available for a very large portion of the population in 1931 – though obviously a substantial portion of the indigenous population of the highlands was disenfranchised on literacy grounds. This literacy criterion was not at all an insurmountable barrier, however, as 85 percent of the registered electorate still had no more than a primary school education (Werlich 1978, 195). Stein (1980, 198), for example, notes that the Lima electorate was "overwhelming lower and to a lesser extent middle class in origin." Backing this up, Herbold (1973, 128) notes that mixed-race mestizos made up 60 percent of the registered electorate and that almost twice as many Indians were registered – despite the suffrage bar – as were "whites."

The 1931 electoral contest – and the events immediately after it – helped to crystallize political dynamics that perpetuated the inability of the Peruvian political system to come to accommodations across party and societal interests that might support the establishment of more effective political institutions. To begin, the conflict had only one organized partisan contender: Haya de la Torre's APRA. Although APRA consciously attempted to build a base among the middle and lower sectors of society, it was not successful in achieving the breadth of support it would need to win majority support on its own. In particular, its penetration into the unorganized informal sector was limited; this instead was the political base of Sánchez Cerro, who could use his nonwhite appearance to generate support on racial grounds, which he coupled with populist appeals founded on the renown he earned for deposing the Leguía dictatorship (Stein 1999, 101). APRA did, however, have very substantial mobilizational capacity, dominant as it was in the *organized* segments of the middle and working classes and given what has been characterized as the almost "blind loyalty" of its followers (Graham 1992, 26). At the same time, despite the upper classes' intense dislike for APRA and what they saw as its "radical" policies, elites were unable to form their own unified and viable alternative electoral vehicle, and they certainly could not attract much mass support (Cotler 1978, 232). Cross-class compromise with APRA was equally impossible given the severe differences in policy positions. Whereas APRA was arguing for statism and industrialization, the Peruvian economy had to that point produced very little in the way of a domestically oriented industrial bourgeoisie that might cooperate with (and moderate) such an undertaking (Cotler 1978, 242). As a consequence, despite the oligarchy's doubts about Sánchez Cerro, and dislike of both his racial background and appeals, as a practical matter, the upper classes lent him their support in an effort to block Haya de la Torre from coming to power.

In the end, the result was not particularly close. Sánchez Cerro polled 152,062 votes, whereas Haya de la Torre managed only 106,007, giving the

Divergence Reinforced

former a clear majority (Herbold 1973, 132).[7] Several important consequences of this electoral defeat followed. First, it became clear that APRA's support – concentrated among the comparatively smaller sector of organized workers and disadvantaged middle sectors – was simply insufficient to produce a straightforward electoral victory. This stands in contrast to Argentina, where the Peronist Party was able to create a substantial enough political base to come to power directly.[8] At the same time, the early advent of competitive politics and working- and middle-class political participation sharply reduced the possibilities for APRA to find political allies, for there was no large middle sector based in public employment that would be a natural ally in pursuit of the kind of statist development and institution building it proposed. Nor had industrialization proceeded far, leaving the possibility of substantial upper-class support around the promotion of national industry lacking. The oligarchy was far more connected to export agriculture on the coasts and concerned with the preservation of its political hegemony in the Sierra. And the fact that the construction of powerful institutions would put a dangerous tool in the avowedly redistributionist hands of APRA made elite opposition all the more implacable.

The response of APRA to defeat in the 1931 elections only served to further impede any hope of the sort of cross-class accommodation that made state building possible in Chile and Uruguay. Not only did Haya de la Torre declare the election's results fraudulent, but on July 7, 1932, APRA launched a civil insurrection centered in the city of Trujillo, its political heartland. But in the waning hours of the insurrection – which was being crushed by government forces – APRA militants assassinated approximately 60 members of the military whom they held prisoner (Pike 1967, 265). The government forces responded with a massacre of approximately 1,000 APRA supporters, and an enduring and bitter enmity between the military and APRA was born (Graham 1992, 24). It was a tension that was reflected in persistent military interventions over the course of the second half of the twentieth century that were designed to keep APRA from coming to power. But this conflict also served to make even more impossible the sorts of political compromises necessary to pave the way for serious institution building. In short order after the election and subsequent rebellion, APRA was banned, and its delegates were expelled from the Constituent Assembly, which was charged with writing a new constitution. But the alternative was not stable either, as President Sánchez Cerro's hold on power was to be short-lived – on April 30, 1933, he was assassinated by an APRA militant. This led to the takeover of power by General Oscar Benavides, who completed the fallen president's term and later seized power on his own,

---

[7] Further minor party candidates polled an approximate combined 41,000 votes.

[8] A variety of factors account for this difference. First, Argentina was a more urban country, given the dominance of ranching instead of agriculture in the countryside. Second, its industrial economy – albeit importantly export linked – had developed much more substantially than that of Peru, making the formal working class a much more important political actor.

166   *Latin American State Building in Comparative Perspective*

remaining in office until 1939.[9] It would not be the last time that the military intervened to block APRA – or an APRA-backed coalition – from coming to power.

BUSTAMANTE Y RIVERO: THE FAILED DEVELOPMENTALIST COALITION

While Haya de la Torre would never become Peru's president, and APRA would not itself manage to take executive office until Alan García's victory in 1985, Peru did experience a brief developmentalist government that was elected principally with APRA support in the immediate wake of the Second World War. In the 1945 election, coming on the heels of the Allied victory over fascism, the global political winds had shifted sharply in favor of democratic competition, making it politically impossible to continue the ban on APRA's political participation. It was an election that also coincided with a high point in APRA's electoral popularity. The result produced a president elected principally with APRA support (though not an Aprista himself) and a legislature in which APRA held large pluralities in both chambers. If ever there were an opportunity to cement a multiclass coalition behind a developmentalist agenda and a program of institution building, this was it.

In the 1945 election, conservative forces were represented by General Eloy Ureta, while a coalition of middle class–led elements, including the formal participation of APRA, formed the Frente Democrático Nacional (National Democratic Front; FDN) under the presidential candidacy of José Luis Bustamante y Rivero. In an open electoral context – and without the populist candidacy of someone like Sánchez Cerro – large swathes of the informal sector and peasantry had become unattached voters that might well swing to APRA; that said, Bertram (1991, 425) points out that APRA had limited success in bringing them into its orbit in a lasting fashion. Bustamante's opponent, however, was a conservative member of the oligarchy, and in this two-way contest, the result was clear: Bustamante won with 69.8 percent of the vote (Graham 1992, 28). In the legislature, the FDN coalition took three-fourths of the seats in both chambers, with the APRA component alone commanding near-majorities by itself (Bertram 1991, 428).

The brief presidency of Bustamante is an important period from the perspective of this book, for it draws a line under the importance of path dependence in understanding the possibilities for creating political coalitions that can pursue effective strategies of state building and administrative reform. This book has argued that Peru was not on a trajectory conducive to state building – an

---

[9] Notably, the 1936 elections were held on schedule, but after Social Democratic Party candidate Luis Eguiguren came in first – having sought APRA's support directly because APRA could not present its own candidate – Benavides intervened to overturn the outcome and remain in power (Bertram 1991, 418–19).

Divergence Reinforced 167

outcome achieved elsewhere in Latin America only through a developmentalist alliance of industrialists, the middle sector, and organized labor. What is critical about the Bustamante period is that it represented the best possibility (in democratic Peru) to launch precisely such a project – under conditions of unusually strong legislative support. And before the alliance collapsed completely, a developmentalist program akin to those common in other parts of the region had been launched. Tariff policy was shifted to favor industrialization, and strict exchange controls and multiple exchange rates were used to allocate resources in accord with state developmental priorities (Frankman 1974, 292). The critical issue we must explore, however, is why this state expansion and developmentalist program could not take root in Peruvian soil when it had prospered in other parts of the region.

President Bustamante initially hewed a politically cautious line, and his first cabinet did not draw on APRA members for the important ministries. Instead, he had pursued a middle ground between the demands of the Apristas and the traditional elite. This, however, produced only political isolation, and thus, in January 1946, he moved to a more strongly developmentalist position and placed APRA members in charge of the crucial Ministries of the Economy, Public Works, and Agriculture (Monge 1993, 263–64). This was also important because APRA and its political allies had a working majority in both houses of the legislature and had initiated an effort to legislate on its own (Bertram 1991, 427). A developmentalist policy was thus married to a legislative majority, and it could in theory have launched Peru's institutional trajectory onto a track more similar to that of Chile and Uruguay. But the context was different, owing to the unfavorable trajectory of political development on which Peru found itself (and the sociopolitical background it implied) as well as the precocious entry of workers into political participation, which further hardened elite opposition to state strengthening.

Given the vituperative reaction on the part of traditional Peruvian elites in the 1940s to the policy reforms supported by APRA, one would not recognize that they were in fact strikingly moderate by comparison both with Peru's Latin American contemporaries and indeed with APRA's policy positions of the 1920s and 1930s. APRA, despite its history of nationalist rhetoric, had begun to very seriously tame its anti-Americanism and had become much more open to foreign investment (Clinton 1970, 286). Indeed, by 1946, the APRA-controlled chamber of deputies had even approved an oil exploration and production contract with the International Petroleum Company (a subsidiary of Standard Oil of New Jersey), despite the intense nationalist flames that this would incite (Thorp and Bertram 1978, 168).[10] Nor did APRA at any time during the Bustamante period propose in the legislature any social or political

---

[10] Pike (1967, 284) even claims that by this point, APRA had even become the United States' "favorite political party" in Peru – a shocking transformation of an attitude that had formerly considered APRA effectively a communist organization.

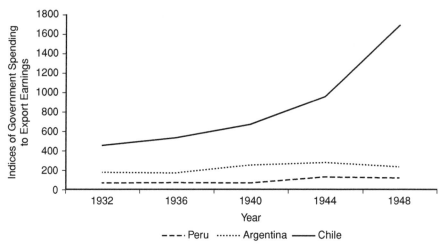

FIGURE 5.3. Ratio of government spending to export earnings (indices 1928 = 100).

reforms that would noticeably change social relations or property rights in a fundamental way (Cotler 1978, 264).

The point, however, is that even the very modest developmentalism of the Bustamante y Rivero era proved to be a bridge too far for the Peruvian-dominant classes. This result was a product of the institutional path that Peru had been on since the formation of its national state. For the powerful landed oligarchies of the highlands and the coast, the centralization of political authority – and the creation of state institutions strong enough to generate and distribute resources substantial enough to lead a program of domestic industrialization – was far too threatening. And an alternative urban–industrial upper class that would profit from such a strategy was all but incipient (Cotler 1970, 747). When this social backdrop was coupled with a surprisingly mobilized and well-organized working class tied to APRA (which, in its early days, had a radical set of policy prescriptions), this only further heightened fears that strong institutions would inevitably lead to unacceptable redistributive outcomes. And so the sorts of state-building compromises necessary to create a viable set of national institutions – and indeed, even much more limited ones – like those that were successfully enacted in Chile and Uruguay were impossible in the Peruvian context.

Indeed, when we consider the spending side of government, there is little sign that Peru made any significant strides in the direction of institution building or greater state activism. In Figure 5.3, we can see data on the ratio between government spending and export earnings during and after the Great Depression and the Second World War. The contrasts are striking – as statist institution building and protectionist development were launched in Chile, spending surged in relation to exports, exceeding a multiple of 16 to 1 by 1948. By contrast, only a gradual rise in spending relative to exports is detectable in

Divergence Reinforced

Argentina – despite the vigorous activity of the first Peronist government – and no meaningful change is detectable in Peru during the course of the Bustamante y Rivero period. Whatever reforms were implemented in Peru, they paled in comparison to the sorts of enormous investments in state activity in which the Chileans engaged.

While the political system proved – repeatedly – incapable of endogenously generating a viable transformative, institution-building coalition, a serious period of institutional creation married to developmentalism did finally occur during the 1968–80 military government. The lessons of that period are, however, an essential piece of evidence that only helps to underscore the path-dependent character of institutional trajectories proposed in this book. For even under sustained, authoritarian auspices, the institutional reforms of the military period left virtually no lasting imprint on Peruvian institutions.

ATTEMPTING TO CHANGE THE PATH: THE REVOLUTIONARY GOVERNMENT OF THE ARMED FORCES

Peru has attracted substantial scholarly interest for having experienced a very unusual form of military rule: a nonsocialist, progressive military government oriented toward national development and extensive social reform. While the development and ultimate failure of this 12-year period of inclusionary authoritarianism (1968–80) has been widely studied in its own terms, it is crucial in a different way for the argument put forward in this book. It is essential because the reforms undertaken in the military period – alongside its status as an authoritarian government – profoundly transformed the variables that this book argued in Chapter 3 had initially launched Peru on an unfortunate path of institutional underdevelopment. But if the path dependence central to the theory proposed in this book is valid, these reforms, coming a century too late, should not have been able to underwrite a turn in Peruvian political development toward the institutionalization of effective government and the deepening of its penetration. This is because path dependence implies hysteresis: the effect of any set of these conditions depends on what came before them, that is, in part, on how and when they were achieved.

This permits us to look at this unique period of military rule in Peru as a specific test of the structural, path-dependent claims laid out in this book. Indeed, it allows us to separately evaluate a series of critical causal dynamics. First, does a transformation of rural social relations – as was accomplished during the military agrarian and labor reforms – change the relationship between political and economic elites and efforts to improve public institutions? Does elite coordination – coercively arrived at in this case – under military leadership committed to quasi-Bismarckian approaches to working-class pacification enable effective long-run investments in the improvement of government and its ability to autonomously penetrate society? And finally, considering the post-Depression dynamics that are central to Chapters 5 and 6, what was the effect of *preexisting* working-class organization and mobilizational capacity on the efforts of the Peruvian military to build an effective and encompassing state where none had theretofore existed?

There are three critical characteristics of the self-denominated "Revolutionary Government of the Armed Forces," most particularly of its more radical phase from 1968 to 1975. First, the military under General Juan Velasco Alvarado aimed at extensive structural reforms, most notably including a fundamental transformation of property and labor relations. In short order, the remaining legacies of a semiservile agrarian economy were finally overcome, and indeed, a fundamental improvement to the basic rights of all workers was enacted. The Industrial Communities Law of 1970 was quite far-reaching; it went so far as to contemplate employee co-management and co-ownership of all but the smallest private firms. By 1971, this approach was broadened to include nonindustrial firms in fishing and mining (Robinson 1976, 24–25). And the problem of elite cooperation was rendered moot by virtue of authoritarian control and the fears that upper-class actors had of the political power that APRA would have as the likely alternative in a democratic political system. This control was further strengthened by the censorship or seizure of important media outlets.

State building was also very much on the agenda of this reformist military government. Its vision was embodied in a concrete plan (called the Plan Inca) for the dramatic expansion and improvement of public institutions as the cornerstone of a developmental strategy to be implemented by a state restructured along corporatist lines (Sanders 1981, 84). Finally, the military even tried – in an inclusionary corporatist fashion – to overcome the legacies of precocious worker mobilization, coupling a host of new benefits with a series of institutional efforts to channel and constrain popular-sector political participation. In short, the military moved aggressively to shift the underlying political and social realities that had long impeded state building and simultaneously sought the rapid and comprehensive reform and expansion of public institutions. The effort failed, and it failed convincingly across a variety of dimensions, underscoring the worrisome possibility that windows of opportunity for real improvement in governance and the construction of a strong state are not always open and, once closed, may remain so for long periods.

The Military Comes to Power

The political dynamics that led up to the military intervention of 1968 made it clear that a substantial program of social reform was unlikely to occur under democratic auspices in Peru. This pre-1968 political reality speaks to the inability of a cross-class coalition of labor and the middle sectors, linked to national industry, to coalesce behind a strategy of economic developmentalism and the strengthening of the state – the road that state building took elsewhere on the continent. Instead, essentially liberal economic policy continued until the abrupt transformation of the military regime under General Juan Velasco

Divergence Reinforced

Alvarado in 1968. Notably, this was in sharp contrast to the developmental strategies undertaken in virtually every other country in the Latin American region.

Why could the democratic political system in Peru not generate a lasting consensus behind institutional development or even industrialization? Part of the reason was the incoherence of the political party system in Peru – for as we have seen, it generally had only one long-lasting, institutionalized party: APRA. In the 1950s, however, the political situation become even more complicated, as APRA, in the face of repression under the Odría dictatorship, concluded the Pact of Monterrico in 1956 with presidential candidate, and representative of the traditional oligarchy, Manuel Prado (Bertram 1991, 441). This politically odd coupling of ideologically dissimilar forces was instrumental. In exchange for APRA support in the election, Prado would legalize the party, which had been banned since Odría's seizure of power in 1948. Further complicating matters, this cynical move suggested a long-term rightward shift in APRA's political ideology: the party chose to place an oligarch in power instead of attempting to compromise with alternative, middle-class reformist candidate Fernando Belaúnde. But Belaúnde and his Acción Popular competed with APRA for some of the same voters.

The beginnings of the military's road to power, and a precursor to the "revolution" of the late 1960s and early 1970s, came in 1962. In that year, the first wholly open electoral contest occurred in Peru since 1931, with General Odría facing APRA's Haya de la Torre and the comparatively new Acción Popular of Belaúnde. The election was inconclusive, with Haya de la Torre achieving a narrow plurality and strong congressional representation. The military, however, made it clear that it continued to be unwilling to permit the ascension of Haya to the presidency (Cotler 1991, 458). Cognizant of this, APRA was ready to transfer its support to Odría, but that option proved similarly unacceptable to the generals, in part because of the negative valence on the military as an institution that the accession of the former dictator would imply (Rozman 1970, 559). The result was a coup that imposed a yearlong period of military rule. But this brief period contained policy initiatives that, for example, foreshadowed what was to come: the military initiated a pilot agrarian reform in part of the Department of Cuzco and created the National Planning Institute, an agency that would later be central to its effort at statist developmentalism (Rozman 1970).

When elections were convoked a year later, this time it was Belaúnde who would win a narrow victory – on a moderate reformist platform. But with APRA and the supporters of Odría holding a majority in the legislature, even his quite modest institutional reforms were consistently blocked. Indeed, even a commitment to basic fiscal stability proved impossible as tax increases were blocked alongside the social reforms (Philip 1976, 40). Despite the fact that both Acción Popular and APRA allegedly shared similar reform priorities, they were locked in irresolvable competition and unable to form the sort of

Latin American State Building in Comparative Perspective

stable compromise that might have undergirded long-run state building. And of course, even had such a compromise been possible – APRA instead threw in its lot with conservatives and the oligarchy to undermine Belaúnde – it remains likely that the intense enmity of the military toward APRA would have prevented its effective consummation. And ultimately, it was just such Belaúnde–APRA cooperation, in this case around a settlement with the International Petroleum Company, that raised nationalist worries to unsupportable levels and provoked a military intervention.

The Structural Transformations

From the perspective of the theory of state building presented in this book, the military government that came to power in 1968 represented something akin to a best chance for Peru to depart from the unfavorable institutional trajectory on which it had been trapped. It embodied an effort, very late in the game, to initiate reforms that would remove historically critical obstacles to serious administrative and state development, including both direct efforts to expand and improve the institutions of governance and social reforms that would sharply weaken the oligarchies that had long inhibited political and institutional development. While the economic and social terrain in which the military operated was not nearly so favorable as in other cases examined in this book, the move to institution building and state-guided industrial development was not without more potential supporters than were present in earlier periods. For example, since the 1959 Industrial Promotion Law, a limited amount of protected industrialization had taken place, and manufacturing as a share of GDP had expanded moderately from 16.6 percent in 1960 to 20.2 percent in 1968 (Ferner 1979, 274). And as we saw, domestically oriented industrialists were an important part of the state-building coalition in the successful cases of Chile and Uruguay.

What is in fact most instructive about this period is that despite moving social and institutional reforms that were in many ways similar to but more ambitious than its peers' in the cases of successful state building (Chile and Uruguay), the military government managed neither to institutionalize a new direction for economic management nor to induce a change of trajectory off the path of administrative and institutional weakness that had characterized Peru since independence. As we shall see, it is precisely this outcome that highlights the critical path dependencies in administrative development: by the time structural change came to Peru, it was too late.

What did the Peruvian military government undertake in its self-denominated "revolution"? Although land reform had been discussed in Peru at least since the 1930s, the military government pursued it with vigor, redistributing some 10 million hectares of land among 340,000 peasant families (Schydlowsky and Wicht 1983, 103) in the form of agrarian cooperatives. While this only benefited a minority of the peasantry, its political consequences were

Divergence Reinforced

173

profound: "With the expropriation of the large *haciendas* under the agrarian reform, the agro-exporters of the coast and the landed quasi-feudal *gamonales* of the Sierra virtually ceased to exist" (Ferner 1979, 273). Thus did a principal barrier to state building – the implacable opposition of traditional landed elites – come to an end.

While the agrarian reform was extensive – easily among the most radical on the continent, surpassed only by Chile (1967–73) – it was only the beginning of the structural transformations undertaken by the military. Other wholesale transformations of property rights were also in the offing, as a massive wave of nationalization dramatically increased the state's direct ownership of the commanding heights of the economy. This began with the seizure of the International Petroleum Company six days into the military government and was succeeded by the creation of public firms in mining, steel, telecommunications, electricity, and even fishing (Schdylowsky and Wicht 1983, 105). Social relations of production were transformed – not simply by bringing wage labor to the countryside but even through efforts at worker self-management and ownership in industry under the Industrial Community Law of 1970.[11] While this effort was not strongly implemented, and ultimately watered down by 1976 (Stepan 1978, 273), it signals a radical break from the previous patterns of repressed, semiservile, or often-unrepresented labor. The reforms amounted, in their sum, to extensive changes to the property rights structure of Peruvian capitalism: between 1968 and 1975, the state-owned share of national production rose from 18 to 42 percent, while foreign firms declined from 34 to 13 percent of output and domestic capital's share declined from 48 percent to 35 percent. A further 10 percent was accounted for by (largely agrarian) cooperative production (Fitzgerald 1976, 62).

The changes in ownership were complemented by dramatic efforts to expand the reach of the state in institutional terms. In an effort to reorganize and make more efficient the public administration, new ministries were carved out of existing jurisdictions for industry, commerce, food, transport, housing, and so on (Schdlowsky and Wicht 1983, 105). The policy strategy was to be woven together by the rejuvenated Instituto Nacional de Planificación (National Planning Institute), an agency that had professionalized in the 1960s and included a "dedicated corps of midlevel planners" (Wise 2003, 89). On the financial side, this was linked to the creation of the Corporación Financiera de Desarrollo (Financial Development Corporation), the Peruvian complement to Chile's CORFO in the arena of development finance (Wise 2003). Associated public employment also surged, from about 225,000 persons in 1969 to more than 424,000 in 1978 (Wise 2003, 91).

---

[11] The law envisioned profit-sharing responsibilities on the part of firms that would be used to purchase equity stakes on behalf of workers, leading to the representation of the latter in corporate governance.

174   *Latin American State Building in Comparative Perspective*

The expansion of the state and public employment also helped the internal political consolidation of the revolutionary military government. At a minimum, it provided (lucrative) employment opportunities for quite a large number of active-duty military officers in the management of parastatal firms – and this employment allowed the officers to collect double salaries: one military, one civilian (Philip 1976, 44). But military reformism was premised mostly on the active support of the military itself, and it took place (at least initially) in the context of a "general passiveness of society" that gave the Velasco government great latitude to impose its transformations (Cleaves and Pease 1983, 217). But at the same time, it was a political project that did not have a solid societal base. Here the military found itself in quite a bind. It had earned the enmity of the traditional oligarchy through its agrarian reforms. But at the same time, the loyalties of large swathes of the middle and working classes were already bound to either Haya's APRA or Belaúnde's Acción Popular. To build a political coalition of beneficiaries of military social reforms, it would not be sufficient to organize the beneficiaries; rather, it would also be necessary to *displace* their existing loyalties.

This was the political legacy of early working- and middle-class incorporation in Peru, particularly as it interacted with decidedly delayed state building. The military government – directly or through a supportive political organization – could not lead the middle and working classes into politics; this had already been done, and durable political identities had already been constructed. The military was well aware of this problem and endeavored to create an inclusionary corporatist institutional edifice that would provide political support and supplant the existing political interlocutors for these groups. To do this, however, it began by attempting to clear the organizational brush, repressing both popular-sector organizations and those of the elite, including both the National Industrial Society and the National Agrarian Society (Wise 2003, 93–94). After 18 months of indecision, the military took a state-corporatist tack to generate a political base, establishing the Sistema Nacional de Apoyo a la Movilización Social (National System for the Support of Social Mobilization; SINAMOS). This was an alternative to the spontaneously born Committees for the Defense of the Revolution, which had emerged in 1970, and a traditional party vehicle, both options that the military rejected (McClintock 1983, 301). Its goal was to organize, channel, and mediate political support for the organic statist project of the military government.

This effort failed decisively. Stepan traces this failure in part to the fact that SINAMOS was a bureaucratic agency rather than a political party. It could thus not autonomously recruit a permanent and loyal cadre, nor could it negotiate flexible patron–client arrangements with local power brokers (Stepan 1978, 314–15). While SINAMOS was also the repository of progressive forces within the military government, it had neither a clear ideology nor a coherent set of institutional rules. The goal of SINAMOS was clear – to combine material incentives with repression to cultivate political support and to use its

Divergence Reinforced 175

institutional structures to replace traditional political intermediaries (Pásara 1983, 321). But instead of demobilizing opponents or creating social peace, SINAMOS paradoxically left the Peruvian popular sectors with increased rather than decreased autonomous mobilizational capacity and was ultimately seen as a failure in its own terms (Wise 2003, 96).

The contrast we have seen between Chile and Peru in the post-Depression era has shown how the second critical juncture – the incorporation of the nonelite sectors into national political competition – can serve to underwrite further political development or to raise ever steeper barriers to it. But these cases are fundamentally about the deepening of a preexisting trajectory. In the next chapter, we begin with two cases – Argentina and Uruguay – that had, by the late nineteenth century, initiated a successful process of institution building. Yet they confronted the dilemma of the social question at different times and in different ways, ultimately leading to a divergence in institutional outcomes. On the one hand, Uruguay (like Chile) experienced a deepening of its state-building trajectory, but Argentina was diverted onto an altogether new path – one of underinstitutionalization and populist–antipopulist cycling in its administrative structure. It is to this contrast, and its causes, that we now turn.

6

The Social Question and the State

Mass Mobilization, Suffrage, and Institutional Development in Argentina and Uruguay

We saw in Chapter 4 that the initial Uruguayan and Argentine state-building trajectories both were favorable – each country had initiated belated, but ultimately successful, national unification and institution-building projects. In this chapter, we consider a subsequent divergence in their paths of political development that came about as the process of state building faced the second great hurdle: the challenge of mass political incorporation. Here the two countries parted ways, as in Argentina, two distinct surges in nonelite political participation induced a dynamic that led to a persistent dynamic of cyclical expansion and contraction of state institutions without the institutionalization of state power. By contrast, in Uruguay, the onset of mass political participation was much delayed and channeled through elite-dominated political parties, permitting the construction of penetrating institutions to govern the political economy well in advance of expanded electoral participation. And these institutions themselves created incentives for political parties that made them self-reinforcing and undergirded their long-run stability even in the face of severe subsequent political and economic challenges. Conversely, in Argentina, the fact that expanded state institutions were the consequence rather than the antecedent of mass working-class political mobilization both undermined their society-wide legitimacy and rendered them ineffective as tools of political management. The result was a spiral of populist institutional expansion and antipopulist retrenchment – tied to cycling periods of democratic and authoritarian politics. Periodic efforts to form cross-class and cross-party compromises over the structure of state institutions were unsuccessful. In Uruguay, expanded political participation, mass mobilization, and inward-looking development were all accommodated within governmental and partisan institutional channels, at least until the breakdown of democracy in 1973. And in Uruguay, meaningful mass political participation tended to strengthen and deepen the state, not weaken it. The consequence was the creation of a firm institutional

The Social Question and the State

foundation – one whose basic contours were not fundamentally changed or effectively challenged by turnovers of partisan control, the collapse of democratic politics, or severe economic crisis.

This chapter thus continues the consideration of the second major branching point in the paths that define contemporary state-building outcomes in Latin America in two cases in which positive trajectories had already been launched. In Chapters 3 and 4, we saw that the absence of labor-repressive agriculture and elite cooperation was crucial to enabling the formation of viable national institutions. These institutions – in all our cases – were then subjected to two distinct subsequent challenges emanating from the political arena that would finally define their long-run trajectories: the political incorporation of, first, the middle sectors and then, more importantly, the working class.

This pair of challenges to the state and political leaders' responses to it – how they "resolve the social question" – are fundamental to understanding institutional development. But why is mass political incorporation a moment during which institutional development trajectories can be substantially changed? It is the inclusion of nonelite actors in national politics for the first time that puts the question of *redistribution* on the political agenda and thereby tests the limits of public institutions and elites' support for them. For by engaging the question of redistribution, institutions must channel and constrain the political activity not just of subaltern actors but also of the political representatives of the dominant economic classes. Whether they are up to this task at the point in time when mass participation becomes important and unavoidable is crucial and ultimately induces very different long-run dynamics depending on how they respond.[1]

What state-building outcomes can we expect in the wake of the inclusion of nonelite political actors, the natural consequence of expanding democratic rights? There is no single answer to this question, and this is why the first critical juncture (see Chapters 3 and 4) is so important. If elites had managed to construct strong central institutions of public administration in the oligarchical era after independence, these provided an institutionalized foundation through which the pressures of the social question could be addressed – in ways that could work to further strengthen and expand governmental institutions themselves. There are two mechanisms through which this can take place. First, well-established existing institutions can serve to shape, channel, and constrain the demand making of working- and middle-class actors as they come onto the national political stage. If such institutions are powerful enough, they are also able to deliver real benefits to popular-sector constituencies, thus providing an important incentive for the political actors representing the masses to operate within the basic institutional parameters of the state.

---

[1] The focus on the class divide and working-class incorporation as a theoretically central moment in political development is hardly unique to this book (see, e.g., Collier and Collier 2002 [1991]; Rueschemeyer et al. 1992; Collier 1999; Boix 2003; Acemoglu and Robinson 2009).

178   *Latin American State Building in Comparative Perspective*

Just as important, however, older and more institutionalized public administrations are more able to constrain *elite* political behavior and interests, for powerful, well-established administrative institutions necessarily have leverage over dominant classes as well, particularly when they are empowered by a broad coalition of middle- and working-class actors cooperating around a program of reform. We should recall, however, from the preceding chapters that such strong institutions were initially the product of elite action and were only created where elites could cooperate around their mutual interests while guaranteeing the exclusion of other actors from the polity. That is, strong institutions were built before the social question became pressing. Indeed, elites risked their construction precisely because their control by middle- and/or working-class political actors was not anticipated.

This very important constraining effect of early institutionalization on elite political behavior can operate through the usual juridical and coercive apparatus of public power. But perhaps more important, it can operate through a self-reinforcing process by which the new public institutions create new segments within the upper classes whose economic interests are linked to institutional persistence and continued development. As time passes and more and more elites find themselves dependent on public institutions for their positions of power and material well-being, efforts at classwide institutional rejection become ever harder to organize.

By contrast, where major expansions of administrative institutions happen as a *consequence* of the entry of the working and middle classes into politics, not only will these institutions have far less legitimacy in the eyes of economic elites but these same elites will be in a material sense disconnected from them: they represent something far closer to a pure loss. Elites will not dominate their staffing at the highest levels, will have limited policy influence, and they will often have direct conflicts with expanding state institutions over the revenue demands that they seek to place on upper-class incomes. That is, the institutions themselves become part of the redistributive struggles among contending political parties and social actors rather than channels that shape the form that redistributive conflict takes. Thus, where institutions emerge as a product of popular-sector mobilization in contexts that nevertheless were on an initially favorable institutional trajectory, they do so typically without substantial upper-class involvement, and administrative development itself thus becomes the terrain on which political conflict is fought, with elites and/or middle-class actors seeking to retrench or transform important institutions and working-class actors seeking to use and expand them to enforce redistribution or developmental goals. This back and forth thus becomes economically and politically polarizing and puts institutional development on a seesaw path of populist expansion and radical retrenchment as extrainstitutional changes to governments of the day – and even the political regime – can become ever more common and severe. And most critically, major governmental institutions will have great difficulty in attaining substantial society-wide legitimacy.

The Social Question and the State

Importantly, however, we must remember that the effect of early mass political participation is different depending on the ex ante path of political development. Institutional cycling occurs where the institutional trajectory was initially favorable. Where it was unfavorable, however, the outcome is not cycles of institutional creation and destruction (as in Argentina) but rather a persistence and deepening of comparative institutional underdevelopment (as in Peru).

The politics of mass entry into national political competition thus is crucial to the ultimate trajectory of national political development. This, in turn, in Latin America, hinged on the *timing* of mass political inclusion. This is true in two senses. First, as noted earlier, assuming that a state is already on a trajectory that permitted the consolidation of national political institutions, ceteris paribus, the longer these institutions have been successfully employed to manage national administration, the more institutionalized they become. Thus, time elapsed relative to the formation of national institutions affects the outcome. But there is also a second, more critical element of timing that has to do with the historical point at which the social question begins to become a serious political issue. The issue hinges on whether this occurred before, or during and after, the Great Depression. The potential consequences of early versus late mass challenges to oligarchical politics are outlined in Figure 6.1. Where inclusion preceded the Depression, middle sectors and middle-class parties develop and mobilize early. They are also typically societally centered in the private sector and linked to export-oriented firms or farms – which, after all, were hegemonic before the calamity that detonated in 1929. By contrast, the later emergence of the social question implies the entry of the middle and working classes into politics in an era in which state expansion and intervention are held in notably higher general esteem and in which middle sectors are much more likely to be socially located in the public bureaucracies. This creates a structure of middle-class material interests that is quite different from their private-sector–based counterparts in the precocious democratizers. And it means in the former that there is a shared material basis for compromise and cooperation between the political representatives of both middle and working classes around a shared political program calling for expanded and economically interventionist state institutions. But where the social question is posed early, there is more typically a conflict of interest between middle- and working-class political actors over the proper role of the state, rendering a political compromise around a shared vision of an empowered state decidedly less likely.

These are the dynamics we observe in Uruguay and Argentina. In Uruguay, critical expansions of governmental institutions occurred early, under Batlle's presidencies (1903–7; 1911–15) – and they occurred before, rather than in response to, substantial working-class or middle-sector protest and political participation. As such, they were created by, and with participation from, elements of both traditional, elite-dominated political parties. And many of these new governmental institutions were constructed in a way that made important sources of wealth for growing segments of the upper classes. They also

FIGURE 6.1. Institutional development and the political entry of the popular sectors.

180

The Social Question and the State

generated substantial hiring, providing the principal source of middle-sector employment, while at the same time driving industrialization and offering modest forms of redistributive social protection for workers and the poor. Thus, while Batlle certainly improved the lot of the working classes, and provided immense opportunities to the middle sectors via public employment, he also did it in a way that fomented a form of industrialization that was simultaneously very beneficial to large, private-sector interests (especially in the protected industrial sector), creating a broad array of institutional stakeholders. More surprisingly, and importantly, these institutions were created without a powerful mobilized societal or electoral presence from popular-sector groups. It was only well into the wake of the creation of these institutions – and the powerful vested interests they came to embody – that suffrage expansion was embarked on. This had two effects. First, it channeled political conflict into a focus on tinkering with the margins of existing institutions rather than creating something radical (or radically redistributive) de novo. Second, it made possible working-class and middle-sector entry into politics through the vehicle of the traditional parties (notably the Colorados but also in part the Blancos) that simultaneously represented important elite interests.

The opposite was true of Argentina. Although national political institutions were created by the 1880s, they almost immediately faced the challenge of rising middle-class and working-class demands for political power. Middle-class actors successfully broke into national political competition far earlier than did the working class. Indeed, a middle-sector political party not only contended effectively for political power by the 1890s but actually won the presidency by 1916. Working-class electoral incorporation came far later, beginning seriously with the ascendance of Juan Perón during the 1943–46 military government and his tenure from 1946 to 1955 as elected president. This period marked the beginning of serious working-class participation in executive power, though as a mobilized economic force, it had been active as far back as the last part of the nineteenth century.

The early emergence of middle-class political mobilization and demand making had two critical consequences. First, it put tremendous pressure on the only recently created institutions of national government. Second, it came during the golden age of economic liberalism, from a middle class that was principally private sector in occupational terms and that had strong economic linkages to export-oriented economic activity. That, in turn, implied an orientation of middle-class political representatives that was broadly supportive of the private sector and the free trade orientation of the pre-Depression Argentine political economy. While the middle-sector actors fought fiercely with traditional elites over *political* reforms and democratization, they held far less divergent views of economic policy and redistributive politics.

When working-class mobilization proved politically explosive in the 1940s, however, neither the institutions to accommodate it nor the material foundations for broad-based political cooperation existed. For the working class

182 — Latin American State Building in Comparative Perspective

entered politics under the auspices of a leadership strongly committed to protectionist and statist industrial development. This set the stage for the radical populist experiment of the Perón era – which was launched without substantial middle-sector or upper-class political support – and it opened a dynamic of persistent inability to institutionalize *any* definitive pattern for subsequent political development; the perspectives of each side were ideologically illegitimate and materially threatening to the other. Instead, a seesaw of populist institutional expansion and antipopulist retrenchment ensued, leaving in its wake a legacy of weak institutions of government and noncooperative politics.

BUILDING AND UNBUILDING THE POPULIST STATE: POLITICAL
INCORPORATION AND INSTITUTIONAL HYPERTROPHY
IN ARGENTINA

The initial period after the consolidation of national political institutions in Argentina could hardly have seemed more auspicious. Economic growth boomed in this golden age, lasting from the 1880s through the onset of the First World War, based on a tremendous expansion of the export economy; this sharply increased national wealth and, largely as a consequence, engendered unprecedented levels of European immigration and the onset of industrialization. It was also a time of political democratization, leading to vast expansion of suffrage and improvements to the probity of elections, especially in the wake of the 1912 Ley Sáenz Peña. One might have expected that this era would simultaneously be a period of institutional development – a consolidation and expansion of national political and administrative institutions, particularly given the unprecedented level of resources available. Instead, however, rapid export-oriented growth and comparatively precocious democratization laid the political foundation for an unstable long-run outcome: cycles of populist hypertrophy and institutional retrenchment, as political conflict was not fought *within* the boundaries of national institutions but instead critically hinged on *what* those boundaries properly should be. Thus did societal interests dominate institutions, rather than institutions serving to constrain interests in a way that would give the former durability and stability and, over the longer term, legitimacy and effectiveness.

But what could be so infelicitous about rapid growth and early democratization? The key here is the way in which they shaped the Argentine response to a challenge shared everywhere in South America: the social question. That is, almost everywhere on the continent, sometime during the first half of the twentieth century, national politics came to confront the question of how to accommodate the entry of middle-class and working-class citizens into a national political arena formerly dominated almost exclusively by members of the oligarchy. This was in all contexts a wrenching transformation, undertaken in the context of civil war and revolution in Mexico; rebellion, authoritarian rule, and

The Social Question and the State 183

military intervention in Chile; and unprecedented labor unrest in Argentina. But the way in which national political systems responded to this shared challenge also represented the final choice point in a long process of path-dependent institutional development.

Argentina confronted the social question earlier than Chile, Uruguay, and Peru, and Argentine middle-class and worker unrest during the era of incorporation was also substantially more vigorous than for its peers. At the same time, national political institutions had just developed with any durability, real unification having been achieved only in the early 1880s. Conversely, demands for popular-sector – initially middle-class and then later working-class – entry into the political arena came in the context of long-run economic growth between 1880 and 1914. This was a fundamentally export- and foreign investment–driven economic boom – and it created a middle class that was dependent on the export sector. As a consequence, its representative in the struggle for political admission – the Unión Cívica Radical (Radical Civic Union; UCR) – would subscribe at this time to a fundamentally liberal economic ideology, a position it shared with the traditional oligarchy. This was a natural consequence of the fact that much of middle-class employment was linked to export sectors of the economy, as opposed to being founded in protected sectors, parastatal enterprises, or the public bureaucracy, as was typical of many other Latin American countries. And because the economic elite was similarly liberal in orientation, no fundamental class cleavage had yet emerged in the political arena.

The problem, however, was that this sort of an economic commitment would later render a cross-class alliance between middle- and working-class political representatives around the expansion of the state and internally oriented industrialization decidedly problematic.[2] This left Argentina without the possibility of a mass political consensus about the role of the state in the broader political economy at the moment of incorporation – instead, it faced intractable political conflict fought in large measure on this very dimension. The working class, while quite mobilized early on, fully entered democratic politics *after* the Great Depression, under the tutelage of Juan Perón, and backed a Peronist Party committed to extensive public intervention, protectionism, and corporatist institutional structures. Indeed, the working class was at once very substantially enlarged – and unionized – in these protected sectors, which grew explosively during Perón's government. The middle-class Radicals, whose base was not so squarely among public employees as in Chile and Uruguay, were also largely in

---

[2] Note that I make no claim that inward-looking industrialization was a better economic choice than an economically liberal development strategy. The crucial issue is that by the time of working-class entry into politics after the Great Depression, there was no political foundation in Argentina for a statist and developmental alliance of middle-class and working-class actors around a protectionist economic policy. And it was just such an alliance – dependent as it is on a large and effective state administration and state-owned enterprise sector – that stabilized national political institutions in Uruguay and Chile.

184   *Latin American State Building in Comparative Perspective*

opposition in this period and thus did not help define the protectionist development strategy. They were, instead, a leading opponent of Perón's corporatism and extreme protectionism and saw their supporters systematically *excluded* from rapidly expanding public employment. At the same time, the economic oligarchy was vituperatively opposed to protectionist industrialization and the corporatist organization of labor while, at the same time, frequently in bitter conflict with the UCR over other issues. This pattern of cross-party and cross-class noncooperation would ultimately become a central feature of postwar Argentine politics, a divide too well established to bridge even when the UCR later (at least in part) abandoned its commitment to small-state economic orthodoxy. And as periods of protectionism brought about the emergence of a new domestically oriented industrial sector, it too was unable to sustain a stable, long-term alliance either with the developmentalist project of the Peronists or with the more liberal project of the traditional agro-oligarchy (O'Donnell 1978).

The consequence in Argentina was a political battle that was organized around the appropriate institutional organization of the state and its relationship to the economy. This underwrote a populist–antipopulist cycle that persisted for two generations, in which popular-sector actors demanded the expansion of state institutions and economic intervention, whereas antipopulists tried to disarticulate corporatist institutions, liberalize economic policy, and emphasize private rather than public enterprise. It was, as a consequence, a period of uninstitutionalized political institutions – they at times expanded rapidly and intervened forcefully (most notably in the 1946–55 Perón administration). But a consensus never developed over the proper structure of state institutions; they were not able to obtain the legitimacy achieved in other contexts and were constantly a central axis of political contestation, all of which made them much more the products of contemporaneous political conflict rather that forces that shaped or constrained it. We will see in the following sections how the legacy of the era of mass political inclusion produced the cyclical trajectory that has proven impossible – for democratic and authoritarian governments alike – to substantially alter. Indeed, the institutional cycling continues to this day as the statism and nationalization of Kirchner and Fernández replaced the liberalism and deregulation of Menem.

ECONOMIC EXPANSION, IMMIGRATION, AND THE RISE OF
THE SOCIAL QUESTION

As we saw in Chapter 4, national unification in the 1880s brought with it access to foreign loans and foreign investment that helped make possible a massive improvement in economic infrastructure, including vertiginous expansion of the rail network and the improvement of the port of Buenos Aires. At the same time, Roca's victory in 1880 consolidated national institutions by abolishing provincial militias, federalizing the city of Buenos Aires (thus undermining the

The Social Question and the State

autonomy of the larger province) and creating a political instrument of governance, the Partido Autonomista Nacional (PAN) (Corblet et al. 1965, 36–44). That state building was on the agenda is obvious even from the government's very slogan – *Paz y Administración* (Peace and Administration).

The postunification period did indeed take off like a shot. Between 1869 and 1914, the national population more than tripled (from 1.7 to 7.9 million), and this was accompanied by rapid urbanization, including a 10-fold increase in the population of some provincial cities. And between 1880 and 1914, economic growth managed to average an astounding 5 percent per year (Gallo 1993, 82–84). This economic growth was inextricably tied to the United Kingdom, with over 80 percent of foreign direct investment coming from the United Kingdom in 1900, declining only to 73.2 percent in 1913 at the onset of the First World War (for 1900, see Merkx 1968, 51; for 1913, see Teichman 1982, 53). This sustained economic investment and development fueled an immense surge of European immigration to Argentina (accounting for the bulk of the population increase), as more than 5.9 million people arrived and more than 3.19 million people settled permanently in the 1871–1914 period (Gallo 1993, 83).

The engine of economic growth for Argentina in this period was squarely in the export sector. It overwhelmingly comprised cereal and meat exports, and these were in turn overwhelming received by the United Kingdom (Merkx 1968, 48). There were political implications of this export-led growth experience that ultimately had profound, and infelicitous, consequences for the development of national institutions, though not necessarily for the national economy. The pre-Depression success of the export economy in Argentina and the deep economic dependence on the United Kingdom, the paramount promoter of free-trade policies in this era, generated a commitment by Argentine political forces – whether oligarchical or middle class – in favor of open economic policies.[3] This was mirrored in the organization of economic activity, for the Argentine oligarchy was firmly tied to the primary sector (Hora 2001). Non-livestock (industrial) investment was left largely in the hands of foreign – especially English – producers, as was much of the carrying trade (Teichman 1982, 48, 55).

Very importantly, the Argentine middle classes experienced substantial, comparatively early growth during this pre–World War I period – this stratum accounted for between 12 and 15 percent of the economically active population in 1869, rising to 35 to 40 percent by 1914. But unlike many other Latin American contexts, this was a middle sector largely linked to export agriculture and agricultural commercialization, not public employment (Gallo 1993, 86). This fact would become crucial in the first half of the twentieth century, as it precluded the formation of a viable cross-class political coalition with working-class representatives behind a shared program of public institution building and government expansion. In Argentina, as we will see later, the

---

[3] Indeed, in the pre–World War I period, even the Argentine Socialist Party supported free trade.

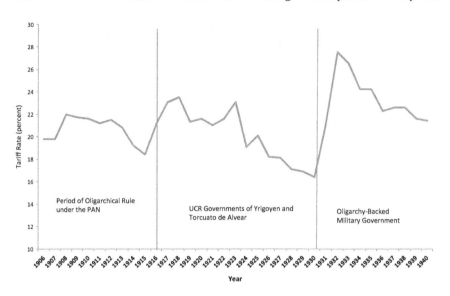

FIGURE 6.2. Import duties in Argentina (tariffs as a percentage of tariff value of merchandise imports).

middle sectors entered politics through the vehicle of the UCR, which held the presidency between 1916, and the collapse of democracy and the onset of oligarchy-linked military rule in 1930, and this party drew its support heavily from individuals linked to the export sector (Gallo and Sigal 1963, 201). During its time in executive power, it became clear that the UCR had irreconcilable differences with the representatives of the Argentine oligarchy, which helped to overthrow it in 1930, but also that it did not differ with the oligarchy on one critical issue: the reliance on free trade and the commitment to the agro-ranching sector. It was not a party, then, committed to the promise of protected industrial development – this would become a core interest, by contrast, of working-class actors, whose serious electoral participation came after the onset of the Great Depression.

This free-trade policy commitment can be seen in data on import duties in Argentina. The total share of import duties as a percentage of the tariff value of merchandise imports varied almost not at all across oligarchical, UCR, and military governments in the first half of the twentieth century. Indeed, in Figure 6.2, we can see that the Radical governments that took power after 1916, if anything, *decreased* the level of protection relative to their oligarchy-backed predecessors, and tariff rates were raised (and not all that dramatically) only after the conservative military government that took power in 1930 was confronted by global trade closure and the Great Depression. And at the levels they imposed, protection was still quite modest by the standards of the day. There

The Social Question and the State

are also indicators of ongoing institutional weakness even in as important an area as the taxation of foreign trade. Díaz-Alejandro (1967, 78) points out that the Argentine state did not even tax imports on a traditional ad valorem basis, which requires accurate information on prices paid for merchandise imports, but instead relied on far simpler *aforos*, assigned estimated unit values for each item, which were in practice rarely updated. Indeed, he concludes that the "Argentine public sector [before 1940], in spite of the efforts of some outstanding civil servants, was not sufficiently energetic to tackle the complicated issue of tariff revision" (Díaz-Alejandro 1967, 97).

And of course, throughout the 1930s, the oligarchy-backed Argentine military government's response to the global catastrophe of the Great Depression was strikingly orthodox. While it is true that convertibility of the currency was suspended – as it was nearly everywhere – this was done in the interests of maintaining the ability to pay the external debt and continue trade (Alhadeff 1986, 103–4). Thus, foreign exchange was rationed and given over preferentially to the payment of external obligations. Moreover, the government locked in the national orientation toward the external sector via the Roca–Runciman pact, which cemented Argentina squarely in the sterling area. The pact committed the United Kingdom to a substantial funding loan in sterling as well as to minimum purchase quotas of Argentine chilled beef in exchange for a strongly preferential trading arrangement for English exports. Substantial tariffs were imposed on manufactured goods from the United States, whereas the United Kingdom was exempted from them – making the United Kingdom Argentina's principal supplier of manufactured goods. And in the process, the low level of protection from English manufactured imports all but precluded a broad-based process of domestic industrialization. The legacies of this agreement would become even more problematic after the Second World War, as Argentina's large accumulated foreign exchange holdings of pounds sterling – then inconvertible – could not be used to purchase much-needed industrial inputs from the United States.

The point here, however, is not about economic policy; rather, it underscores the position of the major players in Argentine politics with respect to state institutions. From the perspective of the export oligarchy, a process of state-guided, domestically oriented industrialization was simply not in the cards. Just as important, the rising mass-based middle-class UCR was also opposed to such an effort, underscoring the fact that its social base was *not* in an extensive public-sector bureaucracy or parastatal manufacturing sector that would benefit from the sort of sharp expansion of public activity that was occurring in other places such as Chile and Uruguay.

These issues were, however, only a prelude, as one final actor had only just entered the scene in Argentina. The industrial working class, whose numbers had expanded sharply during the postunification economic boom, was not in the 1910s through 1930s a major political player. During the era of Radical Party dominance under Yrigoyen and Alvear (collectively, 1916–30), its numbers were heavily concentrated among noncitizen populations, and as such, they

188   *Latin American State Building in Comparative Perspective*

were ineligible to vote. And although there was substantial labor mobilization, both Radical Party and oligarchical governments were anything but tolerant of it. Instead, repression was the modal response.

Timing Is Everything

In two ways, issues of timing became crucial here in ways that had very long-run implications. Every South American country that successfully initiated a process of state building in the nineteenth century would face the challenge of expanding the political arena to middle- and working-class actors. Indeed, even Peru, not on such a path, was also eventually faced with this task. But the timing of this entry, relative to the establishment of viable national political institutions, is important. Institutions work through time – and the longer they are able to survive, the greater effect they have on the society and polity. Generally, where they are effective, they help to channel political competition in ways that are compatible with, and reinforcing of, status quo institutions. That is, they create a set of dynamics that can tend to lock in their structures. This can happen by creating a coordination of expectations – for example, around the de jure and de facto avoidance of successive reelection of presidents, or the possibility of the rotation of power across political factions, or the comparative probity of electoral tabulations – outcomes we saw, for instance, in nineteenth-century Chile. It can also happen by creating actors in society that have vested interest in the survival of governmental institutions (and concomitantly, by weakening the economic and political power of those who might desire substantial institutional transformation). It also reduces the transaction costs of enacting policies that are consistent with existing institutional structures and raises such costs for those that are inconsistent with them. In short, the longer institutions survive, the more likely they are to survive new challenges.

The first problem confronting Argentina at the dawn of the social question was that the consolidation of its national institutions was of very recent vintage – indeed, not really completed until 1880. At the same time, owing in part to its remarkable economic success in the late nineteenth and early twentieth centuries, it was faced with the challenges of the social question before most of its peer nations; governments of the day confronted middle- and working-class actors who were more powerful, more militant, and more mobilized. Sustained economic growth had fueled the rapid expansion of both social groups, and this brought demands for political inclusion. The second way in which timing is critical is with regard to the issue of *when* the social question enters the center of political competition – well before, or during and after, the Great Depression. The critical issue here is the underlying structure of interests in society at the time that popular-sector incorporation takes place. We saw in Argentina that electoral incorporation for the middle class began at roughly the turn of the century and was firmly established after the suffrage expansion of the

The Social Question and the State

Sáenz-Peña law of 1912, which helped produce the subsequent UCR dominance in the electoral arena (from 1916 until the coup of 1930). This move to universal male suffrage and the secret ballot had definitively enfranchised the middle sectors, while still leaving out the bulk of the working class, which was still comprised very heavily of noncitizen immigrants (Borón 1972, 229, 233).

The issue of central importance here is that the middle sectors came to political dominance just at the end of the long export-led boom of the 1880–1914 period – and that the middle sectors themselves were largely creations of that economic boom. Where the middle class entered politics around the onset of the Great Depression or thereafter, by contrast, it was almost always based on a foundation in the public sector. Where it entered well before that date, it almost always had a private-sector, often export-linked background, given the prevailing open economy in the era of the global gold standard.

This matters critically because of its effects on domestic politics. Building strong state institutions happens much more easily when a fairly stable cross-class consensus as to the scope and role of public institutions is developed. But this requires compromise, and typically a substantial cross-class compromise, that is ultimately reinforced by durable political bargains. That is, contending parties eventually have to take the existence of expanded and empowered state institutions off the agenda for debate, focusing instead on policy choices within these institutional confines. But for this to occur, parties of a wide variety of ideological positions have to understand an expanded state as nonthreatening, or perhaps even beneficial, for their diverse underlying core constituencies.

As we have seen, the early emergence of the middle classes – before the trade collapse of the Great Depression – meant that its core societal location was in neither the domestic industrial sector nor the public sector. And this in turn led to a commitment on the part of its political representative – the UCR – to liberal patterns of economic organization (Moran 1970, 28). Moreover, uncommitted in this era to industrialization, the UCR as a party had also been quite hostile to organized labor and the working class. Radical president Yrigoyen, for example, used the navy to crush a meatpacking strike in 1917, and UCR president Alvear refused even to enforce the existing law imposing price limits on beef for domestic consumption (Smith and Sylvestre 1967, 807–17). At the same time, the ties of the UCR governments to the traditional elite were strong: during the first Yrigoyen presidency (1916–22), and that of Alvear (1922–28), 62.5 and 53.9 percent of cabinet positions, respectively, were filled by members of the oligarchy's premier interest group, the Sociedad Rural Argentina (Argentina Rural Society; SRA) (Smith and Sylvestre 1967, 806). Only in the two-year period of Yrigoyen's second term (1928–30) did middle-class actors occupy a majority of cabinet positions. By contrast, the working class in Argentina entered electoral politics in a serious way only in the wake of the Great Depression, at the end of the Second World War. As a consequence, it was increasingly located in a new domestically oriented industrial sector (that itself emerged in important measure because of the collapse of global trade after

1929) and that expanded sharply through the protectionist industrialization of the government of Perón (1946–55).

The *political* entry of the working class – via its massive electoral support for Perón in the 1940s and 1950s – was preceded by very substantial working-class union mobilization on the economic front as early as the 1900s. Workers were unionized and pursued vigorous mobilizational tactics from the 1890s onward, including massive strikes, often followed by brutal government repression. And the absolute size of the industrial working class was simultaneously increasing rapidly as the collapse of world trade in the 1930s drove an unplanned process of import-substituting industrialization. James (1988, 7) reports, for example, that the size of the industrial working class expanded from 435,816 workers in 1935 to 1,056,673 in 1946, all taking place before the massive state-led industrialization campaign of the Perón government. This rapid and mobilized industrialization implied a challenge similar to the one identified by Luebbert (1987) for the interwar incorporation of labor in Europe: only some form of major institutional imposition – corporatism – could possibly stabilize the sudden entry of the working class into politics. And this is precisely what the Perón government essayed, albeit hewing much more closely to the authoritarian variant of corporatism than the democratic. Undergirding this effort was an initial political coalition that encompassed both the newly created bourgeoisie in the expanding industrial sectors as well as (most critically) the large industrial working class. Both were united in their support of protection, public subsidy and regulation, and the increased taxation of the export sector.

The Political Entry of the Working Class

While the middle classes had entered politics via the UCR in the 1910s and 1920s, the real effective participation of the broad mass of the working class would await the 1940s, as expansion of the political arena was interrupted in 1930 by a military coup that precluded real political competition for more than a decade. And this delay also permitted the formerly largely immigrant working class to obtain citizenship (and thus voting rights) either through birth or naturalization. The process of reopening politics began, ironically enough, with the progressive military coup of 1943, in which Juan Perón was a participant. It is well understood that Perón subsequently used his positions in the military government as Secretary of Labor, beginning in December 1943, and later as vice president in 1944, to impose substantial pro-worker policies, encourage unionization, and settle labor disputes in favor of employees – all of which helped him build a powerful following in the industrial working class. This would stand him in good stead, as the military government of which he was a member, fearing his increasing power, placed him under house arrest in October 1945. He was released shortly thereafter on the heels of massive worker mobilization (Ranis 1979, 321), paving the way for his ascendency to the presidency.

The Social Question and the State 191

The initial political incorporation of the Argentine working class thus came with the 1946 elections, convoked by the military junta and won by Juan Perón. Perón won a comparatively narrow victory, based very heavily on working-class voters, against an alliance that spanned the spectrum from most of the middle-class UCR to the traditional oligarchy and even the Communist and Socialist parties (whose support base in the labor movement was rapidly evaporating as workers moved en masse to back Perón and Peronist unions). This election was emblematic of the organization of political conflict as it would occur over the next half-century. Whenever open political competition was allowed, partisan competition centered importantly around a bipolar struggle between the UCR and the Peronists. The sorts of center–left cross-class alliances found in cross-party terms in Chile during the popular front governments (1938–52) or in the form of a progressive, centrist Christian Democratic government of 1964–70, and both within and across parties in Uruguay under Batlle and thereafter, were simply impossible in Argentina. Instead, the UCR would lead the civilian opposition to Peronism for the subsequent half-century.[4]

The turn to a government oriented toward the working class under Perón brought with it a vertiginous process of institutional creation and public policy transformation. It did not, however, bring with it a meaningful process of institutionalization. What was accomplished instead was the anchoring of one pole in the overall axis of political competition in Argentina – a competition that would ultimately be fought over the very structure of the institutions that shaped the organization of the working class, governed the economy, and even imposed the rule of law.

In what would become a decidedly infelicitous precedent, Perón began his administration with a political purge, removing from the public service large numbers of bureaucratic personnel hired by previous governments – so that they could be replaced by Peronist loyalists.[5] This sort of practice was not entirely an innovation of the incoming Peronist government, of course. To that time, the Argentine bureaucracy was not covered by any coherent system of hiring and firing rules. Indeed, only a few general characteristics (e.g., age of 18 years or greater, citizenship) were universally required by law for hiring, and in practice "every federal ministry or board would hire, with or without examination, and dismiss, with or without acceptable reasons" (García-Zamor 1968, 139). But the purging of the bureaucracy just as a massive expansion of the state by Perón was about to begin would have lasting consequences. The expansion of the state was naturally accompanied by its staffing with Peronist

---

[4] The inability to cooperate was so severe as to involve – at different points – Peronist and Radical Party support for military intervention against elected governments of the opposing political stripe.

[5] To be fair, this was not at all unprecedented. Control of the government had long brought with it the power to reward supporters with positions, a tactic employed both by the oligarchical PAN and the UCR when they held executive power. One difference was that of scale, given the massive expansion of the public bureaucracy during the 1946–55 Peronist governments.

loyalists – and thus by definition the civil service could not become an important element in the construction of a cross-party and cross-class collaboration to expand political institutions. For the natural party of the middle sectors – the UCR – had no important role in its expansion, and most of it was not a collaborator with the inward-looking and statist development model launched by Perón in the 1940s and 1950s. Nor were its supporters welcome in the expanding bureaucracy. Indeed, Buchanan (1985, 73) points out that by 1951, the occupants of bureaucratic positions instead "were united by a single factor: ideological allegiance to Perón."

The similarly radical reorganization of the trajectory of economic development during Perón's 1946–55 tenure also involved necessarily the wholesale creation of new governmental institutions. These transformations crossed the entirety of the public administration, covering everything from economic governance (the central bank, nationalizations, protection, and foreign exchange rationing) to the rule of law and the supreme court to the nature of agricultural land tenure and the initiation of a corporatist industrial relations system. In sum, Perón's changes were so consequential that they amounted to a wholesale transformation even of the very definition of private property rights (Adelman 1992, 252).

Perhaps the most far-reaching transformation of the Argentine political economy – and one that certainly helped launch the populist/antipopulist spiral that would define institutional creation and destruction over the ensuing 50 years – was the corporatist organization of labor. The core of the institutional transformation was embodied in the 1945 Ley de Asociaciones Profesionales (Law of Professional Associations), which gave the Secretary of Labor unilateral authority over the recognition or decertification of unions and restricted representation to a single union per occupational category. At the same time, the state could use its authority to ensure favorable contracts were forthcoming to more politically cooperative unions (Little 1979, 343). The consequence of this was profound. Not only was the labor movement effectively united under the Peronist labor central, the Confederación General de Trabajo (CGT), but membership – partly due to active state sponsorship – exploded, from about 400,000 at the inception of Perón's government to about 3 million within five years (di Tella 1981, 45). At its core, the political foundation of the Peronist government rested on a "highly visible exchange of new worker and union benefits for political support," which included a ninefold increase in social security coverage by 1952 and a 60 percent increase in real wages between 1946 and 1949 (Collier and Collier 2002 [1991], 337, 341).

A critical aspect of this incorporation of the working class was that, although labor was subordinated while Perón was in power, this was a personal subordination, not one mediated by the creation of durable state institutions. This fact would prove crucial, for the organizational strength of the labor movement, created during the 1946–55 Peronist government, would create a powerful societal interest that subsequent democratic or military governments

The Social Question and the State

would have enormous difficulty containing, either via political institutions or by force. As Silvert (1961, 162) has suggested, the state had not managed to become the decisive institution in Argentine society, and postwar politics centered more around direct, unmediated interest group representation and less around political parties able to effectively channel and mediate societal pressures and implement policy through the state. This clash was reflected in a constant construction and destruction of governmental institutions, with the long-term consequence of the weakening of the state itself and the inability to form a lasting political consensus around its proper role and structure. Indeed, even under Perón, where the working class and the labor movement were most effectively controlled or coopted by the state, independent economic planning still proved difficult. Instead, "Peronist industrial policy responded to the political pressures of the social forces which had emerged and expanded during the depression and the war years" (Teichman 1982, 64). This problem was only exacerbated in years to come.

And it was not just in the staffing of the public sector, its scope, or the corporatist organization of the labor movement where the institutional seesaw that has been the signal characteristic of postwar political development in Argentina can be seen. The rural sector was host to a wave of transformations that fundamentally altered its mode of operation during Perón's presidency and initiated a cycle of institutional control and liberalization that persisted throughout the postwar era. Most notable in this regard was the creation of the Instituto Argentino de Promoción del Intercambio (Argentine Institute for Trade Promotion; IAPI). In effect, IAPI was simultaneously (1) a marketing board for virtually all important Argentine agricultural products, (2) a state trading agency that dominated external transactions in the late 1940s and early 1950s, and (3) an effective regulator of crucial domestic prices. This institutional behemoth is usually thought of as simply a mechanism to tax the agrarian oligarchy (via its monopsonistic purchase of domestic agricultural products at low, compulsory prices denominated in local currency and their subsequent sale on international markets for scarce foreign exchange). It certainly was this, but it went far deeper. It organized and financed a wave of nationalizations of foreign enterprises, most notably the British-owned railways, and it effectively controlled domestic food prices through its extensive subsidy regime. And as a state trading agency, it became the go-between for those seeking industrial and capital goods imports (for the state and the private sector). Created in 1946, this agency experienced such vertiginous growth that by 1948, it had become the largest state trading entity outside the Soviet Union (*Time*, September 20, 1948).

A second and far less-recognized change involved the regulation of land tenure. The Argentine agrarian political economy had a very important rental sector – a consequence of its fairly concentrated landholding structure (Scalabrini 1963). While some regulation of tenancy contracts had been in the offing since the UCR governments of the 1910s and 1920s, major changes were not made until the 1940s because of effective conservative opposition in the senate and the oligarchy-dominated governments of the 1930s (Gallo 2006). The military government of 1943–46 began the process of land tenure transformation by suspending evictions and imposing a 20 percent decrease in rents – helping to provide a rural base for Juan Perón's 1946 election campaign among the large numbers of tenant farmers (Gallo 2010, 5–6).

Similar institutional instability was initiated – and would continue in the ensuing decades – in two other critical parts of the government. First, monetary policy was rendered fully dependent, as the Central Bank was put under the direct authority of the Treasury Ministry, and thus subject to intense personnel and policy vicissitudes. And through the Central Bank's regulatory efforts, the state effectively seized control over private deposits (Cramer 1998, 546; García-Zamor 1968, 89). Even more worrisome, the supreme court was rendered hardly less dependent on the government of the day. On entering office, Perón forced four of the five supreme court justices off the bench through impeachment, initiating a pattern of continual removal of those supreme court judges deemed undesirable by the government that continues into the contemporary era (Alston and Gallo, 2010, 180). Spiller and Tommasi (2003, 298) point out that this change was initiated in the 1940s – prior to that point, the court's development had been moving in the direction of independence more akin to that of the US Supreme Court. But since the mid-1940s, judicial tenure became quite short, aligning justices with the incumbent government. Alston and Gallo (2010, 194) point out that this interference in judicial institutions subsequently had no partisanship or regime character. In addition to Perón, the subsequent military government removed all five Peronist justices, while the incoming Radical Party president, after the democratic transition in 1958, replaced most of the court and added judges. Meanwhile, from the 1960s to the 1990s, the length of judicial tenure in Argentine was comparable to that of Peru and Zambia, and no president until de la Rúa in 1999 actually faced an opposition majority on the court (Spiller and Tommasi 2004, 298).

The argument here is that while the Argentine Republic had begun life in the 1880s as a unified national state on a trajectory that was favorable to the long development of effective institutions of government, the shock of the social question ultimately deflected this trajectory in the direction of populist and antipopulist cycles of institutional creation and destruction that prevented what Argentina most needed: institutionalization. The consequence of unstable institutions were manifold. They affected economic policy in ways that introduced so much instability that Argentina's position in international economy moved from being wealthy on a par with the United States at the dawn of the twentieth century to underdevelopment, inflation, and economic calamity at century's end. The underinstitutionalization of governmental institutions – very notably the industrial relations regime – also impeded the sorts of political bargains and interparty compromises that might have prevented the frequent recourse to brutal military government in the last half of the twentieth century.

The Social Question and the State

The persistence of problems of institutionalization and the cyclical nature of institutional creation and retrenchment are important to the path-dependent argument set forth in this book. The argument is not simply that the state expansion, impelled by the way in which the social question came to a head in Argentina, did not achieve institutionalization; it is also that this induced subsequent dynamics that continued to make the deepening and institutionalization of any coherent structure – liberal or statist – of the public administration extremely problematic. We can see the effects of this in three subsequent periods: when the Radical government of Frondizi launched a major developmentalist economic strategy and sought (but failed to sustain) the cooperation of the Peronists in a statist campaign of industrial deepening. A belated statist alliance between the Peronists and the middle sector was precluded by the way the initial entry of the working class was accommodated. Similarly, we see a failed effort at institutionalizing a new, economically liberal order under the highly repressive bureaucratic–authoritarian regime of 1976–83. And finally, in the contemporary democratic era, we see that antipopulist–populist cycling over the institutions of the state and the proper role of government continues even across governments of the same political party, as the liberalism of Menem ultimately gave way to the statism of the Kirchner and Fernández.

The long-run problem in Argentina was not, however, the same as the problem of Peru. In the latter, meaningful and sustained efforts at state building were not on the agenda of most political elites, and institution building progressed comparatively more slowly there than in our comparison cases – an institutional backwardness that was only heightened by the entry of the working class into political competition and the added disincentive this created for elites to permit the greater expansion, consolidation, and empowerment of the organs of government. Argentina, by contrast, experienced cycles of aborted, but often ambitious, state-building efforts. Not only were there the tremendous institutional experiments described earlier under Perón but successive governments also initiated efforts at "refounding" and strengthening public institutions, albeit in very different ways. The problem was that the political cooperation necessary to institutionalize such changes over time was simply not to be found; instead, cycles of populist or developmentalist expansion were matched with countercycles of retrenchment and institutional atrophy.

From the perspective of this book, a key barrier to the consolidation of political institutions had arisen out of the timing and fashion of the entry of the middle and working classes into politics – the political representatives of the middle and working classes could not forge a lasting compromise around any particular set of institutions, development policies, or even political regime types. Quite a lot of work has examined the tremendous instability of democracy in Argentina, and it is not the point here to differ with these interpretations.[6]

---

[6] It was very severe. David Pion-Berlin (1997, 46) has pointed out that between 1930 and 1976, "the armed forces cut short the tenure of every democratically elected head of state."

196   *Latin American State Building in Comparative Perspective*

Rather, it is to show how a particular set of structural features of the post-incorporation period renders *institutional development* difficult. For swings in the political regime do not necessarily translate into severe changes to the trajectory of institutional development. For example, major episodes of military rule in Uruguay and Chile did not fundamentally alter the competence and capacity to govern of the public administration – though they certainly did change economic policies, result in egregious violations of human rights, and involve efforts to stamp out whole political ideologies. And of course, political regime was largely irrelevant to state building in Peru, where authoritarian and democratic governments alike proved unwilling or incapable of launching a trajectory of institutional development and capacity improvement.

Importantly for a path-dependent argument such as the one developed in this book, the outcome in Argentina should not be seen as the continual but contingent failures of politicians to endeavor to strike compromise positions that might have stabilized institutions. Instead, the point is that where politicians tried to do so – and both military and democratic leaders did in various ways – a fundamental, lasting collaboration over the scope and nature of government institutions was effectively impossible. One part of this dilemma is not particularly controversial: the traditional agro-export oligarchy in Argentina was implacably opposed to large-scale state expansion, economic protectionism, and associated developmentalist industrialization.

It was the inability to form any lasting middle-class and working-class accommodation between the Radical and Peronist political forces, respectively, that was the most critical problem in Argentina. Similar accommodations proved viable elsewhere – either through cross-party and cross-class alliances in Chile or through intra- and cross-party cooperation in Uruguay. But these cooperative efforts were organized around a shared project of statist industrialization. As we saw earlier, the middle classes and the bulk of the Radical Party in Argentina, however, did not initially support the initiation of a major statist developmental episode, much less one dominated by Perón.[7] There was a material foundation for this reticence, for many middle-sector and most upper-class interests were negatively affected by the terms of Perón's shift to populist developmentalism; even the position of the middle classes within the state bureaucracy was undermined by the systematic purging of the public administration of non-Peronists and its subsequent repopulation by Peronist loyalists.

Instead of compromise and coalition, the Radicals (alongside the Roman Catholic Church and the oligarchy) supported the 1955 military coup that ousted Perón. After a brief interlude that emphasized conciliation alongside

---

[7] The inability to cooperate does not necessarily begin here; even as Perón moved to a protectionist industrial strategy, he was unwilling to rely on the economic plans or personnel of the administrations that preceded him. This was despite the fact that his industrial goals had important elements in common with the 1940 Plan Pinedo, and a central architect of economic policy in that era was none other than longtime proponent of protected industrialization Raúl Prebisch.

The Social Question and the State

de-Peronization, the coup leader, General Eduardo Lonardi, was replaced by General Pedro Aramburu, who instead initiated major transformations of the Argentine state in an effort to eradicate fully the influence of Perón and his policies. The developmental engine and the levers of control the state had over the economy were largely dismantled: the state trading monopoly IAPI was abolished, bank deposits were denationalized, and controls on international transactions were sharply reduced (Torre and de Riz 1993, 266). Indeed, in terms of economic management, this was devastating, as "the institutions of the Peronist government were dismantled, but no lasting institutions were created in their place to take responsibility for economic development" (Sikkink 1991, 83). And of course, the Peronist Party itself was proscribed, its supporters purged from the government and union leadership, and Perón himself went into exile. The institutional seesaw was completed when a Constituent Assembly was called in 1957 to repeal the 1949 Peronist constitution as part of a plan to transition the polity back to electoral competition, albeit in a setting in which Peronist forces were not permitted to compete.

The election of 1958 was an important moment from the perspective of the hypotheses put forward in this book, for it was a direct test of the contention that a lasting rapprochement between middle-class Radicals and working-class Peronists was structurally unviable. In the 1958 election, the contest was essentially between two Radical Party candidates,[8] the result of a schism in the party over the possibility of cooperation with the Peronists. Arturo Frondizi, running on the Unión Cívica Radical Intransigente (UCRI) ticket, confronted Ricardo Balbín of the Unión Cívica Radical del Pueblo (UCRP). The former's position was very important, for not only did he actively (if secretly) seek cooperation with Perón but he also ran on a strongly developmentalist platform, advocating a major expansion of the state's role and specifically aiming to take the import-substituting industrialization of the Peronist era (which had emphasized light industry and consumer goods) into the stage of industrial deepening (durables and capital goods). In so doing, the possibility of an accommodation around an expanded, developmentalist state that might at least have the tacit support of both major electoral blocs was mooted – a move that would have, were it successful, produced an outcome more like that of Uruguay or Chile. With support of Peronist voters who had no candidate of their own to support, and who had been given guidance by Juan Perón to back the UCRI candidate, Frondizi won the 1958 election and attempted to launch a political and economic developmentalist strategy.

It was, however, not to be. To begin, President Frondizi could not even count on solid support from his own side of the political spectrum. Indeed, the forces aligned with the UCRP and Balbín "took up positions of unrelenting opposition almost from the day Frondizi took office" (Sikkink 1991, 90). Frondizi took important and politically costly steps to repay his Peronist supporters, including

---

[8] Openly Peronist candidacies were legally precluded.

the return of the CGT to Peronist control and the reestablishment of monopoly unionism (Torre and de Riz 1993, 272). The political strategy pursued by Frondizi to build a solid statist, developmental coalition, however, began to unravel almost immediately, in 1959, when a major stabilization crisis rocked the economy and forced a turn toward sharply contractionary economic policies – which enraged his erstwhile labor and Peronist allies. In the stabilization that ensued, wages fell as much as 30 percent, and labor conflict exploded (Torre and de Riz 1991, 278). While economic recovery in 1960–61 provided a bit more room to maneuver, Frondizi attempted further outreach to the Peronists by authorizing the party to compete independently in the 1962 congressional elections. If the hope was that this would be repaid with substantial electoral support for his UCRI, it was dashed, with the Peronists returning to their traditional position as an independent and plurality political force and Frondizi's UCRI being forced into third place behind the UCRP. The victory of the Peronists in 9 of 14 provincial gubernatorial elections proved too much for the anti-Peronist military to bear, and it forced Frondizi to annul the results and, shortly thereafter, removed Frondizi himself from office by force.

The inglorious end to Frondizi's administration also signaled the end of the developmentalist effort – in both its political and economic forms. The newly appointed interim president Guido instead returned to a far more orthodox economic strategy of monetary contraction, austerity, and devaluation – even bringing back the 1930s-era liberal Frederico Pinedo to manage the Economy Ministry during the stabilization. The subsequent civilian government of Illía, of the UCRP faction of the Radicals, was much less suited to cooperation with labor and the Peronists than even the ill-fated Frondizi administration. It made an effort to govern from the center but was ultimately sandwiched between the demands of the military and those of the still-proscribed Peronists. And by 1966, even the Peronists initially supported the military intervention against the Radical Party government that brought General Onganía to power – further cementing the difficulties in reaching anything like a meaningful political accommodation. Onganía then launched the first of two force-based efforts to stabilize and refound the Argentine state, in this instance on an authoritarian corporatist foundation. Societal resistance and labor mobilization eventually brought this experiment to an end, resulting ultimately in the return of Perón to the country and the presidency in 1973 and his replacement by his wife, Isabel, after his death shortly thereafter. The 1973–76 return of Peronism to power was characterized by violence and economic instability and ultimately ended with the savage military dictatorship of 1976–83, this time pursuing a strategy of state shrinkage and more orthodox economic policy.

The long-term populist–antipopulist cycles in Argentina, as we have argued earlier, were in large measure a product of the nature and timing of the entry of the middle and working classes into politics. The early entry of the middle-class Radicals, founded on an electoral base that was supportive of liberalism and orthodoxy, had little room to reach an accommodation with a working class

The Social Question and the State

that became politically active much later – but extremely vigorously – around a policy of forced-march statist and protectionist industrialization. And the political foundation for this sort of political bargain that was found in other cases – around the role of the public sector as the principal source for middle-sector employment and advancement coupled to protectionist industrialization that benefited industry and organized labor – was thus not possible. The middle sectors had a much greater private-sector component, and the initial forays into industrialization under Perón, if anything, expelled the Radical Party supporters from state institutions – to make way for Peronists – in a way that further undermined the possibility of any such compromise. Instead, the oligarchy, the military, the Radicals, and the Peronists were at odds for the rest of the postwar era, never managing to coordinate around a consistent role for the state, a set of institutions, or even a set of personnel to staff the bureaucracies. The consequences for state building were pernicious, for expansions of the state were at best episodic and not institutionalized, leading to strikingly low levels of public-sector capacity in the context of a decidedly affluent economy (by Latin American standards). As we see later, a very different pattern of mass political incorporation in Uruguay produced a superior state-building outcome despite substantially lower levels of resources with which the state could work.

FROM THE REVOLUCIÓN ARGENTINA AND THE PROCESO TO MENEM AND KIRCHNER

Indeed, as many have noted, the political and institutional swings in Argentina only became more severe with each subsequent iteration – as the practical reality of repeated inability to compromise compounded the already stark difficulties of reaching political accommodation. And even recourse to the most savage repression failed to force a durable consensus around the nature of the state, its institutions, economic policy direction, or even the political regime. That is not to say that efforts at refounding the institutional landscape were not tried. At least two distinct episodes were initiated by successively more brutal military regimes, the first being General Onganía's Revolución Argentina (Argentine Revolution) and the second being a more collective military project, the Proceso de Reorganización Nacional (Process of National Reorganization). Indeed, the names themselves these dictatorships gave to their regimes make clear their goals in terms of institutional transformation.

Neither was successful, though their approaches were decidedly different. Onganía (1966–70) pursued a nationalist, exclusionary strategy that aimed at laying the foundation for an authoritarian corporatist and organicist conception of the relation between state and society. In the process of trying to create it – through force of arms – he managed to alienate nearly all the major interests in the Argentine political economy. His suspension of collective bargaining earned him the enmity of the unions and the Peronists (who had to some extent supported the coup against the preceding Radical Party government of Illía).

Moves to tax exports and land alienated the oligarchy, while small and medium industrialists faced credit reductions and declining protection (Torre and de Riz 1993, 301–8). In many ways, this dictatorship – brought down in a coup in the wake of mass popular protest in the city of Córdoba in 1969 – made an untenable situation worse by provoking the rise of armed insurrection, as Torre and de Riz (1993, 308) argue:

Onganía had eroded the very bases of the modus vivendi within which, at the price of a high level of institutional volatility, the Argentine people had previously resolved their differences.

The return of democracy in 1973, and shortly thereafter the return of Juan Perón to the presidency, still could not quell the cycles of institutional instability. Despite an overwhelming electoral victory, and a concerted effort to do so, Perón was unable to bring a broad coalition along with him as he turned to an explicitly moderate economic and political project. In the face of high inflation, an effort to stabilize prices and politics through tripartite bargaining and cross-party agreement began to founder as labor conflict escalated and business rebelled against price ceilings (Torre and de Riz 1993, 320–21). With the succession of Isabel Perón after his death on July 1, 1974, these efforts at accommodation were abandoned, and a cycle of economic and political chaos ensued.

The final turn toward military rule during the 1976–83 Proceso marked a qualitative escalation in the use of repression to accomplish political goals, and it earned the Argentine generals a victory as the most murderous military government in the South American region. Yet even this turn toward military rule – now in the interests of a decidedly orthodox economic and institutional vision – did not manage a fundamental reorganization of the state (indeed, it was not seriously attempted), even if economic policy had changed sharply. The inability to cooperate and the cycling of institutions indeed continue into the present, where, for example, the neoliberal government of Peronist Carlos Menem transformed the state by initiating the privatization of the national pension system, transferring the bulk of public enterprise assets to the private sector, and a divide-and-conquer strategy applied to ostensible labor allies. In the wake of this strategy, which ultimately came to an end with a massive economic catastrophe in 2002, yet another set of Peronists came to power – Nestor Kirchner and, subsequently, his wife, Cristina Fernández de Kirchner – behind yet another institutional transformation, this time radically reenlarging the state's organs through the renationalization of important sectors of the economy, returning the pension system to public hands, and through the implementation of administratively imposed prices for core consumer goods. The point is not to dwell on the nature of these changes but rather merely to point out that more than 50 years after the decisive rupture of the social question into the political arena, the question of the proper institutional structure for the Argentine state still remains to be answered.

The Social Question and the State

WE'RE *ALL* STATISTS NOW: POLITICAL CONSENSUS AND THE LONG-RUN DEVELOPMENT OF STATE INSTITUTIONS IN URUGUAY

In many ways, Uruguay should have been the less likely site for the long-run, effective development of state institutions. Although its political economy was in some ways very similar to that of Argentina – it was also a ranching export–based economy – there were also crucial differences. The consolidation of national institutions in Argentina had led, after 1881, to an enormous influx of foreign investment and immigration, sustained high rates of economic development, and the emergence of a large grain-farming agricultural sector (and the settled population this implies). By contrast, in Uruguay, stable political consolidation awaited definitive pacification of the national territory in 1904, and whereas its economy expanded, it experienced nothing like the golden age of development that Argentina did, as its adjustment to a ranching *and* agricultural economy remained retarded.

Yet it was Uruguay that left the second critical juncture for state building on a trajectory that would achieve a cross-class and cross-party consensus over the scope of sharply enlarged state institutions, their role in the economy, and even the staffing of them. Unlike Argentina, where the institutions that shaped the political economy were the crux of democratic- and authoritarian-period political conflict, in Uruguay, only one political institution – the collegial executive – was the center of similar paroxysms of change. Conversely, from their establishment in the two crucial presidential terms of José Batlle y Ordoñez, vast expansions of public-sector institutions – including extensive regulatory bureaucracies and the creation of a large state-owned enterprise sector – received and retained the support of all major political forces. Indeed, underlining the trajectory on which Uruguay was embarked, over most of the period, the trend was to *build* on this foundation of statist economic organization, and even in times of immense economic duress, serious *institutional* (as opposed to fiscal) retrenchment proved essentially impossible. Indeed, neither the consequences of the exceedingly repressive 1973–85 military government nor the economic challenges of the debt crisis and a reorientation of the economy in a more export-oriented direction in the 1980s and 1990s would induce a fundamental restructuring of government institutions. Instead, it was the long-run development of precisely those institutions that helped make possible the economic reorientation of the past 20 years without the political and economic turmoil experienced by Uruguay's Argentine neighbor.

Why did a long-run trajectory of effective state building take root in Uruguay, despite in some ways a less propitious environment than that of Argentina? The differential pathways after national unification of these two countries take us some difference in setting up the distinct fashion in which the challenge of the social question was met, the root cause of the deepening of state institutions in Uruguay. To begin, the extent of economic development in Uruguay during the gold standard era leading up to the First World War was far less than that of Argentina, with two important consequences: both the emergence of a large export-linked middle class and complementary industrialization were quite delayed. Lacking a parallel developmental surge in the pre–World War I boom years similar to that which characterized Argentina, the Uruguayan political economy's middle-sector and working-class strata emerged only very slowly. And very importantly, Uruguay's middle class was far less economically connected to the liberal order than its Argentine counterpart. Indeed, it was a proportionately much more state-dependent middle class that had a strong and early foundation in Uruguay, as it was in part connected to the very early expansion of the primary school system under LaTorre in the 1870s, and then later under Batlle in the 1910s for secondary education. Substantial public employment and relatively early protectionist legacies, and thus middle sectors more linked to local economic activity and government, also had an early history in Uruguay – in sharp contrast, again, to Argentina.

Although all of this may have had infelicitous developmental consequences – after all, for example, protectionism in a small country can be exceedingly economically inefficient – it had positive *political* consequences of the first order. The slower pace of economic development and associated industrialization rendered the mobilized pressure of the urban working class far less powerful and pressing than in Argentina. Similarly, the early middle-sector elements were neither as powerful nor as politically organized as in Argentina and generally made their presence felt within the traditional parties – not via an extraparty effort to seize power on their own. In this way, the pressing of the social question was much delayed in Uruguay relative to Argentina, and mass political incorporation would occur only well after the institution building of the Batlle periods – that is, during and after the Great Depression. The sequencing of institutional development thus contrasts sharply with Argentina. In Uruguay, the bulk of the middle-sector and working-class population would be a *product* of expanded state institutions (and the development policies they pursued) rather than such institutions emerging as a political response to the pressures of a mobilized and expanding middle and working class. And with politics dominated by two heterogeneous and multiclass political parties, there were no insurmountable political barriers to cross-class accommodation, either. Indeed, as we shall see, this compromise was institutionalized as part of the very structure of an expanding state, helping to provide the glue that carried it through good times and bad.

THE SOCIAL QUESTION DELAYED: GRADUAL ECONOMIC EXPANSION AND LIMITED MASS MOBILIZATION

Given their similar comparative advantages in the international division of labor and timing of national unification, Uruguay, like Argentina, experienced an increase in its population. From 1880 to 1910, the total population expanded from 463,867 to 1,081,084 (Rial 1980, 3). But economic growth was

The Social Question and the State

comparatively much slower than in Argentina. While in 1870, Uruguay had a per capita gross domestic product estimated by Angus Maddison at $2,181, by 1914, this had reached only $2,654. By contrast, Argentina expanded from $1,311 to $3,302 per capita over the same time span.[9] Economic development thus came later and more slowly to Uruguay, as it would have to await the end of the long period of intermittent civil conflict in 1904 (Panizza 1997, 673).

Rather surprisingly for a small, export-dependent country in the heyday of the gold standard, Uruguay from an early date also had a comparatively protectionist economic policy. Finch (1981, 161–62) notes that as early as 1875, a general tariff at a rate of 20 percent was in effect, further rising to 31 percent by 1888. The general tariff law, in addition, had "considerably higher rates" for import-competing sectors. This nascent industrial policy was complemented by 1912 by legislation that reduced tariff rates on primary inputs, creating a more consistent pro-industrialization policy that was focused on the domestic market. Ranching exports, however, remained the principal economic engine of growth and source of foreign exchange. Uruguay's main exports were beef and wool, the former most commonly in jerked form (*tasajo*) before the twentieth century. Political stabilization and the expansion of the national territory used for ranching brought a major increase in production, albeit one not founded on increased productivity. From a low point of 1.8 million head of cattle after the disaster of the Guerra Grande (ending in 1851), the stock expanded to 6.8 million by 1900. The sheep economy expanded even more vertiginously, from 0.75 million to 18.6 million over the same period (Arocena 2002, 151). After 1905, the total size of annual cattle slaughter remained in a consistent range but increasingly comprised much higher-value frozen and chilled meat (industrial) exports (Arocena 2002, 168, 348–49), once technological changes made such a trade viable.

A surprising feature of this era in economic development – and one that had social consequences – was the absence of a large farming sector, especially one aimed at the export market. As one economic geographer noted in 1927, "although climate, relief, and soil favor the production of a great variety of crops in most of Uruguay, the products of the soil play an insignificant place in the commerce of the country" (Jones 1927, 369). While local grain production was generally enough to supply the small home market, and sometimes produce an exportable surplus, by mid-century, farming (as opposed to ranching) occupied only a comparatively small 8 percent of the land area (Fitzgibbon 1953, 259). Instead, what occurred was the consolidation of the ranching *estancia* economy, which neither utilized much labor nor produced a more balanced rural occupational structure (Panizza 1997, 680). In so doing, it also limited the extent to which the export economy in Uruguay was linked to an

---

[9] Both countries' output per capita is measured in constant international Gheary–Khamis dollars of 1990, as calculated by Maddison. Data are available at http://www.ggdc.net/MADDISON/Historical_Statistics/vertical-file_02–2010.xls.

204 *Latin American State Building in Comparative Perspective*

accessory middle and working class that might have interests in more liberal economic policy. This contrasted sharply with Argentina, where a much larger and export-capable large- and medium-scale farming sector had emerged.

Conversely, early educational reforms laid the foundation for a more state-oriented middle class. Uruguay is unusual for the very early establishment for such a poor country of an effective national system of public education. This process began during the LaTorre dictatorship, when the 1877 Law of Common Education was imposed, which resulted in a massive expansion of primary education. Critical to the expansion of education was that it was free of charge to parents and, by 1934, compulsory (if enforcement was somewhat varied) (Fitzgibbon 1952a, 69). Under Batlle, educational reform proceeded apace, with major construction initiated to expand the university system and, in 1912, the passage of a law to introduce secondary education to each departmental capital, thus ensuring access to high school across the country, not simply in the environs of Montevideo. This expansion of education was also an expansion of the public sector, especially after the 1909 Law on Lay Education undermined private and confessional educational systems. In addition, as of 1916, public secondary *and* tertiary education were made free of charge (Faraone 1968, 33–34). The effects of the educational reforms were impressive. By 1908, 67.42 percent of the age-eligible population were enrolled in primary school in Montevideo, and by 1930, this number had increased from 28.17 percent to 41.69 percent in the interior departments (Rial 1983, 104). This remarkable educational expansion for such a poor, agrarian country not only produced a comparatively large middle-sector group tied to the educational infrastructure but also provided the human capital from which the public sector and parastatal bureaucracies, expanding vertiginously after the Batlle era, could draw to fill their ranks.

It eventually created a middle class that was both unusually large and state linked, particularly for an agro-export–dependent economy. But the ranching economy in the interior itself created virtually no middle stratum – starkly divided as it was between *estanciero* and *peón*[10] in a system of long-term *latifundia* dominance (Barrán and Nahum 1984, 663–66). In the urban sector, the native-born (and thus voting-eligible) middle class was heavily centered in the "dependent middle stratum" of public employees, the foundation of which had been laid in the educational reforms outlined earlier. Indeed, even at the dawn of the twentieth century, the size of this urban middle sector was comparatively large (Finch 1981, 36–37).

By contrast, the urban working class was underdeveloped as a social or political force. The comparatively small industrial sector that predated the reforms of the Batlle era was not concentrated in large firms or economic enclaves that might have favored labor organization (Collier and Collier 2002 [1991], 83; Panizza 1997, 684). Klaczko (1979, 37) goes still further and argues

---

[10] Roughly, "ranch owner" and "cow hand," respectively.

The Social Question and the State

that most industry by 1908 was still of an artisanal variety and that it showed little likelihood of rapid development. Nor was actual worker mobilization particularly extensive. Finch reports that the number of strikes in the 1908–12 period fluctuated between 9 and 41 per year, the great majority involving defeats for labor. And the labor central of the day, the Federación Obrera Regional Uruguaya (Uruguayan Regional Worker's Federation), could claim a membership estimated to be at most 7,000 (Finch 1981, 54–55). Of course, the rural wage labor force, however meager its conditions of life were, was essentially unorganized (Solari 1956, 262).

Several features of this pattern of social development in Uruguay are important. First, in contrast to Argentina, large portions of the nascent middle sectors – and really rapid expansion of this social stratum would occur as a *consequence* of the reforms of the Batlle era – were from an early date associated with the public sector, and as a consequence, they had no vested material interest in liberal economic policies (Rama 1958, 40). Second, neither middle-class nor working-class actors had erupted onto the national political or economic arena with anything like the severity that characterized Argentina, where worker mobilization was, by the turn of the twentieth century, quite intense, and middle-sector interests allied to the UCR had launched armed rebellions in the first decades of the century, eventually, in 1916, winning control over the presidency itself in an electoral contest. Instead, workers were weakly organized and linked to comparative ineffectual anarchist-inspired organizations, while much of the Montevideo middle class was employed in the public sector and formed a core constituency of the traditional Colorado Party electorate.

The most important difference, however, is in the timing of the emergence of the social question – for ultimately it did emerge. Indeed, in important ways, the social question was answered – in the sense of the creation of an enduring set of institutions to regulate conditions of work, pensions, the stability of employment, and the workweek – long before it was forcefully posed from below. Social reform in Uruguay had a preemptive character. As a consequence, these institutions of economic governance both built support from expanding working- and middle-class sectors and, at the same time, helped channel their political demands through the vehicles of the two traditional parties, which, over time, both participated in the utilization, expansion, and legitimation of these institutions. The point is that the construction of strong, deeply penetrating, and stable state institutions is most possible where working-class and middle-class interests are reconcilable, making it possible for a broad political consensus to emerge over the proper role and scope of the state. This sort of compromise, where it was achieved, was typically organized in Latin America in Depression-era patterns of statist development led by middle-class actors in the public sector and backed by industrial- and working-class interests in the protected local economy. It was decidedly difficult to accomplish where, as in Argentina, the representatives of the middle and working classes differed sharply over their views of the proper role of the state and instead focused political competition in large measure over efforts to define precisely this. In those contexts, rounds of institutional creation were met with rounds of institutional decay, dismantlement, or retrenchment, preventing the institutionalization of much of the public administration and producing instead a populist–antipopulist institutional cycling and a weaker state.

An important point from the perspective of this book is that the "timing" of the social question refers to two related phenomena. It involves the emergence of mobilized, nonelectoral pressures from excluded sectors (the middle classes and/or the working class) serious enough to threaten the stability of national politics if they are not directly addressed. It also involves the incorporation of the working classes as an actor into national politics – typically via the expansion of suffrage. In Uruguay, because of its small scale and delayed industrialization, mobilized working-class pressures did not emerge early – indeed, union demand making was far more serious during and after the Great Depression than it was before. Nor did Uruguay experience an eruption of middle-sector demands for political inclusion that mirror those led by the UCR in Argentina. Instead, in a remarkable act of political foresight, President Batlle created the institutions to harness and channel working-class pressures, and he did so before the force of mobilization made it a political imperative. He also did it in an era in which the actual electoral participation of the working class was very limited, and the middle-sector voters who did exercise their suffrage did so in a context in which ballots were not secret and disloyalty to incumbent politicians would meet sanctions; that is, it was nonthreatening. This underscores the importance of timing in the construction of state institutions – for doing so in advance of political incorporation and mass political participation has serious advantages. First, it implies that mass participation will take place in a context in which critical institutions had already been created, and these in turn shaped the character of subsequent popular-sector participation. Second, it implies the entry of middle- and working-class actors into politics during and after the Great Depression, a time when a practical and intellectual consensus around state-centric and protectionist patterns of development had emerged. This limited the conflicts of interest between these sectors over external orientation and facilitated the making of political bargains to create and stabilize a much-expanded set of state institutions.

The task of the sections that follow is to examine what the institutional innovations of the Batlle era were and their consequences for the development of the Uruguayan state and the social forces that supported its creation. The interaction of these institutional reforms with the expansion of free suffrage that occurred after them is the next step in the argument. Here the influence of timing becomes essential, for in contrast to Argentina, real popular electoral competition served to deepen and stabilize the role of the state and its institutions rather than undermining them, thus helping to create a powerful set of vested interests behind the strong state, and to organize the commitment of all major political forces – by the 1930s – behind the basic vision that Batlle had

The Social Question and the State

launched. The depth of the path dependencies in Uruguay institutional development was, however, severely tested in three distinct periods that came thereafter – each ratifying the hard-to-change character of these pathways. The first was the authoritarian reaction – under President Gabriel Terra in the 1930s – to the profound institutional reforms of the Batlle era. The second began in the mid-1950s and was marked by prolonged economic crisis and the exhaustion of the viability of the protectionist and statist industrialization model. In this period, we see the unwillingness of either of the dominant Uruguayan political parties to fundamentally challenge the institutional underpinnings of the state, even where economic crisis and persistent stagnation made reform seem essential. For, to do so would have challenged the exceedingly powerful vested interests within and outside the public administration that had developed during the process of state building. The final great challenge to institutional development came after the failure of the democratic regime to deal effectively with Uruguay's structural problems, leading to the 1973–85 military government, which, despite an extraordinary level of repression, and a clear goal to dismantle the statism of the past, ultimately was not successful. The post-1985, much more outward-oriented economic system remains among the most statist on the continent, showing the enduring presence of, and popular support for, the massive state and effective institutions that were set in motion approximately a century ago.

It is worth reiterating here that Uruguay's empirical experience makes clear a theoretical point emphasized in the opening chapters: the political and social dynamics that give birth to effective and penetrating state institutions are *not necessarily* the same ones that encourage rapid economic development. The former is a question of institutions, while the latter is in large measure a question of policy choices. While effective institutions can certainly improve the results of wise economic policy choices, they by no means cause their selection. Quite a few political systems with the administrative capacity to implement efficiently major changes in their societies and political economies have nevertheless pursued inefficient and even self-defeating developmental strategies for long periods of time. This was, in fact, likely the case for Uruguay, a low-population, resource-poor country that nevertheless pursued an extremely protectionist developmental strategy for the best part of the twentieth century that was unlikely to be viable in the long term – or even as mixed in its implications as it was in its Brazilian or Argentine neighbors. But it *was*, as we shall see, an economic model quite complementary to a dynamic of state administrative development, professionalization, and institutionalization.

BATLLE, THE INTERVENTIONIST STATE, AND POLITICAL CONCERTATION

It is widely understood that the two presidential terms of José Batlle y Ordóñez (1903–7; 1911–15) represented a sea change in the development of Uruguayan

208   *Latin American State Building in Comparative Perspective*

politics and political institutions. In what Vanger (1980, 119) has called a "rain of programs" that emerged in this era, particularly during his second term of office, not only was the traditional activity of the state massively expanded but its reach for the first time took on a serious role in the productive side of the economy through the creation of parastatal firms, public monopolies, and the ever-stricter regulation of trade and financial flows. This change would, in effect, transform society by dramatically increasing the size and political importance of the middle sectors and, for the first time, engender the emergence – over the subsequent years – of a substantial urban working class.

What is less widely understood is that the sociological emergence and economic incorporation of the middle and working sectors occurred in Uruguay long before they had any meaningful political role: Batlle may have become a hero to the middle and working classes, but he did not come to power based on their political support. Indeed, meaningful democratization and political incorporation for these social actors would be gradual and delayed, not achieving full force until the 1940s. Instead, politics in Batlle's era revolved around a series of essentially elite political bargains between the traditional parties that ultimately gave both political sides a strong stake in the survival and expansion of the political structures that Batlle had launched.

Political competition at the start of the twentieth century in Uruguay was a decidedly elite affair. Presidents were elected indirectly by the national legislature, which itself was elected through a unique institution locally called the "double simultaneous vote." Elections aggregated votes at the level of political parties (*lemas*) on the basis of the total of the vote share obtained by the sum of affiliated sublists (*sub-lemas*) running distinct slates of candidates for office in a particular department (the main political subunit). Thus, several lists of Colorado Party candidates might vie for power, with their votes aggregating to determine the overall winning party. Then, two-thirds of the seats available would be apportioned to the most-voted sub-lema of the most-voted party, while one-third was allocated to the most-voted sub-lema of the second most popular party.[11] This system served to render almost impervious the two-party Colorado–Blanco duopoly on power, while at the same time permitting within-party competition without the risk of schism. Suffrage was in practice at this point in time also quite restricted – with only 46,238 voters exercising their rights in the 1905 congressional elections and even fewer, 44,693 and 31,862, in 1907 and 1910, respectively (Acevedo 1942, 303, 309). This is in the context of a country whose population in 1910 exceeded 1 million residents (Rial 1980, 3).

Even within the limited scope of electoral participation of the era, suffrage was not exercised free of constraint. Most critically, not only was voting not secret but voters were also required even to sign their ballots (Vanger 1980,

---

[11] The various thresholds and shares allocated to winning and losing parties changed slightly, and sometimes varied by department, but the basic structure survived for some time. For a description, see Acevedo (1942, 302–4).

The Social Question and the State

44).[12] This created a situation in which public servants and police were often encouraged to vote, while Blanco supporters in rural areas were sometimes reticent to vote for fear of potential political retaliation (Vanger 1963, 101).

In the end, despite this elite-centric electoral system, the reformist Batlle was elected president in 1903 and 1911 by small majorities of the national legislators. This situation would not change until well after the institutional developments of the Batlle era were launched – with the formation of an Electoral Court and legislation to ensure an actually effective secret ballot approved only in 1924 (Faraone 1968, 60). And even then, serious middle- and working-class electoral pressures would await the enlargement of these groups and, in many cases, the naturalization or generational replacement of the immigrants to Uruguay who often comprised them.

Critically, middle-class support (or, for that matter, the working class) was thus not an important part of Batlle's political power base, though it would later become a crucial part of the Colorado Party's electoral support in the post–World War II era (Vanger 1980, 99; Taylor 1963, 64). At the same time, in marked contrast to Argentina, workers' support was not forthcoming for any alternative political force, either. Indeed, in the elections for the 1916 Constituent Assembly, the Socialists managed to elect only two representatives (Acevedo 1942, 313). Indeed, in the entire period between 1925 and 1950, the Socialist and Communist parties – the principal left opposition in Uruguay – never summed more than seven seats in the Assembly and one in the Senate and, most typically, fewer even than that (Taylor 1955, 25).[13]

So what did Batlle accomplish with his "rain of programs"? The new institutions that populated – and would come to dominate – the Uruguayan political economy were basically established in three principal areas. First, protectionism and strict economic regulation were introduced as part of a conscious strategy to foment domestic industrialization and save scarce foreign exchange reserves. Second, a large state-owned enterprises sector – called *entes autónomos* (autonomous entities) in Uruguay – was created in an effort to break dependence on the foreign sector and achieve developmental goals. Third, a series of social laws were implemented, regulating hours and conditions of work and establishing a national pension system. Finally, and surprisingly, a substantial proportion of these reforms were financed by taxation on the export-oriented agricultural sector. That said, despite the willingness to impose taxes on farmers and ranchers, substantial changes in Uruguay's very inegalitarian patterns of land tenure were never undertaken.

Surprisingly for a small, export-dependent country, protectionism has had a long history in Uruguay, dating from at least 1888. Trade taxes were in fact

---

[12] The first election held under secret ballot rules was for the Constituent Assembly of 1916.

[13] The overall size of the Chamber of Deputies was 123 seats through the early 1930s and 99 thereafter. The senate, after the initiation of direct election in 1934, consisted of 30 representatives.

quite substantial, and Hanson (1938, 13) estimates that tariffs on imported goods averaged about 50 percent of real value already in the 1898–1900 period. This eventually evolved into an industrial policy such that, by the first years of the twentieth century, imports of machinery and inputs for the purpose of local industrialization could receive exemptions from duties. And corresponding tax increases on competing final products that were of imported origin were also imposed (Faraone 1968, 38). Batlle was also focused on more than simple protectionism; he engineered a decided expansion of the role of the state in controlling and coordinating the commanding heights of the Uruguayan economy. To that end, he created a public monopoly over the sale of insurance (to that date dominated by foreign firms), and he completed the takeover of the Banco de la República Oriental de Uruguay (BROU) and the Banco Hipotecario, giving the state a dominant role in mortgage lending. The BROU would quickly come to take on the functions of a dependent central bank, monopolizing the issue of currency, regulating internal credit, and holding the state's gold reserves (Hanson 1938, 75). Complementing control over finance was a move to create public monopolies over basic services. To that end, electrical power and telephone and telegraphic communication parastatals were created, as they were also in railways and trams and the operation of the ports, water, and sewerage (Buzzetti 1969, 206–7).

The reforms of the social arena were also substantially ahead of their time. Batlle began in his first presidency the practice of governmental neutrality during labor disputes – as opposed to the repressive role that had theretofore been practiced (Rama 1958, 46). By his second term, in 1915, he managed to pass a law restricting the ordinary workday to eight hours, with very broad effect (Hanson 1938, 130). By 1920, worker's compensation legislation had been enacted, and in 1919, a system of old age and disability pensions was approved, making Uruguay one of the global leaders in the enactment of a broad-based social insurance system. Very importantly, however, direct political linkages between the state or the Colorado Party and the labor movement were not created (in contrast to the party–union linkages that were central to Argentine Peronism), and the state did not directly encourage unionization. Instead, a pluralist system of labor relations developed, helping to avoid the identification of the labor relations system with one particular political party. This in turn made the social protection and welfare reforms far less controversial to the usually more conservative Blanco opposition and helped to ensure that they performed a conflict resolution function alongside the provision of incentives for popular-sector representatives to frame their demands around the institutional structures that had already come into being.

REINFORCING PATH DEPENDENCY AND INSTITUTIONALIZING
RADICAL REFORM

Uruguay is far from the only place in which forward-looking (or otherwise) executives implemented dramatic changes to the structure and staffing of state

The Social Question and the State

institutions. Indeed, as we saw earlier, the principal problem in Argentina was that changes were all too commonplace. But they rarely outlived the administration (and political regime) that created them and certainly never achieved the stability through times of regime change and economic crisis that they did in Uruguay. What we address next is how the reforms of the Batlle era ended up becoming self-reinforcing, leading to the construction of a large, penetrating, and comparatively effective state. This is the essence of path dependency, and we will subsequently evaluate the durability of government institutions in the face of severe political and economic challenges.

The key to the deep institutionalization of the public administration was the construction of a political consensus among the main *contending* political forces around the general structure of the Uruguayan state. This, at first glance, would seem an unlikely occurrence, given the initial intimate association of critical institutional reforms with the Colorado Party presidency of Batlle, a man who himself accomplished the definitive defeat of the last major armed insurrection of Blanco Party rebels. But in sharp contrast to Argentina, the early transformation of institutions, coupled with the late entry of the social question onto the national stage, produced an underlying social terrain that was far more favorable to the creation and consolidation of a political consensus about the expansion and strengthening of state institutions. By creating middle and working classes that were dependent on the state, and linking important elements of these groups to both of the main political parties through the development of distinctively Uruguayan forms of cross-party stakeholding in the structure of Batlle's new institutions, political conflict was transformed. Uruguayan parties came to clash less and less over the role and structure of the state, in a pattern that was impossible in the Argentine context but that has substantial similarities to the Popular Front–era governments of Chile.

Political cooperation did emerge in Uruguay and was remarkably durable. As we have seen earlier, several factors that distinguished Argentina from Uruguay made this collaboration a much more viable outcome. In Argentina, not only were political forces much more clearly divided along social class lines (particularly middle vs. working classes) but the material interests of these sectors were widely divergent. The Argentine middle classes were far more committed to liberal economic policies at the critical moment, while the existence of much of the working class was heavily dependent on an interventionist state and strong economic protection. In Uruguay, by contrast, the ranching economy had generated virtually no trade-linked middle sector, and the early imposition of protectionist policies meant that what intermediate social sectors did exist were concentrated in the public sector or linked to domestically oriented industry. Uruguayan middle-class citizens generally did not face an obvious material threat from the expansion of the state or the protection of the local economy.

And it is also the case that the political incorporation of the Uruguayan masses was quite tardy – occurring in great numbers only *after* the onset of the

Great Depression, when, in any event, orthodox economic policies were both largely impracticable and in extreme disrepute. We can see this in the figures on political participation. In the 1926 presidential elections, for example, 289,255 votes were cast – a figure that had surged to a turnout of 823,829 in 1950 (representing 18.4 and 37.5 percent of the population, respectively).[14] By contrast, mass political participation had begun in earnest in Argentina after the Sáenz-Peña Law of 1916, incorporating middle-class political actors a full generation before their Uruguayan compatriots. Structurally, Uruguay's political scene was also more conducive to the formation of cross-class alliances. As an almost exclusively ranching economy, there was only a small and declining rural population, making it essential that any party contending for national power have at least a significant urban presence – particularly in Montevideo.[15] This, of course, necessitated support from the urban middle or working classes, who were largely (directly or indirectly) tied to the expansion of the state's institutions under Batlle. And while the Colorados were generally more electorally popular in Montevideo, the Blancos had very important support there as well.

That said, structurally conducive terrain does not make the formation of a lasting political compromise inevitable. In Uruguay, a set of institutional developments that resulted from cross-party political bargains provided the practical cement that gave all the major political players a stake in the extensive set of public institutions born during the Batlle presidencies. Perhaps the most important institution that came out of the critical juncture was the construction of a collegial executive in lieu of the traditionally strong president. Vanger (1980, 164) makes the case that Batlle's initial push for a collegial executive was more about maintaining the unity and dominance of the Colorado Party (against the power of any particular president) and that he pushed for it consciously precisely where there was "not yet mass or powerful social group support for the specifics of the Batlle program."

But the 1916 Constituent Assembly elections did not produce a clear majority for a collegial executive along the lines Batlle desired. Instead, a compromise was struck creating a dual executive. On the one hand, a president would be directly elected and would have authority over the Ministries of the Interior, Foreign Relations, War, and the Navy (Fitzgibbon 1952b, 619). The innovative feature was the creation of a Consejo Nacional de Administración (National Administrative Council) comprising nine members, three of whom were to be elected every two years. Of these seats, two would go to the majority list

---

[14] Data on voter turnout are from Taylor (1955, 40), and population data are from Maddison (2010).

[15] Uruguay was the most urban country in Latin America. The advent of agricultural production (principally cereals) that might have utilized more labor was long delayed until well after that critical moment for state building. Through at least the 1950s, the economy was essentially dependent on the beef and wool trade.

The Social Question and the State

and one to the first minority (Constitution of 1918, Sección VIII, Capítulo I, Artículo 82, reprinted in Gros Espiell 1956). This council would have responsibility for domestic matters, including finance, labor, public health, and industry. And the electoral law that governed its composition all but guaranteed a bipartisan duopoly of power (Fitzgibbon 1952b, 619). Indeed, both sides stood to gain from this compromise: for the Blancos, it gave them a chance, at least, at partial executive authority, which their persistent minority electoral status was very unlikely to provide them in the context of a unitary executive;[16] for the Colorados, it brought a buy-in by the Blancos for an institutional project that was fundamentally a Colorado creation. As Fitzgibbon (1952b, 619) has noted, the collegiate executive "offered for the Nationalist (Blanco) Party representation in the executive branch . . . [and] relieved political tensions that might otherwise have built up to a dangerous point."

This principle of interparty cooperation was extended far further in 1931, with the *pacto del chinchulín* (roughly, "pork barrel pact"). This agreement set in place an arrangement whereby new positions in the public sector and the autonomous entities (parastatal firms) would be shared among adherents of the main political parties in rough proportion to their electoral fortunes (Taylor 1952, 306). This was part of a bargain with the Blanco opposition that made possible the further expansion of the state through the formation of Asociación Nacional de Combustibles, Alcohol, y Portland (ANCAP), which granted the state a monopoly on the import and refinement of petroleum products; the distillation, import, and export of alcohol; and the manufacture of cement.[17] The existing parastatal in electricity production and distribution was also granted a monopoly position as part of the bargain (Faraone 1968, 54n72). This agreement gave both opposing main political parties a strong vested interest in the size and success of the public administration – and frankly, joint responsibility for its shortcomings. It was an institutional structure that, once created, produced its own form of lock-in through the expansions of the public sector and its consequent tremendous increase in political importance as an interest group central to both main political parties. It is also notable for its structure – the expansion and deepening of state institutions was exchanged for the broadening of their political composition. And this implied that any future effort at institutional replacement or retrenchment would strike directly at core supporters of *both* main political parties.

---

[16] González (1991, 15) notes that Colorado Party candidates won almost every election before and after the Second World War through the late 1950s. They also held the presidency continually (in democratic and undemocratic contexts) from at least the time of LaTorre in the 1870s through 1959.

[17] The durability of this institution is remarkable. An effort in 2002 to privatize the firm was rejected in a referendum called for by petitions signed by almost 700,000 citizens and that defeated privatization with a majority of 62%.

SURVEYING THE OUTCOME: THE URUGUAYAN STATE IN THE POST-BATLLE ERA

The long-run institutional development of the post-Batlle Uruguayan state contrasts sharply with that of Argentina. Whereas the latter institutions were created, transformed, eliminated, and reborn through cycles of populist, developmentalist, and orthodox politics, in Uruguay, the core institutions of the state – despite at least three important efforts to transform them – had acquired enough institutional stability and a self-reinforcing set of supporting interests to sustain and expand themselves through time.

The point is not that a perfectly functioning, rational–bureaucratic state was created out of whole cloth in the Batlle era; rather, it is that an institutional and political trajectory was launched that made possible the consistent development and expansion of administrative institutions and that ultimately facilitated their survival even in times of political and economic crises. And over the long haul, this produced a public bureaucracy that was capable of deep penetration into the society and economy, that directly provided many vital goods and services (including education, utilities, energy, and financial services), and that was able to impose high levels of taxation. In so doing, it performed at a level that induced a sense of legitimacy for these state institutions in the eyes of much of the citizenry.

Oszlak (1972, 50), in an evaluation of the Uruguayan state's public bureaucracy for the United Nations Development Program, pointed out that – subsequent difficulties notwithstanding – the Batlle-era administrative developments created a "more coherent state" and a "fundamentally cohesive" administration. Not only was the post-Batlle state comparatively effective but it also expanded rapidly in the scope of its activity. As it took on new functions, staffing increases were vertiginous. From a size of 43,220 employees in 1931, the public bureaucracy expanded to 57,200 in 1941, 166,000 in 1955, and over 200,000 by 1969 (Bergara et al. 2006, 35).

At first it might seem paradoxical that the expansion of the Uruguayan bureaucracy would over time produce – relative to Argentina and most of its Latin American peers – a public sector of substantially higher capacity. After all, entry into the public sector had been subject, from at least 1931, to political conditionality: new positions were allocated to supporters of the main political parties in proportion to their electoral strength. This form of politicization of the administration was not, however, fatal for governance for a series of reasons. First, once appointed, civil servants had very effective life tenure. Indeed, it required a vote of the senate to dismiss such an employee, a procedure retained across constitutional reforms (Constitution of 1934, Sección VII, Capítulo III, Artículo 158-10; Constitution of 1942, Sección IX, Capítulo III, Artículo 157-10; Constitution of 1954, Sección IX, Capítulo III, Artículo 168-10). This provision was intended to – and very effectively did – prevent the use of firings in the bureaucracy to make room for large numbers

The Social Question and the State 215

of patronage appointments for the government of the day. And the civil service system also provided a clear career path – as most non-entry-level positions were filled by means of internal promotion, not external hiring (Hall 1954, 55, 60).

While it was clearly not a perfect system, a variety of analysts have pointed out that the bureaucracy became unwieldy and bloated by the 1950s in part as public employment was used as a mechanism to compensate for inadequate private-sector job growth and to ameliorate social conflicts (see, e.g., Faraone 1968, 121; Bergara et al. 2006, 34) – the structure of the public administration had several features that made it enduring and less prone to maladministration than it might otherwise have been. First, the party-based division of positions implied that all the major political forces in the country bore shared responsibility for the performance of the state, giving them an incentive to avoid actions that would undermine performance despite whatever incumbent might hold power at any particular moment.[18] Nor were conflicts winner-take-all, as tenure regulations meant that even repeated national electoral defeats would not render the state bureaucracy the exclusive purview of any one political force. And finally, as a highly desirable position, public employment attracted individuals with substantial human capital. Oszlak (1972, 95) notes that by 1969, 21.8 percent of the civil service had a university education, in comparison with only 3.8 percent of the adult general population. And the state ultimately employed 68 percent of those with higher education credentials.

Other institutions also showed remarkable independence and stability, in sharp contrast to the Argentine experience. The supreme court, for example, has been credited with considerable independence and authority. Verner (1984, 481), in a review of Latin American supreme courts, locates Uruguay alongside Chile and Costa Rica as having the most "independent, vigorous, and active" courts in the region. The principal lacuna in terms of independence for the first two, however, was their subjugation to military governments in the 1973–85 and 1973–89 periods, respectively. The Uruguayan Supreme Court has usually, however, been influential, having from at least 1,934 judicial review powers; though as is typical in Latin America, it can decree unconstitutionality only in the application of a law in a specific case (Lösing 2002, 123). The tradition of a two-thirds legislative supermajority as a requirement for appointment to the supreme court (e.g., Constitution of 1952, Sección XV, Capítulo II, Artículo 236) has prevented its politicization and manipulation, as such majorities are essentially impossible to obtain without broad cross-party and cross-faction

---

[18] It is worth noting that this sort of a system is not without precedent. A similar form of party-based hiring into public employment was also long utilized in the Austrian *Proporz* system (Engelmann and Schwartz 1974, 960). A similar – if social and confessional rather than partisan at its core – division of society and political resources can be found in the Netherlands as well (Andeweg and Irwin 2002, 29–30). In neither case did the imposition of political or ascriptive criteria prevent the development of some of the world's most effective governments.

216 *Latin American State Building in Comparative Perspective*

support (Bergara 2006, 37). This is particularly true given the fragmentation and minority party representation that is a product of Uruguay's electoral law.

THE POWER OF PATH DEPENDENCY: THREE FAILED EFFORTS TO TRANSFORM THE STATE

Another way of looking at the path dependencies involved in institutional development is to consider how they react in times when a given trajectory is placed under extreme political or economic stress. Does a path of political development survive crisis? If not, the underlying political dynamics are likely not path dependent. It is easy to understand the establishment and/or expansion of public institutions when they occur during periods of sustained economic growth or cooperative, positive-sum politics. But a truly path-dependent argument would also suggest that they have remarkable stability in the face of contemporary pressures that threaten to undermine them in a fundamental way, be it fiscal or political. It is to such an examination that we next turn, considering the actual development of Uruguay's public institutions in three critical moments of stress after they were launched in the Batlle era. In two of them – the dicatorships of the 1930s and 1970s – authoritarian leaders came to power committed to fundamentally restructuring governance and political institutions. In the third, the democratic political system from 1955 to 1973 confronted the realities of severe economic crisis and prolonged stagnation, which produced internal and external efforts to transform the structure of the state. In none of these periods of intense political and/or economic stress were the basic features of the Uruguayan state changed, and indeed the basic patterns of a large, interventionist public bureaucracy remain – and remain very popular – to this day.

The Terra Dictatorship and the Depression

The first major challenge to the Batlle-inspired path of institutional development came from within the Colorado Party itself. Gabriel Terra, elected president in 1930 (governing in conjunction with the then-operative, power-sharing Consejo Nacional de Administración [CNA]), was initially supportive of the 1931 pact that had secured the expansion of state institutions[19] in exchange for coparticipation in public employment (position sharing across parties). But as the economy worsened, Terra turned against this limit on his executive power (as well as vociferously opposing the partial collegial executive that had been established in 1918). Instead, he moved to seize unilateral political power in a self-coup, behind a political and economic vision committed to revising the pro-industry statism of Batlle and his successors.

---

[19] Notably in this regard, including the creation of ANCAP and the establishment of a public electricity-supply monopoly.

The Social Question and the State

The effort to increase personal power as president came alongside a worsening economic climate as the Great Depression set in, which was exacerbated after the 1932 Ottawa accords reduced Uruguayan access to the vital UK market for its beef exports and as the British moved to favor trade among the commonwealth members through the Imperial preference system. This put tremendous pressure on the Uruguayan upper classes, who lacked access to alternative markets, leading them to support Terra's conservative reaction (Jacob 1983, 24; Finch 1991, 198). Despite this core support – and the seizure of dictatorial power and willingness to use repression – we will see that Terra found it impossible to fundamentally change the trajectory on which the Uruguayan state was developing.

This was not for lack of trying. For example, a vituperative opponent of coparticipation and the collegial executive, Terra managed to abolish the CNA and impose a new constitution in 1934. But if his goal was to remove the practice of cross-party power sharing, he was unsuccessful. The new constitution replaced the collegial executive with a senate that was to be equally divided among the Terra faction of the Colorado Party and the Herrera faction of the Nationalist (Blanco) Party, in recognition of the Blanco leader's essential cooperation with the seizure of power. This, if anything, gave the opposition more power insofar as it gained an effective veto over policy initiatives in the senate (Faraone 1968, 81).

Nor – despite the powerful influence of landed, export-oriented elites – were the institutions of protectionist development substantially affected. The recently created ANCAP, for example, proceeded to grow apace, commissioning its first oil refinery under Terra's government in 1937. And the foreign exchange and trade controls imposed as the Great Depression set in were institutionalized rather than substantially liberalized (Finch 1991, 200). Instead of pursuing an agro-ranching–based liberal strategy in line with Terra's core support base, the weight of industrialization and urbanization had already become so great that Terra had little choice but to further pursue import substituting industrialization. In addition to continuing earlier pro-industrial tariff policies, Terra instituted partial market reserves for some sectors and conferred additional effective protection via devaluation (Jacob 1983, 82). This in turn implied continued commitment to powerful and economically invasive state institutions.

Indicative of the failure of even the modest institutional transformations attempted by Terra was the fact that a new constitutional revision was undertaken under his immediate successor, Alfredo Baldomir – who was also Terra's brother-in-law and police chief (Finch 1991, 201). By 1942, a new constitution had been approved in a plebiscite that largely reversed Terra's changes, returning the institutional structure to one quite similar to a more normal democratic one (but without the collegial executive of the 1918 charter). Then, the end of the Second World War brought the Batlle faction of the Colorado Party back to power, and it was further accompanied by an unprecedented economic expansion based on both the accumulated foreign reserves of the conflict era

218   *Latin American State Building in Comparative Perspective*

and the very high international commodity prices that characterized the post–World War II and Korean War periods. This only deepened Uruguayan institutional development in the pattern of the established trajectory, as growth both validated the approach and lessened resource constraints. Indeed, further expansion of the state became the norm: social protection was expanded considerably, the creation of wage councils brought new state intervention into the setting of private-sector wages, and social security benefits were broadened substantially, becoming near universal by 1954 (Finch 1991, 203). Even the collegial executive returned in the 1952 constitutional charter – in a stronger form than its 1918 variant – replacing the office of the president altogether (Taylor 1955, 37; Edelmann 1969).[20]

The Era of the Lean Cows

The next major challenge to the development of the Uruguayan state came as the consequence of a substantial and sustained decline in its trade position coupled with the all-too-predictable exhaustion of the import-substituting strategy of industrialization in such a small economy. As foreign exchange earnings declined and industrial expansion slowed (owing to the saturation of the domestic market and the inability to import sufficient capital goods and raw material inputs), the economy entered a period of prolonged stagnation (Daly 1965). Between 1955 and 1975, the Uruguayan economy experienced almost no net growth in gross domestic product (GDP) and suffered from high and increasing rates of inflation, capital flight, and low rates of investment (Arocena 2002, 201–2).

This posed a severe challenge for a democratic political system. The first response to crisis was to further increase the scope and interventionist character of the Uruguayan state. Oszlak has argued that during this period, public employment came to be used as a substitute for the stagnant private sector, ultimately attempting to absorb social demands and social tensions through its expansion. This strategy may have delayed – but not prevented – the escalation of societal demands, but it also reached its limits by the late 1950s; public employment had reached a whopping 25 percent of the economically active population (Oszlak 1972, 38, 69). Changing paths, especially within a democratic regime, would be extremely difficult. And as Taylor (1963, 71) noted at the time, the public administration

is the heart of the middle sector, and therefore highly functional both as a means of sharing the available national wealth and as a support for the present political system. Relocation of this enormous staff would be impossible; no private alternatives exist.

[20] The plural executive – the Council of Government – even further deepened the principle of coparticipation by making possible the representation of the two factions of the dominant political party (by sharing one of its six council seats). The minority party's dominant faction was guaranteed the remaining three seats on the council.

The Social Question and the State

The Colorado Party majority in the collegial executive responded to this stagnation not with retrenchment but with a deepening of statism. The system of multiple exchange rates expanded, protectionism increased, and subsidies were used in an effort to protect consumers from the consequences of accelerating inflation (Finch 1991, 209). With growth negative in 1957 and 1958, in the latter year, for the first time, the Uruguayan electorate gave a majority to the Blanco Party.

The incoming Blanco government made substantial changes in economic policy – most notably the unification of the exchange rate, devaluation, and the reduction of barriers to trade. This stabilization package had critical outside support from the International Monetary Fund and was politically beneficial to the core Blanco constituency in the agro-export sector (Finch 1981, 239). But in *institutional* terms, very little changed – the size of the public sector increased under the two Blanco administrations of the late 1950s and early 1960s just as it had under the preceding Colorado governments (Finch 1991, 211–12). At the same time, the institutional empowerment of the middle and working classes, coupled with rising inflation and stagnant growth, produced a sharp escalation in social conflict and demands made on the already overburdened state. Two different Blanco governments, led by different party factions, proved as incapable as the Colorados of fundamentally altering the nature and power of public institutions – even as economic pressures put them under immense strain.

As the 1960s wore on, however, the ability of the state to continue to ameliorate social conflict through public employment and subsidies was limited by the already very high fiscal burden and the difficulty of further increasing public indebtedness. Yet the 1966 presidential election was fought in large measure over the collegial executive, which had been blamed by many for Uruguay's persistent problems – and which was repealed and replaced with a traditional unitary presidency. In the wake of this reform, Oscar Gestido, a conservative Colorado, was elected, but he died soon after and was replaced by his vice president, Jorge Pacheco. Pacheco took power in the context of almost triple-digit inflation and serious economic decline, choosing as his response to impose austerity and real wage declines on the population and to bypass the legislature as much as possible. This was complemented by an increasingly repressive approach to strikes and labor mobilization that only escalated as the Tupamaro urban guerrilla insurrection gained force (Finch 1991, 216). Rising political polarization, civil insurrection, and an inability to solve – regardless of recourse to repression – the underlying structural problems of the Uruguayan political economy opened the gateway to the next major crisis that state institutions faced: the military government of 1973–85.

Military Dictatorship and Failed State Reform

It had become abundantly clear to many observers that the Uruguayan political system was poorly equipped to handle the social and economic tensions that buffeted the country in the late 1960s and early 1970s (González 1991, 44–46). At the same time, the traditionally apolitical military had become steeped in anti-Communist national security ideology, and the barrier to its political participation was substantially breached when the Pacheco administration (1967–72) utilized the military directly in the conflict with the Tupamaro insurgency. The military's slide into de facto power – behind the facade of a civilian president – began in February 1973 and culminated in the closure of congress and the creation of a military-dominated national security council (Consejo de Seguridad Nacional; COSENA) that seized executive authority.

The military's early years in power – behind the essentially puppet civilian presidencies of Bordaberry (1972–76) and Méndez (1976–81) – eventually developed a two-pronged strategy for governance, involving first seizing complete political control and subsequently attempting to institutionalize a decidedly different Uruguayan state. The degree of control achieved by the military was remarkable, and it was virtually unchallenged after it had crushed a brief general strike in the early days of its rule. Gillespie has highlighted the depth of this military–technocratic domination, noting that by 1976, Uruguay had more political prisoners per capita than any other country in the world. And its direct reach into civil society was more profound than the three neighboring bureaucratic authoritarian regimes – the military had "even classif[ied] each citizen of the country as A, B, or C according to political reliability, and control[ed] employment on that basis, even in some private-sector activities, such as education" (Gillespie 1991, 50).[21] The intensity of repression had its desired effect of eliminating overt expressions of opposition and enforcing citizen passivity and compliance (Sondrol 1992, 197).

Although the generals themselves may not have had a clear ideology beyond a vituperative and moralistic nationalism and anti-Communism, they turned to a decidedly orthodox set of civilian allies to impose a fundamental transformation of the Uruguayan state. The approach blamed Uruguay's travails on state intervention (Astori 1985, 145), and led by Economy Minister Alejandro Végh Villegas, an orthodox stabilization was initiated. What is notable about the neoliberal episode under the Uruguayan military is how decidedly limited its *institutional* reforms ended up being. Policy was indeed transformed: sharp austerity was imposed, and the economy was substantially opened to trade and capital flows. But structural changes to the public administration were not forthcoming. The direct state ownership over the commanding heights of the economy was not removed – indeed, Finch points out that the only important public entity that was privatized was the Montevideo mass transit system (Finch 1981, 270). This stands in exceedingly sharp contrast to the Chilean military government, which not only engaged in wholesale privatization of

---

[21] Uruguay was *not* a leader in the practice of death-squad terror that was all too common elsewhere in the Southern Cone, most notably in Argentina and Chile.

The Social Question and the State 221

state-owned enterprises but also engendered a complete privatization of the national pension system and a partial one in health care. Even more strikingly, the enormous public-sector labor force was largely untouched. What reduction occurred was generally the result of arbitrary dismissals of suspected opponents, and wages fell no more rapidly in government than in the broader private economy (Finch 1981, 269–70). With complete political control, unions essentially neutered, and a civilian leadership committed to restructuring, still very little was achieved beyond attempts at inflation control and management of external imbalances. Certainly the institutions of the state itself proved remarkably resilient.

The more explicitly political project for the transformation of the Uruguayan state was brought forward in 1977 and put to a vote in a national plebiscite on a constitutional revision in 1980 (Finch 1991, 224). When the constitutional plebiscite was held, in the context of a near-complete media monopoly by pro-regime forces and a high level of repression, the population came out in force and decisively rejected the reforms by a margin of 57.2 to 42.8, with turnout at 85.2 percent (Gillespie 1991, 71). Even the use of the state to build a political support base for the military-inspired political project proved to be exceedingly difficult – existing institutional patterns were deeply entrenched both in the government and in the popular mind. Attempts to deprofessionalize the civil service and misuse public institutions largely failed. As Gillespie (1991, 66) points out, despite the theoretical ability of the military government to hand out employment and provide access to social provision on a clientelistic basis, it faced the "problem that the provision of welfare-state programs could not easily be exchanged for votes when sophisticated Uruguayans had already come to see such programs as their birthright."

This marked the beginning of the end of the military effort at refounding the Uruguayan state along different lines. In recognition of this defeat, the military initiated a process in the early 1980s that led to a democratic transition and the effective restoration of the 1967 constitution. Indeed, the traditional parties and party competition reemerged from the intense repression of the military era in an almost unchanged form, further underscoring the depths to which the patterns of political development and even political contestation had become institutionalized. It was an institutional stability that was to serve Uruguay well moving forward, where when combined with economic strategies more suited to a small country than the intense protectionism of the 1930s to the 1970s, a return to sustained economic expansion was made possible for the first time since the 1950s. What is even more remarkable is the critical role the state and its decidedly robust institutions continue to play in this now much more open economy.[22]

---

[22] This contrast highlights the very imperfect overlap between public institutions and economic policy. It is very possible to have robust state institutions with sensible or self-defeating economic strategies; of course, the reverse is entirely possible as well.

INSTITUTIONALIZATION OVER THE LONGUE DURÉE: POPULIST CYCLING VERSUS CONSENSUAL STATISM

This book has made a fundamentally path-dependent argument about the nature of state-building processes. Most critically, it argues that differences in trajectory of political development are fundamentally persistent – even in the face of potentially severe economic or political pressures. And in the examinations of Argentina and Uruguay earlier, we have examined the hypothesized trajectories (populist cycling vs. state building, respectively) as they faced critical tests in the wake of a second critical juncture marked by the rise of the social question. We saw that in Argentina, subsequent political and economic crises were met with pendular swings of vertiginous institutional creation *or* destruction, leading to the inability to institutionalize and thus legitimate broad swathes of the public administration. In contrast, in Uruguay, severe challenges were met with the stability and sometimes expansion of existing public institutions along the same lines as emerged during the critical juncture. These institutions were not only subject to self-reinforcing dynamics based on the creation of powerful vested interests but they also achieved substantial societal legitimacy that was evidenced in the overwhelming rejection of efforts to transform the statist institutional structure in a series of referenda in the 1990s and 2000s.

But to make the case for a path-dependent explanation, it is also important to show that hypothesized differences outlined here are persistent and/or expand over very long periods of time – that is, that they are truly path dependent rather than the consequent alternative factors of what Collier and Collier (2002 [1991], 31ff.) have termed "constant causes" – that is, those that operate on a contemporaneous and independent basis. It is to this task that we turn here, evaluating the long-term performance of the Argentine and Uruguayan public administrations in two arenas that are core competencies of any national state: taxation and the provision of basic education.[23] If the argument of this book holds, we should see the divergence between Argentina and Uruguay beginning around the time of the critical juncture (that of mass political and electoral inclusion beginning in early–twentieth-century Argentina and during and after the Great Depression in Uruguay).

Taxes

The *type* of taxation that is imposed is the initial point of departure in the examination of long-term patterns. One important measure of the administrative

---

[23] It is important to focus on arenas that are seen as essential activities for virtually all states, to ensure that observed differences are a consequence of variation in the scope, competence, and quality of public administration rather than a reflection of policy preferences. This would, for example, be the case if we examined military spending. States vary widely in their preferences for national defense expenditure. But all states – especially in developing areas – see the raising of revenue and provision of basic schooling as a critical function.

The Social Question and the State

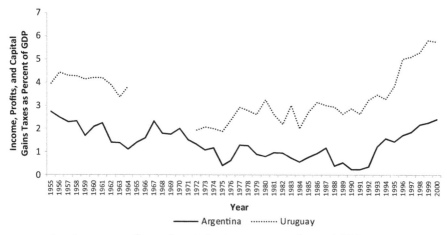

FIGURE 6.3. Income, profits, and capital gains taxes as a share of GDP.

capacity of a state is to consider the degree to which it is able to levy imposts on more sources that are notoriously hard to reach. Particularly in the developing world, this is the case with taxation of individual income, capital gains, or royalties. Unlike taxes on trade that can be collected at a few narrow ports of entry, or indirect taxes, such as the value added tax, that can be made self-enforcing in important ways, levying taxes on individual or corporate income requires accurate information as to the actual income earned (or equivalently, the actual level of profits) and usually some system of withholding. Unfortunately, given taxation, there exist very strong incentives to underreport this income, and without an economy-wide system of withholding for income taxes or the ability to make parallel calculations and engage in complex auditing efforts for corporate profits, the collection of these taxes will tend to fall to levels far below what the nominal rates imply. As a consequence, the relative ability of states to levy such taxes is an indicator of their administrative efficacy, at least in the vitally important arena of taxation.

Figure 6.3 considers the relative importance of direct taxes on individual and corporate income in Argentina and Uruguay. Data are, unfortunately, only available from 1950 onward, but they indicate a persistently higher level of taxation by this source in Uruguay. The order is typically between 1 and 2 percentage points of GDP, which is a very substantial difference, especially when one is considering a single taxation mechanism, and one that is in neither country the principal revenue source. This difference probably understates the actual divergence, as it does not incorporate data on the very large payroll taxes on wages (levied on both employers and employees) that supports the Uruguayan national pension system.

Of course, it is possible that Argentina simply prefers not to level substantial taxes on income but has a large, well-developed state that funds itself through alternative mechanisms. Figure 6.4 considers that ratio of the share of the

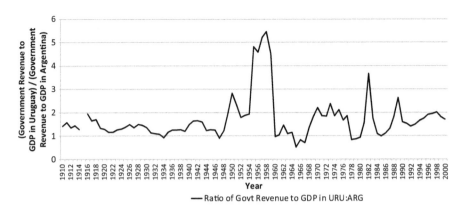

FIGURE 6.4. Ratios of government revenue to GDP in Uruguay and Argentina (Uruguay revenue:gdp/Argentinarevenue:gdp).

economy that government taxation obtains in Uruguay relative to that of Argentina. In this calculation, any number greater than 1 implies a higher overall taxation level in Uruguay – an outcome that obtains for almost every point in time in a 90-year time span. Even given differences in economic cycle, the level of taxation is higher in Uruguay, often far higher. It is commonly more than 50 percent greater than in Argentina and, in some circumstances, double or triple the Argentine level. This finding is all the more surprising when we consider that for this time period, Argentina was always the wealthier country – and taxation levels have been shown to rise with the level of development.

Education

The same pattern holds in an examination of a different core function of the state – the provision of basic public goods in the form of secondary education. We saw earlier that Uruguay was an early innovator in this education, as a consequence, one of the many institutional reforms of the Batlle era, and one can see that this initial advantage was maintained thereafter. In Figure 6.5, we see the percentage of the national population enrolled in secondary education since 1900. Beginning in the 1920s, and uninterrupted thereafter, Uruguay has provided secondary education to more of its population even than wealthier Argentina, and the gap, in addition to being consistent, has generally widened over time.[24]

---

[24] The large jump in the data for both countries for 1970 is the consequence of a change in data source, and operational definition, that affected both countries. Although data before and after that time are not comparable, at any particular point in time, the comparison of Argentina with Uruguay is valid – relying on the same definitions and same data sources.

The Social Question and the State

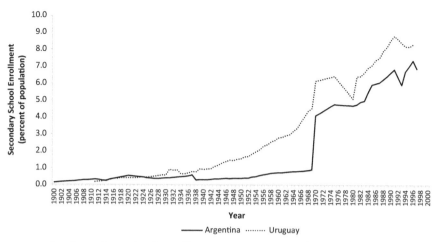

FIGURE 6.5. Secondary school enrollment as a percentage of national population.

Indeed, from roughly the mid-1920s onward, Argentine school enrollment as a share of the population never reached the levels observed in Uruguay. This is particularly striking because Argentina was a substantially wealthier country over this entire period, and presumably, if public resources were underutilized because of institutional deficiencies on the part of the state, private, familial solutions would be comparatively more available. Yet Uruguay still dominated on this metric. Nor do the differences reflect structural dissimilarities, as both countries are highly urbanized and share a similar underlying political economy. Neither has the very large (and hard-to-reach) peasantry more common in many other parts of Latin America.

This chapter has focused analytically on two central goals. First, it examined the differentiation that occurs for states on an initially favorable trajectory of political development that is consequent on alternative resolutions of the social question of mass political inclusion. Thus, Argentina and Uruguay, similar in underlying political economy, delayed state formation, and initially auspicious institutional development, parted ways as a consequence of delayed early middle-class incorporation in the former and much delayed political inclusion of the popular sectors in the latter. These differences produced in Uruguay a deepening of institutional development and profound institutional cycling in populist and antipopulist swings in Argentina that ultimately undermined the institutionalization of any stable set of public institutions. This pendular expansion and contraction of the state also contrasts sharply with the experience of Peru (as seen in Chapter 5), which similarly experienced comparatively early mass incorporation but was not on an initial trajectory favorable to institutional development.

Second, this chapter probed the path dependence of these institutional trajectories by examining their stability in the wake of severe countervailing pressures – when political elites openly sought to change regnant patterns in the context of economic and/or political crisis. Their resilience in the face of determined – and oftentimes authoritarian – efforts at reform highlights the importance of the critical junctures that launch trajectories of political development. And by a variety of metrics, the differences in the scope and capacity of the Argentine and Uruguayan public administrations are stable or expanding and very persistent after the resolution of the second critical juncture, despite myriad political and economic crises confronting both polities.

7

Conclusions, Implications, and Extensions

Social Foundations, Germany–Prussia, and the Limits of Contemporary State Building

This book has laid out a long-term, path-dependent explanation for state-building outcomes in the South American region. The explanation has also taken issue with the theoretical thrust of much of the contemporary literature; its emphasis has been squarely societal and political–economic. Instead of war, the curse of resource wealth, institutional design, leadership, or culture holding pride of place in explaining long-run patterns of political development, the emphasis here has been on underlying social and political dynamics at two key moments – the initial formation of national political institutions in the wake of independence from Spain and the period in which the middle and working classes first gained substantial suffrage and effective entry into national political competition.

RECAPITULATION

The approach taken in this book differed sharply from prevailing approaches to the study of state building. It proposed a path-dependent theory of the development of national political institutions that posited two critical inflection points. The first, which comes at the time of the consolidation of national political institutions in the postcolonial era, depends fundamentally on (1) the servile or juridically free character of prevailing social relations and (2) the ability or inability of elite political factions to cooperate around the formation of national institutions that would work to their collective – and individual – benefit. These two features of the postindependence sociopolitical environment condition the resultant trajectories, for unless both conditions are met (juridically free labor and elite political cooperation), the construction of comprehensive and penetrating state institutions will be unlikely.

Why would this be the case? An economy reliant on unfree labor puts an absolute premium on the *local* control over coercion by dominant economic

227

actors, a control they cannot cede to an administrative center without immediate risk to both life and livelihood. Where elites cannot cooperate, and in particular, where they cannot also collude to exclude nonelite interests from the political system, national political competition takes on a zero-sum character, with political factions or parties most concerned about the empowerment of state institutions leading to the permanent victory of an opposing faction and the imposition of severe costs on the losing side. This fear in turn drives an intense resistance to the building of strong state institutions – born out of a fear of their use against parts of the elite itself. It is only where iterative cooperation is achieved, and the permanent dominance of any particular elite faction is precluded, that the self-taxation to engage in long-run institution building is possible – for only then can there be confidence that the public goods and private benefits of expanded central state activity will be shared across elite factions alongside the costs.

The initial critical juncture thus launches a trajectory – either of institution building or atrophy. But it does not by itself determine long-run outcomes. It must be remembered that the successful cases of institution building in this initial period focus on a small, but comparatively important, set of government institutions. Most important is the construction of a framework for effective taxation – even of elite incomes or wealth – and the juridical and coercive institutions necessary to impose basic rule of law, property rights enforcement, and the primacy of the central state's authority throughout the national territory. This initial institution building is possible in these contexts in large measure because there is no visible threat at the time that the central state authorities thus empowered will be used in a redistributive sense – for the demands of the popular masses are far from being effectively pressed in national political competition. And elites, whatever their factional differences, are united in the desire to maintain this exclusion. The consolidation of the long-run trajectory of political development, however, awaits the resolution of a second crisis faced by all states in the Latin American region: the political rise of the popular classes.

The second crucial moment in the state-building process thus comes when the social question enters national political debate.[1] As economic development progressed in the region, and economic structures became more complex and differentiated, eventually, middle-class and working-class sectors began to expand and produce political representatives that forcefully demanded participation in national governance. This occurred both in mobilized ways (including labor mobilization or insurrectionary activity at different times and in different places by both middle- and working-class parties alike) and through electoral

---

[1] The "social question" is scornfully referenced by Marx (1938) in *Critique of the Gotha Program* as it was associated with the state-based amelioration of the misery of the working classes – rather than self-organized revolutionary transformation. It has since come to signify when the conditions of life for ordinary working-class citizens become a serious issue on the national political agenda and a matter for mobilization and socioeconomic conflict.

Conclusions, Implications, and Extensions

competition, where it existed, and if suffrage was broad enough to include substantial numbers of nonelite voters. In the Latin American context, this challenge to oligarchic dominance generally occurred sometime between 1900 and the Second World War.

How this challenge was resolved – and its effect on the dynamics of state building – depended critically on the preexisting trajectory of political development and the timing of the electoral incorporation of the popular classes. Where the trajectory of institutional development was favorable, and popular incorporation came late – during or after the Depression – the construction of cross-class coalitions between middle-class and working-class parties around the construction of an expansive, developmentalist state became possible. This political bargain underwrote the vertiginous expansion of already relatively effective public institutions, the creation of new protected industrial sectors, and thus a set of new industrial elites with a strong interest in the survival of the statist political economy. And it also took the question of the proper role of the state out of the center of political debate – for powerful actors of all political stripes developed a vested interest in the expansive state. Although there certainly was constant conflict over the character of specific public policies or the degree of redistribution they entailed, few important actors challenged the value of a dominant state role in directing the economy, economic protectionism, or a large public sector in these cases.

By contrast, if popular-sector incorporation came early, but state institutions were already on an initially favorable trajectory, the crucial middle class–working class accommodation would prove difficult, for the former group was much more tied to the private, oligarchy-dominated export economy, was far less reliant on public employment, and thus was frequently opposed to the creation of an expansive or interventionist state. Politically, parties representing the middle sectors in these contexts were economically liberal, rejecting the state subsidy, exchange rate overvaluation, and protectionism widely used in the region to create large, domestically oriented industrial sectors. Should an effort at developmentalism and protectionism nevertheless begin in one of these countries, its institutions would be met with little, if any, cross-class political support.[2] As a consequence, the appropriate role and scope of public institutions became *the* central axis of political conflict among working-class, middle-sector, and oligarchical interests, sparking populist and antipopulist cycles and the inability to consolidate *any* coherent pattern of state institutional structures.

The challenge of middle- and working-class incorporation was even more problematic in contexts in which an initial foundation of solid national institutions did not exist. In such contexts, efforts to incorporate or control rising pressure from below were difficult to enact or sustain. The state lacked the institutional capacity to effectively constrain or tax elite interests, making

---

[2] Indeed, few industrial or middle-sector actors would see themselves as having a stake in the survival of such an invasive state apparatus.

230 *Latin American State Building in Comparative Perspective*

successful redistributive politics nearly impossible, even where popular-sector forces might win political power. On the other side, an oligarchy-dominated government would find it difficult to stabilize national politics either through a confining institutional apparatus that offers some material compromise (as in, e.g., Bismarckian social protection or state corporatism) or through the removal of popular-sector interests from political contestation by force. For both efforts require stronger central institutions than had come to exist in such contexts. Even more crucially, once the irruption of the social question has taken place, even structural reforms that transformed the factors (elite division and unfree labor relations) that had initially impeded the formation of effective and penetrating national institutions were insufficient to create a viable coalition to support long-run institutional development. For once the question of redistribution has entered the national political arena, the elite cooperation that was possible in other settings and that was necessary to initiate the construction of strong political and administrative institutions will not be forthcoming. It will have become all too obvious that such newly empowered institutions could at a future date be turned on their oligarchical enablers. Path dependence here implies, unfortunately, that there is no easy road back.

The utility of an argument is, however, at some level proportional to the scope of its applicability. Thus, in this last chapter, consideration is given to the theoretical and empirical implications of the arguments set forth and the potential reach that this approach to state building might have to contexts beyond the postcolonial Latin American region in which it was born. In theoretical terms, the relevance of the passage of time- and path-dependent dynamics in the consolidation of (good or bad) institutional equilibria necessitated a long-term, comparative examination of development trajectories and an assessment of the over-time stability of the outcomes. At the same time, the social–foundational approach employed here also begs questions of scope not easily answered in an empirical treatment limited to four Latin American cases. For the countries of the region share myriad underlying features that make them potentially quite different from the context in which state building took place in other times and places, from, for example, the anarchic states system of Early Modern Europe for the first wave of state builders to the contemporary era of extensive international integration, more robust popular-sector politics, economic liberalism, and more limited interstate conflict for the late, late developers. It is thus important to consider whether the theoretical patterns posited in this book make a plausible contribution to the understanding of political development in entirely different contexts. This is a possibility that will be probed, in a necessarily preliminary fashion, in an examination of the emergence of the archetypal "strong state" in Prussia and, later, Germany.

THEORETICAL AND PRACTICAL IMPLICATIONS

There are profound theoretical and practical implications that follow from the shift to a society-centric historical approach to long-run state-building

Conclusions, Implications, and Extensions

outcomes. The path-dependent formulation implies that once a trajectory is laid in, it can be decidedly difficult to change long-term outcomes. The path dependency, as we have seen, derives from the over-time development or diminution of societal actors who either have vested interests in the expansion and improved efficacy of governmental institutions or, alternatively, have quite a lot to lose should effective political development take place. Path departure, as a consequence, is as time passes (and vested interests proliferate) increasingly difficult to initiate and, at a minimum, entails not only institutional innovation in inhospitable terrain but also general social–structural transformations. The theory is not, of course, fully deterministic – such structural changes *are* possible, but they ought also to be quite exceptional. And we will examine in the next section an example of just such an exception – nineteenth-century Prussia – that successfully transformed, to some extent endogenously, a partially unfavorable state-building trajectory (albeit under comparatively favorable political conditions).

It is also important to stress that the passage of time – because it provides concrete experiences that condition expectations – will itself also tend to deepen the particular channel in which political development (or underdevelopment) proceeds.[3] Societal expectations of institutional activity and efficacy can make particular institutional configurations (for good or ill) increasingly self-enforcing. Thus, for example, where servile social relations and elite discord undermine the efficacy of national institutions, that very result is likely to induce or reinforce a *subsequent* belief among crucial actors that costly investments in state institutional deepening are unlikely to be collectively or individually worthwhile. As time passes and elites increasingly pursue private alternatives to government action via public goods production, the incentives to invest in institutional development decline still further. The reverse logic obtains, of course, where initial state-building investments produce comparatively desirable outcomes, from the perspective of elites, that help to shape the perceived value of subsequent investments in state power and institutional penetration in other arenas.[4] And as was argued in Chapters 3 and 4, the building of state institutions to provide public goods in such virtuous-cycle contexts was also often simultaneously privately profitable for dominant class actors as well.

Changing an unfavorable state-building trajectory is difficult for reasons independent of the specific path dependencies outlined earlier as well, for it implies a paradox. If one accepts that servile labor relations and elite discord must be overcome to induce cooperation around the development of stronger institutions and to provide the material resources necessary for their creation, then one must consider just how the transformation of such sociopolitical

---

[3] This is very much in line with the mechanisms of institutional reinforcement identified by Greif and Laitin (2004).

[4] After all, where the state is competent enough to successfully provide a public or private good, it can usually attain scale economies, solve coordination dilemmas, and avoid free riding much more easily than through disaggregated private provision of the same good.

patterns can be achieved. But the factors that initially blocked an effective state-building effort – servile labor relations and elite discord – induce a problem for any government that seeks to engage in serious administrative reform. For the comparatively ineffective existing state institutions would themselves have to overcome these twin challenges. This is decidedly difficult under the most favorable of circumstances, for the mitigation of interelite conflict where it exists typically relies on the utilization of complex and *credible* institutions for the sharing of power over time (whether it be via corporatism, consociationalism, limitations on executive tenure, or collegial executives, inter alia).[5] Of course, where institutions are weak and/or unstable, such arrangements are difficult to construct and harder to make credible. Similarly, the emancipation of a large servile labor force – and its replacement with a nonservile alternative – is institutionally, economically, and in all likelihood militarily exceedingly demanding. For it would entail the wholesale restructuring of property rights systems, quite likely an extensive land reform, but of needs must take place where government institutions are weak and central coercive resources are limited. The paradox, of course, is that the servile character of agriculture impeded the formation of the strong central coercive and administrative institutions that would be required to end servility.[6] Were agrarian social relations changed for exogenous reasons – for example, via imposition by a foreign conqueror – at this historical juncture, however, we would expect the possibility that a trajectory of political modernization could initiate (assuming the political conditions were also met).

As noted earlier, none of this implies that a change of trajectory is impossible in the first critical juncture – only that it becomes increasingly difficult, ceteris paribus, as time passes. And of course, in the empirical portion of the book, several changes of trajectory do take place. For example, in Argentina and Uruguay, an initial, serious problem of elite disunity was ultimately overcome, but only after nearly a half-century of bloody civil strife. The temporal contrast with Chile is striking, as the much earlier consolidation of basic oligarchic cooperation precluded deep schisms or cleavages from emerging among elites and rendered the civil conflict that did emerge in the postindependence era both brief and quickly resolved. Looking more broadly, sometimes a powerful

---

[5] The effort to end severe intraelite conflict in the Uruguayan case, as detailed in Chapter 4, proceeded in fits and starts over a very long period of time, often punctuated by violent irruptions before, finally, a more lasting arrangement took root and started to reshape the nature of elite political competition.

[6] We will see later that Prussia managed – belatedly and over great resistance – to bring an end to its feudal land tenure structure. This process took nearly a half-century to complete, began long after the monarch had identified it as a goal, and was accomplished in a context that was *not* simultaneously bedeviled by serious intraelite competition for control over national political institutions. Monarchical absolutism under the Hohenzollerns had overcome that challenge – but only at the enormous price of delegating local public authority and immunity from taxation to the noble landed upper class.

Conclusions, Implications, and Extensions

exogenous force is required to knock a state off an unfavorable trajectory. This is particularly true where dramatic land reforms are required to effectively free labor from the bonds of de jure or de facto servitude. These reforms, where they were actually undertaken, in many cases were the product of intense civil conflict (Mexico, the United States), occurred under foreign occupation (Japan, Korea, Taiwan), or resulted from a calamitous military shock coming from the international states system (Prussia's stunning defeats at Jena and Auerstädt). These cases are also contexts in which only *one* of the two key features identified in this book as necessary for the initiation of a state-building trajectory was absent. Changing paths is most problematic in contexts, like that of Peru, where both social relations and elite political dynamics provide infertile terrain for administrative development, and where the probability of successfully changing trajectories is correspondingly sharply lower.

The problem of changing trajectory becomes even more worrisome in light of the two-stage argument outlined in this book. And the outcome of the second critical juncture – the institutional response to the entry of nonelite classes into serious political contestation – depends importantly on the developmental pathway launched during the formation of national political institutions (the first critical juncture). After the second critical juncture, the potential for unfavorable institutional trajectories to harden becomes even more severe. For the emergence of an effective state-building dynamic in the first period was in part premised on the exclusion of working- and middle-class actors from an important role in national politics. This removed the potential for the redistributive use of newly strengthened public power, making it unthreatening to the elites who would have both to undertake it as a political project and pay the bulk of the taxes to support state building.[7] Indeed, where the masses are not yet politically relevant, institutional development could be quite materially beneficial to those elites in collective and individual terms. If, however, time had passed to the point where the social question had come to take an important place on the national political agenda and the popular sector had gained political entrée, elite incentives to cooperate around institution-building processes – even in the most otherwise favorable of social contexts – diminish sharply. Where this is the case, what, then, can induce elites in a polity governed under weak institutions but also beset by the reality of mass popular mobilization and participation to make investments that can constrain, tax, and coerce even powerful interests?[8] As the potential for redistributive policies becomes real where mass participation has emerged, this makes institution building a

---

[7] This, of course, refers only to those cases in which neither servile labor relations nor zero-sum intraelite conflict was characteristic. Where either or both of these conditions obtained, state building was threatening to elites for reasons unrelated to the potential for redistribution.

[8] I do not contend that this is impossible or that only elite actors can launch state-building processes. In revolutionary settings, for example, dramatic institutional expansion and strengthening are quite possible. But these comparatively rare setting are outside the theoretical scope of this book, even if they represent one (however improbable) path to institutional reform. In this case,

234   *Latin American State Building in Comparative Perspective*

decidedly risky endeavor for dominant class actors. For once the masses participate in politics, the possibility of viable antielite political coalitions emerges, or at a minimum, distributional coalitions that do not work to the benefit of important dominant class segments or sectors are readily imaginable.

This raises real and pressing policy questions about what realistically can be done to promote the development and improvement of governmental institutions in unfavorable sociopolitical settings. Will institutional reforms have their intended consequences where the social terrain is not fertile? Can even decisive social transformation induced from without – for example, the penetration of free wage labor relations and agrarian reform that undermines a traditional oligarchy – reset the political clock and allow a jump from an unfavorable to a favorable institutional trajectory?

Considering external influences raises the question of whether countries can be induced to improve the quality of governmental institutions through conditions placed on the provision of aid. The implication of the argument put forward here is, however, that the recent turn toward such conditionality on institutional and governance improvement may end up having the unintended consequence of redirecting support to the places that least need it. For if the path-dependent theoretical claims made in this book hold, the polities most in need of institutional improvement will have the greatest difficulties doing so and will need far greater external support to generate even modest improvements than contexts less burdened with an infelicitous socioeconomic and political history. But to hold developing states to a single standard, in a world where hysteresis characterizes the process of political development, is likely counterproductive.[9] Not all states will be equally able to make improvements, and in particular, if benchmarks inherently rate states relative to the performance of their peers, this problem is only exacerbated.[10]

The challenges to contemporary theory in the academic literature on state building are equally stark. This book has argued forcefully for the bringing back of society into the center of our analyses of state building and away from an emphasis on institutions, the international system and international conflict, and the consequences of ecological endowments that have formed the core of

---

    the obstacles to state building found in the structure of elite interests are obviated by removing the elites themselves.

[9] This is, of course, in addition to the problem that specifying an institutional best practice is at best difficult according to Rodrik (2008), in a world where there may be multiple good solutions to a problem and contextual factors are critical to successful implementation of institutional reforms.

[10] This is one of the features of prominent contemporary measures like the Worldwide Governance Indicators, which is one of the components on which aid allocations through the Millennium Challenge Account are decided. This metric explicitly norms the position of each county's performance relative to the distribution of other countries at a particular point in time rather than using a time-invariant metric that would be suitable for cross-time comparisons. Thus, a country's governance quality rating could decline simply because others' improved at a rate more rapid than its did – without any actual decline in institutional quality taking place. And for this, it would, presumably, be punished.

Conclusions, Implications, and Extensions

scholarship on state building in particular and comparative and international political economy more generally. In this way, it is a book that hearkens back to the spirit of Barrington Moore (1966) or Gregory Luebbert (1991), or James Mahoney (2010), more recently, and forms part of what Weyland (2007) identifies as a recent pendular swing in the direction of more structuralist, society-centric scholarship in contemporary Latin American political economy. The argument presented here is emphatically not, however, calling for a return to the determinism of some dependency theory, structural Marxism, or, for that matter, classical modernization theory. But it does raise questions about the notion that long-term, deep reform and modernization of state institutions are typically amenable to change by means of international aid or incentives, are largely a matter of proper institutional design, are something good leadership itself can produce, or are the straightforward product of changing forms of partisan competition. Path dependence as used here implies that strengthening the state at time t can be much harder or easier – or an entirely different challenge – depending on what happened at a specific historical juncture at time $t - n$. History thus matters, and the effort in this book has worked to show exactly how, where, and to what extent this is so.

A theoretical focus on the *social* foundations of state building also confronts us with the implication that the strengthening of state institutions may actually not be mainly a question of institutional reform. This may at first blush seem paradoxical, because any serious effort at state building necessarily involves substantial institutional transformation. The point here is, however, that the ability of institutional reforms to actually produce sustainable changes in the infrastructural power of the state hinges critically on the social and political environment and the timing of their implementation. That is, as one example, one might more fruitfully pursue administrative modernization by supporting land reform in a semiservile political economy than by seeking to create anticorruption commissions, reforming electoral systems, or rationalizing bureaucratic organization. For the claim here is that unless state building can be rendered compatible with the interests of powerful social actors – and later further linked to organized middle- and working-class actors – institutional reforms will remain dead letters or fall quite far from their intended goals.[11]

SCOPE

The arguments put forward in the preceding pages about the social foundations of state building also raise implicit questions about its scope conditions that attach to the theoretical claims. The empirical focus in this book has been

---

[11] Indeed, Acemoglu and Robinson (2006, 2008) have made the case that even quite substantial institutional reforms that change the formal distribution of political power may ultimately be turned back in practice by elites making investments in countervailing informal power – implying that it is very difficult to take elites out of the political game and thus to change the on-the-ground practices that define the real character of political institutions.

on states in the South American region, although one could reasonably see the argument as one that is potentially relevant to most late-institutionalizing polities.[12] The term *relevant* is used instead of directly *applicable* for three principal reasons. First, one potentially important variable – the institutional and political-economic legacies of colonialism – is not examined directly, given a research design that relies on cases in the Spanish–American colonial world.[13] Second, it is possible that very recent state-building efforts in new countries or recently independent territories face substantially different challenges from the nineteenth- and twentieth-century experiences examined here. Notably, the development of strong state institutions in the Latin American region in the mid-twentieth century was temporally conterminous and politically reliant on a statist and inward-looking model of economic development. The postwar protectionist state was, to oversimplify slightly, often the institutional embodiment of an important form of middle class–working class political compromise that underwrote and sustained the massive investments in institution building that occurred in the successful cases in the region.[14] In the postdebt-crisis era of globalization and international economic integration, however, this sort of a strategy of economic development may be – as a consequence of international pressures and opportunity costs – effectively precluded, making the prospects of establishing the sociopolitical foundation of large-scale, sustained investments in institutional development (through this pathway) seem decidedly grim. And finally, of course, without an expanded empirical focus, strong out-of-sample claims are best avoided.

Probing the scope of the theory outlined in this book, thus, is a principal task for this final chapter. There are two quite distinct senses in which this will be undertaken. The first is the question of how far the theoretical claims made here can reasonably travel. The second focuses on the state-building consequences of empirical combinations of conditions not observed in the South American context. In Figure 2.2, we saw that there was a notable empty cell: where elite cooperation and coordination was nevertheless achieved despite the presence

---

[12] By "late institutionalizing," the emphasis is on distinguishing the challenge of developing strong state institutions in the first wave of cases in northern and central Europe and North America from those that began the state-building process at a much later point. In Gerschenkronian fashion, there are potential advantages to backwardness that might be specific to this set of states, and they generally emerged in a very different – and far less bellicose – international environment, which further differentiates them from institutions that developed in the anarchic states system of Early Modern Europe.

[13] That said, however, *variations* in the pattern of Spanish colonialism in Latin America are evaluated directly.

[14] It is critical to note that while statism – when applied in a national political context that was already on a favorable institutional trajectory, and before the onset of effective mass political participation – was quite conducive to institutional development, this did *not* necessarily make it an effective strategy of economic development. The record on the economic front is poor to mixed. Nor does this claim imply that statism is necessarily associated with state building where underlying conditions are unfavorable – indeed, the opposite may well be true.

Conclusions, Implications, and Extensions 237

Intra-Elite Political Dynamics

Zero-Sum/Non-exclusionary Competitive Establishment

		Institutional Atrophy	Constrained Central State Building
Social Relations	Servile	Peru	Prussia, to ~1806
	Free	**Inter-Elite Conflict and Local Institution Building** Argentina, to 1881 Uruguay, to 1876	**National Institution Building** Prussia, after ~1806 Chile Argentina, after 1881 Uruguay, after 1876

FIGURE 7.1. From absolutist elite coordination and unfree labor to emancipation and state building in Prussia.

of a servile agrarian economy. This combination of conditions was not an outcome that characterizes the cases examined in this book, nor is it observed elsewhere in the South American context. It has, however, been characteristic of historically significant examples of ultimately successful state-building endeavors.

To probe both these issues, in the section that follows, a schematic reanalysis is undertaken of one of the canonical cases of European state building: the emergence of a militarily and institutionally powerful Prussia–Germany in the eighteenth and nineteenth centuries.[15] This case is in many ways quite instructive. For although the German state that Bismarck helped to create on a Prussian backbone has long been seen as infrastructurally powerful, the historical record suggests that this was not always the case. Moreover, the political development of Prussia and, later, a united Germany evidences a profound change on a central determinant of state building – the Prussian peasantry (and that of the other German princely states) were emancipated very late, beginning in 1806 in Prussia and in the near-vicinity of that date in other soon-to-be German states and complete only around 1850. Conversely, the Prussian bureaucracy and dominant class was organized and coordinated well before this in an absolutist fashion under Frederick William I (1713–40) and Frederick the Great (1740–86), and concurrently, the Prussian military underwent precocious expansion (see Figure 7.1).

---

[15] This section cannot, however, be thought of as a full-fledged engagement with the voluminous literature on European state building in general and Prussia–Germany in particular. Rather, it will be an examination of whether the basic theoretical model developed for the South American contexts comports with the broad outlines of political development and socioeconomic history in Prussia–Germany.

238 *Latin American State Building in Comparative Perspective*

Two major omissions in the main text of this book are thus confronted squarely in the Prussian case, which is why a further examination is undertaken here. First, it provides insight with respect to the consequences of managing to successfully integrate the dominant landed classes under central leadership and thus solving the political barrier to state building, but in a context in which the *social* underpinnings of long-term state building were initially largely absent. Then, the belated emancipation (by West European standards) of the Prussian serfs in the early to middle nineteenth century sets up a crucial contrast: did the pattern of Prussian and, later, German political development change when this social underpinning was transformed, as the argument of this book would imply?

An examination of Prussian political development also probes the limits of this book's theory in the core terrain of alternative accounts. Prussian–German state building took place in a time and place far removed from the institutional legacies of Spanish colonialism, in the context of some of the fiercest and most persistent of external security threats and set in a decidedly different Protestant, if not Calvinist, political culture. These have long been identified as crucial factors in the emergence of a strong state. If the society-centric factors highlighted in this book can be shown to have substantial explanatory power even in this case, it is likely that the reach of the theory extends well beyond the postindependence Latin American region. It is critical to point out that the reexamination of the Prussian case in no way pretends to be a definitive engagement with the immense scholarly literature on that case. Rather, it is meant as an effort to see whether the arguments developed in this book might plausibly travel to a very different context and therein provide a useful additional optic for understanding political development in this paradigmatic strong state.

PROBING THE LIMITS: SOCIAL FOUNDATIONS OF PRUSSIAN AND GERMAN STATE BUILDING

The Prussian experience with state building is in important ways quite different from the experiences of the Latin American cases that were explored earlier in this book. In those chapters, we saw trajectories of political development that ultimately saw the creation of a comparatively strong and deeply penetrating governmental bureaucracy that was capable of imposing its will on the whole of civil society (in Chile and Uruguay), one that was sidetracked into populist and antipopulist cycles of expansion and contraction and into persistent institutional instability (Argentina), and one that was unable to launch a sustained or effective process of institutional improvement and deepening (Peru). What we observe in Prussia can be divided into two periods, the pre-1806 period characterized by bureaucratic modernization of central governmental institutions *without* a concomitant-level societal penetration and the ability to enforce governmental policy at the local level or against the will of the landed elite.

Conclusions, Implications, and Extensions   239

This was followed by a period of transition between 1815 and 1848 called the Prussian Vormärz,[16] during which radical reforms to property rights, the emancipation of the serfs, and the restructuring of state institutions were completed. The second period – in the wake of these reforms – finally sees the emergence of the very strong and penetrating Prussian and, later, German state with which we have much greater familiarity.

This characterization of the Prussian state may seem somewhat jarring – after all, a traditional view of the Prussian state dates the rise of a strong state to the alleged defeat by Frederick William I (the "Great Elector," who ruled from 1640 to 1688) of the noble estates and the emergence of a large standing national army (e.g., Downing 1988, 17). But the comparatively early emergence of a centralized, bureaucratic form of central administration was not enough, and the "famed Prussian war machine [was burdened] with internal contradictions which eventually led to its collapse" (Ertman 1997, 245). For as we shall see, the prereform Prussian state did not have a deep, autonomous reach into civil society, was hamstrung in its ability to collect revenues, and was unable to introduce the sorts of basic liberal reforms into the political economy that would be imperative to induce the industrialization and economic growth necessary to support an expansive state or a modern military apparatus. This equation changed decisively during the period of reforms and quickly provided the sociopolitical underpinning for the Prussian state that decisively defeated the French in the Franco-Prussian War and was able to challenge the collective powers of the rest of Western Europe, Russia, and the United States in two successive world wars.

The existing explanations for the ultimate development of exceedingly powerful Prussian and German state are myriad – including those that emphasize the pressures of war, associated organizational and technological change, Calvinist culture, absolutist-era tax and administrative reforms, or various combinations of these (see, inter alia, Tilly 1990; Porter 1994; Gorski 2003; Anderson 1974). And it is not the intention in the limited number of pages that follow to rebut these accounts. Instead, two principal points will be made. First, the commonly held belief in the strength of the Prussian state from roughly the time of Frederick the Great is mistaken. Instead, substantial historical literature supports the notion that until the reforms of the early to middle nineteenth century, it would more appropriately be thought of as a centralized but constrained hybrid state. On the one hand, administrative reorganization had been undertaken, and a disproportionately large military apparatus was constructed, but property rights remained entangled in a complex web of feudal and guild rights and obligations, agrarian elites retained formal juridical authority over their

---

[16] Literally, this means "pre-March" and is used in German history to signify the crucial period between the definitive defeat of Napoleon and the Revolution of 1848, which had its beginnings in March of that year.

estates, the ability to tax the income or property of the nobility was sharply restricted, and even the staffing of central institutions was strongly tied to status at birth. Thus, from a theoretical perspective, the comparison of Prussia before and after the end of serfdom highlights this book's contention that the impact of agrarian social relations on state building is critical, even in a case long central to alternative accounts of political development.

The Prussian State before Emancipation

The Prussian state in the preemancipation (before 1806–50) era was decidedly dualistic in its structure. On the one hand, the consolidation of the Prussian central state took place under Frederick William I (1713–40), who fused the resources extracted from various offices that had governed his own personal estates, regalian dues owed him by nobles under feudal custom, and the newly created central military and taxation institutions into a single hierarchical unit (Rosenberg 1958, 38–41). Central to this was the creation of the *Generalkriegskommisariat* (General War Commission), which was charged with raising funds for warfare but which also quickly took on responsibilities for foreign trade, the promotion of domestic manufacturing, and the guilds (Downing 1988, 21). At the same time, the enlargement of the military and the effective recruitment of soldiers via the cantonal system allowed Prussia to exit the Seven Years' War (1756–63) without being defeated by (or defeating) a numerically superior Austrian foe. But at the same time, surviving the war nearly bankrupted the Prussian state, devastated its territories, and killed some 180,000 soldiers (Showalter 1994, 308–9). The Prussian state's ability to defend itself had been pushed to the very limit by the fiscal constraints inherent in its still-feudal social underpinnings.

The early centralization of authority under monarchical absolutism and the creation of a large, standing national army was, thus, an incomplete measure of the capacity of the Prussian state. For the bargain that created the central absolutist state left the landed oligarchy (Junkers) in juridical control of local government in the countryside (Gutsbezirke) into the twentieth century (Rosenberg 1958, 43). The landlords also were directly responsible for the collection of taxes from peasants resident on their estates, leaving the central state with "no direct jurisdiction at all over the mass of the rural population" (Anderson 1974, 264). Moreover, the bargains that had created central authority and the right to maintain a national standing army had simultaneously exempted the nobility from direct taxation (other than the regalian obligations due the monarch as a product of traditional feudal obligations). At the same time, the formal and practical juridical control of the estates in the hands of the nobility was confirmed, including the right to inflict corporal punishment on peasants for what the Junkers themselves could legally determine was an infraction of law or feudal obligation. Junker property was further allodialized under Frederick William, cementing the bargain of national power for increased local

Conclusions, Implications, and Extensions

autonomy.[17] But this is not what is usually thought of as a powerful and penetrating organization of central state institutions.

At its core, the absolutist state created by the Hohenzollerns was founded on a political bargain, by which national power could be sharply expanded and centralized but only insofar as it ratified the existing servile character of East Elbian productive relations, exempted the nobility from most taxation, and gave them privileged access to the upper reaches of the bureaucracy and military. But this bargain firmly ensconced a precapitalist form of economic organization that sharply delimited the possibilities for Prussian state building in the prereform era. The Prussian state could thus raise large numbers of troops, fight wars, and impose taxes on nonnobles. But it could not reach into the nobles' estates directly either for governance or for taxation.

What did the prereform society look like in Prussia? To begin, the agrarian economy of the eighteenth century (and the national economy was centered very strongly in agriculture) was founded on the system of Gutherrschaft. While widely varied in its specific practices, its core features were relatively constant. In this system, often enormous nobles' estates (Rittergüter) were worked by a dependent peasantry tied to the land in a system of hereditary serfdom (Erbuntertänigkeit).[18] In addition to commanding very substantial labor service from the servile estate-resident peasantry (including the labor of peasant family members), the lord was also charged with police and judicial functions as well as with the implementation of national policy within the boundaries of the estate (Jackson 1964, 9). The maintenance of servility in the context of the centralization of authority was solidified by this and one other key feature: the absolute dominance of the military officer corps by the landed elite. And the unity and class character of the nobility was maintained by a property rights regime that prohibited the sale of estate property to nonnobles (or, for that matter, the taking up of bourgeois occupation by the nobility). Ultimately, it was a largely precapitalist economic environment, where labor was recruited on a nonwage basis, much property was neither individual nor freely alienable, and even the concept of ownership was complex, entailing a variegated system of asymmetrical but reciprocal service obligations, duties, and unsufructory rights.

This created a servile peasantry that, although not property in the sense of chattel slavery, was directly bound to the land and subject to the police and juridical authority of the lord. Serfs were required to pay national taxes (from which the nobility were exempt), and male serfs and their male progeny were

---

[17] The conversion into allodial property – instead of feudal property – removed the military and other service obligations, and relations of vassalage, that the latter implied and exempted the property from the imposition of tax exactions by the monarch.

[18] This differed from chattel slavery insofar as the serfs were not moveable property subject to sale by their lords but rather tied to the estates themselves in a complex web of service obligations and unsufructory rights that could not be renounced.

242   *Latin American State Building in Comparative Perspective*

required to provide military service (Witte 1951, 5). Peasants could not leave the estate, they could be forced to return should they attempt to flee, and they could be disciplined – including corporal punishment – for disobedience to their lord or for shirking. Marriage required permission and the demonstration of an increase in value of the proposed new serf family to the estate. Indeed, even the learning of a trade required both permission and the demonstration of its value to the lord (Ford 1919, 368).

Prussia before 1806 is thus a mixed case with respect to the variables identified as central to state building in this book. Although administrative centralization (and we will see the creation of a corporate coherence to the civil service and a notable esprit de corps) proceeded, and the usual bitter enmity of rural elites to the formation of a national military force was overcome, the fiscal sinews that held together the state were exceedingly weak and ultimately proved crippling. And the penetration of national institutions largely stopped at the estates' gates.

Land Reform, Absolutist Bureaucracy, and the Rise of the Verwaltungsstaat in the Prussian Vormärz

The Prussian Vormärz was a crucial time in the development of what would ultimately become the exceedingly strong and deeply penetrating Prussian (and later German) administrative state. But the initiation of a trajectory of social transformations that unleashed the state-building potential of the Prussian state actually occurred in a period of great weakness, following catastrophic defeat in war and with fiscal conditions in a parlous state. But the 1806–48 period was also the moment in which serfdom was abolished – albeit gradually – and the already consolidated national-level administrative apparatus was able to overcome the legacies of feudal servility, establish a solid fiscal foundation for the first time, and, by the end of the period, come to grips with a massive, revolutionary mobilization on the part of its politically and economically marginalized subjects.

The end of Prussian serfdom was nothing short of a revolution from above – and it was not a reform that could be undertaken in ordinary circumstances. But it was one that was desperately needed from the perspective of the monarchy – which had to contend with an inadequate fiscal, administrative, and economic apparatus for some time. In short, the weakness of the Prussian state threatened its very survival – and had for some time.[19] This seems paradoxical, as we saw earlier that the Prussian state was in a military sense seemingly very strong. It could field an unusually large and competent army relative to its subject population; indeed, this is a principal reason for the comparatively commonplace assumption that it was in fact a very powerful state. But the fiscal basis of the

---

[19] These problems had become quite clear from *at least* the time of the Seven Years' War (1754–63).

Conclusions, Implications, and Extensions

Prussian state was grossly inadequate to the task of supporting the military – and the scope of the military was possible only because of the extraordinary economies imposed on other major public functions. Indeed, Prussian finances were, as late as 1779, still operating in large measure on the traditional feudal basis – which assumed that, save in times of war, the costs of operating the state were to be paid for based on the proceeds generated on the monarch's own personal estates. As Braun (1975, 295) notes, at this point in time, fully 45.7 percent of all public revenues came from the profits earned on the Crown's own estates.[20] The remainder was raised from the taxation of nonnoble activities and property in the urban areas or through the limited commutation into cash payments of traditional feudal service obligations on the part of the nobility. For the political bargain that had made possible the administrative centralization of Prussian absolutism – and overcame the Junker opposition to it – had cemented the effectively allodial status of their property and the general exemption from taxation of the first estate.

Indeed, the centrality of peasant labor servility, and the monarchical interest in overcoming it, can be seen on a variety of dimensions. To begin, before it was able to compel an emancipation of the serfs, the Prussian monarchy endeavored to induce such behavior on the part of the Junker class on a voluntary basis by imposing reforms first on Crown lands. The hope – but not reality – was that this would, by virtue of a demonstration effect, induce similar activity on the part of the broader nobility. The impetus for this reform was, of course, far from humanitarian. The problem was that Prussia was economically and industrially underdeveloped, and any effort to launch a serious industrialization drive was effectively prevented by the large investments in public infrastructure that must first be made (R. Tilly 1966, 484–85). But with so much of the wealth of the country tied up in the nontaxable property of the nobility, the fiscal resources were unavailable, and even the effort to tax the (in any event impoverished) peasantry directly in the pre-1806 period also induced conflict with the Junkers, for such exactions tended in practice to trade off against the servile levies on which the lords themselves relied (Hagen 1989, 334).

Similarly crucial to the launch of a major industrial economy in Prussia would be an end to the decidedly inefficient property rights system that characterized the East Elbian region. Landownership there did not mean clear individual and exclusive title with rights to transfer. Instead, it was a complex interweaving of nontransferable peasant holdings situated on the lords' estates that came with a variety of unsufructory rights (including wood gathering, foraging, gleaning, and grazing on demesne lands) and service obligations that were inherited but not easily shed. Estate ownership itself (or perhaps, more properly, lordship) was transferable only *within* the noble classes. It was a property rights regime that rendered most basic market arrangements

---

[20] Braun (1975, 295) notes, by comparison, that by the year 1700, the equivalent revenues were of negligible importance to the British state.

all but impossible. There was no obvious way to replace the dispersed strip-farming system of the estates with economically much more efficient, compact holdings,[21] nor was there a way to strip landed property of its serfs or their customary rights. Any emancipation reform would thus not only have to grapple with the question of the abolition of heritable servitude but also make a settlement that would address the property rights peasants held to a wide variety of usufruct. Would a peasant be entitled to receive as individual property the land he had been allotted to farm as a serf? What compensation would be due the lord in recognition of his property rights in the form of serfs' labor obligations? What of the recognition of the peasants' commons rights or rights to secondary usufruct on directly farmed demesne property?

The catalyst for the *initiation* of the structural transformation of the Prussian political economy that would end serfdom and make possible the rapid strengthening of state institutions was, ironically, a catastrophic military defeat that underscored its very weakness. The experience of the Seven Years' War (1756–63) had had a long-lasting impact on Prussian leadership – on both Frederick II and Frederick William III – insofar as it nearly destroyed the kingdom and stretched the capacity of the state to finance war to its limits. In fact, simple survival had been made possible only through external fiscal dependence on Britain. Indeed, the contributions of the British subsidy were so great as to equal the direct revenue-raising capacity of an economically prostrate Prussia, and even together, these funds were grossly insufficient to pay for the war effort without simultaneous recourse to the debasement of the currency. Even the civil service was left unpaid (Longman 1912, 157).

The period between the end of the Seven Years' War and the decisive battle with Napoleon's armies at Jena and Auerstädt (1806) was one, however, characterized by intensive efforts to modernize the military and improve logistics, command, and control (Showalter 1994). Despite an obvious need, Prussia simply could not, however, make more than marginal improvements in state strength. And the important fact was *not* that these reforms were unsuccessful – they were, in large measure, in their own terms – but they were of little avail in the coming conflict with the French. This became clear when Napoleon's army won a crushing victory on October 14, 1806, "virtually annihilating the enemy's [Prussia's] entire military establishment" (Heyman 1966–67, 186). The Prussians were left devastated and were forced to cede half their prewar territory to Napoleon's France in the Treaty of Tilsit.

What came next, however, was a radical reorganization of Prussian political economy, initiated shortly after the Napoleonic Wars and completed by the time of the revolutions of 1848. Most critically, as will be seen later, while reforms occurred in the context of massive interstate conflict, the subsequent

---

[21] I.e., peasant-farmed parcels and demesne property were divided into many narrow strips and were profoundly interspersed. Even a single peasant family would in all likelihood farm a variety of distinct strips of land in different locations on the estate.

Conclusions, Implications, and Extensions

transformation of Prussia was not consonant with the usual renderings of the war-makes-states literature. After all, Prussia had been in an intensely conflictual strategic environment for a very long time – indeed, it faced an existential struggle in the Seven Years' War – and while this did drive military modernization and expansion, it did not change the fiscal underpinnings of the state or make the Junker class more cooperative with the centralization of taxation and expenditure authority necessary to turn Prussian absolutism into the military–industrial behemoth it would become beginning with Bismarck and ending with Hitler. As early as Frederick William I's reign as Great Elector, the Junker class had become exceedingly concerned that arming the peasantry for war might undermine labor servility, and they regularly negotiated with the Crown to exchange a loss of their influence in national politics (as in the Landtags-Recess[22] of 1653) for further tightening of the restrictions on the serfs and for the maintenance and expansion of their local juridical and enforcement authority.

Indeed, the reaction to the crushing military defeat was less military than it was fiscal and administrative. Frederick William III responded to the calamity by convening a commission with a charge to "investigate the condition of the country to restore the war-devastated economy and to devise means of securing new revenues to meet the impending indemnity payments" (Jackson 1964, 30). The ultimate result was the October Edict of 1807, which, among other things, (1) eliminated the estate-based restrictions on property ownership or entrepreneurial undertaking and (2) marked an end to hereditary serfdom and gave serfs an immediate right to depart the land (Witte 1951, 9). In one fell swoop, the structural change that had long been sought by the Prussian monarchy was imposed in the (remaining) national territory.

This was, at the end of the day, a social–structural revolution. But it is important to keep in mind that it was ultimately a revolution from above. For with emancipation came also an end to the royal protection of serfs against excessively abusive practices on the part of their lords, without at the same time ending the local juridical authority of the estate owners. It would not be until 1872 that local law and its enforcement became a public rather than a private function (Rosenberg 1958, 219). And as the regulations governing the actual division of formerly feudal property emerged, they worked to the severe disadvantage of the peasants. To begin, while hereditary servitude was abolished, the enforcement of traditional obligations of service were not commuted. Thus, while a peasant could in theory achieve unencumbered ownership of a plot of land by ceding between one-third and one-half of her customary plot of land held in unsufructory tenure to the landlord in commutation of feudal obligations (the proportion depending on the specific type of feudal tenure), this was

---

[22] This involved the indefinite suspension of the estate-based representation of agrarian elites and the concession of some tax authority to the Crown in exchange for the strengthening of lords' local juridical authority and the allodialization of their property.

246 *Latin American State Building in Comparative Perspective*

only sometimes achieved in practice. Instead, to continue in farming her plot of land after emancipation, a serf remained obligated to provide full customary labor service. And further regulations of 1816 limited this commutation possibility only to larger holdings (those large enough to support a team of plow oxen), and only if the resident tenant could prove unsufructory occupancy since the Seven Years' War (Bowman 1993, 67). The result was that in general, peasants faced a choice of land loss to achieve freedom or continued servitude.

The result was a tremendous process of land concentration and a transfer of much of the land held in usufruct by former serfs into the hands of the estate holders (Witte 1951, 12). Liberation from feudalism in this particular fashion, if anything, only heightened inequality, while at the same time creating capitalist social relations. Peasant living conditions worsened still further as traditional feudal obligations of estate owners to provide lodging, food in times of dearth, and help to maintain the serf in possession of his plot of land – in sharp contrast to the labor obligations of peasants – were abolished between 1807 and 1811 (Hamerow 1958, 47). In 1821, the rights to use of the common lands of the estates (forests and pasture) were divided, with 80 percent being transferred to the full control of noble landholders. But the land taxes owed to the state by peasants (but not by the nobility, who were long exempted) continued unabated – making the continuation of what small-scale independent landownership survived reform exceedingly difficult (Bowman 1993, 69). At the same time, the end of estate-based prohibitions on landownership brought an influx of capitalist investment into agriculture as the urban bourgeoisie began to undertake agricultural investment. This led to rapid capitalist modernization of the estates, and as early as 1855, only 55 percent of estates remained in the hands of the nobility, declining still further to 32 percent by 1889 (Gillis 1968, 113).

In short order, then, the Prussian countryside was subject to tremendous transformation. The new bourgeois landowners purchased and modernized the estates, and the remaining nobles were those willing to undertake the transition to modernizing agrarian capitalism themselves (Bowman 1993, 66). The dispossession of peasants from their traditional plots also served this end by increasing the available labor supply for nascent urban industrialization and the shift to wage labor in estate agriculture. The sale of formerly noble-held lands also brought a shift in the character of the dominant class, for instead of relying on agriculture for its wealth, large numbers of the nobility entered the direct service of the state. Indeed, they came to dominate its upper reaches – a dominance that was ironically facilitated by the meritocratic standards for entry into the civil service that were simultaneously strengthened. For, as education requirements for entry were tightened and long (unpaid) apprenticeships were required of prospective applicants for public service, a position in the bureaucracy was effectively restricted to the well-to-do who could afford costly schooling and long periods of unpaid labor (Rosenberg 1958, 213). This shift in income source for large numbers of nobles in turn tended to reduce

Conclusions, Implications, and Extensions

their long-standing resistance to the strengthening and expansion of the reach of the state – on which they now increasingly depended for employment and status. And a modernizing (and more profitable) agricultural sector became increasingly capable of providing expanded tax revenues to the central state without risking economic calamity for its new capitalist landowners. Increases in taxation soon followed, and by 1851, the income tax was made much more effective; in 1861, the land tax was modernized – providing the revenue foundation for a state that used it to make a powerful public commitment to industrial development (R. Tilly 1966, 490, 492). Perhaps as important, the state also embarked on a program of mass, compulsory schooling by the early nineteenth century – one to two generations earlier than even the French or British achieved (Schleunes 1979, 315).

We have seen, thus, that Prussia was consistently beset by external strategic threats since the seventeenth century. And it is also quite clearly the case that Prussian monarchs were intent on creating a powerful central bureaucracy, with great reach into society and the economy. But external threat did not drive modernization – for as long as Prussian rural society continued to be dominated by servile labor relations, the necessary cooperation of the aristocracy in a power-centralizing effort, even in this absolutist era, was fruitless. Neither the redirection of resources into urban, industrial ventures; the massification of education; nor the imposition of serious taxation on the first estate was possible in such a context. But after "emancipation" of the serfs in 1807–50,[23] this changed. The combination of the shift toward capitalist agriculture, an agricultural crisis, and the consequent bankruptcy of many noble estates led to large-scale entry into public service and the military, an outcome that left the nobility "virtually dependent on the support of the state" (Gillis 1968, 111, 126). And consequently, they were in no position, then, to resist the long-in-coming modernizing reforms pursued from above.

The remainder of the story of state building in Prussia is well known. The impoverished, agrarian state that was defeated decisively by Napoleon in 1806 would, by 1870–71, become the industrializing, military powerhouse that defeated France in the Franco-Prussian War. And of course, by the early to middle twentieth century, Germany had become an industrial and military giant, capable of challenging, simultaneously, the dominant powers of its day.

Although in a few short pages it is impossible (and unwise) to rewrite the history of Prussian–German state building, the Prussian case was explored here with an eye to demonstrating the degree to which the ideas developed in this book can inform an earlier, important, and decidedly different process of institutional development. I have tried to show the centrality of the transformation of rural economic relations as part of this process; it was a key change that

---

[23] I take 1850 as the ending point here as it was in the 1850 constitution that a commitment to full juridical equality was enshrined, and it was in that year that an effective mechanism for the definitive liquidation of remaining feudal dues was put into place (Hamerow 1958, 221).

248   *Latin American State Building in Comparative Perspective*

rendered monarchical efforts to strengthen the state politically and economically viable and can be seen in the rapid education, industrialization, and mobilization of Prussian and, later, German society. Although a measure of national *political* unification among elites had been accomplished through bargains that traded national dominance for local autonomy, larded as well with substantial preference for the nobility in the upper civil service, it was the transformation of underlying social relations that finally unlocked the door to long-run state building.

Indeed, the history of political modernization in Germany–Prussia is also quite consistent with the central argument made in this book about the second critical juncture – at the time of the irruption of the masses as a political force. Like the successful cases of state building in Latin America, problems of elite coordination and structural transformation of agriculture were solved well before the onset of severe demands from below in either the cities or the countryside. And it was thus *because* powerful state institutions existed by 1848 that the truly massive popular uprisings of that time were not only successfully repressed but were also contained via a large and expanding set of public institutional channels. As Gerschenkron (1962) has argued, late economic development in Germany was achieved through a large, invasive, and effective state. At the same time, mass political demand making was contained within a conservative institutional synthesis through the provision of extensive social welfare – as early as 1854, formerly guild-based welfare funds were operated under state control, and this model was famously expanded under Bismarck. As Hamerow (1958, 236) has pointed out, "a monarchism of public welfare developed in Germany, which won the allegiance of the nation with its program of political legitimism and economic stability." This, in Rosenberg's (1958, 233) terms, resulted in

the Bismarckian synthesis, as consolidated after 1871, [that] brought peace, great national prestige, an almost spectacular long-term upswing of material growth, highly competent and honest public administration, with a profound respect for law and order, a substantial measure of personal rights, civil liberties, and social security, and a flourishing of intellectual and artistic life to the German people.

CONCLUSION

This volume began with an illustration of the importance that effective governmental institutions can have for the well-being of citizens. It developed a society-centric explanation for the emergence of path-dependent trajectories of institutional and political development and underdevelopment. And it ends now with a warning: social scientists have for too long been overly concerned with the elucidation of the institutional reforms that might improve the effectiveness of governance, reduce corruption, or cause the imposition of the rule of law. While such outcomes are rarely achieved without accompanying institutional

Conclusions, Implications, and Extensions

reforms, we cannot simultaneously ignore that near-countless reform laws and anticorruption campaigns left bureaucratic or judicial practices effectively unchanged or transformed them in ways that ultimately did not improve performance much. More is needed if effective governance is to be achieved.

What this book has tried to show is that state-building reforms can be effective only if they are embedded in a favorable social and political context, one in which labor is free and elites are able to coordinate and cooperate – if only to strengthen public institutions for their own selfish ends. It has also shown that history and sequence matters – the launch of a state-building trajectory is something best done well before the entry of the masses into politics, for should the latter come early relative to institutional development, the populist temptation will be great, and the ability of public institutions to channel and contain mobilized action is limited. Distressing as it may be, if elite cooperation is essential to *early* institutional development, it is difficult to understand how this can be achieved in a context of truly free democratic politics – for, where the institutions to be empowered could plausibly be used by democratic majorities in ways harmful to the interests of elites whose cooperation was required to construct powerful institutions in the first place, such cooperation would very likely not be forthcoming. Fortunately, this dynamic is not the same if viable institutions are created prior to democratization – as institutions strengthen, and nonelite social actors in the middle and working classes grow larger and more organized as a consequence, over time, effective state institutions no longer rest exclusively on elite support, and these new social actors typically act to strengthen and expand them as well as use them for new purposes. Thus, the argument here suggests that democracy does not cause, and may impede, the earliest stages of political development. But when it comes *after* the formation of solid institutions, the effect is the opposite – it will help to consolidate and improve institutional development.

What does this mean for the future of institutional reform in developing countries? The point is not that political development is somehow foreclosed. But this book *does* suggest that social contexts – and serious efforts to change them – are essential components of the state-building process. And in intellectual terms, it requires us to return to a series of topics lately less central to scholarship in the political science and sociology of political development: the importance of land reform, social composition and the openness or closure of the dominant strata of society, and the political party alliances and economic strategy chosen at the time at which mass actors make a definitive entry into national politics. And it suggests that in contexts where mass incorporation has preceded the development of effective institutions, the challenge of political development may be markedly more severe. It is a challenge that we must all hope is somehow solved.

References

Acemoğlu, Daron, and James Robinson. 2006. "De Facto Political Power and Institutional Persistence." *American Economic Review, Papers and Proceedings*. Vol. 96:2 (May):325–30.

——. 2008. "Persistence of Power, Elites, and Institutions." *American Economic Review*. Vol. 98:1 (March):267–93.

——. 2009. *Economic Origins of Dictatorship and Democracy*. New York: Cambridge University Press.

Acemoğlu, Daron, Simon Johnson, and James Robinson. 2001. "The Colonial Origins of Comparative Development: An Empirical Investigation." *American Economic Review*. Vol. 91:5 (December):1369–1401.

——. 2005. "Institutions as a Fundamental Cause of Long-Run Growth." In Philippe Aghion and Steven N. Durlauf, eds., *Handbook of Economic Growth, Volume 1A*. Amsterdam: North-Holland.

Acevedo, Eduardo. 1942. *Manual de historia uruguaya después de Artigas. Tomo segundo*. Anales de la Universidad, Year XLIX, No. 151. Montevideo: Universidad de la República de Uruguay/Talleres Gráficos "33" S. L.

Adelman, Jeremy. 1992. "Reflections on Argentine Labour and the Rise of Perón." *Bulletin of Latin American Research*. Vol. 11:3 (September):243–59.

Alexander, Robert J. 1949. "Social Security in Chile." *Social Forces*. Vol. 28:1 (October):53–58.

Alhadeff, Peter. 1986. "The Economic Formulae of the 1930s: A Reassessment." In Guido di Tella and D. C. M. Platt, eds., *The Political Economy of Argentina, 1880–1946*. London: Macmillan.

Alston, Lee, and Andrés Gallo. 2010. "Electoral Fraud, the Rise of Peron and Demise of Checks and Balances in Argentina." *Explorations in Economic History*. Vol. 47:2 (April):179–97.

Alvarez, Juan. 1938. *Estudio sobre guerras civiles argentinas*. 3rd ed. Buenos Aires: Círculo Militar – Biblioteca del Oficial.

——. 2001 [1936]. *Las guerras civiles argentinas y el problema de Buenos Aires en la república*. Buenos Aires: Taurus.

References

Amsden, Alice. 1991. "Diffusion of Development: The Late-Industrializing Model and Greater East Asia." *American Economic Review.* Vol. 81:2 (May):282–86.

———. 2001. *The Rise of "the Rest": Challenges to the West from Late-Industrializing Economies.* Oxford: Oxford University Press.

Anderle, Adam. 1985. *Los movimientos politicos en el Perú entre las dos guerras mundiales.* Havana: Ediciones Casa de las Américas.

Anderson, Lisa. 1987. "The State in the Middle East and North Africa." *Comparative Politics.* Vol. 20:1–18.

Anderson, Perry. 1974. *Lineages of the Absolutist State.* London: Verso Press.

Andeweg, Rudy B., and Galen A. Irwin. 2002. *Governance and Politics of the Netherlands.* New York: Palgrave/Macmillan.

Angell, Alan. 1993. "Chile since 1958." In Leslie Bethell, ed., *Chile since Independence.* Cambridge: Cambridge University Press.

Arellano, José-Pablo. 1985. "Social Policies in Chile: An Historical Overview." *Journal of Latin American Studies.* Vol. 17:2 (November):397–418.

Arndt, Christiane, and Charles Oman. 2006. *Uses and Abuses of Governance Indicators.* Paris: OECD.

Arocena Olivera, Enrique. 2002. *Proceso histórico de la economía uruguaya: Del mercantilismo colonial al encierro dirigista.* Montevideo: Linardi y Risso.

Aston, T. H., and C. H. E. Philpin, eds. 1987. *The Brenner Debate: Agrarian Class Structure and Economic Development in Pre-industrial Europe.* Cambridge: Cambridge University Press.

Astori, Danilo. 1985. "Neoliberalismo autoritario en el Uruguay: Peculiaridades internas e impulsos externos." *Revista Mexicana de Sociología.* Vol. 47:2 (April–June):123–53.

Ayres, Robert L. 1972. "Economic Stagnation and the Emergence of the Political Ideology of Chilean Underdevelopment." *World Politics.* Vol. 25:1 (October):34–61.

Bailey, Norman A. 1961. "Inflation in Chile and Argentina." *Journal of Interamerican Studies and World Affairs.* Vol. 3:4 (October):539–47.

Ballesteros, Marto A., and Tom E. Davis. 1963. "The Growth of Output and Employment in Basic Sectors of the Chilean Economy, 1908–1957." *Economic Development and Cultural Change.* Vol. 11:2, Part 1 (January):152–76.

Barrán, José Pedro, and Benjamín Nahum. 1984. "Uruguayan Rural History." *Hispanic American Historical Review.* Vol. 64:4 (November):655–73.

Barrera, Manuel. 1980. "Desarrollo económico y sindicalismo en Chile: 1938–1970." *Revista Mexicana de Sociología.* Vol. 42:3 (July–September):1269–96.

Barsky, Osvaldo, and Julio Djenderedjian. 2003. *Historia del capitalismo agrario pampeano: Tomo 1. La expansión ganadera hasta 1895.* Buenos Aires: Siglo XXI.

Bates, Robert. 1981. *Markets and States in Tropical Africa: The Political Basis of Agricultural Policies.* Berkeley: University of California Press.

Basadre, Jorge. 1947. *La multitud, la ciudad, y el campo en la historia del Perú.* 2nd ed. Lima: Editorial Huascarán.

———. 1976. "Para un esquema histórico sobre las elecciones peruanas: La ruptura del consenso legal (1919–1929) y la aparente transformación radical en el sistema (1931)." *Revista de Derecho y Ciencias Políticas.* Vol. 40:1–3 (January–December):87–154.

Bauer, Arnold. 1975. *Chilean Rural Society: From the Spanish Conquest to 1930.* Cambridge: Cambridge University Press.

References

Bauer, Arnold, and Ann Hagerman Johnson. 1977. "Land and Labour in Rural Chile, 1850–1935." In Kenneth Duncan and Ian Routledge, eds., *Land and Labour in Latin America: Essays on the Development of Agrarian Capitalism in the Nineteenth and Twentieth Centuries*. New York: Cambridge University Press.

Bengoa, José. 1990. *Haciendas y campesinos: Historia social de la agricultura chilena*. Tomo II. Santiago, Chile: Ediciones Sur.

Berg, Ronald, and Frederick Weaver. 1978. "Toward a Reinterpretation of Political Change during the First Century of Independence." *Journal of Interamerican Studies and World Affairs*. Vol. 20:1 (February):69–84.

Bergara, Mario, Andrés Pereyra, Ruben Tansini, Adolfo Garcé, Daniel Chasquetti, Daniel Buquet, and Juan Adrés Moraes. 2006. "Political Institutions, Policymaking Processes, and Policy Outcomes: The Case of Uruguay." Research Network Working Paper R-510. Washington, DC: Inter-American Development Bank.

Bergman, Marcelo S. 2003. "Tax Reforms and Tax Compliance: The Divergent Paths of Chile and Argentina." *Journal of Latin American Studies*. Vol. 35:3 (August):593–624.

Berry, Albert. 1990. "International Trade, Government, and Income Distribution in Peru since 1870." *Latin American Research Review*. Vol. 25:2:31–59.

Bertram, Geoffrey. 1991. "Peru, 1930–1960." In Leslie Bethell, ed., *The Cambridge History of Latin America, Volume III: Latin America Since 1930, Spanish South America*. Cambridge: Cambridge University Press.

Blakemore, Harold. 1974. *British Nitrates and Chilean Politics, 1886–1896: Balmaceda and North*. London: Athlone Press.

———. 1993. "From the War of the Pacific to 1930." In Leslie Bethell, ed., *Chile since Independence*. New York: Cambridge University Press.

Boix, Carles. 2003. *Democracy and Redistribution*. Cambridge: Cambridge University Press.

Bonilla, Heraclio. 1978a. "The Indian Peasantry and 'Peru' during the War with Chile." In Steve Stern, ed., *Resistance, Rebellion, and Consciousness in the Andean Peasant World: 18th to Twentieth Centuries*. Madison: University of Wisconsin Press.

———. 1978b. "The War of the Pacific and the National and Colonial Problem in Peru." *Past & Present*. No. 81 (November):92–118.

———. 1984. "Continuidad y cambio en la organización política de estado en el Perú independiente." In Inge Buisson, Günther Kahle, Hans-Joachim König, and Horst Pietschmann, eds., *Problemas de la formación del estado y de la nación en Hispanoamérica*. Cologne, Germany: Böhlau.

Borón, Atilio. 1972. "El estudio de la movilización política en América Latina: La movilización electoral en la Argentina y Chile." *Desarrollo Económico*. Vol. 12:46 (July–September):211–43.

Borzutzky, Silvia. 2003. "Social Security Privatization: The Lessons from the Chilean Experience for Other Latin American Countries and the USA." *International Journal of Social Welfare*. Vol. 12:86–96.

Boucoyannis, Deborah. 2005. *Land, Courts, and Parliaments: The Hidden Sinews of Power in the Emergence of Constitutionalism*. Vol. I. Unpublished PhD dissertation, Department of Political Science, University of Chicago.

Bowman, John, and Michael Wallerstein. 1982. "The Fall of Balmaceda and Public Finance in Chile: New Data for an Old Debate." *Journal of Interamerican Studies and World Affairs*. Vol. 24:4 (November):421–60.

Bowman, Shearer Davis. 1993. *Masters & Lords: Mid-19th-Century U.S. Planters and Prussian Junkers.* New York: Oxford University Press.

Braun, Rudolf. 1975. "Taxation, Sociopolitical Structure, and State-Building: Great Britain and Brandenburg-Prussia." In Charles Tilly, ed., *The Formation of National States in Western Europe.* Princeton, NJ: Princeton University Press.

Brenner, Robert. 1977. "The Origins of Capitalist Development: A Critique of Neo-Smithian Marxism." *New Left Review.* No. 104 (July):25–81.

———. 1987. "Agrarian Class Structure and Economic Development in Pre-industrial Europe." In T. H. Aston and C. H. E. Philpin, eds., *The Brenner Debate: Agrarian Class Structure and Economic Development in Pre-industrial Europe.* Cambridge: Cambridge University Press.

Buchanan, Paul. 1985. "State Corporatism in Argentina: Labor Administration under Perón and Onganía." *Latin American Research Review.* Vol. 20:1:61–95.

Buchbinder, Pablo. 2002. "Estado nacional y provincias bajo la Confederación Argentina: Una aproximación desde la historia de la provincia de Corrientes." *Desarrollo Económico.* Vol. 41:164 (January–March):643–64.

Burga, Manuel, and Alberto Flores Galindo. 1979. *Apogeo y crisis de la república aristocrática: oligarquía, aprismo, y comunismo en el Perú, 1895–1932.* Lima: Ediciones Rikchay Peru.

Buzzetti, José. 1969. *Historia económica y financiera del Uruguay.* Montevideo: Departamento de Inversiones y Planamiento/Ministro de Obras Públicas.

Campbell, John L. 1993. "The State and Fiscal Sociology." *Annual Review of Sociology.* Vol. 19:163–85.

Cariola, Carmen, and Osvaldo Sunkel. 1985. "The Growth of the Nitrate Industry and Socioeconomic Change in Chile, 1880–1930." In Roberto Cortés Conde and Shane Hunt, eds., *The Latin American Economies: Growth and the Export Sector 1880–1930.* New York: Holmes and Meier.

Cavarozzi, Marcelo. 1978. "El orden oligárquico en Chile, 1880–1940." *Desarrollo Económico.* Vol. 18:70 (July–September):231–63.

Centeno, Miguel. 1997. "Blood and Debt: War and Taxation in Nineteenth-Century Latin America." *American Journal of Sociology.* Vol. 102:6 (May):1565–1605.

———. 2002. *Blood and Debt: War and the Nation-State in Latin America.* University Park: Pennsylvania State University Press.

Chang, Ha-Joon. 1999. "The Economic Theory of the Developmental State." In Meredith Woo-Cumings, ed., *The Developmental State.* Ithaca, NY: Cornell University Press.

Chaudhry, Kiren. 1989. "The Price of Wealth: Business and State in Labor Remittance and Oil Economies." *International Organization.* Vol. 43:1 (Winter):101–45.

———. 1994. "Economic Liberalization and the Lineages of the Rentier State." *Comparative Politics.* Vol. 27:1 (October):1–25.

Chelliah, Raja T. 1971. "Trends in Taxation in Developing Countries." *Staff Papers – International Monetary Fund.* Vol. 18:2 (July):254–331.

Cleaves, Peter S., and Henry Pease García. 1983. "State Autonomy and Military Policy Making." In Cynthia McClintock and Abraham F. Lowenthal, eds., *The Peruvian Experiment Reconsidered.* Princeton, NJ: Princeton University Press.

Clinton, Richard Lee. 1970. "Apra: An Appraisal." *Journal of Interamerican Studies and World Affairs.* Vol. 12:2 (April):280–97.

References

Cohen, Youssef, Brian R. Brown, and A. F. K. Organski. 1981. "The Paradoxical Nature of State Making: The Violent Creation of Order." *American Political Science Review*. Vol. 75:4 (December):901–10.

Collier, Ruth Berins. 1999. *Paths toward Democracy: The Working Class and Elites in Western Europe and South America*. New York: Cambridge University Press.

Collier, Ruth Berins, and David Collier. 2002 [1991]. *Shaping the Political Arena: Critical Junctures, the Labor Movement, and Regime Dynamics in Latin America*. Notre Dame, IN: Notre Dame University Press.

Collier, Simon. 1977. "The Historiography of the 'Portalian Period' (1830–1891) in Chile." *Hispanic American Historical Review*. Vol. 57:4 (November):681–82.

———. 1993. "From Independence to the War of the Pacific." In Leslie Bethell, ed., *Chile since Independence*. New York: Cambridge University Press.

Collier, Simon, and William F. Sater. 2004. *A History of Chile, 1808–2002*. Cambridge: Cambridge University Press.

Comité Interamericano de Desarrollo Agrícola. 1966. *Chile: Tenencia de la Tierra y Desarrollo Socio-económico del sector agrícola*. Santiago: CEPAL/IICA/FAO/ OEA/BID.

Corblett, Oscar E., Ezequiel Gallo, and Alfredo O'Connell. 1965. "La generación del 80 y su proyecto: antecedentes y consequencias." In Torcuato di Tella, Gino Germani, and Jorge Graciarena, eds., *Argentina: sociedad de masas*. Buenos Aires: Editorial Universitaria de Buenos Aires.

Correa, Sofía, Consuelo Figueroa, Alfredo Jocelyn-Holt, Claudio Rolle, and Manuel Vicuña. 2001. *Documentos del siglo XX chileno*. Santiago: Editorial Sudamericana.

Correlates of War [COW]. 2011. http://www.correlatesofwar.org/COW2%20Data/ MIDs/MID310.html.

Cortes-Conde, Roberto. 2001. "Estudio Preliminar." Preface to *Las guerras civiles argentinas y el problema de Buenos Aires en la república*. Buenos Aires: Taurus.

Cotler, Julio. 1970. "Crisis política y populismo militar en el Perú." *Revista Mexicana de Sociología*. Vol. 32:3 (May–June):737–84.

———. 1978. *Clases, estado y nación en el Perú*. Lima: Ediciones Instituto de Estudios Peruanos.

———. 1991. "Peru since 1960." In Leslie Bethell, ed., *The Cambridge History of Latin America. Volume VIII: Latin America since 1930, Spanish South America*. Cambridge: Cambridge University Press.

Cramer, Gisela. 1998. "The Argentine Ridde: The Pinedo Plan of 1940 and the Political Economy of the Early War Years." *Journal of Latin American Studies*. Vol. 30:3 (October):519–50.

Criscenti, Joseph T. 1961. "Argentine Constitutional History, 1810–1852: A Re-examination." *Hispanic American Historical Review*. Vol. 41:3 (August):367–412.

Cumings, Bruce. 2005. "State Building in Korea: Continuity and Crisis." In Matthew Lange and Dietrich Rueschemeyer, eds., *States and Development: Historical Antecedents of Stagnation and Advance*. New York: Palgrave/Macmillan.

Daly, Herman E. 1965. "The Uruguayan Economy: Its Basic Nature and Current Problems." *Journal of Interamerican Studies and World Affairs*. Vol. 7:3 (July): 316–30.

Davis, Stanley M. 1970. "The Politics of Organizational Underdevelopment in Chile." *Industrial and Labor Relations Review*. Vol. 24:1 (October):73–83.

Desch, Michael. 1996. "War and Strong States, Peace and Weak States?" *International Organization.* Vol. 50:2 (Spring):237–68.

Díaz-Alejandro, Carlos F. 1967. "The Argentine Tariff, 1906–1940." *Oxford Economic Papers, New Series.* Vol. 19:1 (March):75–98.

Dirección de Contabilidad. 1914. *Resumen de la hacienda pública de Chile desde 1833 hasta 1914.* London: Spottiswoode.

Di Tella, Torcuato. 1981. "Working-Class Organization and Politics in Argentina." *Latin American Research Review.* Vol. 16:2:33–56.

Dollar, David, and Aart Kraay. 2003. "Institutions, Trade, and Growth." *Journal of Monetary Economics.* Vol. 50:1 (January):133–62.

Donoso, Ricardo. 1942. *Desarollo político y social de Chile desde la Constitución de 1833.* Santiago: Imprenta Universitaria.

Downing, Brian M. 1988. "Constitutionalism, Warfare, and Political Change in Early Modern Europe." *Theory and Society.* Vol. 17:1 (January):7–56.

Drake, Paul W. 1993. "Chile, 1930–1958." In Leslie Bethell, ed., *Chile since Independence.* Cambridge: Cambridge University Press.

———. 1999. "Chile's Populism Reconsidered, 1920s–1990s." In Michael L. Conniff, ed., *Populism in Latin America.* Tuscaloosa: University of Alabama Press.

Dunning, Thad. 2008. *Crude Democracy: Natural Resource Wealth and Political Regimes.* New York: Cambridge University Press.

Edelmann, Alexander T. 1969. "The Rise and Demise of Uruguay's Second Plural Executive." *Journal of Politics.* Vol. 31:1 (February):119–39.

Edwards V., Alberto. 1976 [1927]. *La fronda aristocrática: Historia política de Chile.* 8th ed. Santiago: Editorial del Pacífico.

Einhorn, Robin. 2000. "Slavery and the Politics of Taxation in the Early United States." *Studies in American Political Development.* Vol. 14 (Fall):156–83.

———. 2008. *American Taxation, American Slavery.* Chicago: University of Chicago Press.

Engelman, Frederick, and Mildred Schwartz. 1974. "Partisan Stability and the Continuity of a Segmented Society: The Austrian Case." *American Journal of Sociology.* Vol. 79:4 (January):948–66.

Ertman, Thomas. 1997. *Birth of the Leviathan: Building States and Regimes in Medieval and Early Modern Europe.* Cambridge: Cambridge University Press.

———. 2005. "Building States – Inherently a Long-Term Process? An Argument from Comparative History." In Matthew Lange and Dietrich Rueschemeyer, eds., *States and Development: Historical Antecedents of Stagnation and Advance.* New York: Palgrave/Macmillan.

Evans, Peter. 1992. "The State as Problem and Solution: Predation, Embedded Autonomy, and Structural Change." In Stephan Haggard and Robert Kaufman, eds., *The Politics of Economic Adjustment.* Princeton, NJ: Princeton University Press.

———. 1995. *Embedded Autonomy: States and Industrial Transformation.* Princeton, NJ: Princeton University Press.

Evans, Peter, and James Rauch. 1999. "Bureaucracy and Growth: A Cross-National Analysis of the Effects of 'Weberian' State Structures on Economic Growth." *American Sociological Review.* Vol. 64:5 (October):748–65.

Faraone, Roque. 1968. *El Uruguay en que vivimos.* Montevideo: Bolsilibros Arca.

Faúndez, Julio. 2007. *Democratization, Development, and Legality: Chile, 1831–1973.* New York: Palgrave/Macmillan.

References

Fazal, Tanisha. 2004. "State Death in the International System." *International Organization*. Vol. 58:2 (Spring):311–44.

Feder, Ernest. 1960. "Feudalism and Agricultural Development: The Role of Controlled Credit in Chile's Agriculture." *Land Economics*. Vol. 36:1 (February):92–108.

Felix, David. 1960. "Structural Imbalances, Social Conflict, and Inflation: An Appraisal of Chile's Recent Anti-inflationary Effort." *Economic Development and Cultural Change*. Vol. 8:2 (January):113–47.

Ferner, Anthony. 1979. "The Dominant Class and Industrial Development in Peru." *Journal of Development Studies*. Vol. 15:4:268–88.

Finch, Henry. 1991. "Uruguay since 1930." In Leslie Bethell, ed., *The Cambridge History of Latin America, Volume VIII: Latin America since 1930, Spanish South America*. Cambridge: Cambridge University Press.

Finch, M. Henry. 1981. *A Political Economy of Uruguay since 1870*. New York: St. Martin's Press.

Finer, Herman. 1947. *The Chilean Development Corporation: A Study in Planning to Raise Living Standards*. Montreal, Canada: International Labour Office.

Fisher, John. 1984. "La formación de estado peruano (1808–1824) y Simón Bolívar." In Inge Buisson, Günther Kahle, Hans-Joachim König, and Horst Pietschmann, eds., *Problemas de la formación del estado y de la nación en Hispanoamérica*. Cologne, Germany: Böhlau.

Fitzgerald, E. V. K. 1976. "Peru: The Political Economy of an Intermediate Regime." *Journal of Latin American Studies*. Vol. 8:1 (May):53–71.

Fitzgibbon, Russell H. 1952a. "Uruguay's Remarkable Educational Achievement." *History of Education Journal*. Vol. 3:3 (Spring):65–77.

———. 1952b. "Adoption of a Collegial Executive in Uruguay." *Journal of Politics*. Vol. 14:4 (November):616–42.

———. 1953. "Uruguay's Agricultural Problems." *Economic Geography*. Vol. 29:3 (July):251–62.

Ford, Guy Stanton. 1919. "The Prussian Peasantry before 1807." *American Historical Review*. Vol. 24:3 (April):358–78.

Frankman, Myron J. 1974. "Sectoral Policy Preferences of the Peruvian Government, 1946–68." *Journal of Latin American Studies*. Vol. 6:2 (November):289–300.

Fukuyama, Francis. 2004. *State-Building: Governance and World Order in the 21st Century*. Ithaca, NY: Cornell University Press.

Gallo, Andrés. 2006. "Political Institutions and Economic Policy: Rural Renter Legislation in Argentina, 1912–1942." *Revista de Historia Económica*. Vol. 24:2 (Autumn):251–96.

———. 2010. "The Political Economy of Property Rights: Rural Rents Legislation in Argentina, 1912–1960." Working Paper, Department of Economics and Geography, University of North Florida.

Gallo, Carmenza. 1991. *Taxes and State Power: Political Instability in Bolivia, 1900–1950*. Philadelphia: Temple University Press.

Gallo, Ezequiel. 1993. "Society and Politics, 1880–1916." In Leslie Bethell, ed., *Argentina since Independence*. Cambridge: Cambridge University Press.

Gallo, Ezequiel, and Silvia Sigal. 1963. "La formación de los partidos políticos contemporáneos: La Unión Cívica Radical (1890–1916)." *Desarrollo Económico*. Vol. 3:1/2 (April–September):173–230.

Gamson, William. 1968. "Stable Unrepresentation in American Society." *American Behavioral Scientist*. Vol. 12:2:15–21.

Garavaglia, Juan Carlos. 2003. "La apotheosis del leviathan: El estado en Buenos Aires durante la primera mitad del siglo XIX." *Latin American Research Review*. Vol. 38:1:135–68.

García-Zamor, Jean-Claude. 1968. *Public Administration and Social Changes in Argentina: 1943–55*. Rio de Janeiro: Editorial Mory.

Garretón, Manuel Antonio. 1982. "Modelo y proyecto politico del regimen militar chileno." *Revista Mexicana de Sociología*. Vol. 44:2 (April–June):355–72.

Gerring, John, and Strom Thacker. 2004. "Political Institutions and Corruption: The Role of Unitarism and Parliamentarism." *British Journal of Political Science*. Vol. 34:2 (April):295–330.

Gerschenkron, Alexander. 1962. *Economic Backwardness in Historical Perspective*. Cambridge, MA: Harvard University Press.

Ghosn, Faten, Glenn Palmer, and Stuart Bremer. 2004. "The MID3 Data Set, 1993–2001: Procedures, Coding Rules, and Description." *Conflict Management and Peace Science* Vol. 21:133–54.

Giddens, Anthony. 1987. *The Nation State and Violence. Volume Two of a Contemporary Critique of Historical Materialism*. Berkeley: University of California Press.

Gillis, John R. 1968. "Aristocracy and Bureaucracy in Nineteenth-Century Prussia." *Past & Present*. Vol. 41 (December):105–29.

Glaeser, Edward L., and Andrei Shleifer. 2003. "The Rise of the Regulatory State." *Journal of Economic Literature*. Vol. XLI (June):401–25.

Glaeser, Edward L., Rafael La Porta, Florencio López-de-Silanes, and Andrei Shleifer. 2004. "Do Institutions Cause Growth?" *Journal of Economic Growth*. Vol. 9:271–303.

Global Financial Data Inc. 2005. "A Global History of Currencies." Compiled by Brian Taylor. http://www.globalfindata.com/gh/index.html.

Gómez, Rudolf. 1969. *The Peruvian Administrative System*. Boulder: University of Colorado, Boulder Bureau of Governmental Research.

González, Luis E. 1991. *Political Structures and Democracy in Uruguay*. Notre Dame, IN: Notre Dame University Press.

Gootenberg, Paul. 1989. *Between Silver and Guano: Commercial Policy and the State in Post-independence Peru*. Princeton, NJ: Princeton University Press.

Gorski, Philip. 2003. *The Disciplinary Revolution: Calvinism and the Rise of the State in Early Modern Europe*. Chicago: University of Chicago Press.

Graham, Carol. 1992. *Peru's APRA: Parties, Politics, and the Elusive Quest for Democracy*. Boulder, CO: Lynne Rienner.

Grant, Geraldine. 1983. "The State and the Formation of a Middle Class: A Chilean Experiment." *Latin American Perspectives*. Vol. 10:2/3, Part II (Spring–Summer):151–70.

Greif, Avner, and David Laitin. 2004. "A Theory of Endogenous Institutional Change." *American Political Science Review*. Vol. 98:4 (November):633–52.

Gros Espiell, Hector. 1956. *Las constituciones del Uruguay: Exposición, crítica y textos*. Madrid: Ediciones Cultura Hispánica.

———. 1966. *Esquema de evolución constitucional del Uruguay*. Montevideo: Biblioteca de publicaciones oficiales de la Facultad de Derecho y Ciencias Sociales de la Universidad de la República.

References

Grove, David L. 1951. "The Role of the Banking System in the Chilean Inflation." *Staff Papers – International Monetary Fund.* Vol. 2:1 (September):33–59.

Grugel, Jean. 1992. "Populism and the Political System in Chile: Ibañismo (1952–1958)." *Bulletin of Latin American Research.* Vol. 11:2 (May):169–86.

Haber, Stephen, and Victor Menaldo. 2011. "Do Natural Resources Fuel Authoritarianism? A Reappraisal of the Resource Curse." *American Political Science Review.* Vol. 105:1 (February):1–26.

Hagen, William W. 1989. "Seventeenth Century Crisis in Brandenburg: The Thirty Years' War, the Destabilization of Serfdom, and the Rise of Absolutism." *American Historical Review.* Vol. 94:2 (April):302–35.

Haggard, Stephan. 1990. *Pathways from the Periphery: The Politics of Growth in the Newly-Industrializing Countries.* Ithaca, NY: Cornell University Press.

Hall, John O. 1954. *La administración pública en el Uruguay: Sugerencias para una reforma de la organización administrativa.* Montevideo: Instituto de Asuntos Interamericanos de los Estados Unidos de América.

Halperín Donghi, Tulio. 1995. *Proyecto y construcción de una nación (1846–1880).* Vol. 2. Buenos Aires: Ariel.

Hamerow, Theodore S. 1958. *Restoration, Revolution, Reaction: Economics and Politics in Germany, 1815–1871.* Princeton, NJ: Princeton University Press.

Hanson, Simon G. 1938. *Utopia in Uruguay: Chapters in the Economic History of Uruguay.* New York: Oxford University Press.

Haring, Clarence H. 1931. "Chilean Politics, 1920–1928." *Hispanic American Historical Review.* Vol. 11:1 (February):1–26.

Heller, Patrick. 1996. "Social Capital as a Product of Class Mobilization and State Intervention: Industrial Workers in Kerala, India." *World Development.* Vol. 24:6 (June):1055–71.

Herbold, Carl F. 1973. *Developments in the Peruvian Administrative System, 1919–1930: Modern and Traditional Qualities of Government under Authoritarian Regimes.* Unpublished PhD dissertation, Yale University.

Herbst, Jeffrey. 2000. *States and Power in Africa: Comparative Lessons in Authority and Control.* Princeton, NJ: Princeton University Press.

Heyman, Neil M. 1966–67. "France against Prussia: The Jena Campaign of 1806." *Military Affairs.* Vol. 30:4 (Winter):186–98.

Higley, John, and Michael G. Burton. 2006. *Elite Foundations of Liberal Democracy.* Lanham, MD: Rowman & Littlefield.

Hinks, Peter. 2006. *Encyclopedia of Antislavery and Abolition.* Westport, CT: Greenwood Press.

Hintze, Otto. 1975. *The Historical Essays of Otto Hintze.* Edited by Felix Gilbert. New York: Oxford University Press.

Hirschman, Albert. 1963. *Journeys toward Progress: Studies of Economic Policymaking in Latin America.* New York: Twentieth Century Fund.

Hora, Roy. 2001. "Landowning Bourgeoisie or Business Bourgeoisie? On the Peculiarities of the Argentine Economic Elite, 1880–1945." *Journal of Latin American Studies.* Vol. 34:3 (August):587–632.

Horowitz, Donald. 1971. "Three Dimensions of Ethnic Politics." *World Politics.* Vol. 23:2 (January):232–44.

Howe, Edward T., and Donald J. Reeb. 1997. "The Historical Evolution of State and Local Tax Systems." *Social Science Quarterly.* Vol. 78:1 (March):109–21.

Hui, Victoria Tin-bor. 2004. "Toward a Dynamic Theory of International Politics: Insights from Comparing Ancient China and Early Modern Europe." *International Organization*. Vol. 58:1 (Winter):175–205.

———. 2005. *War and State Formation in Ancient China and Early Modern Europe.* New York: Cambridge University Press.

Hunt, Shane. 1971. "Distribution, Growth, and Government Economic Behavior in Peru." In Gustav Ranis, ed., *Government and Economic Development.* New Haven, CT: Yale University Press.

———. 1985. "Growth and Guano in Nineteenth Century Peru." In Roberto Cortés Conde and Shane Hunt, eds., *The Latin American Economies: Growth and the Export Sector 1880–1930.* New York: Holmes and Meier.

Huntington, Samuel. 1991. *The Third Wave: Democratization in the Late 20th Century.* Norman: Oklahoma University Press.

Ibáñez Santa María, Adolfo. 1981. "Los ingenieros, el estado y la política en Chile: Del Ministerio de Fomento a la Corporación de Fomento, 1927–1939." *Estudios Históricos 7.* Santiago: Instituto de Historia, Pontificia Universidad Católica de Chile.

Jackson, William S. 1964. *Prussian Peasant Emancipation: The Genesis of the October Edict.* Unpublished MA thesis, Department of History, University of South Carolina.

Jacob, Raúl. 1983. *El Uruguay de Terra, 1931–1938: Una crónica del terrismo.* Montevideo: Ediciones de la Banda Oriental.

James, Daniel. 1988. *Resistance and Integration: Peronism and the Argentine Working Class, 1946–1976.* Cambridge: Cambridge University Press.

Jones, Clarence F. 1927. "The Trade of Uruguay." *Economic Geography.* Vol. 3:3 (July):361–81.

Jones Luong, Pauline, and Erika Weinthal. 2010. *Oil Is Not a Curse: Ownership Structure and Institutions in Soviet Successor States.* New York: Cambridge University Press.

Karl, Terry Lynn. 1997. *The Paradox of Plenty: Oil Booms and Petro-States.* Berkeley: University of California Press.

Kaufman, Robert R. 1972. *The Politics of Land Reform in Chile, 1950–1970: Public Policy, Political Institutions and Social Change.* Cambridge, MA: Harvard University Press.

Kaufmann, Daniel, Aart Kraay, and Massimo Mastruzzi. 2009. "Governance Matters VIII: Aggregate and Individual Governance Indicators, 1996–2008." World Bank Policy Research Working Paper 4978. Washington, DC: World Bank.

Kay, Cristóbal. 1977. "The Development of the Chilean Hacienda System, 1850–1973." In Kenneth Duncan and Ian Routledge, eds., *Land and Labour in Latin America: Essays on the Development of Agrarian Capitalism in the Nineteenth and Twentieth Centuries.* New York: Cambridge University Press.

Klaczko, Jaime. 1979. "El Uruguay de 1908: Obstáculos y estímulos en el mercado de trabajo: La población económicamente activa." Working Paper 36. Montevideo: Centro de Informaciones y Estudios del Uruguay.

Klarén, Peter. 1977. "The Social and Economic Consequences of Modernization in the Peruvian Sugar Industry, 1870–1930." In Kenneth Duncan and Ian Routledge, eds., *Land and Labour in Latin America: Essays on the Development of Agrarian Capitalism in the Nineteenth and Twentieth Centuries.* New York: Cambridge University Press.

References

261

_____. 2000. *Peru: Society and Nationhood in the Andes.* New York: Oxford University Press.

Klein, Herbert S., and Mario R. dos Santos. 1973. "Las finanzas del virreinato del rio de la plata en 1790." *Desarollo Económico.* Vol. 13:50 (July–September):369–400.

Kofas, Jon V. 1999. "Stabilization and Class Conflict: The State Department, the IMF, and the IBRD in Chile, 1952–1958." *International History Review.* Vol. 21:2 (June):352–85.

Krebs, Ricardo. 1984. "Orígenes de la conciencia nacional chilena." In Inge Buisson, Günter Kahle, Hans-Joachim Konig, and Horst Pietschmann, eds., *Problemas de la Formación del Estado y de la Nación en Hispanoamérica.* Cologne, Germany: Böhlau.

Krueger, Anne. 1974. "The Political Economy of the Rent-Seeking Society." *American Economic Review.* Vol. 64:3 (June):291–303.

Kurczy, Stephan, Leigh Montgomery, and Elizabeth Ryan. 2010. "Chile Earthquake Facts: Chile vs. Haiti, in Numbers." *Christian Science Monitor.* March 2. http://www.csmonitor.com/World/Global-News/2010/0302/Chile-earthquake-facts-Chile-vs.-Haiti-in-numbers.

Kurtz, Marcus J. 2004. *Free Market Democracy and the Chilean and Mexican Countryside.* Cambridge: Cambridge University Press.

Kurtz, Marcus, and Andrew Schrank. 2007a. "Growth and Governance: Models, Measures, and Mechanisms." *Journal of Politics.* Vol. 69:2 (May):538–54.

_____. 2007b. "Growth and Governance: A Defense." *Journal of Politics.* Vol. 69:2 (May):563–69.

Kurtz, Marcus, and Sarah Brooks. 2011. "Conditioning the 'Resource Curse': Globalization, Human Capital, and Growth in Oil-Rich Nations." *Comparative Political Studies.* Vol. 44:6 (May):747–69.

Laite, Julian. 1980. "Miners and National Politics in Peru, 1900-1974." *Journal of Latin American Studies.* Vol. 12:2 (November):317–40.

Levi, Margaret. 1989. *Of Rule and Revenue.* Berkeley: University of California Press.

Lijphart, Arend. 1969. "Consociational Democracy." *World Politics.* Vol. 21:2 (January):207–25.

Little, Walter. 1979. "La organización obrera y el estado peronista, 1943–55." *Desarrollo Económico.* Vol. 19:75 (October–December):331–76.

Lomnitz, Cinna. 2004. "Major Earthquakes of Chile: A Historical Survey, 1535–1960." *Seismological Research Letters.* Vol. 75:3 (May–June):368–78.

Longman, F. W. 1912. *Frederick the Great and the Seven Years War.* New York: Charles Scribner's Sons.

López Alves, Fernando. 1996. "The Authoritarian Roots of Liberalism: Uruguay, 1810–1886." In Vincent Peloso and Barbara Tenenbaum, eds., *Liberals, Politics, and Power: State Formation in Nineteenth Century Latin America.* Athens: University of Georgia Press.

Lösing, Norbert. 2002. "La justicia constitucional en Paraguay y Uruguay." In *Anuario de Derecho Constitucional Latinoamericano. Edición 2002.* Montevideo: Konrad-Adenauer-Stiftung.

Loveman, Brian. 1976. *Struggle in the Countryside: Politics and Rural Labor in Chile, 1919–1973.* Bloomington: Indiana University Press.

_____. 1988. "Government and Regime Succession in Chile." *Third World Quarterly.* Vol. 10:1 (January):260–80.

262 References

———. 1999. *For la Patria: Politics and the Armed Forces in Latin America*. Wilmington, DE: Scholarly Resources.

Lower, Milton. 1968. "Institutional Bases of Economic Stagnation in Chile." *Journal of Economic Issues*. Vol. 2:3 (September):283–97.

Luebbert, Gregory. 1987. "Social Foundations of Political Order in Interwar Europe." *World Politics*. Vol. 39:4 (July):449–78.

———. 1991. *Liberalism, Fascism, or Social Democracy: Social Classes and the Political Origins of Regimes in Interwar Europe*. Oxford: Oxford University Press.

Maddison, Angus. 2010. "Historical Statistics of the World Economy, AD 1–2008." http://www.ggdc.net/MADDISON/Historical_Statistics/vertical-file_02–2010.xls.

Mahoney, James. 2001. *The Legacies of Liberalism: Path Dependence and Political Regimes in Central America*. Baltimore: Johns Hopkins University Press.

———. 2003. "Long-Run Development and the Legacy of Colonialism in Spanish America." *American Journal of Sociology*. Vol. 109:1 (July):50–106.

———. 2010. *Colonialism and Postcolonial Development: Spanish America in Comparative Perspective*. Cambridge: Cambridge University Press.

Mallon, Florencia. 1987. "Nationalist and Antistate Coalitions in the War of the Pacific: Junín and Cajamarca, 1879–1902." In Steve Stern, ed., *Resistance, Rebellion, and Consciousness in the Andean Peasant World: 18th to Twentieth Centuries*. Madison: University of Wisconsin Press.

Mamalakis, Markos. 1976. *The Growth and Structure of the Chilean Economy: From Independence to Allende*. New Haven, CT: Yale University Press.

Mann, Michael. 1993. *The Sources of Social Power Volume II: The Rise of Classes and Nation-States, 1760–1914*. Cambridge: Cambridge University Press.

Manning, Roger B. 1977. "Violence and Social Conflict in Mid-Tudor Rebellions." *Journal of British Studies*. Vol. 2:1 (Spring):18–40.

Markoff, John. 1991. *The Abolition of Feudalism: Peasants, Lords, and Legislators in the French Revolution*. University Park: Pennsylvania State University Press.

Marx, Karl. 1938. *Critique of the Gotha Programme*. New York: International Publishers.

McAdam, Doug. 1982. *Political Process and the Development of Black Insurgency, 1930–1970*. Chicago: University of Chicago Press.

McClintock, Cynthia. 1983. "Velasco, Officers, and Citizens: The Politics of Stealth." In Cynthia McClintock and Abraham F. Lowenthal, eds., *The Peruvian Experiment Reconsidered*. Princeton, NJ: Princeton University Press.

McLynn, F. J. 1979. "The Argentine Presidential Election of 1868." *Journal of Latin American Studies*. Vol. 11:2 (November):303–23.

Méndez Vives, Enrique. 1975. *El Uruguay de la modernización, 1876–1904*. Montevideo: Ediciones de la Banda Oriental.

Merkx, Gilbert W. 1968. *Political and Economic Change in Argentina from 1870 to 1966*. Unpublished PhD dissertation, Department of Sociology, Yale University.

Mitchell, Brian. 2003. *International Historical Statistics: The Americas, 1750–2000*. New York: Palgrave/Macmillan.

Monge, Carlos. 1993. *If the People Are Sovereign, the People Must Be Fed: Agricultural Policies and Conflicts during the Bustamante y Rivero Administration, Peru, 1945–1948*. Unpublished PhD dissertation, University of Miami.

Monteón, Michael. 1982. *Chile in the Nitrate Era: The Evolution of Economic Dependence, 1880–1930*. Madison: University of Wisconsin Press.

References

263

———. 1998. *Chile and the Great Depression: The Politics of Underdevelopment, 1927–1948*. Tempe: Arizona State University Press.

Moore, Barrington. 1966. *Social Origins of Dictatorship and Democracy: Lord and Peasant in the Making of the Modern World*. Boston: Beacon Press.

Moran, Theodore. 1970. "The 'Development' of Argentina and Australia: The Radical Party of Argentina and the Labor Party of Australia in the Process of Economic and Political Development." *Comparative Politics*. Vol. 3:1 (October):71–92.

———. 1974. *Multinational Corporations and the Politics of Dependence: Copper in Chile*. Princeton, NJ: Princeton University Press.

Mueller, John. 2009. "War Has Almost Ceased to Exist: An Assessment." *Political Science Quarterly*. Vol. 124:2 (Summer):297–321.

Muñoz Goma, Oscar, and Ana María Arriagada. 1977. "Orígenes políticos y económicos del estado empresarial en Chile." *Estudios CIEPLAN* 16. Santiago: CIEPLAN.

Nahum, Benjamín. 2009. *Estadísticas históricas del Uruguay, 1900–1950*. Montevideo, Uruguay: Comisión Sectorial de Investigación Científica/Universidad de la República.

Nahum, Benjamín, and José Pedro Barrán. 1972. *Historia rural de Uruguay moderno, 1851–1885. Compendio del Tomo I*. Montevideo: Ediciones de la Banda Oriental.

Nordlinger, Eric. 1968. "Political Development: Time Sequences and Rates of Change." *World Politics*. Vol. 20:3 (April):494–520.

North, Douglass. 1981. *Structure and Change in Economic History*. New York: W. W. Norton.

———. 1990. *Institutions, Institutional Change, and Economic Performance*. Cambridge: Cambridge University Press.

North, Liisa, and Mario Dos Santos. 1970. "Orígines y crecimiento del partido aprista y el cambio socioeconómico en el Perú." *Desarrollo Económico*. Vol. 10:38 (July–September):163–214.

Nunn, Frederick. 1970. "Emil Körner and the Prussianization of the Chilean Army: Origins, Process, and Consequences, 1885–1920." *Hispanic American Historical Review*. Vol. 50:2 (May):300–22.

O'Donnell, Guillermo. 1978. "State and Alliances in Argentina." *Journal of Development Studies*. Vol. 15:1:3–33.

OECD. 2011. "Revenue Statistics – Comparative Tables." http://stats.oecd.org/Index .aspx?DataSetCode=REVCHL.

Olivarría Bravo, Arturo. 1962. *Chile entre dos Alessandri: Memorias políticas*. Vol. I. Santiago: Editorial Nascimento.

Olivera, Enrique Arocena. 2002. *Proceso histórico de la economía uruguaya: Del mercantilismo colonial al encierro dirigista*. Montevideo: Ediciones Linardi y Risso.

Olson, Mancur. 1993. "Dictatorship, Democracy, and Development." *American Political Science Review*. Vol. 87:3 (September):567–76.

Ortega, Luis. 1984. "Nitrates, Chilean Entrepreneurs and the Origins of the War of the Pacific." *Journal of Latin American Studies*. Vol. 16:2 (November):337–80.

Oszlak, Oscar. 1972. *Diagnóstico de la administración pública uruguaya. Informe técnico*. New York: United Nations Development Program.

———. 1982a. "Reflexiones sobre la formación del estado y la construcción de la sociedad argentina." *Desarrollo Económico: Revista de Ciencias Sociales*. Vol. XXI (January–March):1–18.

264 References

_____. 1982b. "La conquista del orden político y la formación histórica del estado argentino" Typescript. Buenos Aires: Centro de Estudios de Estado y Sociedad.

_____. 2004 [1997]. *La formación del estado argentine: Orden, progreso, y organización nacional.* Buenos Aires: Grupo Editorial Planeta/Ariel.

Oxford Economic History Database. 2011. "The Montevideo–Oxford Latin American Economic History Database." http://oxlad.qeh.ox.ac.uk/search.php.

Paige, Jeffery M. 1975. *Agrarian Revolution: Social Movements and Export Agriculture in the Underdeveloped World.* New York: Free Press.

_____. 1997. *Coffee and Power: Revolution and the Rise of Democracy in Central America.* Cambridge, MA: Harvard University Press.

Palma Zuñiga, Luis. 1967. *Historia del Partido Radical.* Santiago: Editorial Andrés Bello.

Panizza, Francisco. 1997. "Late Institutionalization and Early Modernization: The Emergence of Uruguay's Liberal Democratic Political Order." *Journal of Latin American Studies.* Vol. 29:3 (October):667–91.

Pásara, Luis. 1983. "When the Military Dreams." In Cynthia McClintock and Abraham F. Lowenthal, eds., *The Peruvian Experiment Reconsidered.* Princeton, NJ: Princeton University Press.

Payne, James L. 1965. *Labor and Politics in Peru: The System of Political Bargaining.* New Haven, CT: Yale University Press.

Peloso, Vincent. 1996. "Liberals, Electoral Reform, and the Popular Vote in Mid-Nineteenth-Century Peru." In Vincent Peloso and Barbara Tenenbaum, eds., *Liberals, Politics, and Power: State Formation in Nineteenth-Century Latin America.* Athens: University of Georgia Press.

Petras, James, and Elida P. Guiard Grenier. 1969. "La política de integración: La burocracia chilena." *Desarrollo Económico.* Vol. 9:33 (April–June):67–93.

Philip, George. 1976. "The Soldier as Radical: The Peruvian Military Government, 1968–1975." *Journal of Latin American Studies.* Vol. 8:1 (May):29–51.

Pike, Fredrick B. 1963. "Aspects of Class Relations in Chile, 1850–1960." *Hispanic American Historical Review.* Vol. 43:1 (February):14–33.

_____. 1967. *The Modern History of Peru.* New York: Praeger.

Pion-Berlin, David. 1997. *Through Corridors of Power: Institutions and Civil-Military Relations in Argentina.* University Park: Pennsylvania University Press.

Polidano, Charles. 2001. "Why Civil Service Reforms Fail." *Public Management Review.* Vol. 3:3 (September):345–61.

Porter, Bruce D. 1994. *War and the Rise of the State: The Military Foundations of Modern Politics.* New York: Free Press.

Queisser, Monika. 1998. "Regulation and Supervision of Pension Funds: Principles and Practices." *International Social Security Review.* Vol. 51 (February):39–55.

Quiroz, Alfonso. 1988. "Financial Leadership and the Formation of Peruvian Elite Groups." *Journal of Latin American Studies.* Vol. 20:1 (May):49–81.

Rama, Carlos M. 1958. "El movimiento obrero y social uruguayo y el Presidente Batlle." *Revista de Historia de América.* No. 46 (December):399–426.

Ramírez Necochea, Hernán. 1969. *Balmaceda y la contrarrevolución de 1891.* Santiago: Editorial Universitaria.

Ranis, Peter. 1979. "Early Peronism and the Post-liberal Argentine State." *Journal of Interamerican Studies and World Affairs.* Vol. 21:3 (August):313–38.

References

Rauch, James E., and Peter B. Evans. 2000. "Bureaucratic Structure and Bureaucratic Performance in Less Developed Countries." *Journal of Public Economics*. Vol. 75:49–71.

Remmer, Karen. 1977. *Party Competition in Argentina and Chile: Political Recruitment and Public Policy, 1890–1930*. Lincoln: University of Nebraska Press.

Rial, Juan. 1980. *Estadísticas históricas de Uruguay 1850–1930*. Cuaderno 4. Montevideo: Centro de Informaciones y Estudios del Uruguay (CIESU).

———. 1983. *Población y desarrollo de un pequeño país: Uruguay 1830–1930*. Montevideo: Centro de Informaciones y Estudios del Uruguay (CIESU)/Acali.

Robinson, Richard D. 1976. "The Peruvian Experiment: The Theory and Reality of the Industrial Community." Alfred P. Sloan School of Management Working Paper WP 851–76. Cambridge: Massachusetts Institute of Technology.

Rock, David. 2000. "State-Building and Political Systems in Nineteenth-Century Argentina and Uruguay." *Past & Present*. No. 167 (May):176–202.

Rodrik, Dani. 2008. "Second-Best Institutions." *American Economic Review, Papers and Proceedings*. Vol. 98:2 (May):100–4.

Rosenberg, Hans. 1958. *Bureaucracy, Aristocracy, and Autocracy: The Prussian Experience, 1660–1815*. Cambridge, MA: Harvard University Press.

Ross, Michael. 2001. *Timber Booms and Institutional Breakdown in Southeast Asia*. Cambridge: Cambridge University Press.

———. 2004. "Does Taxation Lead to Representation." *British Journal of Political Science*. Vol. 34:2 (April):229–49.

———. 2012. *The Oil Curse: How Petroleum Wealth Shapes the Development of Nations*. Princeton, NJ: Princeton University Press.

Rozman, Stephen. 1970. "The Evolution of the Political Role of the Peruvian Military." *Journal of Interamerican Studies and World Affairs*. Vol. 12:4 (October): 539–64.

Rueschemeyer, Dietrich. 2005. "Building States – Inherently a Long-Term Process? An Argument from Theory." In Matthew Lange and Dietrich Rueschemeyer, eds., *States and Development: Historical Antecedents of Stagnation and Advance*. New York: Palgrave/Macmillan.

Rueschemeyer, Dietrich, Evelyne Huber Stephens, and John Stephens. 1992. *Capitalist Development and Democracy*. Chicago: University of Chicago Press.

Sanders, Thomas G. 1981. "The Politics of Transition." In Howard Handelman and Thomas Sanders, eds., *Military Government and the Movement toward Democracy in Latin America*. Bloomington: Indiana University Press/American Universities Field Staff.

Sater, William F. 2004. *A History of Chile, 1808–1994*. Cambridge: Cambridge University Press.

Saylor, Ryan. 2008. *Commodity Booms, Political Coalitions, and State Building in Latin America and Africa*. Unpublished PhD dissertation, Department of Politics, University of Virginia.

Scalabrini, Raúl Pedro. 1963. *Reforma agraria argentina*. Buenos Aires: D. Francisco A. Colombo.

Schleunes, Karl. 1979. "Enlightenment, Reform, and Reaction: The Schooling Revolution in Prussia." *Central European History*. Vol. 12:4 (December):315–42.

Schrank, Andrew. 2004. "Reconsidering the Resource Curse: Selection Bias, Measurement Error, and Omitted Variables." Unpublished manuscript, Yale University.

Schumpeter, Joseph A. 1954. "The Crisis of the Tax State." Translated from the German by W. F. Stolper and R. A. Musgrave. In Alan Peacock, Wolfgang Stolper, Ralph Turvey, and Elizabeth Henderson, eds., *International Economic Papers*, No. 4. London: Macmillan.

Schydlowsky, Daniel M., and Juan Wicht. 1983. "The Anatomy of an Economic Failure." In Cynthia McClintock and Abraham F. Lowenthal, eds., *The Peruvian Experiment Reconsidered*. Princeton, NJ: Princeton University Press.

Scott, James. 1987. *Weapons of the Weak: Everyday Forms of Peasant Resistance*. New Haven, CT: Yale University Press.

_____. 1990. *Domination and the Arts of Resistance: Hidden Transcripts*. New Haven, CT: Yale University Press.

Scully, Timothy. 1992. *Rethinking the Center: Party Politics in Nineteenth- and Twentieth-Century Chile*. Stanford, CA: Stanford University Press.

Shafer, D. Michael. 1994. *Winners and Losers: How Sectors Shape the Developmental Prospects of States*. Ithaca, NY: Cornell University Press.

Shefter, Martin. 1977. "Party and Patronage: Germany, England, and Italy." *Politics & Society*. Vol. 7:4 (December):403–51.

Showalter, Dennis E. 1994. "Hubertusberg to Auerstädt: The Prussian Army in Decline?" *German History*. Vol. 12:3 (October):308–33.

Sikkink, Katherine. 1991. *Ideas and Institutions: Developmentalism in Brazil and Argentina*. Ithaca, NY: Cornell University Press.

Silva, Patricio. 1994. "State, Public Technocracy and Politics in Chile, 1927–1941." *Bulletin of Latin American Research*. Vol. 13:3 (September):281–97.

_____. 2006. "Los tecnócratas y la política en Chile: Pasado y presente." *Revista de Ciencia Política*. Vol. 26:2:175–90.

Silvert, K. H. 1961. "Liderazgo político y debilidad institucional en la Argentina." *Desarrollo Económico*. Vol. 1:3 (October–December):155–82.

Skowronek, Stephen. 1982. *Building a New American State: The Expansion of National Administrative Capacities, 1877–1920*. Cambridge: Cambridge University Press.

Slater, Dan. 2008. "Can Leviathan Be Democratic? Competitive Elections, Robust Mass Politics, and State Infrastructural Power." *Studies in Comparative International Development*. Vol. 48:3–4 (September):252–72.

Smith, Gavin. 1989. *Livelihood and Resistance: Peasants and the Politics of Land in Peru*. Berkeley: University of California Press

Smith, Peter, and Graciela Sylvestre. 1967. "Los radicales argentinos y la defensa de los intereses ganaderos, 1916–1930." *Desarrollo Económico*. Vol. 7:25 (April–June):795–829.

Snow, Peter G. 1972. *Radicalismo chileno: Historia y doctrina del partido radical*. Santiago: Editorial Francisco de Aguirre.

Soifer, Hillel. 2006. *Authority over Distance: Explaining Variations in State Infrastructural Power in Latin America*. Unpublished PhD dissertation, Department of Government, Harvard University.

_____. 2008. "State Infrastructural Power: Approaches to Conceptualization and Measurement." *Studies in Comparative International Development*. Vol. 48:3–4 (September):231–51.

_____. 2009. "The Sources of Infrastructural Power: Evidence from Nineteenth-Century Chilean Education." *Latin American Research Review*. Vol. 44:2:158–80.

References

267

———. 2011. "The Institutional Origins of State Infrastructural Power: Historical Evidence from Latin America." Unpublished manuscript, Department of Politics, Princeton University.

Soifer, Hillel, and Matthias vom Hau. 2008. "Unpacking the Strength of the State: The Utility of State Infrastructural Power." *Studies in Comparative International Development*. Vol. 48:3–4 (September):219–30.

Solari, Aldo. 1956. "Las clases sociales y su gravitación en la estructura política del Uruguay." *Revista Mexicana de Sociología*. Vol. 18:2 (May–August):257–66.

Sondrol, Paul C. 1992. "1984 Revisited? A Re-examination of Uruguay's Military Dictatorship." *Bulletin of Latin American Research*. Vol. 11:2 (May):187–203.

Spiller, Pablo, and Mariano Tommasi. 2003. "The Institutional Foundations of Public Policy: A Transactions Approach with Application to Argentina." *Journal of Law, Economics, and Organization*. Vol. 19:2 (October):281–306.

Spiller, Pablo, Ernesto Stein, and Mariano Tommasi. 2008. "Political Institutions, Policymaking, and Policy: An Introduction" in Ernesto Stein and Mariano Tommasi, eds., *Policymaking in Latin America: How Politics Shapes Policies*. New York: Inter-American Development Bank/David Rockefeller Center for Latin American Studies, Harvard University.

Spruyt, Hendrik. 1994. *The Sovereign State and Its Competitors*. Princeton, NJ: Princeton University Press.

Standard and Poor's. 2011. "Standard and Poor's Sovereign Ratings List." http://www .standardandpoors.com/ratings/sovereigns/ratings-list/en/us?sectorName=null& subSectorCode=39&filter=C.

Stein, Steve. 1980. *Populism in Peru: The Emergence of the Masses and the Politics of Social Control*. Madison: University of Wisconsin Press.

———. 1999. "The Paths to Populism in Peru." In Michael L. Conniff, ed., *Populism in Latin America*. Tuscaloosa: University of Alabama Press.

Stepan, Alfred. 1978. *The State and Society: Peru in Comparative Perspective*. Princeton, NJ: Princeton University Press.

Stevenson, John Reese. 1942 [1970]. *The Chilean Popular Front*. Westport, CT: Greenwood Press.

Stijns, Jean-Phillippe. 2005. "Natural Resource Abundance and Economic Growth Revisited." *Resources Policy*. Vol. 30:2 (June):107–30.

———. 2006. "Natural Resource Abundance and Human Capital Accumulation." *World Development*. Vol. 34:6 (June):1060–83.

Stinchcombe, Arthur. 1961. "Agricultural Enterprise and Rural Class Relations." *American Journal of Sociology*. Vol. 67:2 (September):165–76.

Stuart, Graham. 1928. "The Administration of President Leguía of Peru." *American Political Science Review*. Vol. 22:2 (May):416–20.

Suárez, Rubén, and Bonnie Bradford. 1993. "The Economic Impact of the Cholera Epidemic in Peru: An Application of the Cost of Illness Methodology." Water and Sanitation Health Project Field Report 415. Washington, DC: US Agency for International Development.

Sulmont, Denis. 1980. *El movimiento obrero peruano (1890–198): reseña histórica*. Lima: TAREA.

Tantaleán, Javier. 1983. *Política económico-financiera y la formación del estado: Siglo XIX*. Lima: Centro de Estudios para el Desarrollo y la Participación.

Tax Foundation. 2011. "Alaska's State and Local Tax Burden, 1977–2009." http://www.taxfoundation.org/taxdata/show/440.html.

Taylor, Philip B. 1952. "The Uruguayan Coup D'etat of 1933." *Hispanic American Historical Review*. Vol. 32:3 (August):301–20.

———. 1955. "The Electoral System in Uruguay." *Journal of Politics*. Vol. 17:1 (February):19–42.

———. 1963. "Interests and Institutional Dysfunction in Uruguay." *American Political Science Review*. Vol. 57:1 (March):62–74.

Teichman, Judith. 1982. "Businessmen and Politics in the Process of Economic Development: Argentina and Canada." *Canadian Journal of Political Science*. Vol. 15:1 (March):47–66.

Thies, Cameron. 2004. "State Building, Interstate and Intrastate Rivalry: A Study of Post-colonial Developing Country Extractive Efforts, 1975–2000." *International Studies Quarterly*. Vol. 48:1 (March):53–72.

———. 2005. "War, Rivalry, and State Building in Latin America." *American Journal of Political Science*. Vol. 49:3 (July):451–65.

Thomas, M. A. 2010. "What Do the Worldwide Governance Indicators Measure?" *European Journal of Development Research*. Vol. 22:1 (February):31–54.

Thorp, Rosemary, and Geoffrey Bertram. 1978. *Peru, 1890–1977*. New York: Columbia University Press.

Tickner, Joel, and Tami Gouveia-Vigeant. 2005. "The 1991 Cholera Epidemic in Peru: Not a Case of Precaution Gone Awry." *Risk Analysis*. Vol. 25:3:495–502.

Tilly, Charles. 1975. "Reflections on the History of European State-Making." In Charles Tilly, ed., *The Formation of National States in Western Europe*. Princeton, NJ: Princeton University Press.

———. 1990. *Coercion, Capital, and European States, A.D. 1990–1992*. Cambridge, MA: Blackwell.

Tilly, Richard. 1966. "The Political Economy of Public Finance and the Industrialization of Prussia, 1815–1866." *Journal of Economic History*. Vol. 26:4 (December):484–97.

Time. 1948. "Argentina: To Benefit the People." September 20.

Torre, Juan Carlos, and Liliana de Riz. 1993. "Argentina since 1946." In Leslie Bethell, ed., *Argentina since Independence*. Cambridge: Cambridge University Press.

Transparency International. 2012. "Corruptions Perceptions Index." http://cpi.transparency.org/cpi2011/results/.

Trinidade, Helgio. 1985. "La construcción del estado nacional en Argentina y Brasil (1810–1900)." *Revista Mexicana de Sociología*. Vol. 48:1 (January–March):137–66.

US Geological Survey. 2011a. "Magnitude 8.8 – OFFSHORE BIO-BIO, CHILE." http://earthquake.usgs.gov/earthquakes/eqinthenews/2010/us2010tfan/#summary.

———. 2011b. "Magnitude 7.0 – HAITI REGION." http://earthquake.usgs.gov/earthquakes/eqinthenews/2010/us2010rja6/#summary.

Vanger, Milton I. 1963. *José Batlle y Ordóñez: The Creator of His Times, 1902–1907*. Cambridge, MA: Harvard University Press.

———. 1980. *The Model Country: José Batlle y Ordóñez of Uruguay, 1907–15*. Hannover, NH: Brandeis University Press/University Press of New England.

Varshney, Ashutosh. 2001. "Ethnic Conflict and Civil Society: India and Beyond." *World Politics*. Vol. 53:3 (April):362–98.

References

Venczel, Linda. 1997. *Cholera Prevention in Latin America: Implications for Diarrheal Disease Control and Environmental Health Indicators*. Metepec, Mexico: Centro Panamericano de Ecología Humana y Salud.

Verner, Joel. 1984. "The Independence of Supreme Courts in Latin America: A Review of the Literature." *Journal of Latin American Studies*. Vol. 16:2 (November):463–506.

Vernon, Raymond. 1977. *Storm over the Multinationals: The Real Issues*. Cambridge, MA: Harvard University Press.

Villanueva, Víctor. 1975. *El APRA en busca del poder, 1930–1940*. Lima, Peru: Editorial Horizonte.

Werlich, Peter. 1978. *Peru: A Short History*. Carbondale: Southern Illinois University Press.

Weyland, Kurt. 2007. "The Political Economy of Market Reform and a Revival of Structuralism." *Latin American Research Review*. Vol. 42:3 (October):235–50.

White, C. Langdon, and Ronald H. Chilcote. 1961. "Chile's New Iron and Steel Industry." *Economic Geography*. Vol. 37:3 (July):258–66.

Wise, Carol. 2003. *Reinventing the State: Economic Strategy and Institutional Change in Peru*. Ann Arbor: University of Michigan Press.

Witte, Hermann. 1951. *Bauernbefreiung und Städteordnung und die Ostpreussen*. Kitzingen am Main, Germany: Holzner.

World Bank. 2011a. "World Development Indicators Online." http://databank.world bank.org/ddp/home.do?Step=12&id=4&CNO=2.

———. 2011b. "Worldwide Governance Indicators: Government Effectiveness (Data for 2009)." http://info.worldbank.org/governance/wgi/mc_chart.asp.

Weber, Max. 1978. *Economy and Society*. Vol. I. Berkeley: University of California Press.

Whigham, Thomas L., and Barbara Potthast. 1999. "The Paraguayan Rosetta Stone: New Insights into the Demographics of the Paraguayan War, 1864–1870." *Latin American Research Review*. Vol. 34:1:174–86.

Wright, Gavin, and Jesse Czelusta. 2002. "Exorcizing the Resource Curse: Minerals as a Knowledge Industry, Past and Present." Unpublished manuscript, Stanford University.

———. 2003. "Mineral Resources and Economic Development." Paper prepared for the Conference on Sector Reform in Latin America, Stanford Center for International Development, November 13–15.

Yaffé, Jaime. 2000. "Política y economía en la modernización: Uruguay 1876–1933." Avance de Investigación 7/00. Montevideo: Instituto de Economía, Universidad de la República.

Yepes del Castillo, Ernesto. 1981. *Perú 1820–1920: ¿Un siglo de desarrollo capitalista?* 2nd ed. Lima: Signo Universitario.

Zeitlin, Maurice, and Richard Ratcliff. 1988. *Landlords and Capitalists: The Dominant Class of Chile*. Princeton, NJ: Princeton University Press.

Zum Felde, Alberto. 1941. *Evolución histórica del uruguay y esquema de su sociología*. Montevideo: Librerias Maximino García.

Index

Acción Popular (Peru), 162, 171
Acemoglu, Daron, 4, 31, 33, 59
Alessandri, Arturo, 142, 145
  social reforms of, 143
Alessandri, Jorge, 139, 151
  effort at state retrenchment, 151–153
  liberalization strategy, 152
ANCAP, 213
Aparicio, Timoteo, 127
APRA, 137, 157, 163
  composition of supporters, 161, 164, 165
  election of 1945, 166
  resort to insurrection, 165
Argentina
  barriers to developmentalist coalition, 183,
    187, 196, 198
  center-periphery conflict, 109
  conflict with indigenous population, 109
  corporatist institutions, 192
  decline of regionalism, 112–113
  delayed working class incorporation, 183,
    190–191
  early middle sector incorporation, 181
  emergence of elite cooperation, 99
  formation of national institutions, 111–112
  government expenditures, 102
  importance of export economy, 185
  institutional cycling, 184, 193, 194,
    199–200
  middle and working class suffrage, 52, 188
  middle class social composition, 183, 185
  political economy, 99–101
  post-unification expansion, 185

trade monopoly of Buenos Aires, 104
upheaval in public administration, 191

Balmaceda F., José, 88, 139
Banda Oriental. See Uruguay
Barros Borgoño, Luis, 142
Batlle y Ordóñez, José, 116, 204
Belaúnde Terry, Fernando, 162
bellicist theories of state building, 8, 21–22
  causal mechanisms, 19, 22
  changing nature of war in, 35
  role of taxation in, 21
  selection problems in, 49, 248
Blancos. *See* National Party (Uruguay)
Bustamante y Rivero, José Luis, 157, 166

Cáceres D., Andrés Avelino, 79
Caseros, Battle of, 110
Castilla, Ramón, 74
Centeno, Miguel, 21, 22
Chaudhry, Kiren, 27
Chile
  agrarian political economy, 85
  early statism in, 135
  economic downturn's effects, 152
  elite cooperation in, 87–89
  indigenous population, 67, 73, 83
  industrial development, 149
  late mass incorporation, 136, 149
  middle sector social composition, 141
  neoliberalism in, 153
  Parliamentary Republic, 88, 139
  persistent suffrage restrictions, 142

271

272 Index

Chile *(cont.)*
  Portalian State, 87
  post-Depression state building, 138
  public employment, 93
  slavery and indenture, 74
  social mobility of elites, 86
  social relations, 83–86
  tax collection in, 68, 93, 154
  timing of mass incorporation. *See* mass
    political incorporation
  union membership, 149
COFIDE, 173
collegial executive (Uruguay), 212
Collier, David, 222
Collier, Ruth Berins, 222
colonial legacy, 18
  Argentina and Uruguay compared, 97
  Argentine social relations, 101
  center-periphery conflict (Argentina),
    106–107
  Chile and Peru compared, 66–67, 83
  weak administrative infrastructure
    (Uruguay), 114–115
Colorado Party (Uruguay), 115, 205
  militarista era, 125
  relationship to labor, 210
Communist Party (Chile), 149
Confederación Argentina, 109, 111
  weakness of, 111
Consejo Nacional de Administración
  (Uruguay), 212
Constitution of 1925 (Chile), 143
co-participation, 116, 120
CORFO, 148, 149
COSENA, 220
critical junctures. *See also* path dependence
  formation of national institutions, 36–42,
    52, 227–228
  mass political incorporation, 42–48, 52–54,
    131, 228–229
  sequencing of, 43

double simultaneous vote (Uruguay), 208
Dunning, Thad, 23

ecological theories. *See* resource curse theories
  of state building
education
  Argentina and Uruguay compared, 224–226
  Chile, 93
  as measure of state capacity, 12–14, 63

electoral incorporation 9. *See also* mass
  incorporation
  early, 9
  late, 9
elite compromise
  Argentina and Uruguay compared, 95–96
  institutional foundations (Argentina),
    114
  institutional foundations (Chile), 88
  institutional foundations (Uruguay),
    127
  social foundations (Chile), 88
elite conflict, and property rights (Argentina),
    105, 108
elite cooperation, 9
Ertman, Thomas, 32, 33
exclusionary oligarchy, 9

Frederick II, 244
Frederick William I, 239
Frederick William III, 244, 245
free labor 37. *See also* social relations
Frondizi, Arturo, 197

García, Alan, 155
Generalkriegskommisariat, 240
Gerschenkron, Alexander, 34
González Videla, Gabriel, 149
Gorski, Philip, 19, 239
governance. *See* state capacity
Grove, Marmaduke, 143
Guerra Grande, 116, 126
Gutherrschaft, 241

Haya de la Torre, Victor Raúl, 161,
    163
Hintze, Otto, 21
Hui, Victoria Tin-bor, 21, 22, 35, 49

IAPI, 193, 197
Ibáñez, Carlos, 136, 143, 144, 150
indigenous rebellion, effect on state building,
    78
infrastructural power. *See* state capacity
inquilinaje. See social relations
institutional theories of state building, 19,
    28–29
interstate conflict
  aggression versus defense, 89
  effect on taxation in Peru, 75
  in Peru and Chile, 51

Index

Jena and Auerstädt, Battles of, 244

Landtags-Recess of 1653, 245
Latin America
  contrast with Europe, 230
  limits of regional focus, 236
  prevalence of war, 35
Latorre, Lorenzo, 117, 122, 127
Leguía, Augusto, 80, 93, 159, 163
Levi, Margaret, 33
Luebbert, Gregory, 235

Mahoney, James, 16, 66, 73, 235
mass political incorporation
  consequences of early occurrence, 133, 178
  consequences of late occurrence, 177
  defined, 206
  relation to state building, 134–135
  timing in Chile and Peru, 131–132
  timing of, 43–48, 179
middle class. *See* middle sectors
middle sectors
  accommodation with working class, 132,
    179, 229
  attitude toward protectionism, 132
  early mobilization in Argentina, 181
  public v., private employment, 9–10
Mitre, Bartolomé, 101
Moore, Barrington, 37, 235
Mueller, John, 35

national institutions. *See* critical junctures,
    formation of national institutions
National Party (Uruguay), 115
  militarista era, 125
nitrates, 79
  effect of loss in Peru, 79
  end of monopoly, 140
  and state expansion in Chile, 140
North, Douglass, 33

Onganía, Juan Carlos, 199

Paraguayan War. *See* War of the Triple
    Alliance
path dependence
  efforts at path departure, 53, 231–233
  implications of, 230–231
  sequencing of critical junctures, 230,
    233–234
  and theory testing, 49, 50

Pavón, Battle of, 109
Perón, Juan Domingo, 183, 190
  relation to labor movement, 193
Peru
  Aristocratic Republic, 79, 80
  barriers to developmentalist alliance, 163,
    164, 168, 174
  early labor unrest, 160
  early mass suffrage, 164
  efforts at state expansion, 162
  elite resistance to independence, 73
  failed developmentalism, 167
  guano boom effects, 74
  indigenous population, 73, 78
  land reform, 172
  Leguía administration, 80–81
  limited industrialization, 136, 158, 160, 172
  middle sector social composition, 160
  military era reform effort, 172–175
  peasant insurrections, 77
  radical reforms of military government, 170
  slavery and indenture, 73, 77–78
  tax collection in, 68
  weak administrative infrastructure, 74, 159
Pinochet, Augusto, 151
  effort at state retrenchment, 153–156
political development. *See* state building
Popular Front (Chile), 136, 138, 148
Proceso de Reorganización Nacional, 199
Prussia
  absolutism before emancipation, 240–241
  British fiscal subsidy, 244
  characterization of state capacity, 239
  civil service dominance by military, 246
  as complementary case, 237–238
  contrasts with Latin America, 238–239
  early weakness of state, 239
  emancipation and the industrial economy,
    243
  emancipation process, 245
  emancipation's effects on peasantry, 245–247
  empancipation process, 242–243
  feudal legacies, 239
  fiscal conditions, 243
  military dominance by nobility, 241
  pre-emancipation political economy,
    241–242, 243–244
  reorganization after Napoleonic Wars, 244
  taxation, 247
public administration, partisan composition
    of, 48

Radical Party (Argentina). *See* UCR
Radical Party (Chile), 136, 152
railway network
as measure of state capacity, 14–15, 63–64
and national unification (Argentina), 113
redistribution, 133, 135
resource curse theories of state building, 8, 23
causal mechanisms, 23, 25
functionalism in, 26–28
measurement problems in, 24
temporal selection bias in, 24
Revolutionary Government of the Armed
Forces (Peru), 169
Rosas, Juan Manuel de, 109
Rosenberg, Hans, 240, 245, 246, 248
Ross, Michael, 26

Sánchez Cerro, Luis Miguel, 163
Schrank, Andrew, 24, 25
scope conditions, 230, 235–238
servile labor, 37. *See also* social relations
Argentina, 99
Peru, 77–78
Seven Years War, 240, 244
SINAMOS, 174
social foundations, 36–48
versus bellicist and ecological approaches,
234
versus institutionalism, 235
versus structuralism, 235
social question. *See* critical junctures, mass
political incorporation
social relations, 9
effect on state building, 37–39
free labor in Uruguay, 119
free labor vs. agrarian capitalism, 96
and indigenous population, 73–74, 83
inquilinaje in Chile, 83, 84–85
and military capacity, 76, 91
Soifer, Hillel, 10, 19, 28, 40, 60
Spruyt, Hendrik, 33
state building, 6. *See also* state capacity
advantages of backwardness, 34–35
definition of, 54–58
elite cooperation and, 40–42
initial trajectory, 51
long-run outcomes, 52, 135–137
organizational knowledge's effects on, 32
path dependencies in, 32–34
and rents, 28
role of external influences, 234
role of time, 30

selection processes in, 32
servile labor and, 37–39. *See also* social
relations
versus economic development, 30–32, 102
state capacity, 3. *See also* state building,
definition of
and bureaucracy, 56
consequences of, 3
and economic development, 4
importance of, 3–5
as 'infrastructural power', 56
measurement of, 58–64
and principal/agent problems, 55
and public policy, 58
versus property rights, 57
and wealth, 3, 5–6, 98
state strength. *See* state capacity
Stinchcombe, Arthur, 121
suffrage
early expansion in Peru, 81
early restrictions in Argentina, 113
landlord control in Chile, 86
late expansion in Chile, 87
limitations in Uruguay, 129

taxation
Argentina and Uruguay compared, 222–224
Argentine regional conflict over, 104
Chile and Peru compared, 68–71, 90, 92,
138
as measure of state capacity, 11, 12, 61–63,
228
nitrate exports and, 92
Peruvian elite opposition, 75
and the "resource curse," 26, 92
Terra, Gabriel, 207, 216
Tilly, Charles, 21, 68, 239
Treaty of Tilsit, 244

UCR, 183, 186
conflict with working class, 189
free trade orientation, 186
Urquiza, Justo José de, 110
Uruguay
administrative development, 214
class structure transformed, 124
developmentalist institutions, 209
early industrialization, 203
educational reforms, 204
electoral system, 128
emergence of elite cooperation, 126–129
era of the lean cows, 218–219

expansion of institutions under Batlle,
179–181, 208
failed retrenchment under military,
219–221
formation of institutions under Latorre,
117–118
foundations for developmentalist alliance,
212
free labor. *See* social relations, free labor in
Uruguay
inclusion before mobilization, 181
institutional foundation of compromise,
212
interparty cooperation, 213
land enclosures, 123
land values in, 117
limited mass mobilization, 202, 204–205
middle sector social composition, 204
military professionalization, 127
partisan power sharing, 117
political economy, 115, 120–122, 203

post-independence conflict, 116–117
post-unification expansion, 201, 202
post-war institutional deepening, 218
property rights establishment, 122–124
servile labor, 125
social composition of elite, 126
social relations after Guerra Grande, 121
suffrage restrictions, 208
tax collection in, 118
timing of mass incorporation, 53

Velasco Alvarado, Juan, 170

war. *See* interstate conflict
war makes states. *See* bellicist theories of state
building
War of the Pacific, 75, 79, 91
causes of Peruvian weakness, 76
War of the Triple Alliance, 14, 103
working class, delayed incorporation in Chile,
141

For EU product safety concerns, contact us at Calle de José Abascal, 56–1°, 28003 Madrid, Spain or eugpsr@cambridge.org.

www.ingramcontent.com/pod-product-compliance
Ingram Content Group UK Ltd.
Pitfield, Milton Keynes, MK11 3LW, UK
UKHW011320060825
461487UK00005B/209